the pinckaers reader

Servais Pinckaers, O.P.

the pinckaers reader

Renewing Thomistic Moral Theology

Edited by John Berkman and Craig Steven Titus

Translated by Sr. Mary Thomas Noble, O.P.,

Craig Steven Titus, Michael Sherwin, O.P.,

and Hugh Connolly

The Catholic University of America Press
Washington, D.C.

LIBRARY OF CONGRESS CATALOGING-IN-PUBLICATION DATA

Pinckaers, Servais.

[Essays. English. Selections]

The Pinckaers Reader : renewing Thomistic moral theology / edited by John Berk-

man and Craig Steven Titus / translated by Mary Thomas Noble . . . [et al.].—1st ed.

p. cm.

Includes bibliographical references and index.

ISBN 13: 978-0-8132-1408-5 (cl. : alk. paper)

ISBN 10: 0-8132-1408-4 (cl. : alk. paper)

ISBN 13: 978-0-8132-1394-1 (pbk. : alk. paper)

ISBN 10: 0-8132-1394-0 (pbk. : alk. paper)

1. Christian ethics—Catholic authors.   I. Berkman, John, 1964–   II. Titus, Craig

Steven, 1959–   III. Title.

BJ1249.P54717 2005

241´.042—dc22

2004003344

Contents

Abbreviations   vii

Acknowledgments   ix

Introduction by John Berkman   xi

Section I. Thomistic Method and the Renewal of Moral Theology

1. The Sources of the Ethics of St. Thomas Aquinas (2002)   3

2. The Body of Christ: The Eucharistic and Ecclesial Context
of Aquinas's Ethics (2000)   26

3. Scripture and the Renewal of Moral Theology (1995)   46

4. The Place of Philosophy in Moral Theology (1999)   64

5. Dominican Moral Theology in the 20th Century (1993)   73

Section II. Beatitude and Christian Anthropology

6. Aquinas's Pursuit of Beatitude: From the *Commentary
on the Sentences* to the *Summa Theologiae* (1993)   93

7. Beatitude and the Beatitudes in Aquinas's
Summa Theologiae (1998)   115

8. Ethics and the Image of God (1989)   130

9. Aquinas on the Dignity of the Human Person (1987)   144

Section III. Moral Agency

10. Aquinas and Agency: Beyond Autonomy
    and Heteronomy? (1978)   167

11. A Historical Perspective on Intrinsically Evil Acts (1986)   185

12. Revisionist Understandings of Actions in the
    Wake of Vatican II (1982)   236

Section IV. Passions and Virtues

13. Reappropriating Aquinas's Account of the Passions (1990)   273

14. The Role of Virtue in Moral Theology (1996)   288

15. Capreolus's Defense of Aquinas: A Medieval Debate about
    the Virtues and Gifts (1997)   304

16. Conscience and Christian Tradition (1990)   321

17. Conscience and the Virtue of Prudence (1996)   342

Section V. Law and Grace

18. Aquinas on Nature and the Supernatural (1992)   359

19. The Return of the New Law to Moral Theology (1999)   369

20. Morality and the Movement of the Holy Spirit:
    Aquinas's Doctrine of *Instinctus* (1991)   385

Bibliography of Servais-Théodore Pinckaers   397

Index of Holy Scripture   413

Index of Patristic, Ancient, and Medieval Sources   415

Index of Proper Names   417

Index of Works of St. Thomas Aquinas   421

Subject Index   423

Abbreviations

Aquinas, St. Thomas

Ad Rom.	*In epistolam ad Romanos*
De Verit.	*Quaestiones disputatae de veritate*
I ad Cor.	*Super I ad Corinthianos*
Sent.	*Scriptum super libros sententiarum*
SCG	*Summa contra Gentiles*
ST	*Summa theologiae*
Super Mat.	*Lectura super evangelium secundum Matthaeum*

Bible and Magisterial Documents

CCC	*Catechism of the Catholic Church*
OT	*Optatam totius*
RSV	*Revised Standard Version*
VS	*Veritatis splendor*

Patristic, Ancient, and Medieval Sources

Conf.	St. Augustine, *Confessiones*
Fin.	Cicero, Marcus Tullius, *De finibus bonorum et malorum*
De Doc. Christ.	St. Augustine, *De doctrina Christiana*
De Fide Orthod.	St. John Damascene, *De fide orthodoxa*
De Offic.	St. Ambrose, *De officiis*

De Trin.	St. Augustine, *De Trinitate*
In Ioan. Evang.	St. Augustine, *In Ioannis evangelium tractatus*
In Sent.	Peter Lombard, *Sententia in IV libris distinctae*

Journals, Dictionaries, Encyclopedias

PL	*Patrologia Latina,* Mignes
NRT	*Nouvelle revue théologique*
NV	*Nova et Vetera*
RSPT	*Revue des sciences philosophique et théologique*
RTh	*Revue thomiste*
RTAM	*Recherches de théologie ancienne et médiévale*
TS	*Theological Studies*

Acknowledgments

Having been at work preparing *The Pinckaers Reader* for a good number of years, the editors have accumulated numerous debts, which they are eager to acknowledge. We are particularly keen to thank Sr. Mary Thomas Noble, O.P., the major translator of the volume. For many years now she has indefatigably translated the works of Servais-Théodore Pinckaers. Her dedication is surpassed only by her extraordinary ability to translate moral theology into felicitous English prose.

A number of scholars have assisted us throughout the process of bringing this book to completion: Fr. Romanus Cessario, O.P., has supported the project in innumerable ways, and has been a source of wisdom on all manner of details; Fr. Michael Sherwin, O.P., has likewise been very supportive, having contributed to the translation and editing process at several points, and has also assisted in obtaining permissions for the volume; Prof. William Mattison assisted in the editing of several essays while he was in Fribourg, and gave helpful comments on the introduction to the volume; Prof. Tobias Hoffmann assisted John Berkman in the conception of the project back in 1997, and offered advice on the introduction and on points of translation as the project drew to completion in 2004.

The editors would also like to give special thanks to the Dominican community at the Albertinum in Fribourg, Switzerland, which over the years has shown the editors considerable hospitality and many kindnesses. We would like to mention especially Fr. Guy Bedouelle, O.P., who as prior of the Albertinum has greatly supported this project.

Many others offered assistance at particular points. Fr. John Corbett offered helpful suggestions on the selection of the essays for the volume. As research assistants to John Berkman at the Catholic University of America,

Aaron Massey, John Rziha, and particularly Robert Alspaugh contributed extensive labor, finding and checking English-language citations, and formatting and proofreading the essays and the bibliography. John Berkman, Craig Steven Titus, and Aaron Massey collaborated on creating the indices. Aaron's hard work was an indispensable aid to making them as comprehensive as possible.

We also want to express our appreciation to David McGonagle, director and editor-in-chief of the Catholic University of America Press, for his steadfast support of the volume over the last six years. Thanks are also due to Susan Needham for her coordination of the process by which this book came to be, to Elizabeth Benevides for her work in marketing, and especially to Ellen Coughlin for her excellent copyediting, as well as her patience and flexibility.

Craig would like to thank his wife, Giovanna, who has brought her linguistic talents and French expertise to the project.

John is particularly grateful to Jennifer for her willingness to be there until death do us part, and for her delightful presence in the midst of it all.

Finally, we offer our gratitude to Servais-Théodore Pinckaers, whose person and work have made this volume possible. Over the years Père Pinckaers has been unfailingly generous to each of us in many different ways. While the indisputable importance of Pinckaers's writings have made our editing this volume important, his extraordinary person has make our labors on this project a joy.

1 ∾ Introduction

John Berkman

What Is *The Pinckaers Reader*?

You have in your hands a collection of twenty essays by the Dominican priest and theologian Servais-Théodore Pinckaers. *The Pinckaers Reader* represents a selection of Pinckaers's constructive work in academic moral theology since the mid-1980s.[1] Pinckaers is one of the foremost Catholic moral theologians of this past generation, one whose work has not been adequately introduced to the English-speaking world. Furthermore, Pinckaers has an important and distinctive approach to moral theology, one that in seeking to be thoroughly "recoverist" turns out to offer a distinctive and refreshingly original approach to the Christian life.

Pinckaers writes primarily in French, and only a relatively small selection of his corpus has been translated into English. While a number of his introductory and spiritual works have been recently translated (e.g., *The Desire for Happiness* [1998], *Morality: The Catholic View* [2001]), the most important scholarly work of Pinckaers that has been translated into English is his *Sources of Christian Ethics* (1995). In *Sources*, Pinckaers provides one of the most im-

---

1. The exceptions are two earlier essays in the section on moral agency. Not surprisingly, these essays have a more critical (in addition to constructive) function in the volume. "Aquinas and Agency: Beyond Autonomy and Heteronomy?" (1978) is Pinckaers's analysis of aspects of the "autonomous ethics" that has been popular in the European context of moral theology. "Revisionist Understandings of Actions in the Wake of Vatican II" (1982) is his analysis of revisionist moral methodology that was very popular and influential among moral theologians in the decades immediately following the Second Vatican Council. These essays have been included as examples of Pinckaers's engagement with alternative approaches to moral theology while working out a very different approach to the Christian moral life.

portant and comprehensive histories of Catholic moral theology, ranging from studies of the Sermon on the Mount and Saint Paul to an analysis of recent trends in the discipline. However, far more than a history of the discipline (and a pointed one at that), Pinckaers's *Sources* offers a constructive Thomistic moral theology. *Sources* is original and unusual, not only in that its emphasis on the virtues in St. Thomas predates much of the recent interest in this area, but also in its digging deeper into Thomas's account of them, emphasizing the interrelationship between morality and spirituality, between the virtues and the Thomistic gifts and beatitudes. Whereas *Sources* is oriented historically, *The Pinckaers Reader* is ordered systematically, and presents many of Pinckaers's key themes at a length and depth not possible in that earlier volume. *The Pinckaers Reader* is a collection of his most significant scholarly publications over the last two decades, and represents a kind of sequel to *Sources*.

The editors faced great difficulty in trying to decide which essays should be included in *The Pinckaers Reader*. Originally, the essays chosen were enough to fill three volumes, and so in limiting the selection to one volume, many difficult choices had to be made. There are numerous other articles that we would have liked to include on questions of method in moral theology, on the nature of actions, on the passions, on specific virtues, etc. Most especially the editors would have liked to include other writings that elucidate Pinckaers's argument regarding the fateful separation between systematic, moral, and spiritual theology in the modern period. Since one of Pinckaers's preoccupations is to show the integral relationship between these contemporary disciplines (and especially show their integral relationship in the *Summa theologiae),* the editors selected those essays which best display not only the innovative elements of Pinckaers's project, but also Pinckaers's distinctive integration of these various elements in his constructive Thomistic moral theology.

Who Is Servais-Théodore Pinckaers?

Pinckaers was born in 1925 in Belgium. Though his father was Dutch-speaking, his mother was Walloon, and young Servais grew up in the Walloon part of Belgium. At home he spoke Walloon, at school French. He entered the Dominicans and received his formation and basic theological training at the

Dominican house of studies based at the Dominican priory of La Sarte, in the town of Huy in Belgium. He went on to receive his doctoral degree in Rome. He taught moral theology—both "fundamental" and "special"—at La Sarte from 1953 until the *studium generale* (i.e., house of studies) closed in 1965. Pinckaers spent the years 1965 until 1973 preaching at the Dominican priory of Liège in Belgium. In 1973, he accepted the position of professor of fundamental moral theology at the University of Fribourg, where he taught until his retirement in 1997. In teaching moral theology there, Pinckaers followed in the line of major twentieth-century Dominican moral theologians at Fribourg, such as the moral manualist Dominic Prümmer, the Thomistic commentator Santiago Ramirez, and the historian of moral theology Thomas Deman.[2] Since 1973, he has lived in the Albertinum, a Dominican priory for foreign professors and students in Fribourg.

One can also see in Pinckaers's education various key influences on his work. Pinckaers went to study at La Sarte immediately following World War II, while the institution was still in its infancy (it had first opened in 1942). La Sarte was established by theologians committed to the "historic method" in theology, and its founder, Louis Charlier, found himself in trouble with ecclesiastical authorities from the institution's beginning. He gathered a group of young theologians who were committed or at least sympathetic to the historical method, such as Jerome Hamer (later Cardinal), Augustine Leonard, and Bernard Olivier, who were also in conversation with other French theologians sympathetic to this approach, such as Marie-Dominique Chenu, Jacques Leclerc, and Jean Daniélou.[3]

Rebelling against the understanding of the moral life embodied in the manuals still dominant in the discipline of moral theology, the theologians at La Sarte were instead turning to what they understood to be the important sources of morality. Emphasis was given to studying the Scriptures and patristic writings, especially for understanding human agency and action. A major impetus for this "return to the sources" was that it was seen as a key to a superior understanding of the writings of Thomas Aquinas, especially his *Summa theologiae*. Whereas other moralists sought to understand St. Thomas prima-

2. See essay #5 in *The Pinckaers Reader*.

3. For a general discussion of this movement, see Marcellino D'Ambrosio, "*Ressourcement* theology, *aggiornamenta,* and the hermeneutics of tradition," *Communio* 18:4 (Winter 1991): 530–55.

rily through study of his commentators, Pinckaers and others at La Sarte were introduced to the approach of reading those who influenced Thomas's writings, focusing on Thomas's own sources. In so doing, they were seeking to inaugurate a renewal of moral theology. Given that their founder had been prohibited from teaching at La Sarte, and that their approach was considered suspect in the time leading up to the publication of *Humani Generis,* it was an exciting, even daring, time and place to be studying theology.

After completing his seminary training, Pinckaers completed his STL at La Sarte under Jerome Hamer, submitting his eighty-five-page licentiate thesis on Henri de Lubac's *Surnatural* in 1952.[4] Unlike many other Dominicans, and the dominant theological opinion of the time, Pinckaers is clearly sympathetic to de Lubac, as Pinckaers saw it as being in essence a faithful representation of the viewpoint of Aquinas.[5] Pinckaers's own defense of the "natural desire to see God" can be found in many of his essays.[6]

Pinckaers wrote his doctoral dissertation at the Pontifical University of Saint Thomas Aquinas (Angelicum) in Rome under the direction of Reginald Garrigou-Lagrange, the Dominican scholar famous not only for his commentaries on St. Thomas and his writings on the spiritual life, but also for his opposition to the historic method in theology. His dissertation, completed in 1958, was entitled "The Virtuous Nature of Hope, from Peter Lombard to Thomas Aquinas."[7] Unlike his director, Pinckaers was very interested in the importance of the historical method for work on the moral theology of St. Thomas Aquinas. This can be seen both in his dissertation and in early essays, such as "L'utilité de la méthode historique pour l'étude de la morale thomiste" ["The usefulness of the historical method for the study of Aquinas's ethics"] and "Les différences du langage scolastique et du langage courant"

4. *Le "Surnaturel" du P. De Lubac* (S.T.L. Thesis, La Sarte, 1952).

5. For an extensive discussion of the significance of de Lubac's thesis in relation to Thomistic theology, see the *RTh* 101:1 (2001), an issue devoted to his *Surnaturel: études historique.* See also Fergus Kerr, "Quarrels about Grace," in *After Aquinas* (Oxford: Blackwell Publishing, 2002), 134–48.

6. For example, see "Aquinas's Pursuit of Beatitude: From the *Commentary on the Sentences* to the *Summa Theologiae*" (essay #6 in *The Pinckaers Reader*), "Beatitude and the Beatitudes in Aquinas's *Summa Theologiae*" (essay #7 in *The Pinckaers Reader*), "Aquinas on Nature and the Supernatural" (essay #18 in *The Pinckaers Reader*), as well as "Le désir naturel de voir Dieu," *NV* 51 (1976): 255–73.

7. *La vertu d'espérance de Pierre Lombard à St. Thomas d'Aquin* (S.T.D. Thesis, Angelicum, 1958).

["The differences between scholastic and contemporary language"], which would appear in his first book.[8] It is also attested to by the fact that the introduction to the book was written by none other than Marie-Dominique Chenu. Of his generation of Dominicans, Chenu was perhaps the most influential advocate of historical studies as a means of recovering and reappropriating the richness and fullness of the message of St. Thomas.

In Pinckaers's early essays, all written while he was in his thirties, and culminating in *Le renouveau de la morale,* he focused on questions having to do with the nature of human actions and of the virtues, primarily seeking to understand and articulate the viewpoint of St. Thomas for a contemporary audience.[9] However, perhaps more significant was that it was the genesis of an approach to moral theology that was at once completely unsympathetic to the manualist tradition which had dominated Catholic moral theology for the past three hundred years, and yet was not at all moving toward the proportionalist approach to moral theology that would arise in the late sixties and quickly become extremely influential in Catholic ethics through the 1970s and 1980s.

As it would turn out, Pinckaers's critique of the manualist approach to moral theology was deeper, methodologically speaking, than the proportionalist critique. Whereas proportionalists continued to share with the manualists a juridical conception of the moral life—continuing to uphold the view that the moral life is primarily about what one is "obligated," "permitted," or "forbidden" to do in this or that situation—Pinckaers was articulating a very different conception of the moral life, the virtue-oriented approach which dominates Aquinas's work, where discernment and pursuit of the good, the excellent, and the holy underlie the evaluation of an act as being permissible or forbidden.

Pinckaers's fundamental objection to the juridical approach of the manualists and proportionalists is its failure to adequately address the nature and telos of the human person. His understanding of the human person is most vivid in his extensive writings on "spiritual" topics, many of which originate in homilies or retreats Pinckaers has given. It can also be seen in his writings on the spirituality of wonder, which he understands as a form of adoration. Although

8. See *Le renouveau de la morale* (Tournai: Casterman, 1964), 44–60 and 61–74.

9. *Le renouveau de la morale* has never been translated into English, with the exception of one chapter, published as "Virtue Is Not a Habit," trans. Bernard Gilligan, *Cross Currents* (Winter 1962): 65–81.

some may see Pinckaers's strong and abiding commitment to "spiritual" writings as largely unrelated to his writings in "moral" theology, the reader who understands Pinckaers's methodological commitments will know that these "spiritual" works are not in fact unrelated works, but part and parcel of Pinckaers's approach to moral theology. As can be seen throughout this volume, Pinckaers's vision of moral theology is ultimately oriented neither to understanding the demands of the natural law, nor to elucidating the nature of acts and virtues, but to articulating an adequate understanding of the telos of the human person, a key element of which being the integral response of the believer to the call of the Triune God as revealed in the Scriptures and tradition.

Although Pinckaers's education put him in a particularly good situation to actively participate in and contribute to the renewal of moral theology called for by the Second Vatican Council, events do not always develop as might be expected. In 1965, the house of studies at La Sarte was closed. This was the educational institution where Pinckaers had been educated and was teaching. It was also the institution with which Pinckaers had been intimately involved for nearly its entire existence, and for Pinckaers's entire adult life up to that time. From La Sarte, Pinckaers was assigned to a Dominican priory in Liège, Belgium, preaching, leading retreats, and eventually serving as prior of the community. Pinckaers would spend most of his forties at the priory, and over that decade would write relatively little, but in retrospect this can be seen as a time when he came into a deeper contact with Scripture and one that prepared him for the work that would occupy him in the decades to come.

In 1973, Pinckaers returned to academia, when he was appointed to the French-speaking chair in fundamental moral theology at the bilingual University of Fribourg in Switzerland. Not long after arriving in Fribourg, Pinckaers would begin to publish extensively. Over the next decade he would gradually publish the contents of his lectures in fundamental moral theology, first as articles in *Nova et Vetera* in the late 1970s, and then gathered up into *Les Sources de la morale chrétienne [Sources of Christian Ethics]*, first published in French in 1985.

During his first decade in Fribourg, Pinckaers would also continue his studies of human beatitude (i.e., happiness) and on the nature of actions, publishing a commentary on parts of the *Summa theologiae* that address these topics. He would begin to publish extensively on topics seeking to show the integral unity of the spiritual life and the moral life, as exemplified in his book *La quête du bonheur [The Question of Beatitude]*, first published in French in 1979.[10]

During this decade Pinckaers would also become extensively involved in the controversy over the "revisionist" perspective in moral theology. In the late 1970s, Cardinal Jean-Jérôme Hamer sought to bring together advocates of an "innovator" perspective with moral theologians who held to a "classicist" position. In March of 1981, a symposium was held aiming at a dialogue and even a rapprochement in methodology in Catholic moral theology, and for this symposium Pinckaers contributed essays on the topic of absolute moral norms. Unfortunately, little fruit seems to have come from this symposium.[11] The essays that Pinckaers prepared were published in 1982 and later were expanded and integrated into his 1986 book, *Ce qu'on ne peut jamais faire [On What One Can Never Do]*. The two main chapters from this book have been translated and incorporated into *The Pinckaers Reader*.

Since this work on questions of revisionist methodology, Pinckaers has continued to be involved in serving the Church through writing and consultations. In 1988 he became a member of the International Theological Commission, of which he was a member for twelve years. In addition, in the late 1980s, Pinckaers became involved with the writing of the moral part of the *Catechism of the Catholic Church*. Although it is usually very difficult to discern with any certitude the degree of participation of any individual in the composition of Church documents, it is clear from both the style and the contents of the moral section of the *Catechism* that Pinckaers's way of approaching the moral life was influential with regard to both its structure and content.

The original French edition of *Sources of Christian Ethics* (1985) was published the year of Pinckaers's sixtieth birthday. The two decades since its publication have witnessed the full flowering of Pinckaers's contribution to moral theology. In 1989 Pinckaers published *L'Evangile et la morale (The Gospel and Ethics)*, an extensive collection of his essays written over the previous decade.[12] In his 1996 *La Vie selon l'Esprit: Essai de Théologie spirituelle selon*

10. This book was published in English as Servais Pinckaers, *The Pursuit of Happiness—God's Way: Living the Beatitudes* (New York: Alba House, 1998).

11. For Pinckaers's discussion of the purpose and outcome of these meetings, see "Un symposium de moral inconnu," *NV* 76 (2001): 19–34. This essay was recently translated into English as "An Unnoticed Symposium on Moral Theory," *NV* (English edition) 1:2 (2003): 341–57.

12. See Pinckaers, *L'Evangile et la morale* (Fribourg: Editions Universitaires, 1989). The

saint Paul et saint Thomas d'Aquin (Life in the Spirit: The Spiritual Theology of St. Paul and St. Thomas Aquinas), Pinckaers provides his most sustained effort toward a synthesis of the moral and spiritual life.[13] Pinckaers has continued to write and revise commentary on St. Thomas's *Summa theologiae,* has written extensively on the *Catechism* and *Veritatis splendor* and other ecclesial documents, and has published more popular works on the moral and spiritual life.[14] Finally, Pinckaers has written extensively in what might be called "constructive academic moral theology," which is what *The Pinckaers Reader* seeks to make available to an English-speaking audience.

I had the pleasure of spending time in Père Pinckaers's company in the spring of 1997, when I lived and worked at the Albertinum for three months. Pinckaers had just retired from his chair at Fribourg, but was continuing to teach at the university. My impression of Pinckaers was that of a quiet and contemplative man, one completely dedicated to his priestly and scholarly vocation. While slight of stature, he was fit and vigorous. A highlight of my time with Pinckaers was our three-hour walks into the hills around Fribourg during the afternoon, discussing moral theology and other matters. Pinckaers clearly enjoyed vigorous give and take in individual conversation, and was typically more animated in individual conversations than in large gatherings. In my time with Pinckaers, it became clear to me that his integration of morality and

---

twenty-one essays in this volume had previously been published between 1976 and 1988, with one essay, "Ce que le Moyen-Age pensait du mariage," dating back to 1967.

13. Pinckaers, *La vie selon l'Esprit. Essai de théologie spirituelle selon saint Paul et saint Thomas d'Aquin* (Luxembourg: Saint-Paul, 1996).

14. Pinckaers's work in the tradition of Thomistic commentary can be seen in his translation and commentary, *La béatitude* (Ia–IIae, qq. 1–5), Editions le Revue des jeunes (Paris: Cerf, 2001). His writings on ecclesial documents can be seen in "An Encyclical for the Future: Veritatis splendor," in *Veritatis Splendor and the Renewal of Moral Theology,* ed. J. A. Di Noia and Romanus Cessario (Chicago: Scepter, 1999), 11–71 (originally published as *Pour une lecture de "Veritatis splendor"* [Paris: Cahiers de l'Ecole Cathédrale, Mame, 1995]); in essays such as "L'encyclique 'Dives in misericordia,'" *Sources* 7 (1981): 49–58, and "L'Evangile de la vie face à une culture de mort," *NV* 70 (July 1995): 5–17; as well as "Scripture and the Renewal of Moral Theology (1995)" and "The Return of the New Law to Moral Theology (1999)," essays #3 and #19 in *The Pinckaers Reader.* Many of his more popular writings on the spiritual life are gathered in *La justice évangélique* (Paris: Téqui, 1986); *La prière chrétienne* (Fribourg: Editions Universitaires, 1989); *Un grand chant d'amour. La passion selon saint Matthieu* (Saint-Maur: Socomed Madiation, 1997); and *La spiritualité du martyre* (Versailles: Editions St. Paul, 2000).

spirituality was not primarily an academic conviction. He was preaching regularly and giving numerous retreats, which he took most seriously, as evident from the fact that he regularly published these talks. His extraordinary work habits were fully evident when I was with him, as he was preparing numerous papers for publication and working on multiple book projects. In my time with him, Pinckaers left a deep impression on me of a dedicated and generous priest-scholar.

How Did *The Pinckaers Reader* Come to Be?

The Pinckaers Reader has been a work long in progress. Its genesis dates to my stay at the Albertinum in 1997, when I was working on the history of moral theology. In my many conversations with Père Pinckaers, I came to the conviction that a collection of his more recent essays should be available in English. Over the next two years, difficult decisions had to be made as to what essays from Pinckaers's very large corpus of work should be chosen. The elegant and literary translation skills of Sister Mary Thomas Noble were secured, and she began work on translating essays for the volume in 1999. In the spring of 2000, Craig Steven Titus, then a doctoral student and a research and teaching assistant at the University of Fribourg, was recruited. To make these essays as technically accurate as possible, Craig Titus and Pinckaers agreed to double-check the translation. It soon became apparent that Titus's contribution to the volume was such that the project should be co-edited by Berkman and Titus. Titus's contribution to the volume was further expanded in the fall of 2001, when Sister Mary Thomas's election as Abbess at her monastery in Buffalo, New York, precluded her continuing the translations. Titus took over the job of primary translator as well as editor, and was the sole translator of three essays for *The Pinckaers Reader*. Over the last three years Berkman and Titus have worked together on *The Pinckaers Reader*. Their collaboration has extended not only to securing excellent translations, but also to further decisions about the essays to appear in the volume, and the compilation of a bibliography of Fr. Pinckaers specifically geared toward English speakers.

What Is in *The Pinckaers Reader?*

The Pinckaers Reader aims to bring to an English-speaking audience a selection of Pinckaers's most significant writings since the original, 1985 publication of *Sources of Christian Ethics.* Throughout the volume one cannot fail to see the guiding and regulating influence of St. Thomas Aquinas on Pinckaers's work. Pinckaers constantly seeks to capture not only Aquinas's substantive views on the fundamentals of morality, but also Aquinas's own guiding spirit. Like Jean-Pierre Torrell, his Dominican confrere in Fribourg, Pinckaers seeks to convey the key spiritual convictions that animate Aquinas's discussion of a wide range of questions on the moral life. Behind what at times appears to be the "rationalist" façade of the *Summa theologiae,* Pinckaers discerns a spiritual passion in Aquinas for the things of God. Pinckaers sees this, for example, in Aquinas's accounts of the natural desire for God, in his account of the New Law as the interior movement of the Holy Spirit, in Thomas's defense of the mendicant vocation to the contemplation and preaching of evangelical truth, and in his meditations on the Eucharist.

Although some critics accuse Pinckaers of being so preoccupied with Thomas and his outlook that he fails to attend adequately to the specifics of our contemporary situation, Pinckaers's preoccupation with understanding Aquinas—especially in relation to his sources—has led to a rich recovery of elements of Aquinas that are ignored by almost all other contemporary Catholic moralists. Pinckaers's willingness to pursue his line of interpretation of Aquinas outside of the conceptual boundaries of what typically is thought to constitute "moral theology" has enabled him to develop an extraordinarily rich and deep account of St. Thomas that is truly original in our contemporary situation. Pinckaers's account of St. Thomas on the moral life is also rather foreign to a great majority of what currently passes as representing the ethics of St. Thomas Aquinas.

The first section of *The Pinckaers Reader* begins with a focus on three distinctive elements of Pinckaers's approach to moral theology: his historical method and fascination with Aquinas's sources as a key to understanding Aquinas (essay #1); the ecclesial and sacramental assumptions embodied in Aquinas's thought and hermeneutics (essay #2); and the priority of scriptural interpretation for moral theology, both for Aquinas and for our contemporary context (essay #3). In addition, this section provides an essay on Pinckaers's understanding of the relationship between philosophy and theology, occasioned by the promulgation of John Paul II's 1998 encyclical, *Fides et ratio* (essay #4). Finally, this section also provides Pinckaers's most extensive discussion of his particular tradition of moral and intellectual enquiry in the Thomistic tradition, the tradition of French Dominican moral theology in the twentieth century (essay #5).

The second section of *The Pinckaers Reader* takes us to the topic of beatitude, perhaps the topic that has provoked some of Pinckaers's harshest criticisms of moral theology in the modern period, and similarly most captivated Pinckaers's imagination with regard to its centrality and possibilities for a truly renewed moral theology. "Aquinas' Pursuit of Beatitude: From the Commentary on the Sentences to the *Summa Theologiae*" (essay #6) is a particularly powerful introduction to Aquinas's thought on the subject, an essay truly in the spirit of Aquinas in the way it not only informs, but also existentially draws in the reader. The other essays on beatitude (essay #7), the imago Dei (essay #8), and human dignity (essay #9) fill out the picture of Aquinas's theological anthropology, among other things showing the integral connections that Thomas makes throughout the *Summa theologiae* (e.g., here between the *prima pars* and the *secunda pars*).

The third section of *The Pinckaers Reader* presents Pinckaers's analysis of two alternative moral perspectives. The essay on autonomy and heteronomy seeks to contrast Thomas's moral theology with the assumptions of Kantian moral philosophy (essay #10). The next two essays constitute Pinckaers's contextualization of and response to proprotionalists moral methodology. The historical analysis of the question of intrinsically evil acts is in fact a history of action theory in Catholic moral theology from the patristics, through Augustine, the medievals, Suarez, and on down to Billuart (essay #11). His essay on post-Vatican II revisionist understanding of actions first examines the moral methodology of proportionate reason, and then places it historically in relation to the moral methodology of the manuals, showing how it shares some of the key problems endemic in the manualist tradition (essay #12).

The fourth section of *The Pinckaers Reader* focuses on the interior principles and dispositions whose cultivation directs us in the pursuit of beatitude. Pinckaers describes convincingly how and why the passions function in Aquinas's *Summa theologiae* as an indispensable aspect of the moral life (essay #13). The three essays on the virtues provide us with Pinckaers's evaluation of the recent revival of interest in the virtues by the "mainstream" of moral philosophy and moral theology in the United States (essay #14), take us into a historical debate among theologians in the centuries following Aquinas over the proper understanding and role of the virtues and the gifts (essay #15), and show us how the understanding of a central virtue (i.e., prudence) has in turn influenced the understanding of "conscience" (essay #16), and how a recovery of the classical understanding and practice of prudence might help us recast what we think of what it means to act in "good conscience" (essay #17).

The fifth and final section of *The Pinckaers Reader* is particularly revealing of how far Pinckaers's work has stood outside the mainstream of Thomistic moral theology in the last decades. Pinckaers's attempt to reorient moral theology in light of the New Law of the Gospel, his view of the interrelationship of grace and action, and his reflection on the significance of the Holy Spirit in guiding the believer through the infused moral virtues, the gifts, and a more general "spiritual instinct" all reveal a side of St. Thomas's moral doctrine that finds little resonance in the contemporary academy. As such, *The Pinckaers Reader* presents a powerful case that there remain important sources in the tradition waiting to be recovered as part of the ongoing renewal of moral theology.

The editors of *The Pinckaers Reader* have also provided a bibliography of Pinckaers's writings. While it does not claim to be exhaustive, it is comprehensive and seeks to assist readers in finding Pinckaers's writings on different topics and in different genres. To this end, it lists in boldface all of Pinckaers's writings that have been translated into English. It also shows which of his essays are reproduced in books of his collected essays, such as *Le renouveau de la morale* (1964) and *L'Evangile et la morale* (1989). The essays translated for *The Pinckaers Reader* are also included in the bibliography, so readers can gauge the size of the selection from Fr. Pinckaers's writings in relation to his corpus as a whole. The editors hope that the bibliography will allow readers to find other of Pinckaers's essays that address these topics at further length.[15]

15. Thanks to Tobias Hoffmann, Bill Mattison, Craig Titus, and especially Daniel Ferris for their helpful comments on earlier drafts of this essay.

Renewing Thomistic Moral Theology

In our time, moral theology may be seen as a discipline still in search of a methodology. The main methodology of moral theology for centuries prior to the Second Vatican Council—the manualist tradition—has been shown at best to be inadequate for the various tasks moral theologians now understand to be before them. In the midst of the widespread call for the renewal of moral theology, the message and method of Servais-Théodore Pinckaers's work are important, and their importance has not been commensurate with the availability of his work for English-speaking audiences. The editors of *The Pinckaers Reader* hope that this volume may go some ways to rectifying this situation, displaying the importance of Pinckaers's distinctive approach to the moral life, and encouraging further examination of his work as a whole. Ultimately, it is hoped that this volume will help inject Pinckaers's perspective into the ongoing debate in English-speaking context as to how moral theology is to be renewed and reinvigorated. Ideally, it will contribute to a debate about the strengths and weaknesses of Pinckaers's approach, and in so doing to the growth and development of ongoing conversation needed for the discipline's continued renewal. In that way, we hope this volume will be of service not only in the academy and in the seminary, but also in the wider renewal of the Church and of society.

SECTION I ❧ Thomistic Method and the Renewal of Moral Theology

1 ❧ The Sources of the Ethics of St. Thomas Aquinas (2002)

A study of the sources of St. Thomas's moral teaching can be very beneficial, for it gives us new insights into his texts and broadens and deepens our understanding of his thought. To a traditional reading that makes use of the commentators who came after Thomas, it adds an interpretation of the master in light of the authors who preceded him, and of the sources that inspired him and provided him with the materials for his theological project. Thus, a speculative examination of his work is rounded out by a historical consideration that reveals the genesis and unfolding of his thought, helping us to perceive better its vitality and richness. Such a study also aids us in discovering the timeliness of a teaching nourished by the great scriptural and patristic traditions and those of Augustine and Aristotle.

Within the limits of this chapter, I shall focus upon the moral section of the *Summa theologiae,* the *secunda pars,* always with an eye to the possible contributions of other works. It is not difficult to discover the sources of Thomas's teaching, since he himself indicates them. The method is simple enough: it suffices to list the authors he cites, the authorities he appeals to in his articles. Thus, one can easily establish a list of explicit citations, question by question, taking into account the need to pay special attention to works mentioned in the *sed contra* and in the body of the articles, for these are more likely to refer to a substantial source of his teaching.

Originally published in *The Ethics of St. Thomas Aquinas,* ed. Stephen Pope (Washington, D.C.: Georgetown University Press, 2002). Translated by Sister Mary Thomas Noble, O.P., with the assistance of Father Michael Sherwin, O.P. Edited for publication in *The Pinckaers Reader* by Craig Steven Titus.

List of Sources of St. Thomas's Ethics According to His Citations

Using Busa's concordance, I shall begin with a list of citations of authors. Here are the principal authors cited, arranged according to the number of citations in the *secunda pars* of the *Summa:* Augustine, 1,630; Aristotle, 1,546; Gregory the Great, 439; Pseudo Dionysius, 202; Cicero, 187; Jerome, 178; John Damascene, 168; Ambrose, 151; Isidore of Seville, 120; Roman law, 102; Nemesius of Emesa (under the name Gregory of Nyssa), 41; Macrobius, 33; Boethius, 30; Prosper of Aquitaine, 19; Benedict, 18; Basil, 13; Plato, 12; Hilary of Poitiers, 12; Bernard, 9; Caesar, 8; Ptolemy, 1. There are also citations from schools of philosophy: Stoics, 25; Peripatetics, 13; Platonists, 7; Epicurians, 2.

Citations of Scripture are found in all the questions and are the most numerous. Confining myself to the *secunda pars,* I have counted 1,839 from the Old Testament and 2,003 from the New Testament. Most frequently quoted from the Old Testament are the Psalms, the Pentateuch, the Sapiential Books, and the Major Prophets. Here is the picture in detail: Psalms, 246; Deuteronomy, 192; Sirach, 172; Proverbs, 166; Exodus, 136; Isaiah, 132; Wisdom of Solomon, 103; Genesis, 99; Job, 72; Jeremiah, 56; Ezekiel, 38; Daniel, 29; 1 Samuel, 25; 1 Kings, 22; Hosea, 21; 2 Kings, 17; Malachi, 14; 2 Chronicles, 13; Joshua, 11; 2 Maccabees, 10; Judges, 9; 2 Samuel, 9; Amos, 8; Tobit, 8; Zechariah, 7; Song of Solomon, 7; 1 Maccabees, 6; Jonah, 5; Micah, 4; Esdras, 4; Esther, 4; Nahum, 3; Lamentations, 3; Judith, 3; 1 Chronicles, 2; Baruch, 2; Habakkuk, 1; Ruth, 1. The remaining Old Testament authors are not quoted: Obadiah, Zephaniah, Haggai, and Nehemiah. Among citations from the New Testament, Matthew, Paul, and John predominate: Matthew, 335; Romans, 313; 1 Corinthians, 270; John, 126; Luke, 120; Hebrews, 111; 2 Corinthians, 105; Ephesians, 81; 1 Timothy, 81; Galatians, 80; 1 John, 67; James, 63; Acts, 56; Philippians, 29; Colossians, 29; Revelation, 23; 1 Peter, 21; 1 Thessalonians, 15; 2 Peter, 15; Mark, 14; Titus, 12; 2 Thessalonians, 4; Philemon, 2; 2 John, 1; Jude, 1. Only John's Third Letter is not quoted.

In addition to these explicit citations, one also needs to take into account the special category of references indicated by *quidam* and *aliqui,* designating authors not considered as authorities but who may constitute important sources of teaching, beginning with Peter Lombard, the *"Magister,"* and the theologians who have commented on him and who belong to a generation close to that of Aquinas.

The Use of Citations in Scholasticism

Now that I have established a material, one-dimensional list of citations, I need to highlight the contours of the intellectual landscape that they represent. The first important point is the purpose of these citations, which is very different from our modern use of them. In our scientific books, in theology, exegesis, or history, citations give the opinions of authors, particularly contemporary ones. Such references either confirm the position of the writer or advance the discussion. Numerous citations and an abundance of footnotes all serve, it would seem, to bear witness to the author's vast erudition.

With Thomas, the citations of authors are an application of the Scholastic method used in the universities. Citations are placed by the Scholastics in the text and not in the notes; they form part of the structure of the argument. Moreover, thirteenth-century Scholastics cite by name only ancient authors, those who enjoy accepted authority in their field. They do not name contemporary theologians, with whom they are at times engaged in very direct discussions, except by way of anonymous references that historians today are seeking to elucidate: *"Aliqui dicunt . . . alii dicunt"*; "Certain people say . . . others say."

This difference has its foundation and takes its significance from the Scholastic method itself. This method, inspired by St. Augustine, who made listening to the teachings of an authority anterior to the work of reason (*De moribus ecclesiae catholicae* 1.2), contains two complementary operations: the reading *(lectio)* and dialectical disputation *(disputatio)*. Reading refers to the teaching of the master, which draws upon great works whose authority stems from their recognized quality. The first function of the master is to explain such works and comment on them. There are the books of Scripture, whose explanation is the prerogative of masters of theology; the writings of the Fathers of the Church, from which the *Sentences of the Fathers* presented by Peter Lombard are derived, upon which all bachelors had to comment; the works of Aristotle, introduced at the University of Paris in the mid-thirteenth century, and so forth. These authors are cited by name. As for recent and contemporary theologians, they are not named, even though their influence might be great. Thus, St. Albert, who was the greatest living authority in the time of St. Thomas, in the modern sense of the word, was reproached for allowing himself to be quoted by name in university disputations.

Grafted onto the reading of great texts and their commentaries is the second operation of the Scholastic method: the disputation. It proposes for discussion, in the form of "questions" *(quaestiones),* problems encountered in the sentences of authorities, questions that even reach the point of pitting one authority against another, as Abelard had done in his celebrated *Sic et non.* This connection between reading and disputation gives a dialectical structure to the questions and articles in Scholastic works: *"Videtur quod non . . ." "Sed contra . . ." "Respondeo dicendum . . ." "Ad primum . . . dicendum . . ."* which can be translated as: "Objections," "On the contrary," "A main response," and "Reply to the objection."

The citations made by St. Thomas in the *Summa* constitute elements of the reading, especially in the *sed contra* and the body of the article or the solution *(determinatio)* of the master. They then furnish arguments in the discussion of the objections. They thus verify their character as sources of knowledge far better than do our modern citations. Their function is to transmit the riches of the theological heritage into the structure of the teaching and to furnish, at the same time, the material for the rational reflection that it helps to insert into the stream of Christian tradition.

If one counts the authors cited by St. Thomas, it is apparent that they are not very numerous in comparison with the bibliographies of our modern publications; however, their significance far outweighs their numbers. First, within each article, the citations are nonetheless abundant and interconnected. Above all, they are rich in content and play a considerable role in the structure of the argument. They have, in fact, a very precise function: their purpose is not erudition but strictly research and the manifestation of the truth of things. The citations of the *sed contra* and of the body of the article usually serve to build up the master's response to the question posed. In the objections, they demonstrate complementary aspects or solve difficulties.

One should note, too, that in citing his sources, Thomas practices a fine economy. One well-chosen citation is enough for him, sometimes two, rarely three, in order to expose the truth he wishes to affirm or defend. His interest bears less on authors and their authority, which might be strengthened by numbers (does he not say that the argument from authority is the weakest in comparison with reason?), than on the truth itself that they interpret. This is why a single citation, if adequate, suffices to support a truth that enlightens research and sustains argument.

The Hierarchy of Sources in St. Thomas's Teaching

If one wished to construct a table of the sources used in St. Thomas's teaching, one cannot place them all on the same plane, simply listing them alphabetically or chronologically. The Scholastics distinguish different levels among the authors they cite, according to their degree of authority, their capacity to communicate knowledge, and manifest truth, or, in a word, their luminosity.

At the highest level of authority is the Word of God, expressed in Scripture. This is what furnishes the prime substance of theology[1] and constitutes its principal source, the highest and surest one. It is rounded out by the teaching of the great councils, which interpret it in an authentic way in the name of the Church, and by the confessions of faith which summarize their teaching.

Next, at a second level of authority are the teachings of the Church Fathers, considered as qualified interpreters and commentators of Scripture. The works of the Fathers show Christian thought and experience to be in continuity with apostolic tradition, at the same time confronting it with the philosophical wisdom whose sources they endeavor to utilize while safeguarding the supremacy of revelation. In the transmission of patristic teaching, the *Sentences* of Peter Lombard play a determining role as the required manual for theological teaching. St. Thomas for his part will, throughout his life, be concerned to develop his knowledge of the Fathers, Augustine (whom he will read and reread personally), and the Greek Fathers (whose works he will research). I should mention, also, a certain authority accorded the glosses of Scripture, which are of varied origin.

To the Fathers one could add, without attributing to them the same authority, however, representative authors of the height of the twelfth century such as Hugh and Richard of St. Victor. Finally, it is well to consider as direct but more hidden sources the thirteenth-century theologians with whom St. Thomas holds discussions in all freedom and whom he utilizes quite frequently. These are the *quidam,* among whom one can distinguish the "ancients," of the three preceding centuries, and the "moderns," of the last generation. These authors can be evaluated according to the quality of their opinions. Certain masters, such as Philip the Chancellor with his teaching on the virtues, Albert the Great in his teaching at Cologne and Paris, and Franciscan

---

1. *ST* I 1.

colleagues, such as Alexander of Hales and Bonaventure, provide St. Thomas with much information and many ideas.

Turning to the philosophers, one also finds important sources of authoritative teaching. Philosophers share in reason's authority and can furnish theologians with probable arguments. They bear witness to human reflection and experience. For Thomas, the chief philosophical source is obviously Aristotle, "the Philosopher," whom he uses throughout his work, even when treating specifically Christian questions. St. Thomas considers Aristotle an expert on human nature and borrows from him the basic structure of his morality: the ordering to beatitude as our final end, the organization of the moral virtues, and the analysis of friendship that serves him in defining charity.[2] In Thomas's project of constructing a morality of virtues, he also exploits authors such as Cicero and Seneca in dealing with the virtues, Boethius for the treatise on beatitude, and Nemesius for the analysis of human acts. Finally, at this level, Thomas is also in contact and in discussion with the *quidam* of his time, consisting notably of the masters in the Faculty of Arts. Furthermore, one must not forget the Arab (Averroes and Avicenna) and Jewish (Maimonides) philosophers. These commentators on Aristotle are for St. Thomas both adversaries and collaborators in researching the truth about God and the human person.

In considering this rapidly constructed table, I can truly say that the work of St. Thomas, particularly the moral section of his *Summa theologiae,* constitutes the convergence of all the great currents of thought known in the thirteenth century, meeting in the cultural center represented by the University of Paris, in their full theological and philosophical flowering. It should be noted, however, that these currents not only exert a historical influence upon Thomas, but, with the contribution of revelation and the different traditions, they provide him with solid materials for a construction at once faithful and original.

2. [Editors' note: The editors have chosen to translate *"bonheur"* as "beatitude" rather than "happiness," both to remind the reader of Aquinas's particular understanding of the end or goal of human life, and to avoid the senses of "happiness" which are more psychic and transient that what Aquinas understood by *"beatitudo."*]

The Utilization of the Sources and Their Articulation

How does Thomas utilize his sources and establish order among them? To answer this question, there is a capital point that needs to be clarified first: the "authorities" that he cites do not play a deontological role for him, but an epistemological one. In other words, their *sentences* do not impose an obligation to hold one or another proposition as true, even if not understood; rather, they are seen as sources of light and truths to be understood, even if they are as yet understood only imperfectly. The "authorities" (the term designated the person who had authority, and equally the propositions taught) address the intellect first, and not merely the will. As for the latter faculty, it is not constrained by the "authorities," but attracted by the love of truth that they inspire. St. Thomas's teaching is thus situated in the context of an intellectual education, a pedagogy exercised by a teacher toward his disciples, whom he forms as theologians, under the aegis of reason and revelation.

Scripture Commented On by the Fathers

From this perspective of intellectual research and formation, our doctor does not use his sources in haphazard fashion; rather, he arranges them in careful order. The citations from Scripture, his first source, because it is the divine Word, are explained with the help of the Fathers and the contributions of philosophers, for revelation presupposes reason.

I can affirm that the citations from Scripture in the *Summa,* decisive for a question, are often accompanied by references to patristic works. This reveals that St. Thomas does not read Scripture in isolation but interprets it within the Church with the help of authoritative representatives of the best tradition, such as Augustine, Gregory the Great, or Dionysius the Areopagite. Let us take the case of the definition of the Evangelical Law as an interior law.[3] The *sed contra* cites the Letter to the Hebrews, which takes up the prophet Jeremiah's proclamation of a new covenant, consisting of divine laws inscribed in hearts. The body of the article appeals to precise texts from the Letter to the Romans and interprets them in light of St. Augustine's *De spiritu et littera,* which is precisely a lengthy meditation on all of these scriptural passages. Article two, on justification through the New Law, cites the Letter to the Romans

3. *ST* I-II 106.1.

in the *sed contra* and repeats the teaching of *De spiritu et littera* in the body of the article.

The procedure is not mechanical, however. In articles three and four of the same question, the scriptural quotations are placed in the *sed contra* and the principal response, while the references to Augustine and Dionysius are found in the answers to the objections. Nonetheless, the fact remains that the teaching on the nature of the New Law, which underlies the three questions devoted to it, gets its start from Paul, on whom Augustine comments. A similar connection between Scripture and Augustine will appear again as a key issue in the explanation of the Sermon on the Mount, directly inspired by the commentary of the Bishop of Hippo.[4] One finds this link between the Gospel and Augustine once again in the question on the Beatitudes[5] and, to a lesser degree, in the discussion of the fruits of the Holy Spirit.[6]

From this, one can conclude that, in Thomas's view, the Fathers are the necessary interpreters of Scripture, authentic representatives of the Church's thought. They express the tradition, which it is the task of theologians to transmit, defend, and develop. In this role, the Fathers serve as models: first, in listening to and explaining the Word of God, and, then, in their intellectual work, placing the resources of reason at the service of the Gospel in order to form a sacred science, a solid theology corresponding to the needs of Christians and of all men and women called by God. Thomas, as a doctor and master of theology, is aware that he is continuing the work of the Fathers by incorporating them into the new Scholastic method.

I should add an important remark about scriptural quotations. Inserted into the Scholastic text with its strongly rational structure, scriptural quotations at first sight may appear artificial, because they introduce a different type of thought and expression that does not have the same rational structure. They also can be taken too easily as secondary illustrations or proof-texts, which is often the case in modern manuals of moral theology. In reality, these words of Scripture usually play a leading role because they possess a status of their own: they are sparks of a higher light coming from the intellect *(intellectus)*, which is superior to discursive reason. This is why they are presented as simple words, rays of light that theological reflection should refract in its rea-

---

4. *ST* I-II 108.2.   5. *ST* I-II 69.
6. *ST* I-II 70.4.

soning. Such is the case, for example, with the phrase from Psalm 4, "The light of your face has shown upon us, O Lord" *("Signatum est super nos lumen vultus tui, Domine"),* quoted several times in connection with natural law: in *prima secundae,* question 91, article 2, to show that a natural law exists within us; question 19, article 4, concerning the relationship of a good will to the eternal law; and in *De veritate,* question 16, article 3, on the subject of synderesis and its permanence in the human person. This light, which shows us the good and presides over moral judgments, belongs to the very nature of the soul and flows from the domain of intellect. Finally, this verse signifies the interior light, which is the principal cause of knowledge in teaching given by an external master.[7]

It is thus possible to do some very fruitful research on the enlightening role of the Psalms Thomas quotes. In this connection, one needs to mistrust the rationalistic mentality, which sees as important only what possesses the drawing power of argumentation. For Thomas, the words of Scripture, even when very simple in their formulation, can open up more direct access—far more than even the most elaborate Scholastic reasonings—to the reality theology addresses. This is particularly true of those books and authors of the Bible that he himself comments upon and quotes most frequently, such as the Psalms, Isaiah, Job, the Gospels, Paul, and John. According to Thomas, simple and direct understanding is loftier than the reason it guides. It, in fact, enables communication with angelic and divine intelligence.[8]

The Utilization of Philosophical Sources

The second source of light for St. Thomas is human reason, expressed particularly through the philosophers, with Aristotle as their principal representative. The Philosopher plays a basic role in the St. Thomas's ethical theory. He furnishes Thomas with the categories and analyses that serve as the foundation of his morality of virtues. Aristotle is quoted in the majority of articles in the *Summa.* However, Thomas does not separate the two principal sources, revelation and reason, theology and philosophy, as would be done later. On the contrary, one can see in him a very close collaboration in the use of authorities between the content of faith and reason, the Gospel and Aristotle.

7. *ST* I 117.1 ad 1.
8. *ST* I 79.8.

While discerning perfectly the difference between these two kinds of light, Thomas endeavors to show their convergence, which rests on a fundamental harmony. He is thus heir to the Fathers, who saw in nature the work of the creator God of Genesis, and in the human person—through reason and free will—the image of God called to fulfillment in the divine vision and union.

This explains why St. Thomas apparently experiences no hesitation in incorporating Aristotle into the solution of specifically Christian questions arising from the order of grace. In his view, grace and nature are in harmony and call out to each other, in such wise that, by basing oneself upon the movements of spiritual nature, one can discern how grace proceeds in conformity with the wisdom of God.[9] As a witness to humanity, Aristotle becomes in St. Thomas's eyes a servant of the Gospel. Moreover, this daring perspective authorizes him discreetly to correct and transform the teaching of the Stagirite so as to open it to Christian truth.

This unabashed coordination between the Gospel and Aristotle is shown, for example, in the definition of the principal Christian virtue, charity.[10] In order to fashion this cornerstone of the treatise on charity, Thomas associates a quotation from John in the discourse after the Last Supper, "No longer do I call you servants, but friends," with a quotation from the *Nicomachean Ethics* that recalls the entire Aristotelian analysis of friendship in Books VIII and IX. In the study of the virtuous character of charity, there follow quotations from Augustine's *De doctrina Christiana*[11] and *De moribus ecclesiae catholicae*,[12] and, of course, from 1 Corinthians 13, which provides the *sed contra* of articles 4 to 7. Thus, the study and experience of human friendship serve as a substratum for the study of charity, conceived as friendship with God, with Christ, who is called *"Maxime . . . amicus,"*[13] with one's brothers and sisters, and with all people. It is obvious that charity surpasses human friendship, for Aristotle does not think one could enter into friendship with God because of the extreme inequality that separates humanity from Him,[14] nor with enemies.[15] Therefore, Thomas makes profound changes in the Aristotelian analysis so as to adapt it to a higher experience. Nonetheless, it is from that analysis that he borrows the structure of friendly relationships, to apply it to charity and to all

9. *ST* I-II 5.7; 110.2–3.
11. *ST* II-II 23.2, *sed contra.*
13. *ST* I-II 108.4.
15. *ST* I-II 23.1, obj. 2.

10. *ST* II-II 23.1.
12. *ST* II-II 23.3, *sed contra.*
14. *ST* I-II 23.1, obj. 1.

the movements it engenders. For him, the experience of human friendship provides the best analogy for the description of divine love. Doubtless he is thinking of, among other things, fraternal friendship in the religious life. Aelred of Rievaulx described it a century earlier in his *De spiritali amicitia,* but stopped short of defining charity as friendship, unable to see how the love of enemies, which is characteristic of charity, could be explained in terms of friendship.

There exists, therefore, a close coordination between theological and philosophical sources in Thomas's moral works. It is based upon the fundamental harmony between revelation and reason, each of which, according to its own level and its own method, flows from the divine truth.

St. Thomas's broad and open use of philosophical sources is confirmed in his analysis of the moral virtues, and particularly in his handling of the related virtues. For these questions, Cicero, in his two books *Rhetorica* and *De inventione,* is Aquinas's guide, along with Aristotle, whom Cicero rounds out, Macrobius, who commented on Cicero's *Dream of Scipio,* and Andronicus of Rhodes. These authors are quoted and analyzed together in question 48 of IIa IIae, to establish the parts of prudence. In question 49, on the integral parts of prudence, Cicero furnishes most of the *sed contra,*[16] with Macrobius,[17] Isidore of Seville,[18] and finally, Paul's Letter to the Ephesians.[19] Aristotle intervenes in the body of the articles. In regard to the parts of justice, in question 80, one once more finds Cicero, followed by Aristotle, Macrobius, and Andronicus. One again finds the same constellation in question 128, which establishes the parts of fortitude, and in question 143 on the parts of temperance.

Philosophical divisions are thus adopted by Thomas to construct the organization of the virtues that underlie morality. This approach is not without its drawbacks, for it does not always allot to the specifically Christian virtues the place they deserve. This is the case, for example, with humility, which is practically nonexistent in the lists used (Andronicus defined it as modest bearing in the matter of clothing: q. 161, obj. 4), and is connected with modesty in Cicero's list, which is itself a part of temperance. Humility thus receives an overly modest position, which is understandable among pagan authors, but St. Thomas knows perfectly well its importance in Christian tradition: the

---

16. *ST* I-II 23.1; 23.2; and 23.6.

17. *ST* I-II 23.3; 23.5–7.

18. *ST* I-II 23.4.

19. *ST* I-II 23.8.

New Testament;[20] among the Fathers: Origen,[21] Augustine,[22] John Chrysostom,[23] and Gregory the Great;[24] and, in the monastic tradition, with the degrees of humility according to St. Benedict, explained in article 6. It is fitting, moreover, to group this question with the two following questions on pride and Adam's sin, in which, by contrast, the fundamental importance of humility appears to better advantage.

The same is true of vigilance or watchfulness, a typically Christian virtue as presented by Paul, a waiting for the coming of Christ, filled with hope.[25] Thomas identifies vigilance with solicitude, a part of prudence, according to an etymology of Isidore of Seville,[26] and thus loses the opportunity to expose its Christian dimension.

Such an overt use of Aristotle, Cicero, and other philosophers may explain the reproach often leveled at St. Thomas, that he gives too much space to philosophical sources in his ethics, especially the moral virtues. As a matter of fact, it certainly would be beneficial to compare his total presentation of the virtues with those of Paul and the Fathers, notably Augustine, in order to make some clarifications from a Gospel perspective.

The Theological Orientation of the Ethics of St. Thomas: The Virtues and Beatitudes

One can find in Thomas's treatises on the virtues the same theological perspective as is present in the entire *secunda pars*. One could say that in each instance philosophical analysis rises toward Christian experience and places itself at the service of revelation. It is patently clear in the case of the virtue of fortitude, whose principal act is not so much courage in war as the witness of the martyr.[27] One can see it, also, in the questions on obedience, in which Scripture and Gregory the Great are the principal sources, and in the study of humility, which ends, as I have indicated, with an explanation of the twelve degrees of humility as described by St. Benedict.

---

20. *ST* I-II 161.1; 161.3, *sed contra;* 161.5, *sed contra.*
21. *ST* I-II 161.1, *sed contra;* 161.4, *sed contra.*
22. *ST* I-II 161.2, *sed contra;* 161.5, obj. 2 and 4.
23. *ST* I-II 161.5, obj. 1.   24. *ST* I-II 161.5, obj. 4.
25. 1 Thes 5:5–6; Rom 13:11–12, among others.
26. *ST* I-II 47.9.   27. *ST* II-II 124.

Finally, one needs to remember that the virtues form an organism whose head is constituted by the theological virtues. These animate and inspire the moral virtues from within, to such an extent that they transform the measure of the moral virtues. This leads St. Thomas to support the existence of infused moral virtues, needed to proportion the action of the Christian to the supernatural and theological end to which he is called. Furthermore, he associates with each of the virtues, including the moral virtues, a gift of the Holy Spirit that disposes us to receive divine inspirations that empower us to act according to a higher measure. This is shown in the exposition on the evangelical Beatitudes, which are attained differently according to whether they are attained through the virtues or through the gifts.[28]

The problem of the theological orientation of an analysis employing philosophical sources arises particularly with regard to questions about our final end and beatitude, which constitute the backbone of the entire Thomistic moral theology. It is precisely by means of a study of the sources of this treatise that its evangelical dimension can be better demonstrated, appearances to the contrary notwithstanding.

Let me now take the question of the relationship of this treatise to the Gospel Beatitudes. The connection is not apparent from a simple reading of the first five questions of the *prima secundae,* in which one finds only one quotation from the Beatitudes: the Beatitude of the pure of heart in the *sed contra* of question 4, article 4. This fact seems to confirm the common opinion that the treatise is a purely philosophical, Aristotelian study. But, all one need do is read the explanation of the Beatitudes in Thomas's commentary on the Gospel of Matthew to change one's opinion. In the Beatitudes, Thomas sees Christ's answer to the question of beatitude, which no philosopher had ever truly been able to resolve, not even Aristotle. Here, already, one finds the categories later to be used in the *Summa:* Christ overturns both the false answers of those who place beatitude in a life of pleasure and the incomplete answers of those who place it in the active and contemplative life in this world. Thus, Christ is shown as the philosopher and sage *par excellence,* bringing the complete answer through the promise of the Kingdom of God. This commentary on the Beatitudes already follows that ascending movement, passing from external and bodily goods to interior and spiritual ones and culminating in the

28. *ST* I-II 69.3.

vision of God, which one finds again in the argumentation of the *Summa*. In St. Thomas's view, the teaching on the Beatitudes underlies the questions concerning beatitude and provides their chief answer. The same approach is found in the first two drafts of this treatise, in Book IV of the *Commentary on the Sentences,* distinction 49, and in Book III of the *Summa contra Gentiles,* chapters 1 through 63. Moreover, in his outline of the Sermon on the Mount, which contains all moral teaching *("totam informationem christianae vitae"),* Thomas gives the Beatitudes exactly the same position as in the treatise on happiness in the *Summa:* they establish beatitude as the end of human life (*"Post declaratum beatitudinis finem . . ."* [Ia IIae, q. 108, a. 3]).

The fact that St. Thomas studies the Beatitudes separately results from the question of the relationship among the virtues, gifts, and Beatitudes, which had become classic in Scholastic tradition after Peter Lombard.[29] This problem is important for Aquinas, because it conditions the organization of his ethics, whose point of departure is the virtues. It is for this reason that, in the *Summa,* he is led to treat the Beatitudes not with the questions on beatitude, but after the virtues and gifts,[30] and to associate with each of the seven principal virtues a gift and a Beatitude. This plan immediately poses a difficulty: it rarely occurred to readers of the questions on beatitude then to read in turn the study of the evangelical Beatitudes, which appeared to them to be a spiritual supplement and a slightly artificial refinement of the teaching on the virtues and gifts. Let me add, however, that the list of citations in the first questions of the *prima secundae* shows that the scriptural and patristic sources are used as frequently as the works of Aristotle or Boethius's *De consolatione.*

The Methodological Usefulness of the Study of St. Thomas's Sources

One might think that the study of Thomas's sources is, in the end, only of historical interest. This opinion is reinforced by the idea of many Thomists that the master extracted from his sources the essence of their teaching, their rational substance. It, therefore, does not seem necessary to have recourse to the texts employed by St. Thomas, since they are grasped in his own texts and

29. III *Sent.,* dist. 34.
30. *ST* I-II 69.

assembled with conciseness and precision. Thus, all the theological materials—Scripture, the Fathers, and the philosophers—are summarized and gathered together in the work of Thomas. The study of his text, therefore, suffices for theological reflection. But, on the contrary, it seems to me that if St. Thomas were to come back today, he would tell us almost the opposite: "If I made so many, and such well-chosen citations from authorities, it was not to dispense you from consulting their authors, but, on the contrary, to invite you to read their works. All the more so because some of them, beginning with the sacred authors, enjoy a higher theological authority than mine."

In order to show the interest of this reading of sources, it would be well first to pick out the principal texts that inspire Thomas, which vary according to the questions. These works usually are indicated by repeated references. In the questions on beatitude, for example, one finds as references: Aristotle, especially the *Nicomachean Ethics* and the *De anima;* Boethius's *De consolatione;* Augustine's *De moribus ecclesiae catholicae, De genesi ad litteram,* and *De civitate dei,* to name a few. Book XIV of *De civitate dei* is the basis for the study of the passions and their morality. In the analysis of love, Dionysius takes his place with Augustine, particularly in regard to the effects of this first passion.[31]

Upon close examination, the citations, usually limited to a sentence, often prove to be merely the tip of an iceberg. The study of beatitude refers to Books I and X of the *Nicomachean Ethics,* which take in the entire field of morality. Again, an attentive reading shows that the *De consolatione* supplies the Christian philosophical substratum of the treatise. The comparison between the two works brings out both St. Thomas's dependence and his originality, especially in connection with Christian beatitude in the next world. All the same, the definition of beatitude as "the perfect state of possessing all goods" would seem rather flat had one not read Book III of *De consolatione,* which shows how this is realized in God, the source of every good thing.

Let us take another example. Approaching the question of beatitude by discussing the goods of the soul,[32] Thomas quotes, from memory apparently, a half sentence from Augustine's *De doctrina Christiana:* "That which constitutes the blessed life is that which should be loved for its own sake."[33] Behind

31. *ST* I-II 27.1, *sed contra;* 27.3–6, *sed contra.*
32. *ST* I-II 2.7.
33. *De Doc. Christ.* bk. I, ch. xxii, 20.

this brief quotation is hidden a long and profound reflection by Augustine about the goods that one should use and enjoy, and about love of oneself, of others, and of God in connection with the two commandments of love. This gives all its fullness to Thomas's thought, and indicates at the same time the bond that joins the study of beatitude to charity.

I could produce similar examples in all the questions of the *Summa* and demonstrate repeatedly the usefulness of reading the principal sources cited in order to throw light on the text and show the richness of the ideas that Thomas has in mind as he writes. Of course, I realize too that he does not write in isolation but is always in living communion with what is truest and best in ecclesial and philosophical tradition, in order to transmit it according to the method taught in the Gospel: he is the wise scribe who draws forth from the treasure he has received things new and old, the latter being the guarantor of the former.

The Need to Know St. Thomas's Sources

I have been talking about the usefulness of reading St. Thomas's sources in order to understand him better. I need to go further and speak of its necessity, both because of who Thomas is and because of who his modern readers are.

I could characterize Thomas's thought and style in two words: rational precision. Thomas speaks the language of reason plainly, abstracting from sensible, imaginative, and affective connotations in order to express as precisely as possible the essence of things. This rational purpose leads him to an extreme conciseness; he seeks to formulate the essential and nothing more. One can see this rational process at work in the elaboration of his definitions, such as that of law, which is reduced to its four constitutive elements in the four articles of Question 90 of the *prima secundae*. At the same time, Thomas has the art of choosing, from among the texts he uses, the sentence or the phrase that expresses the essence of the issue and provides the exact argument he needs. Such conciseness offers incontestable advantages for the precision and strength of his argumentation. But it has a disadvantage. Separated from Thomas by seven centuries of history and placed in an altogether different cultural setting, practically speaking, one can no longer by solely reading his text discern the richness of its content nor of the traditions that it evokes. Each group of questions is a gold mine to be explored anew. In consulting the sources he indicates, one can manage this task without too much difficulty. The modern reader even has the advantage of wider and easier access to ancient texts than was possible in the Middle Ages.

Yet, when one considers the modern reader's condition, the difficulties increase; any modern student is an heir to modern rationalism, whose earliest roots can already be detected close to Thomas's time, from the end of the thirteenth century. No longer can one conceive spontaneously the relationship of reason to the other human faculties, nor to faith, in the same way as did St. Thomas, and, therefore, one risks interpreting him badly or in an impoverished way.

For Thomas, reason is always in direct relation to, and in natural harmony with, the intuitive intelligence *(intellectus)*, the source of light through the knowledge of first principles;[34] with the will, whence proceeds love of the good and the desire for beatitude; with affectivity, as witnessed by his beautiful study of the passions; and with the senses, and the body itself, naturally united to the soul. For him, reason operates in synergy with sensible and spiritual experience, and in fruitful collaboration with faith and tradition.

However, the predominance of reason has given rise to certain humanly inevitable limitations in the master's work. He speaks little of affectivity. It is enough to read a few pages of Augustine, Gregory, or Chrysostom, so appreciated by St. Thomas, to see the difference. Nor does Thomas have a great deal of imagination, as is shown by the small number of examples he gives and his schematic way of presenting them. Reading his sources eases this difficulty and makes his teaching more expressive. His teaching brings out the essence and structure of things, of human and divine realities, but it is so rigorous and so finely delineated that it sometimes evokes images of a blueprint. The modern reader needs the help of the authors Thomas cites, in order better to gauge the dimensions of his thought and feel the life breath that animates it.

Between Thomas and the modern reader, a real rupture was created in regard to the concept of the human person with the advent, in the fourteenth century, of nominalism, which separates the human faculties from each other. From that time on, rationalism has opposed voluntarism. In its attempt to dominate them, reason has cut itself off from affectivity, sensitivity, and the nat-

---

34. *ST* I 79.8.

ural and acquired inclinations, and has become increasingly conceptual, even mathematical. Theology loses touch with spiritual and human experience. In line with Descartes, the mind, with its ideas, stands in opposition to the body and to matter, and science establishes itself through a break with tradition, by separating itself from faith, as philosophy separates from theology.

It was inevitable that the reading of St. Thomas by his modern interpreters was influenced by the rationalistic context of the day, which to all appearances can claim to have its roots in the heavily rational character of Aquinas's thought. This was even legitimate to the degree that every reader of an ancient work needs to express the teaching from within the context of his own time. But, perhaps, the time has come to become more aware of the influence of rationalism on our minds, its limitations and shortcomings, the error it occasions in our reading of the great theological and philosophical works, and the resulting impoverishment of our reflections on the problems of our day.

The reading of St. Thomas directly and deeply enriched by the concomitant reading of his scriptural, patristic, and philosophical sources is certainly a good way to overcome the narrowness of a rationalistic theology and to rediscover in ourselves the spiritual sources that have nourished all renewals throughout the course of history, in theology as well as in philosophy.

Interior Sources

The question of St. Thomas's sources is actually broader and deeper than one sometimes thinks. To this point, I have been speaking of the textual sources of Thomas's teaching, indicated principally by the authorities cited. This perspective, which could remain in the purely historical order, is actually not enough, for these external sources would have no effectiveness, according to Thomas's own teaching, without the interior and spiritual sources that play a leading role in the formation of theology.

Personal Reason, Source of Light in Teaching

In his lengthy analysis of the act of teaching,[35] which undoubtedly testifies to his personal experience even though he establishes it by bringing to the fore Aristotle and Paul, the Teacher of the Gentiles, Thomas distinguishes a

---

35. *ST* I 117.1, and parallel places.

twofold action. First, the external action of the master, who helps the mind of the disciple to acquire knowledge by presenting him the pathways of reasoning to be followed, which he himself has traveled; this is *disciplina.* Second, the interior action of the disciple's mind, growing in knowledge thanks to the light of the agent intellect and to the first principles that the intellect possesses naturally as a participation in divine truth. As a physician serves nature in procuring the recovery of health, so the master who teaches is at the service of the disciple's mind. God alone can act directly on the latter and exercise the role of interior master.

This analysis applies directly to my question about sources. The authorities Thomas cites are masters who lend their aid to the acquisition of theological knowledge and to the discovery of truth in every question under discussion. Whatever their importance and their number, nonetheless, one can never forget that these authors address an interior source within each person, the light of truth, which shines at the summit of the mind and in the depths of the heart, presiding over judgments about truth and goodness and particularly over one's receptivity to the teaching and opinions of others.

In this connection, St. Thomas is an exemplary case. In each of his works, in each question of the *Summa,* he places himself alongside his disciples and readers in the school of the masters, to receive all the fragments of truth contained in their teaching. But, at the same time, his interior source, his personal genius, is manifested in the way in which he organizes and disposes the materials he has gathered, to form of them a new synthesis, original and worthy of the great architects of his age. Thanks to this intimate light, Thomas enters into a living and fruitful communion with his sources, so close that, in large measure, it breaks down historical separations. Can one not say that through his dialogue with Aristotle, Thomas has become a contemporary of the Philosopher, or, if you will, that he has introduced him into his own age, and into the University of Paris, as a contemporary master? Can one not likewise think that Aristotle and Thomas may become our contemporaries, masters present to the modern reader as well, if one knows how to read them by the light of the truth, which shines within us as it does in them? They can be even closer to us than many contemporary authors, through their response to our most intimate questions, such as those about beatitude and love, truth and goodness. This is, perhaps, still clearer in the case of Augustine, who has been called the most modern of the Fathers of the Church.

The Word of God as the Principal Interior Source in Theology

When it comes to studying and teaching theology, there is obviously a still higher and more interior source: the Word of God with the grace of the Holy Spirit. St. Thomas recognizes perfectly the predominant action of this source and expresses its interiority, particularly in his teaching on the New Law. Above the natural law, which expresses our spontaneous sense of the true and the good, he recognizes the existence of a source of light and an inclination that are higher and very interior; this he identifies as the grace of the Holy Spirit, penetrating us through faith and operating through charity. As the natural law has been placed in the heart of everyone by the Creator, so the New Law is inscribed by the Spirit in the hearts of believers and endowed with a strength of grace for action.[36] Thus, the Spirit becomes our master in a unique way; the Spirit is above all interiorly so by the light of the Spirit's intimate Word, obtaining for us an understanding of the Scriptures and a knowledge of the ways of providence in our own lives and in the history of the Church.

Thomas clarifies what the rays of this spiritual light are by associating the gifts with the virtues. To faith are joined the gifts of understanding and knowledge, to charity the gift of wisdom, to prudence the gift of counsel, and so forth. This is the first source of theological knowledge and of Thomistic moral teaching. This is all the more certain, and St. Thomas's originality in this domain is all the more manifest, when one compares him with the theologians of his day: in his definition of the New Law as an interior law identified with the grace of the Spirit; in his definition of the gifts as dispositions to receive spiritual inspirations; and, finally, in his construction of morality around the virtues and the gifts that perfect them.

The recognition of this interior source at the origin of theological work transforms historical relationships and creates a kind of spiritual contemporaneity from Pentecost to our own day, among the Christian faithful and among theologians. When Thomas cites the Gospel (for example, the Beatitude of the pure of heart who shall see God), he is not merely accepting a text drawn from a venerable passage; through his faith he receives this verse of the Gospel as a word of the Lord bearing within it a present truth, capable of throwing light upon contemporary life. The Beatitude of the pure of heart in-

36. *ST* I-II 106.1 ad 2.

vites every person to seek the vision of God as his or her ultimate end and supreme beatitude. For Thomas, this promise of Christ is not only a historical word, a subject for exegetical study; thanks to the light of the Spirit, it becomes a present Word, opening up to him and to humanity a future that surpasses anything Aristotle and the pagan philosophers could have imagined. In this light, a new concept of time emerges, centered upon the person of Christ, the teacher *par excellence.* This vision of history is divided into three periods: the preparation for the coming of Christ, the accomplishment of his work of salvation in the Gospel, and the Church's journey toward the kingdom. It will be expressed in the reading of Scripture according to the three spiritual senses,[37] and through it passes into theology. One finds it again at the foundation of Christian liturgy from the beginning.

Owing to the action of the Spirit, Thomas enters into profound communion, in the love and the search for truth, with all the authors whom he consults: with the Fathers, as commentators on the Word in the name of the Church, and with the philosophers, as witnesses to the humanity and the nature that God has created in his image and likeness and that remain subject to the wisdom of his Providence in spite of sin. In writing the *Summa,* Thomas is aware that he is listening to the Lord teaching on the mountain, in the company of the Fathers and the holy Doctors of the Church, in the same fellowship with all those, philosophers and others, who, without having been able to hear this voice directly, had nonetheless known how to welcome, even if imperfectly, the light of truth shining at the summit of their souls. For him, it is not merely a beautiful picture or an ideal, but a living communion in the light of the truth poured into hearts by the Spirit, who had already hovered over the waters at the beginning of creation.

Those reading St. Thomas today are invited to enter actively into this communion. In order to do so, however, one cannot be content merely to read his works and study them with methods that are considered scientific, however useful these may be in theological work. In doing so, the reader runs the great risk of seeing them only as monuments of the past or as aspects of a powerful and cold rational system. In my opinion, the indispensable condition for penetrating to the heart of St. Thomas's thought is to begin by opening ourselves to the first source of his teaching: the Word of the Lord spoken by the

---

37. *ST* I 1.10.

Holy Spirit in the Scriptures and in our hearts. Before opening the *Summa theologiae,* therefore, we should open the Gospel and meditate upon it in prayer as St. Thomas himself did, without forgetting to put it into practice, so that we may acquire by experience a living knowledge of the realities of which he speaks. Then, nourished by the same spiritual source, we can enter into communion of mind and heart with St. Thomas and engage in fruitful dialogue with him, as well as with the authors whom he quotes, as he invites us to listen to them in our search for the truth. Thus, we will better grasp the timeliness of his teaching, discerning its human riches and limitations. We will know, also, how to find the words needed today to transmit the intellectual treasure contained in his works.

SELECTED FURTHER READING

Aubert, Jean Marie. *Le droit romain dans l'oeuvre de saint Thomas.* Paris: J. Vrin, 1955.

Bataillon, Louis J., O.P. "Saint Thomas et les Pères: de la *Catena* à la *Tertia Pars.*" In *Ordo sapientiae et amoris,* ed. Carlos-Josaphat Pinto de Oliveira, O.P. Fribourg Suisse: Éditions Universitaires, 1993.

Bellemare, Rosaire, O.M.I. "La Somme de théologie et la lecture de la Bible." *Église et Théologie* 5 (1974): 257–70.

Boyle, John F. "St. Thomas Aquinas and Sacred Scripture." *Pro Ecclesia* 4 (1995): 92–104.

Dondaine, H.-F., O.P. "Note sur la documentation patristique de saint Thomas à Paris en 1270." *Revue des sciences philosophiques et théologiques* 47 (1963): 403–6.

———. "Les scolastiques citent-ils les Pères de première main?" *Revue des sciences philosophiques et théologiques* 36 (1952): 231–43.

Elders, Leo J., S.V.D. "Santo Tomás de Aquino y los Padres de la Iglesia." *Doctor Communis* 48 (1995): 55–80.

Geenen, G. "En marge du Concile de Chalcédoine. Les texts du Quatrième Concile dans les oeuvres de Saint Thomas." *Angelicum* 29 (1952): 43–59.

———. "The Council of Chalcedon in the Theology of St. Thomas." In *From an Abundant Spring.* The Walter Farrell Memorial Volume of the *Thomist.* New York: J. P. Kennedy, 1952.

———. "Les Sentences de Pierre Lombard dans la *Somme* de saint Thomas." In *Miscellanea Lombardiana.* Novara, Spain: Istituto geografico De Agostini, 1957.

———. "Saint Thomas et les Pères." In *Dictionnaire de théologie catholique* 15:1. Paris: Letouzey et Ane, 1946.

Grillmeier, Aloys. "Du 'symbolum' à la *Somme théologique.* Contribution à l'étude des relations théologico-historiques entre la patristique et la scolastique." In *Eglise et Tradition,* ed. Johannes Betz and Heinrich Fries. Le Puy-Lyon, France: Xavier Mappus, 1963.

Marc, P., C. Pera, and P. Caramello. "De Modo citandi auctoritates a Sancto Thoma usurpato." In *Liber de Veritate Catholicae Fidei contra errores infideliumqui dicitur Summa Contra Gentiles*. Vol. 1, introductio, excursus 3. Turin: Marietti, 1967.

Pera, C. *Le Fonti del pensiero di S. Tommaso d'Aquino nella Somma teologica*. Turin: Marietti, 1967.

Pinckaers, Servais, O.P. "Notes." In *Saint Thomas d'Aquin, Somme Théologique, Les actes humains*, vol. 2 *(Ia IIae, QQ. 18–21)*. Paris: Desclée et Cie, 1966.

———. *Le Renouveau de la morale*. 2nd ed. Tournai, Belgium: Casterman, 1964.

———. *Sources of Christian Ethics*. Trans. Mary Thomas Noble. Washington, D.C.: The Catholic University of America Press, 1995.

Pinto de Oliveira, C.J. "A teologia de S. Tomás e a Biblia." *Theologica* (1958): 201–7.

Prete, B. "Bibbia e teologia nell'opera di S. Tommaso d'Aquino." *Bollettino S. Domenico* 55 (1974): 79–92.

Principe, Walter H., C.S.B. "Thomas Aquinas' Principles for Interpretation of Patristic Texts." *Studies in Medieval Culture* 8–9 (1976): 111–21.

Valkenberg, W. *"Words of the Living God": The Place and Function of Holy Scripture in the Theology of St. Thomas Aquinas*. Wilhelmus G.B.M., Leuven: Peeters, 2000.

Vansteenkiste, C., O.P. "Cicerone nell'opera di S. Tommaso." *Angelicum* 36 (1959): 343–82.

Waldstein, Michael M. "On Scripture in the *Summa Theologiae*." *Aquinas Review* 1 (1994): 73–94.

2 ∾ The Body of Christ

The Eucharistic and Ecclesial Context
of Aquinas's Ethics   (2000)

Our topic finds its inspiration in the encyclical *Veritatis splendor:* "The presence of Christ to men of every time is actualized in his Body, which is the Church" (no. 25). The text elucidates moreover that it is the work of the Holy Spirit that accomplishes this presence in our time. The Holy Spirit calls us and makes us understand the Lord's commandments, and he accords us grace that strengthens our new life. Such is the New Law, which gives us "life in Christ" and "life in the Spirit," according to the main headings in the *Catechism of the Catholic Church*'s section on morality.

The episode of the rich young man illustrates that the Christian life, understood as a response to the Lord's call, is neither a solitary nor a purely personal affair. The Christian life takes place in communion with the Church, the Body of Christ. Each Christian enters into the New Covenant through faith in the person of the Son of God; every Christian receives, from the living tradition entrusted to the apostles and to their successors, the moral prescriptions that need to be conserved faithfully and fulfilled permanently in different cultures, throughout history. These precepts are summed up as to follow and to imitate Christ, according to the words of St. Paul: "For me, to live is Christ" (Phil 1:21). Thus the moral life of the Christian is bound to the person of Christ forming his Body, the Church, by the work of the Holy Spirit.

Originally published as "La morale et l'Eglise: Corps du Christ," in *RTh* 100 (2000): 239–58. Translated and edited for publication in *The Pinckaers Reader* by Craig Steven Titus.

Difficulties

This striking doctrine confronts serious obstacles that come particularly from the modern presentation of morality that has shaped our education. We shall concisely note the difficulties.

Our conception of moral action has inherited a largely individualist bent from the classical manuals of the last centuries that marked their preaching, catechesis, and ideas. In this notion, morality results from the confrontation between freedom and law that limits it. This involves specifically the freedom of indifference that is conceived as the individual's essential power to say yes or no to legal prescriptions, to obey or to disobey them, whether they come from the will of God or from reason. The moral law is expressed in the Decalogue, which is identified with the natural law. In regard to individual freedom, the Church is the guardian of this law: she teaches its precepts and she confirms its obligations and proscriptions in the name of the divine authority that she receives from Christ. Based thus on the natural law, the teaching of the moral manuals makes little reference to the Gospel, and mentions only in passing the New Law and the Sermon on the Mount. One would not dream above all to consult St. Paul, who presents the Church as the Body of Christ in relation to morality. One would consign such teaching to dogmatic theology, while relegating Gospel teaching to spirituality.

Such a conception of morality leads effectively and logically to a marked separation between, on the one hand, morality—limited to legal obligations—and, on the other hand, dogmatic theology, as well as ascetic and mystical theology, which seek the perfection of the counsels beyond obligations. These divisions are found in the exegete, among others, who separates dogma, morality, and parenesis, considered as simple exhortation. In this context, it is hardly possible to establish cohesion between this individualistic and authoritarian morality on the one hand, and the presentation of the Church as the mystical Body of Christ on the other. Current moralists and ethicists mostly tend to shift morality's focus from law to freedom, moving from the universalism that the natural law assures toward a pluralism that legitimates individualism and leads to compromises always open to discussion and revision. Moreover, one cannot say that these moralists hasten to reestablish close ties between morality and the Gospel or the thought of St. Paul. They dream rather of instituting a rational and secular morality, distant from a morality of the Church and the mystical Body.

St. Thomas's Position

St. Thomas offers a more favorable interpretation of this relationship. Aquinas does not separate morality from spirituality. In the *Summa theologiae*, he closely ties the moral and dogmatic parts together in order to form a unified theology. In his eyes, the old law and the natural law find their completion in the Evangelical Law, the treatise that introduces grace, as the summit of morality. Special moral theology, treated in the *secunda secundae*, rests on the virtues, both theological and moral, of which the commandments of the Decalogue are like its servants. Aquinas's moral vision grants pride of place to the gifts of the Holy Spirit that confer on the virtues a superior perfection, in addition to the charisms studied as the special and necessary graces for the organization of the Church.

Nonetheless a serious objection arises: throughout the whole moral part of the *Summa*, the *secunda pars*, St. Thomas almost never speaks of either Christ or the mystical Body. We have remarked, with the help of Roberto Busa's concordance, 306 uses of *Christus* in the *prima secundae* and 397 in the *secunda secundae*, which shows its significant presence; however, the name of Christ appears in only one of the article titles of this last part: "Whether it is necessary for the salvation of all, that they should believe explicitly in the mystery of Christ."[1] Only one article equally treats the mystical Body, concerning the diversity of the states and duties in the Church, in the treatise on the states of life.[2] The study of Christ and of his mystical Body is reserved for the *tertia pars*. Does not then the *Summa* plainly separate dogma from morality in such a way that we might envisage an account of moral theology without needing to speak of Christ and the Church?

The response principally resides in the organic character of the *Summa theologiae*, the different parts of which are profoundly unified. There is no real separation between the moral part of the *Summa* and its two dogmatic parts; the doctrine on the Trinity, in particular on the Word and on the Holy Spirit, found in the *prima pars*, pertains to the morality set forth in the *secunda pars* that we can thus identify as Trinitarian and spiritual. In a parallel way, the doctrine of the *tertia pars* on Christ and the mystical Body is intimately linked to

1. *ST* II-II 2.7.
2. *ST* II-II 183.2.

Aquinas's moral teaching, which we can call Christological and ecclesial. Thus we can say that all the virtues studied in the *secunda secundae* form a dynamic whole; they are directed to Christ through faith, hope, and charity.

The contemporary reader experiences difficulty because Aquinas's thought predominantly analyzes reality; he dissects it—the virtuous life, for example—in its multiple elements in order to successively study them, somewhat as in anatomy one dissects the human body, organ after organ. But Aquinas always completes this division with synthetic statements that demonstrate how the virtues form a whole and are ordered to each other so that they act together concretely, in a harmonious and efficacious way.

The following key text demonstrates the intimate connection that links the *Summa*'s moral and dogmatic parts. It is the prologue to the *tertia pars:*

"Forasmuch as our Savior the Lord Jesus Christ, in order to 'save His people from their sins'" (Mt 1:21), as the angel announced, showed unto us in His own Person the way of truth, whereby we may attain to the bliss of eternal life by rising again, it is necessary, in order to complete the work of theology, that after considering the last end of human life, and the virtues and vices, there should follow the consideration of the Savior of all, and of the benefits bestowed by Him on the human race.

This long phrase intimately ties the morality set forth in the *secunda pars,* including its perspective of the last end and the virtues, to the doctrine on Christ and his work of salvation proposed in the *tertia pars;* this is done since Christ revealed himself, in his own person, as the way to truth that leads to full beatitude. This correlation between morality and the person of Christ is studied in his Incarnation after this prologue. Christ is not only the preacher and the model of the moral life; he is, in person, the veritable way of salvation and flourishing. This link is actualized by the sacraments, grouped around the Eucharist, which builds the Body of Christ, the Church. The entire *tertia pars* is connected to the *secunda pars:* the person of Christ, the incarnate Word, becomes the source and the object of the virtues and of the gifts. We shall return to this point later.

This synthetic and personal aspect, however, does not appear in the foreground of Aquinas's works. The predominant features of his thought patterns and written style are the rationality that abstracts and the analysis that divides. He speaks above all to reason, in the universal, by dissecting reality into its parts in order to define exactly its complexity. He differs in this regard from St.

Augustine, whose way of expressing himself is always personal, and who at the same time addresses intelligence, as well as heart and imagination; he bases his writings in a concrete perception of things, which nonetheless sometimes hinders clarity and precision. They have two different, but complementary, forms of thought and modes of expression. In order to understand Aquinas, it is often useful to read Augustine at the same time, as well as the other Fathers of the Church that our doctor regularly cites and employs. Thus we can better perceive the personal dimension of Thomas's ethics in relationship with the person of Christ.

The Apostolic Catechesis: the Paraclesis of St. Paul

In order to understand better the bonds between morality and the Church as the Body of Christ, we will now borrow a path that St. Thomas has followed himself: first, to consult a principal source of Christian moral teaching, the epistles of St. Paul; second, to go to Aquinas's commentaries, in order to return at last to the *Summa theologiae.*

We have chosen this approach with the conviction that the apostolic catechesis provides us the first Christian syntheses of moral teaching; Aquinas considered it the superior source for theology, which serves as an authority and deserves careful study. These texts unfortunately have been completely neglected by later ethicists who relegated them to spirituality or to simple parenesis. Thanks to the *Catechism of the Catholic Church,* these texts (along with the Sermon on the Mount) have been reintroduced into Christian ethics; focusing on St. Paul's contribution, they involve: Romans 12–15, 1 Corinthians 12 and 13, Colossians 3 and 4, and Ephesians 4 and 5. These texts propose moral teaching in the form of exhortation, or more exactly, of paraclesis, according to the term that Paul regularly employs. The Apostle prefers exhortation to imperatives (orders), since he addresses believers who have received the grace of the Holy Spirit, who inspires charity. Thomas understood this when he explained that the Apostle "uses exhortation with the Christians of Rome because he prefers to motivate them through love by imploring them, rather than through fear by commanding them with authority, imperatively."[3]

St. Paul's teaching is obviously moral for Aquinas, whose commentary on

3. *Ad Rom.,* Cap. XII, lect. I, no. 955.

the beginning of chapter 12 of the Letter to the Romans demonstrates the organization of the two great parts of this letter: "After having demonstrated the necessity and origin of grace, the Apostle teaches us about the use of grace, which involves moral instruction."[4] Chapters 12 and 15 offer us a remarkable synthesis of the apostolic moral catechesis. In this regard, it is worth comparing the paracleses of the Letters to the Romans, Corinthians, Colossians, and Ephesians, which represent the theme of the mystical Body; the idea of Christ, as Head of the Church, appears only in the last two.[5]

The Moral Paraclesis of the Epistle to the Romans

We shall briefly examine the moral paraclesis of the Epistle to the Romans with a look at St. Thomas's *Commentary*. Because of our interest in its moral synthesis, we shall study this commentary first, even though it follows by several months Aquinas's commentary on the First Epistle to the Corinthians, which dates to Easter 1257. We shall start by focusing on the translation of a key text: "I appeal to you therefore, brothers and sisters, by the mercies of God, to present your *bodies* as a living sacrifice, holy and acceptable to God" (Rom 12:1—RSV). The Greek term for *bodies* is clear: *sôma*. "Body" makes a rich reference that is lost in some translations.[6] Paul uses the same term, *sôma*, in verse 4, to speak of the Body of Christ, the Church. This word might well have evoked for the original recipients of the letter the personal body of Christ offered in sacrifice through the Eucharist in place of Jewish ritual animal sacrifices.[7] We shall retain the term *body*, while remembering that it evokes the whole person. St. Paul thus begins his moral teaching presenting us the Christian life as spiritual worship, literally a *logical* worship *[logiken]*, reasonable according to God's wisdom, and different from Jewish and pagan worship. This worship consists in offering our bodies, not dead, but living; this includes all our action and work, conforming them as good and perfect to God's

4. *Ad Rom.*, Cap. XII, lect. I, no. 953.
5. Cf. Col 2:19; and Eph 1:22; 4:15.
6. [Translator's note: Pinckaers compares two French translations of the Bible *(Bible de Jérusalem* and *Traduction Œcuménique de la Bible)*. We can find the meaning behind his analysis by comparing recent English translations. Like the *RSV, The Jerusalem Bible, The New American Bible,* and *The Bible: King James Version* translate *sôma* as "bodies." In contrast, the New Testament in *Today's English Version* and *The Good News Bible* translate *sôma* as "yourselves."]
7. Cf. 1 Cor 10:16–17; 6:15–16.

will. Morality appears as a kind of living sacrifice that directly recalls the Eucharist, the sacrament of the body and blood of the Lord.

Paul then enlarges the horizon to the dimension of the Church. In a faith perspective, he compares the body to its members in order to situate and direct the gifts and the virtues that Christians receive and are called to put into practice. The Apostle, however, outstrips the common comparison of a society with a body, by the living bond that is established with Christ by faith and love. This relationship with Christ is the principle of unity between Christians in their sentiments and activities. Paul exhorts them to do everything henceforth in view of Christ and his Body, the Church. He speaks first of gifts or charisms, like prophesy, service, and teaching. Next, in a text that directly echoes the Lord's Sermon on the Mount in Matthew and Luke,[8] he treats the virtues, beginning with charity, which ranges from fraternal affection to blessing persecutors. Paul then expresses this union between Christians, which we dare call *corporal*, by insisting on charity—the plenitude of the Law—through the invitation to become children of light clothed in the Lord Jesus, and more concretely through sensitivity to the weak concerning food sacrificed to idols. Paul concludes: "Let us then pursue what makes for peace and for mutual upbuilding."[9]

The place of moral teaching in the framework of the Church, the Body of Christ, is essential for Paul. This teaching rests on the bond of faith and love that unites each Christian to the person of Jesus. It finds its practical source in the charity that: reunites the members of the Church in fraternal love, directs the charisms for the good of all, unifies the virtues, and accomplishes the precepts of the Law, concerning civil authorities and pagans as well. We also find this bond of morality with the Body of Christ in the other Pauline epistles.

The Paraclesis of the Epistles to the Corinthians, Ephesians, and Colossians

In the First Epistle to the Corinthians, after having spoken of the Lord's Supper, which is a communion with his Body and Blood,[10] Paul addresses more directly and thoroughly the question of the spiritual gifts. He directs them to the common good according to the unity of the Spirit, who distributes them. Then he continues his reflection with the help of the comparison of the body and the members applied to the relationships in the Church between the

---

8. Cf. Rom 12:14–21.　　　　　　　　9. Rom 14:19 (RSV).
10. Cf. 1 Cor 11:17–34.

Christians that form the Body of Christ enlivened by the same Spirit. As in the Epistle to the Romans, Paul applies this thought to the charisms, indicating the priority of apostles, prophets, and doctors. He then addresses the virtues through the hymn to charity, which regroups them: "Love is patient; love is kind; love is not envious [. . .] it endures all things."[11]

In the Epistle to the Ephesians, at the end of the first chapter, which deals with the mystery of salvation accomplished in Christ raised to the glory of the Father, we find the new idea that St. Thomas stresses in his theology: Christ has been constituted "head over all things for the church, which is his body."[12] The catechesis of chapters 3 and 4 is presented, as in the Epistle to the Romans, in the form of paraclesis ("I exhort you"). Paul thus invites a response through conduct that is fitting to the call one receives. He introduces right away, without any development, the idea of unity: there is only one Body, one Spirit, only one Lord, one unique God and Father of all.[13] He then explicates the teaching on gifts, linked to the Ascension of Christ who is its source: apostles, prophets, evangelists, and pastors (which is new in the list) and doctors, organized in view of building up the Body of Christ. Paul then returns to the idea that Christ is the Head "from whom the whole body [is] joined and knit together."[14] Next he places the teaching on the virtues and the vices under the themes of the New Man and Christians as children of light. Afterwards, the epistle addresses domestic morality, and concludes with the invitation to spiritual combat, which means to put on God's armor formed by the virtues: justice, faith in the Gospel Word, and prayer.

In its hymn on the primacy of Christ, the firstborn of all creation and the first to be born from the dead, the Epistle to the Colossians also contains the theme of Christ the Head of the Body, the Church.[15] Paul presupposes this theme as the framework of morality. He nonetheless does not mention it until the end, in connection to the peace of Christ: "to which indeed you were called in the one body."[16] Emile Mersch remarks that in his captivity epistles, Paul adds the article "to" to the expression "sôma Christou" employed in the Letter to the Romans; this concretizes the image.[17]

---

11. 1 Cor 13:4 (RSV).
12. Eph 1:22–23 (RSV).
13. Cf. Eph 4:4.
14. Eph 4:16 (RSV).
15. Cf. Col 1:18.
16. Col 3:15 (RSV).
17. Emile Mersch, *Doctrine de l'Ecriture et de la tradition grecque*, vol. 1 of *Le Corps mystique du Christ* (Louvain, 1933), 162.

The comparison between these Pauline epistles reveals that the theme of the Body of Christ constitutes the principal framework of their moral catechism. This theme establishes its unity by the relationship to Christ in faith and by the predominance of charity that directs the charisms and virtues toward the good of the members of the Body. Such a unity surpasses the natural bonds that establish the nations and the classes: Jew and Greek, slave and free man.[18] The major agreement between these letters is that the Body of Christ is really the Christian's base for action.

Reading these superb texts manifests, among other things, that insertion in the Body of Christ is the source of a grace that changes the human in his very being—he becomes a new man—and in his behavior is inspired henceforth by the *agape* under the movement of the Holy Spirit. Thus an essential connection links the two principal parts of our epistles—the dogmatic and the moral. Paraclesis is the direct consequence and the concrete accomplishment of faith in Christ, in his person and in his work of salvation. This is what the little conjunction "therefore" (*oun,* in Greek) indicates, in the first verse of chapter 12 of the Epistle to the Romans: "I appeal to you, therefore, brothers." *Oun* similarly appears in verse 1 of chapter 4 of the Epistle to the Ephesians: "I, the prisoner in the Lord, implore you therefore," and at the beginning of chapter 3 of the Epistle of the Colossians: "if you have been raised with Christ, seek the things that are above." We are dealing with a structural connection in St. Paul's thought. Clearly these moral syntheses that the apostolic catechesis presents us do not constitute works of theological reasoning, elaborated in the manner of medieval Scholasticism. Nonetheless, in the eyes of the Fathers and of St. Thomas, who revives and comments on them, these scriptural texts are superior to theological labor; they are like an intellectual inspiration that reason then endeavors to differentiate, to refine and deepen. In this perspective, Aquinas builds his moral doctrine in his commentaries on the epistles and in his *Summa theologiae.*

St. Thomas's Commentaries on St. Paul

The commentary on chapter 12 of the Epistle to the Romans is very elaborate. This masterpiece analyzes the text's content. Thomas begins treating the theme of the Body of Christ in *lectio* 2 and continues in *lectio* 3.

18. Cf. Col 3:11.

The text compares the mystical Body of Christ, the Church, to a natural body through three aspects: unity of body, plurality of members, and diversity of function. The Church has a multitude of members, even if they seem few in the world. It gathers them together in the spiritual unity of the mystical Body. Formed by faith and charity, this unity is given to us by the Spirit of Christ, who unites us to each other and to God. The Church also has a diversity of offices aimed at a mutual utility; thus the beneficiary of one charism, such as prophecy, needs someone who has received another, such as the gift of healing.

Aquinas then divides Paul's account into two parts. The first concerns the graces that are not common to everyone, or *gratiae gratis datae*. The second involves that which is common to all Christians: the gift of charity with the virtues that it engenders. We shall not enter further into the distinctions of the commentary, which branch out to consider the text's intricate details while always relating them to the whole. Let us simply mention the division of this little treatise on charity: it is exercised in regard to those who are in need and extends as far as one's enemies. It takes a triple form: benevolence, harmony, and beneficence.

The commentary on the First Letter to the Corinthians, chapters 12 and 13, aims above all to demonstrate that the multiplicity of members of the Body of Christ does not thwart its unity, which is the particular work of the Holy Spirit. Aquinas clearly distinguishes two types of grace given by the Spirit: (1) the graces *gratis datae* (freely given), which do not imply the indwelling of the Holy Spirit in the person who enjoys them, but rather in the Church; and (2) the grace *gratum faciens*, which realizes the personal indwelling of the Spirit. Such are, on the one hand, the charisms, and, on the other hand, charity.[19]

Thomas astutely extends the thought of St. Paul and applies to the Church what he says about the members of the human body.[20] First, the foot is the humble member, since it touches the ground, while the hand is nobler. These members represent those in the Church who are dedicated to an active life: the feet signify the subordinates, and the hands, the prelates, according to Proverbs: "The glory of a king is a multitude of people."[21] The eye and the ear serve to apprehend and acquire wisdom. Sight is superior: it is the organ of

19. *I ad Cor.* Ch. XII, lect. 2.   20. *I ad Cor.* Ch. XII, lect. 3.
21. Prov 14:28 (RSV).

discovery, since it demonstrates the many differences of things. The ear serves to acquire a discipline that is conveyed through the word. In the Church, the eyes represent the doctors who by themselves discern truth, while the ears signify the disciples who receive the truth by listening to the doctors. Thomas judiciously adds, for his audience, that both are necessary. The nose signifies those who are not able to understand words of wisdom (e.g., the teaching of theology), but who perceive it from indications, as from afar through the sense of smell, according to the Song of Songs: "delicate is the fragrance of your perfume."[22]

These members, however, need each other, including the less honorable ones. Thus contemplatives need active members, as Mary received services from Martha. Each of us also needs our lower organs, such as the intestines that represent, in the Church, farmers, among others. Without farmers we could not live; thus they are more necessary even than those who give themselves to contemplation and to wisdom for the Church's adornment and perfection. No matter what the differences, Aquinas insists on mutual care and devotion that motivate the Church's members. He revives the hierarchy established by St. Paul: apostles, prophets, doctors, miracle workers, and he explains them. The power of miracles is ordained to the doctrine of the faith, and the latter to the government of the people. Governing and teaching is entrusted principally to apostles; but certain other members participate in the doctrinal function, like prophets who receive divine revelations, and doctors who instruct the people about things thusly revealed. Thomas finally mentions those who bring their aid to governing the people: the archdeacons, who assist the bishops and the parish priests to whom a part of the faithful are entrusted.

Aquinas devotes his commentary on chapter 13 to charity, which is inseparable from the grace *gratum faciens* and offers us a higher and more perfect path than all the charisms. St. Paul demonstrates it in three points: (1) charity is necessary, for no gift suffices without it; (2) it is the most useful, since through it we avoid every evil and acquire every good; and (3) it is permanent, because it never comes to an end. We would add, in this same perspective, that through charity all the members of the Church, with their own functions, collaborate and unite for the good of the whole Body, which is the Church; charity also infuses in all the virtues their unity of action.

22. Cant 1:3 (Jerusalem Bible). Also: "your anointing oils are fragrant" (RSV).

These two commentaries demonstrate that the theme of the Body of Christ makes two parallel appearances: (1) in the organization of the Church by charisms, and (2) in the disposition of the virtues around charity, for through charity all the works of the virtues are accomplished.[23] Nonetheless, while highlighting the primacy of charity, Thomas does not outline here the organization of the virtues that he develops in the *Summa theologiae* around the theological and moral virtues.

The doctrine of the mystical Body establishes a correspondence between ecclesial and moral dimensions, with the gift of sanctifying grace and of charity giving a priority to the moral dimension. If we are able to speak, according to the Epistle to the Romans, of a liturgical morality exercised in spiritual worship, we can also speak of an ecclesial morality; indeed, the same charity, which builds up the moral life, constructs and inspires the ecclesial Body with the aid of the charisms. The Church is thus the privileged and necessary arena for moral action. The commentary on the Epistle to the Ephesians is shorter. The explanation of verse 22 of chapter 1: "[God] has made him [Jesus Christ] the head over all things for the church" (RSV), which plays a predominant role in Aquinas's theological systematization, is not very long. Christ is the Head of the pilgrim and triumphant Church, formed of humans and angels. He is spiritually their Head by his preeminence and by his virtue, surpassing even the higher angels, whom he enlightens and inspires. He is particularly the Head of humans by his sharing human nature.

In chapter 4 concerning verse 3: be "eager to maintain the unity of the Spirit in the bond of peace. There is one body and one Spirit" (RSV), Aquinas's moral catechesis affirms the importance of unity. He relates the unity of the members of the human body (which signifies the unity of the faithful coordinated among themselves in order to form a body) to spiritual unity (constituted by the unity of body and soul, which denotes the spiritual consensus achieved by the unity of faith and charity). Later, he explains the doctrine of Christ, the Head of the mystical Body, by a triple influence. In the human body, we distinguish the coordination *(compactio)* between the members, the links that the nerves establish, and the collaboration between the members that facilitate growth. In parallel, Christ, as Head of the Church, acts on it in three ways: (1) he coordinates its parts through faith; (2) he ties together the

23. Cf. *I ad Cor.* Ch. XIII, lect. 11, no. 771.

members of the mystical Body through bonds of faith and charity, in order that they may serve each other; finally, (3) by making them grow spiritually, he moves them to act according to each one's measure and competence.

The commentary on the Epistle to the Colossians, chapter 3, verse 15 ("let the peace of Christ rule in your hearts, to which indeed you were called in the one body"—RSV) is laconic: "in the one Body" simply signifies "that you form one unique Body."

The *Summa Theologiae*

When we turn to the systematic works of St. Thomas, we notice an important shift in perspective: he addresses the theme of the mystical Body from a standpoint that is less ecclesial than Christological, based upon Christ as Head of the Body.[24] The key text is Ephesians 1:22–23 (RSV): "he has put all things under his feet and has made him the head over all things for the Church, which is his Body, the fullness of him who fills all in all." This passage follows the great prayer of benediction that opens the letter and constitutes the apex of the description of salvation achieved through the resurrection of Christ and his enthronement at the right of the Father, above the angels, for all ages. In the *tertia pars* of the *Summa*, Aquinas studies the grace of Christ under three aspects: first, the grace of the hypostatic union (q. 3–6); then his personal grace, as man (q. 7), and finally his grace as Head of the Church (q. 8). This distinction originates from the *Sentences* of Peter Lombard.[25]

Here is a brief presentation of the teaching explicated in question 8. The idea of the Church as the mystical Body rests upon the comparison with the human body, where the head dominates through ordering the members, for it is the superior part of the body. It surpasses the others by its perfection, for it reunites all the senses, starting with touch; likewise for virtue, since the head has the power to govern the entire body. Thus, Christ is more elevated in the Church because of his proximity to God and because of the primacy of his grace. Concerning his virtue—his power to act—he infuses grace in all the members of the Church (a. 1). We find here the teaching of Aquinas's commentaries on St. Paul, although focused on the role of Christ as Head of the Church.

24. Cf. III *Sent.* 1.2.1; *De Verit.* 29.4–5; *Compendium theologiae* cap. 214; *ST* III 8.
25. Cf. *In Sent.* III 13.

We find an interesting detail in the response to the third objection. Thomas compares the Holy Spirit to the heart, who vivifies and unites the Church, in an invisible way. He compares Christ to the head, in his visible nature, inasmuch as a human being can be placed before others as a superior member. In the *De veritate*, he still hesitates in front of the objection:

The heart is a hidden member, but the head is apparent. By the heart, accordingly, the divinity of Christ or the Holy Spirit can be meant; but by the head, Christ Himself in His visible nature, which is under the influence of the nature of the invisible divinity.[26]

Thomas then demonstrates that while the humanity of Christ acts principally on the souls, it acts as well on the bodies of humans, the members of which become *instruments of justice* and are submitted by the soul to the action of the Holy Spirit (art. 2). Christ is the Head of all humans, at least potentially and according to different degrees (art. 3). He is the head of the angels, who constitute a part of his mystical Body as well (art. 4). Capital grace, in its reality, is the same as the personal grace of Christ and as the grace of union: it is only distinguished conceptually (art. 5). This grace belongs properly to Christ in that which concerns the interior influence on his members, but it can be communicated to others for the exterior action of governing, as to the bishops for a local church and to the pope for the whole Church. As vicars of Christ, the latter are called heads of the Church (art. 6). The perspective of Christ as the Head is so predominant that Thomas studies its opposite: the devil and the antichrist, as heads of all the wicked (art. 7–8). Concerning morality, this teaching puts forward Christ as the source of every grace, and thus, of the virtues and the gifts.

Let us quickly outline what follows in the *tertia pars.* The theme of Christ as Head of the mystical Body intervenes as a first principle in the account of the effects of the passion of Jesus:

Grace was bestowed upon Christ, not only as an individual, but inasmuch as He is the Head of the Church, so that it might overflow into His members; [. . .] Consequently Christ by His Passion merited salvation, not only for Himself, but likewise for all His members.[27]

---

26. *De Verit.* 29.4.7.
27. *ST* III 48.1.

This particularly applies to the atonement of sins, which was superabundant, and since Christ and the members of the Church form one unique mystical person (art. 2, ad 1).

The theme arises in the study of the sacraments and the Eucharist. Concerning the unity of the sacraments, Thomas evokes the Eucharist: "In the Sacrament of the Altar, two things are signified, viz. Christ's true body, and Christ's mystical body."[28] Each sacrament involves thus a real relation with the mystical Body, but Aquinas does not develop the idea explicitly. The theme reappears, although rather moderately, in the same treatise on the Eucharist. It intervenes as a principle to demonstrate the necessity of this sacrament: "the reality *(res)* of the sacrament is the unity of the mystical body, without which there can be no salvation."[29] Thomas invokes, in this regard, a passage of St. Augustine on St. John (6:54): "by 'This food and this drink,' namely, by His flesh and blood: 'He would have us understand the fellowship of His body and members, which is the Church.'"[30] He contributes more detail later on:

There is a twofold reality of this sacrament: one which is signified and contained, namely, Christ Himself; while the other is signified but not contained, namely, Christ's mystical body, which is the fellowship of the saints.[31]

Aquinas further specifies that the unity of the mystical Body is the fruit of the reception of the true Body of Christ.[32] In order to explain the order of Eucharistic ceremonies, Thomas adopts the principle that the words and gestures signify three things: the passion of Christ, the mystical Body, and finally due devotion and reverence.[33]

The theme of the Body of Christ is present often in the treatises on the sacraments and the Eucharist. It seems to us, however, to remain somewhat in the background: he does not directly dedicate any article to it. We offer an explanation: in the treatise on the Eucharist, the apex of the sacraments, Thomas's study is focused by its content, the true Christ, nourishment for the mystical Body; in a word, everything concentrates on the real presence. This

---

28. *ST* III 60.3, *sed contra*. [Translator's note: This article asks: "Whether a Sacrament is a sign of one thing only?"]

29. *ST* III 73.3.

30. *ST* III 73.3 ad 1, in which Aquinas quotes Augustine, *In Ioan. Evang.*, Tract. 26, n. 13.

31. *ST* III 80.4, which refers to III 76.6.   32. *ST* III 82.9 ad 2.

33. *ST* III 83.5.

orientation confers on the treatise of the Eucharist a personal dimension that we find in Thomas's liturgical compositions.

The Church, Body of Christ and Morality

Let us ask the question one last time: how do morality and the theme of the Church, the Body of Christ, interrelate? As we mentioned, for the reader of Aquinas, the difficulty remains in the fact that the theme of the mystical Body is rarely mentioned in the whole *secunda pars.* It merely appears in three places in the *secunda secundae.* The principal text is found in the treatise on the states of life, at the end of which St. Thomas asks whether it is good that there is a diversity of functions and states of life in the Church.[34] He employs the Epistle to the Romans (chapter 12) and the Epistle to the Ephesians (chapter 4) to demonstrate that the Church—compared to a body with its different members, of which Christ is the head—has a diversity of actual functions and states that contribute to its perfection, to the proper functioning of its activities, to its dignity, and to its harmony. This theme also requires a response to the question of schism, in the treatise on faith.[35] Thomas explains that the unity of the Church offers a double aspect: the connection of the Church's members with each other and their relationship to Christ as the unique Head of the Church, of which the pope is the vicar. The theme is also evoked with regard to religious vows.[36]

Apparently, there are only a few references to this theme. The principal text involves the Church's organization; but we would like to demonstrate how it acts as a matrix of all the virtues. Indeed Thomas seems to study extensively the virtues without thinking to make a reference to the mystical Body of Christ, which is the Church.

Certainly, the basically analytical character of the *Summa,* required by its rigorous organization and for clarity's sake, helps to explain this quasi-absence of the theme of the Church, Body of Christ, from the moral part of this work. What Aquinas writes in the Christological part, where he specifically treats this theme, ought to apply, in his eyes, to the whole of the *Summa*'s theology. Nonetheless, we would expect him to indicate the connections in certain places. That is what we shall now seek.

34. *ST* II-II 183.2.   35. *ST* II-II 39.1.
36. *ST* II-II 88.4 ad 3; 88.12.

The Connective Texts

The prime text that interests us immediately precedes the question (8) dedicated to Christ as Head of the mystical Body. It evokes the personal grace of Christ, which emanates from his grace of union.[37] Thomas establishes first that Christ had habitual grace from his union with the Word of God, because of the dignity and elevation of his soul; then, through his bond with humanity, he bestows his grace on all humans (art. 1). He demonstrates next that the perfect grace that Christ possessed nourished all the virtues, which perfected his faculties in their acts. He describes that Christ had a supreme degree of generosity, magnanimity, and even temperance, even though he did not experience wicked desires (art. 2). Christ also possessed all the gifts, for his soul was perfectly moved by the Holy Spirit (art. 5). He enjoyed moreover all the graces *gratis datae,* or the charisms, which are directed to manifest faith and spiritual doctrine. Thus Christ is the first and principal Doctor (art. 7).

Indeed, grace, the virtues, and the gifts constitute the principal branches of the architecture of the *secunda pars.* The *secunda secundae,* which presupposes the treatise on grace, is divided according to the virtues, associated to the gifts, without forgetting the Beatitudes that start the Sermon on the Mount of our Lord and Doctor. The charisms are studied next among the special graces, with the states of life. None of these treatises, as we can observe, receives a place in the moralities of obligation or duty, which concentrate on commandments, imperatives, and interdictions.

The fullness of Christ's grace, acting through the virtues, the gifts, and the charisms, constitutes the spiritual reserve that spreads over the Church's members, through Christ who is its Head, for three reasons: his proximity to God by his grace of union, the perfection of his grace from which proceeds virtues and gifts, and his power to communicate his grace to all the Church's members, through the virtues, the gifts, and the charisms. Thus, the moral agency of Christians all together, with the virtues and the gifts, has its source in the grace of Christ and its place in the Church, which is his Body.

The second text concerns redemption and liberation from sin through Christ's passion. In the *tertia pars,* question 48, article 4, Thomas shows that the Redemption, which is liberation from sins and from the penalty due to sin,

37. *ST* III 7.

involves two domains: it is the direct work of Christ as a human being, he who gave his blood and his life as the ransom for the sins of humankind; but it is first of all the work of the whole Trinity, as the principal and distant cause, for the Trinity is the origin of Christ's life, and it inspired him to suffer for us in his humanity.[38] All the parts of theology converge here: the *prima pars,* which treats of the Trinity; the *secunda pars,* which studies sins after the virtues (starting with original sin, as opposed to humility);[39] and finally the *tertia pars,* which speaks of Christ and his work.

In question 49, from the first article on, Thomas denotes the liberation from sin by appealing to the theme of the Church, the Body of Christ:

Christ's Passion causes forgiveness of sins by way of redemption. For since He is our head, then, by the Passion which He endured from love and obedience, He delivered us as His members from our sins, as by the price of His Passion: in the same way as if a man by the good industry of his hands were to redeem himself from a sin committed with his feet. For, just as the natural body is one though made up of diverse members, so the whole Church, Christ's mystic body, is reckoned as one person with its head, which is Christ.[40]

This remission of sins is attributed to charity; the Redemption can be considered to provoke charity. Thus all of morality, which involves the virtues linked to charity and sins, is attached to the Redemption enacted by Christ, Head of the mystical Body, whose members we are. The third text that can aid us is the treatise on the New Law. In this treatise—which is also left aside by ethicists of obligation and duty—we do not find mention of the Church, Body of Christ, but the involvement is direct. Aquinas presents this Law as the work of the Holy Spirit. In effect, Thomas demonstrates, in an original way, that the New Law does not consist principally in a written text, like the Gospels. Rather the New Law involves the grace of the Holy Spirit written, in its unique way, in the hearts of those who believe in Christ.[41]

Toward a More Concrete Presentation

These texts are sufficient to provide a solid foundation to coordinate the morality of the virtues of the *secunda pars* and the doctrine of the Body of the

38. *ST* III 48.4.
40. *ST* III 49.1.

39. *ST* II-II 163.
41. *ST* I-II 106.1.

Church whose Head is Christ, which is presented in the *tertia pars.* But if we want to adopt a perspective which is less analytical, less cut up than the structure of the *Summa theologiae,* a more concrete and catechetical presentation like the one of St. Paul, it is our task to show how each virtue—far from being purely individual—has an ecclesial dimension which is combined with the personal dimension. In order to achieve this goal, we can choose as a starting point charity's dynamic and unifying role, in connection with prudential discernment. Moreover, we can refer to St. Thomas's anthropology, which is based on the natural inclination toward social life that he recognizes in human beings; this inclination develops particularly through justice and friendship, but also in the other virtues like courage and temperance inasmuch as they help us to relate to others. According to Aristotle, courage finds its highest expression in war, which is usually not led by one person, and temperance manifests itself particularly with respect to sexual desire, which leads us naturally toward the other sex in the perspective of giving life in the family context. Thomas revives this doctrine and transforms it according to the Christian perspective. The highest expression of courage resides in martyrdom as a witnessing of faith and love for Christ and for the Church. Temperance culminates in the virginal consecration to Christ, which is recognized by the Church and is a basic principle for ecclesial communities.

As we can see, it would not be too difficult to highlight the ecclesial dimension of each virtue, as well as of St. Thomas's morality as a whole. However, we could not perform this task in a clear and coherent way without referring to our Doctor's sources: the Gospels and St. Paul, as well as the Church Fathers, particularly St. Augustine, whose language—which is more pastoral—expresses spiritual experience more clearly.

The Office of *Corpus Christi*

In conclusion, I would like to suggest an idea, or rather an intuition that I had. I wonder if the core of St. Thomas's doctrine on the mystical Body of Christ, the Church, the concrete and personal spiritual source of his theology—including his moral theology—does not lie in his devotion to the sacrament of the Body of Christ, in his faith in the real presence of the Lord in the Eucharist.

The most persuasive argument to support this thesis lies in his composition of the liturgy of Corpus Christi,[42] particularly in the hymns, including *Adoro te*. Indeed, while they reproduce in their own way the content of the treatise on the Eucharist, they are written in a very personal and passionate style, which reveals a literary talent and mystical genius. By reading his theological works, one could not foresee it. We can veritably speak of a spirituality and even of a mysticism in the best sense of the word, which is at once personal because of its expressive mode, scriptural by its evangelical and Pauline sources, theological by its doctrine, and ecclesial by its scope and liturgical form. Thus, we would dare say that faith and devotion to the Body of Christ in the Eucharist and also in his ecclesial Body—in their strongest meaning—are a primary inspiration and source of St. Thomas's theology. It is like a primary experience, hidden under the toil of reflection, which belongs to the realm of prayer and spiritual attraction, as the Holy Spirit forms them in us.

42. Its authenticity has been demonstrated. Cf. P.-M. Gy, "Office liégeois et office romain de la Fête-Dieu," in *Fête-Dieu (1246–1996)*, Actes du Colloque de Liège (September 12–14, 1996), ed. André Haquin (Louvain-la-Neuve, 1999), 117–26.

3 ∾ Scripture and the Renewal of Moral Theology (1995)

The Second Vatican Council ratified the biblical renewal that had prepared the way for it. It truly gave Scripture back to the Catholic people, and
recommended it as "the very soul of sacred theology."[1] The Council invited
theologians to show the inner coherence of the mysteries of salvation proposed
by the Scriptures. Theologians were exhorted to make use of the teaching of
the Church Fathers and to engage in speculative reflection, with St. Thomas as
a guide, in order to search for the solutions to human problems in a manner
suitable to our contemporary times. In particular, the Council affirmed:

Special care should be given to the perfecting of moral theology. Its scientific presentation should draw more fully on the teaching of Holy Scripture and should throw light
upon the exalted vocation of the faithful in Christ and their obligation to bring forth
fruit in charity for the life of the world.[2]

The document on the formation of future priests published on February 22,
1976, by the Congregation for Catholic Education makes the directives in this
conciliar text beautifully explicit and helps us to perceive its main lines. It
states:

An earlier version was published as "L'usage de l'Ecriture dans la théologie morale," *NV* 2
(1995): 23–36. A similar version is "The Use of Scripture and the Renewal of Moral Theology:
The Catechism and *Veritatis splendor,*" *The Thomist* (January 1995): 1–19. Translated by Sister
Mary Thomas Noble, O.P., with the assistance of Craig Steven Titus. Amended and edited for
publication in *The Pinckaers Reader* by John Berkman.

1. *Dei Verbum* 24; English translation by Liam Walsh, O.P., *Vatican Council II,* ed. Austin
Flannery, O.P., revised edition (Collegeville, Minn.: The Liturgical Press, 1992), 764. See *OT* 16.

2. *OT* 16; English translation by B. Hayes, S.M., S. Fagan, S.M., and Austin Flannery, O.P.,
Vatican Council II, 720.

In the past, moral theology exhibited at times a certain narrowness of vision and some lacunas. This was due in large part to a kind of legalism, to an individualistic orientation, and to a separation from the sources of Revelation. To counter all this, . . . it is necessary to clarify the method by which moral theology ought to be developed in close contact with Holy Scripture (n. 96).

The *Catechism of the Catholic Church* and Pope John Paul II's 1993 encyclical *Veritatis splendor* have each in its own way effected the reestablishment of the bonds between Scripture and moral theology. I propose to touch upon the principal points of this scriptural renewal in the teaching of moral theology.

In order to get an idea of the novelty of these recent developments, a comparison will help. We shall look at the presentation of Catholic moral teaching given in the manuals which have served as textbooks in seminaries and which have oriented preaching and moral catechesis over the last four centuries, i.e., since the Council of Trent. These manuals developed and transmitted a certain systematization of moral theology based on categories which have become classic. Even those who criticize the manuals (e.g., proportionalists and consequentialists) still use these categories. The moral theory of the manuals constitutes a common cultural base, one whose concepts and categories (for the most part connected with certain currents in modern philosophy such as Kantian ethics) have exercised a determining role in the relationship between the teaching of Christian ethics and Scripture.

In our effort to delineate the principal elements of scriptural renewal proposed to us by the *Catechism* and *Veritatis splendor,* we shall examine six points: firstly, the use of Scripture; next, the great moral texts it offers us, the Decalogue, the Sermon on the Mount, apostolic catechesis, and the treatment of cases of conscience; finally, we shall respond to the difficulty created by new ethical problems and by recent cultural changes.

Scriptural Quotations

We need only run through the moral section of the *Catechism* to see that biblical citations there are far more numerous than in the manuals of former times. These citations appear even in the section titles, such as "Life in Christ" and "Life in the Spirit," taken from St. Paul in order to describe the moral life. The table of contents of *Veritatis splendor* is likewise sprinkled with biblical citations.

Looking more closely, we see that the quotations are not simple illustrations or proof texts, but constitute the primary source of the doctrine being proposed. Such is the case with the Beatitudes, placed at the beginning of the moral section of the *Catechism*.[3] It is also the case with the story of the rich young man who poses the fundamental moral question: "What good must I do to have eternal life?"[4]—the question which traces the entire framework of *Veritatis splendor*.

This renewal of contact with the Gospel leads to a profound modification of the conception of moral theology. Christian moral teaching cannot be reduced to the observance of a code of obligations and prohibitions. It consists principally, as *Veritatis splendor* says, in "holding fast to the very person of Jesus."[5] And so for every believer, "following Christ is the essential and primordial foundation of Christian morality."[6]

The Question of Obligation and the Question of Beatitude

In order to reestablish a solid bond between moral theology and the Gospel, it is not enough to multiply quotations from Scripture. We are facing a problem that I shall try to reduce to its bare essentials: it is a matter of knowing what is the first and characteristic question for moral theology.

We have here a choice between two questions that embody two concepts of moral theology. I shall mention first the one that is still the most widespread. Since the end of the Middle Ages, moral theology has focused on the idea of obligation imposed by law, to such an extent that moral teaching has become the domain of obligations, commands, prohibitions. The first moral question has therefore become: What is obligatory? What is allowed or forbidden? In consequence, moral theology has been divided according to the Decalogue, understood as the expression of the obligations and prohibitions imposed by the law of God. It has been cut off from all that goes beyond obligation and from all that concerns the free search for perfection. These have been relegated to another science, to the domain of asceticism and mysticism, or of spirituality, or perhaps of what Scripture scholars refer to as parenesis (exhortation).

As far as the relationship between Scripture and moral theology is con-

3. *CCC*, n. 1716–29.
4. *VS*, n. 6ff.
5. *VS*, n. 19.
6. *VS*, n. 19.

cerned, the result of all this is direct and logical: since they began with the question of obligation, moral theologians were only interested henceforth in scriptural texts which established obligations or formulated commands, that is to say the Decalogue, seen as a legislative code, and passages of the New Testament which could be related to this, such as the teaching on the indissolubility of marriage.[7] Moral theologians were no longer interested in sapiential and exhortatory texts. They did not realize that they were overlooking the principal texts of apostolic moral teaching. Thus the contact between Catholic moral teaching and Scripture narrowed by focusing on the Decalogue, which was identified, moreover, with natural law.

To aid us in reestablishing the connection between Catholic moral teaching and Scripture, the theological tradition fortunately offers us another model, one that comes to us from the Church Fathers. The approach of the patristic authors to moral teaching began with the question which St. Augustine expressed in these terms, "What is the blessed life?" and which St. Thomas later posed at the beginning of the moral section of the *Summa,* asking, What is true "beatitude"? In this way, they were rephrasing the question of the rich young man to Jesus: "What good must I do to gain eternal life?" That is also the question of salvation, according to another biblical formulation.[8]

With the moral question formulated in this way—"What is the true good, the true beatitude?"—the horizon of moral theology is opened up broadly, beyond legal obligations, and the scriptural texts evoked in response flow abundantly, beginning with the Gospel Beatitudes, which are like a summary of God's promises to his people. The Beatitudes bring us Christ's answer to the question of beatitude—a question that, according to St. Thomas's commentary on Matthew, philosophers of all schools tried in vain to resolve.

The *Catechism* (together with the encyclical *Veritatis splendor*) orients us in this direction when it introduces at the beginning of fundamental moral teaching—before the study of liberty, human acts, conscience, and law—a chapter on "Our Vocation to Beatitude," with its triple division: the Beatitudes, the desire for beatitude, and Christian beatitude. Since the appearance

7. See Mt 19:9.

8. [Editors' note: The editors have chosen to translate *"bonheur"* as "beatitude" rather than "happiness," both to remind the reader of Aquinas's particular understanding of the end or goal of human life, and to avoid the senses of "happiness" which are more psychic and transient that what Aquinas understood by *"beatitudo."*]

of the first manuals in the seventeenth century, the treatment of beatitude had been separated from fundamental moral theology without a word being said. So complete was the separation that one could discuss the entire field of moral theology without mentioning the question of beatitude or thus of the Beatitudes. This is borne out by the thematic indexes of these treatises on moral theology.

What is at stake is of prime importance for us. If we approach the Bible from the perspective of the question of beatitude, the entire body of Scripture will give us answers, by showing us the ways that lead to the promised beatitude and by furnishing us with examples to support us in our pursuit of it. We then rediscover this patristic idea: the entire Bible possesses a moral meaning centered upon the application of the teaching and the life of Christ to our own conduct. Having rediscovered the path to scriptural renewal in ethics, thanks to the question of true beatitude, we can now approach the principal moral texts offered to us by Scripture.

The Reinterpretation of the Decalogue

Throughout Christian tradition, the Decalogue has provided the basic foundation for moral teaching, but the interpretation given it varies according to the place attributed to it in the theological systematization. For St. Thomas, for example, the Decalogue is at the service of the virtues, beginning with the theological virtues that form the heart of the New Law. In the study of each virtue, he examines each corresponding commandment, as determining that without which no virtue is possible. In the modern manuals, the structure of moral theology is formed by the Decalogue, seen as the expression of moral obligations, while the virtues are practically speaking dropped from fundamental moral theology in favor of the study of sins. They serve merely as points of reference for classifying obligations and sins.

The *Catechism* proposes to us a broadening of the concept of moral law and its domain. It directs the natural law and the Decalogue to the New Law as to their fulfillment. Thus it places the Decalogue within the framework of the Covenant and makes of it a preparation for the Gospel, at the service of love of God and neighbor.

Veritatis splendor, in its turn, adopts this viewpoint and adds a clarification which is of great importance for the interpretation of the Decalogue. The

Decalogue is not simply a list of commandments demanding obedience under pain of sin and punishment; it is a gift of God's Goodness, a manifestation of God's Wisdom and Holiness. And here is the decisive point: more than legal obedience, the Ten Commandments require of us a response of love,[9] a love that will take on the twofold form of love of God above all and love of neighbor; these in turn are refracted into the precepts of the first and second halves of the Decalogue.

This last point is of great significance. In placing the response of love as the basis of the observance of the Decalogue, *Veritatis splendor* is making a fundamental change. *Veritatis splendor* raises the question explicitly in a quotation from St. Augustine: "Does love bring about the keeping of the commandments, or does the keeping of the commandments bring about love?"[10] In other words, which is first and fundamental? Is it obedience to the imperative that a commandment formulates, or is it love, which is the object of the commandment? By thinking of morality as the domain of obligations, and particularly by reducing the treatment of charity to a listing of the duties it imposes and the sins contrary to it, Catholic teaching in recent centuries had given priority to commands in moral theology. *Veritatis splendor* invites us to a conversion: to give love primacy over command, and to return legal observance to its role as the servant of charity. This is indeed St. Augustine's answer to his question: "But who can doubt that love comes first? For the one who does not love has no reason for keeping the commandments."[11] In moral theology, the point is not to observe the commandments of the Decalogue materially, to obey them so as to fulfill one's obligations or through a sense of duty; the point is to observe them out of love, with the heart. This is precisely the work of the Holy Spirit, infusing charity in our hearts, and forming the New Law within us as an interior law.

The very crux of moral theology is being modified. The Decalogue is being reestablished on the foundation of charity and put in direct contact once more with the New Law. It presides like a tutor over the first stage of the formation of charity, a formation whose further growth will develop under the aegis of the Gospel Law. This change of perspective has direct and profound

---

9. *VS*, n. 10.

10. Augustine, *In Ioan. Evang.*, Tract. 82, n. 3; *VS*, n. 22.

11. Augustine, *In Ioan. Evang.*, Tract. 82, n. 3.

consequences for the relationship between moral theology and Scripture, if it is true, as St. Augustine thinks, that love of God and of neighbor constitutes the principal criterion for interpreting all of sacred history; for charity is the soul and the end of Scripture.[12]

The Sermon on the Mount and the Law

A major innovation in the *Catechism* and in *Veritatis splendor* is that the New Law and the Sermon on the Mount have been reintroduced into the domain of Christian moral teaching. As the Decalogue stood to the Old Law, so the Sermon on the Mount stands to the New Law, as its specific text. This is a return to the tradition of the Church Fathers and to St. Thomas. It is also an essential point for the return to the Gospel.

The Sermon on the Mount is indeed a major part of apostolic catechesis. The evangelist Matthew made of it the summary of Jesus' teaching on justice, that is to say, on the moral life. It has rightly been called the charter of the Christian life. For this reason, it became a principal source of preaching and moral theology among the Church Fathers, Greek as well as Latin, and among theologians up to the thirteenth century.

The discreet rejection of the Sermon on the Mount from moral theology in the modern era is easily explained. The teaching of the Sermon on the Mount cannot be integrated into a systematization of moral theology based on obligations. It is impossible to reduce it to strict commands. On the one hand, moral systems of obligation or command are by nature static; they fix limits and determine minimal requirements.[13] On the other hand, the teaching of the Sermon on the Mount is fundamentally dynamic; it is animated by a continuous tendency toward exceeding and surpassing, a tendency toward the progress and perfection of love in imitation of the Father's goodness.

While taking up again the precepts of the Decalogue, the Sermon on the Mount radicalizes and maximizes them by placing itself at the level of the heart (i.e., of interior acts, in St. Thomas's terms), ordering these precepts to the perfection of charity. We are dealing here with two different kinds of moral

12. *De Doc. Christ.* bk. I, ch. xxxv, 39.

13. On this point, see Henri Bergson's *The Two Sources of Morality and Religion* (Garden City, N.J.: Doubleday, 1954).

teaching. Obligations do indeed remain a necessary basis in Christian moral teaching, but they can only fulfill their role and acquire evangelical significance by being ordered, as servants, to the increase of charity, whose ways the Sermon on the Mount traces out for us.

The reintegration of the Sermon on the Mount in moral teaching will not be easy, however, because it requires a modification in the moral categories we have inherited from our education. A sign of this difficulty can be seen in the subject indexes of the *Catechism:* no index, not even that in the 1994 English edition, mentions the Sermon on the Mount, even though it is explicitly treated in the body of the text.[14] Still, in the Index of Citations from Sacred Scripture there are 139 citations to the chapters of Matthew's Gospel which comprise the Sermon on the Mount.

In order to adequately take account of the teaching of the Sermon on the Mount, moral theology must begin with the question of beatitude and develop by following the virtues grouped around charity, as the structure of the Sermon on the Mount itself indicates. The Sermon on the Mount first teaches us the blessings of the Kingdom and then describes the attitudes of heart and the conduct that lead to them—in other words, the virtues which prepare the blessings of the Kingdom and which will be more explicitly indicated in the catechesis of the New Testament epistles.

The *Catechism* and *Veritatis splendor* seek to accord with the Sermon on the Mount by recovering the teaching on the New Law, defined by St. Thomas as an interior law formed by the grace of the Holy Spirit, received through faith in Christ, and operating through charity. This teaching on the New Law includes, as secondary elements, a) the text of the Sermon on the Mount as the moral center of Scripture, and b) the sacraments as the instruments that communicate the grace of the Spirit. Thus the Holy Spirit once more enjoys a preponderant role in Christian moral teaching. The Spirit's indispensable action is exercised notably through the gifts, which St. Thomas links closely to the virtues.

---

14. *CCC,* n. 1965–70. [Editor's note: Reference to the Sermon on the Mount appears in the later Index Analyticus of the Latin Typical Edition of the *Catechism of the Catholic Church,* which was promulgated on August 15, 1997.]

Apostolic Catechesis and Paraclesis

The Sermon on the Mount is not the only source of New Testament moral teaching. It is not an isolated text; it appears as summary and completion of biblical sapiential doctrine, and should be seen in relation to the other texts of apostolic catechesis, of which it is a principal component, representing the direct authority of the Lord.

The *Catechism,* even more clearly than *Veritatis splendor,* points us to the principal texts of apostolic moral catechesis: Romans 12–15, 1 Corinthians 12–13, Colossians 3–4, Ephesians 4–5, and so forth.[15] In these texts we see the work of the apostles and the first Christian communities, impelled as they were by the desire to obtain for their preaching, catechesis, and meditation summaries of moral teaching in a formulation which would lend itself to being passed on and learned by heart.

We encounter here, however, an exegetical obstacle derived from the fact that many Scripture scholars simply assume the appropriateness of the commonly accepted moral categories that have been challenged so far in this essay. Scripture scholars (and the New Testament translations they influence, e.g., the Jerusalem Bible) typically place the texts we have cited under the heading of "parenesis." Parenesis designates an exhortation that is distinct from moral teaching, which ordinarily takes the form of an imperative. In this view, because these texts do not present imperatives, Scripture scholars thus conclude that such texts belong to the field of spiritual exhortation and are not, "properly speaking," moral teaching. This is effectively the opinion of "proportionalist" writers, who consequently remove these texts from their ethical system. Therefore, it seems that the New Testament has little to teach us about morality understood in this way. One could thus construct the science of morality without in fact any need to consult Scripture, by basing it solely on rational arguments and norms. These moral theologians proceed on the assumption that the first generations of Christians had little interest in moral teaching and their few ideas were confused; in this view, the early Christians are seen to have been content to add some spiritual exhortations to the Decalogue. This interpretation is based on a rigid application of the separation between morality and spirituality.

15. *CCC,* n. 1971.

This rather surprising conclusion is the sign of what we might call an incompatibility of systems in the conception of moral theology. When these moral theologians question the New Testament from the viewpoint of their own system, focused on obligations and imperative norms, they obtain only a disappointing response. The end result of their efforts is at best paltry.

However, the teaching of the authors of the New Testament is indeed linked to a moral system, to a presentation and organization of moral teaching which responds to the question of beatitude and salvation and which is based upon the teaching of the virtues, beginning with faith in Christ and charity. Thus, their manner of presentation differs from the imperative mode. It is properly called "paraclesis," i.e., apostolic and fraternal exhortation.

This is obviously a decisive point with regard to the subject we are discussing: the use of Scripture in moral theology. If we continue to think of Christian moral teaching as a set of obligations and imperatives, the exegetical situation will continue to be one of frustration, with constant difficulties arising over scriptural interpretation. If the impasse is to be overcome, we must extricate ourselves by amending our categories and by being attuned to those used by the sacred writers when they are teaching about morality.

Paraclesis

To do so, we first need to clarify our terms. As was noted earlier, Scripture scholars have tended to refer to the apostolic texts of which we have been speaking as taking the form of "parenesis." This term is inadequate; it does not belong to the moral vocabulary of the New Testament.[16] The term "paraclesis," meaning urgent exhortation, is preferable.[17]

Paraclesis is practically a technical term for St. Paul, who usually uses it to introduce his moral teaching, as in the Letter to the Romans: "I appeal to you therefore, brethren, by the mercies of God. . . ."[18] In either the substantive or verbal form, the word occurs 38 times in the Pauline letters and more than a hundred times in the New Testament. Paraclesis is the apostle's preferred teaching mode when transmitting the Lord's teaching to disciples who have become his brothers and sisters. He no longer issues orders or commands as

---

16. The verb *parainein* appears only twice, in the account of the storm in Acts 27:9, 22.

17. See Heinrich Schlier, *Die Zeit der Kirche: Exegetische Aufsätze und Vorträge* (Freiburg: Herder, 1956), 74–89.

18. Rom 12:1.

he would to servants, for the disciples have opened their hearts to love, to *agape;* Paul exhorts them by word and example, as brothers and sisters in Christ. Paraclesis is perfectly suited to the regime of the New Law, to a morality of charity and of the virtues, one that calls for each person's initiative. Thus, paraclesis should be considered the form of moral teaching in apostolic catechesis, and should be seen as a major resource for Christian ethics.[19]

Chapters 12–15 of St. Paul's Letter to the Romans are a model of this form of apostolic catechesis. Here St. Paul presents the Christian life as a spiritual worship in which we offer our bodies and our persons to God as a living and holy sacrifice, in active communion with the Body of Christ, which is the Church. The moral teaching here parallels the Sermon on the Mount. It focuses on charity, which acts through the virtues: fraternal love, humility, devotion, constancy under persecution, piety, and hospitality. These virtues are then specified in concrete cases such as obedience to civil authority and consideration for the weaker brethren in the matter of eating foods that have been offered to idols. Thus, we are dealing with a main source of Christian teaching and of moral theology.

It is important to note that the moral catechesis of Romans 12–15 cannot be separated from the earlier part of the Epistle to the Romans, which focuses on the faith that justifies.[20] The moral teaching is the direct consequence and active realization of faith working through charity. This is indicated by the conjunction which connects the two sections of the letter: "*Therefore,* I exhort you, brethren. . . ." So Luther should not be followed when he separates the faith that justifies, taught in the first section, from the works described in the second part. Nor should we follow Catholic moralists who produce a similar separation. In the desire to safeguard the meritorious value of works, moralists have removed them so far from faith that they have established two separate domains as it were, dogma being concerned with faith and morality with works. Here again the *Catechism* indicates the path to renewal by its explicit reference to the principal texts of the apostolic catechesis: "To the Lord's Sermon on the Mount it is fitting to add the *moral catechesis of the apostolic teach-*

---

19. [Editor's note: The following three paragraphs have been drawn from S. Pinckaers, *La Parole de Dieu et la Morale—Discours Universitaries no. 52* (Fribourg: Editions Universitaires, 1996), 14–16.]

20. Cf. S. Pinckaers, "La méthode théologique de la morale contemporaine," *Seminarium* 43 (1991): 313–27.

ings, such as Romans 12–15, 1 Corinthians 12–13, Colossians 3–4, Ephesians 4–5, etc. This doctrine hands on the Lord's teaching with the authority of the apostle, particularly in the presentation of the virtues that flow from faith in Christ and are animated by charity, the principle gift of the Holy Spirit."[21]

Here the *Catechism* refers us to major New Testament sources of moral teaching. These texts nourished the moral reflection of the Church Fathers and of theologians and spiritual writers up to the modern period. Happily, the liturgy has preserved them for us. We, in our turn, face the challenge of allowing this heritage to bear its fruit. There is an obstacle in our path, however, stronger and more tenacious than we may realize. We must succeed in discarding the mental categories we have received in the recent past, such as the idea that morality is solely a matter of law and obligation, commandments, and prohibitions. The Sermon on the Mount begins with the promises of the Beatitudes and engages us in the way of wisdom that finds its perfection in love, given even to enemies. We have, therefore, to conform our idea of morality to the truth, widening it to the measure of the Gospel.

These texts of apostolic catechesis, in the same way as the Sermon on the Mount, often constitute small syntheses of moral teaching, syntheses that are well organized and formed out of bits or pieces that have been carefully worked over (even on a literary level) in the light of the tradition (primarily oral) and above all in the light of practice. These presentations teach us to follow the logic of the Holy Spirit, rather different from Cartesian or Kantian logic, or even Scholastic logic. As in the Gospel, the center of moral teaching in these texts is the intelligent and loving heart. We have here real treasures to be rediscovered; they are part of our heritage. If moral theologians have neglected them too much, we have to note that the liturgy has fortunately continued to repeat them to us through the centuries.

Discernment in Cases of Conscience

With the help of the *Catechism* and *Veritatis splendor,* we have shown how Catholic moral theology can renew itself by contact with the principal scriptural sources of moral teaching. I should like at this point to complete this general overview by examining how the sacred authors treat the concrete cases

21. *CCC,* n. 1971.

proposed to them, cases of conscience as we call them. St. Paul, among others, provides us with models in the series of cases that he resolves in 1 Corinthians. Yet, what is his method, what are his criteria?

The method is constant. We could characterize it as a compenetration of criteria of two orders. First of all, there are the criteria belonging to the order of reason, such as can be found in the thought of the philosophers and rabbis. In the case of fornication, for example: "Every other sin which a man commits is outside the body; but the immoral man sins against his own body."[22] At the same time, criteria based on faith come into play: our relationship to Christ, to the Spirit, and the bond of charity: "Do you not know that your body is a temple of the Holy Spirit?"[23] We thus see here an intimate link between the understanding of the human and the understanding of Christ. Each penetrates and reinforces the other, but the Christian criteria become predominant, particularly through the work of charity which unites believers as brothers and sisters, as members of the same Body by the impulse of the Spirit. Pauline moral teaching in the Epistle to the Romans, as well as in that to the Ephesians, is also situated within this framework of the Church seen as the Body of Christ.

In brief, we already find in Paul what later theology will develop—a close union between the moral virtues (e.g., sobriety, justice, chastity, gentleness, discernment) and the theological virtues—the latter providing the higher and decisive criteria. Charity in particular penetrates so deeply into the other virtues that they become aspects or forms of *agape*. "Love is patient and kind. . . . Love bears all things, believes all things, hopes all things, endures all things."[24]

However, St. Paul does not furnish his correspondents with "ready-made" solutions to be applied without variation. He proposes to them models for solutions of cases of conscience; he gives them the basic principles and conclusions; he teaches them how to judge according to right reason and the Gospel, so that they will be able to discern for themselves when other situations arise. In this way, he educates their Christian conscience.

In the cases examined, we notice that the apostle is not content to determine what is permitted and what forbidden. His reflection is always directed to the formation of charity in the hearts of the faithful and in the ecclesial com-

22. 1 Cor 6:18.   23. 1 Cor 6:19.
24. 1 Cor 13:4–7.

munity, so that they may acquire wisdom in docility to the Spirit. In this concrete teaching, he aims primarily at progress in charity and in every virtue.

Nevertheless, in Paul's nuanced teaching on formation in charity—as in the case of eating food offered to idols, where he wishes to take into account the conscience of the weak—Paul shows himself intractable in regard to negative precepts and the vices involved: "Do you not know that the unrighteous will not inherit the Kingdom of God? . . . neither the immoral, nor idolaters, nor adulterers, nor sexual perverts, nor thieves, nor the greedy, nor drunkards, nor revilers, nor robbers will inherit the Kingdom of God."[25] These vices corrupt *agape*. One must choose. On this level, no compromise, no accommodation is possible.

It is clear that moral judgment takes place first at the level of the heart, in the conscience, where virtues and vices are formed beneath God's gaze and where actions are engendered. Paul is categorical in his reprobation of vices. But the consideration of sins is not predominant for him, as it will be in casuistry. It is the work of grace through charity which is uppermost in his thought. His catechesis is wholly oriented toward salvation in Jesus and sanctification in the Spirit through the practice of the Gospel virtues: "You were washed, you were sanctified, you were justified in the name of the Lord Jesus Christ and in the Spirit of our God."[26]

The study of the cases of conscience is truly a model for us, showing the range of criteria to be used, with their ordering and interconnection, as well as showing how faith, hope, and charity should guide a Christian's concrete behavior.

New Ethical Problems and Cultural Changes

We now need to respond to two difficulties frequently presented in regard to the application of Scripture to concrete moral judgment. The advances of science and technology have created new ethical problems. How can Scripture give us norms and prescribe to us a line of conduct in the case of problems which were not imagined in former times, such as those posed by bioethics? Or again: the biblical authors and the first Christians lived in a cul-

25. 1 Cor 6:9–10.
26. 1 Cor 6:11.

tural context far different from ours, which has been transformed with the advent of "modernity" and the progress of the sciences. It seems that the solutions worked out in their time cannot apply such as they are in our time. How can there be a continuity between biblical culture and our own, as far as moral norms and their application are concerned? This difficulty calls into question not only the recourse to Scripture for the solution of concrete cases, but also the universal and permanent character of moral laws. Here we are at the heart of the current debate raised by "proportionalism."

To respond to these questions, we should distinguish three levels in human action, levels that are contained and united in action in the concrete.

1) We can consider the human act at the level of the external act, as St. Thomas put it. Later moral theologians would rigidify matters by speaking of a physical level, and the "proportionalists" of a pre-moral or ontic level. At this material level, it is clear that the progress of the sciences and technological inventions have produced changes which have modified conditions of life and mentalities, creating a certain "scientific" or "technological" culture. These are material and cultural facts that we need to take into consideration in assessing the circumstances of action.

The danger exists, however, of in effect reducing moral judgment to this level and of conceiving it according to the model of a technical calculation of profit and loss in view of a desired goal. We would be basing our judgment on a comparison of the good and evil consequences of the action, which the Germans call a *Güterabwägung*, a weighing out of goods. In this view, the moral teaching of Scripture would be considered as one cultural datum among others, more or less applicable to our times. For example, if we take a judgment about abortion, the unborn child will be assessed first of all as a datum in the biological order that will be weighed against the interests of the mother in the physical, psychological, or social order. If we are not careful, in this way of looking at things we will end up using money as the measure, because money lends itself best to the calculation of profit and loss. This method by way of comparison of consequences could lead to a revision of the norms themselves, if general conditions were modified to an important degree, as in the case of the establishment of freedom of abortion by civil legislation.

2) Such a view of human action is partial. Although it suits our technological mentality, it should not be allowed to hide from us the properly moral di-

mension of the human act: it is the work of the human person and qualifies her in her personality. Human action is directly moral at the level of the interior act. If we rise to this plane, which touches us in our state as persons, the perspective changes profoundly. The moral plane is constituted by the qualities of the human person at the level of reason, will, and heart, where she has mastery over her actions. That is the domain of the virtues, the virtues that make both the act and the one who does it good.

At this higher level that is concerned with the human person as human, the changes noted on the material level are reduced. The virtues preached by Paul, such as self-control, patience, truthfulness, purity, as well as the virtues taught by the philosophers, Plato, Aristotle, and Cicero, which have become our cardinal virtues—all these qualities of mind and heart with their contrary vices remain relevant for us, whatever the changes which have occurred over the centuries. These qualities enable us precisely to measure the profundity of such changes, notably by means of prudential judgment. These moral perfections witness to the permanence of the human vocation in the multiplicity of peoples and civilizations. It is with regard to them that the greatness or corruption of a culture can be judged; they stand at the very source of civilization. It is on this same common human base that we can establish the universality of human rights, as well as obligations.

At this level, the view on abortion that we took as an example, is also modified: here the unborn child appears as a human person as much as her mother. The child has the seeds of virtue already within her and is, morally speaking, a subject possessing rights. If justice is the will to render to everyone his or her due, it will, by combining with the mother's natural affection, inspire in her the will to bring her child to birth and to her full human formation, to the point of the active enjoyment of the child's rights. This will for justice will then be an integral part of the mother's love.

3) If we wish to return fully to the Scriptures, we must rise still higher, to the level of our relationship with God, to which faith in Christ and charity give us entrance. Here the initiative belongs to the Word of God, resonating in the hearts of believers and using Scripture as its instrument. According to the definition of the New Law, we are the recipients of an interior Word given by the grace of the Holy Spirit, received through faith in Christ and operating through charity. Together with the sacraments, the text of Scripture is the instrument used by grace in order to speak to us and enlighten us.

Scripture scholars, in my humble opinion as a moral theologian, have fixed our attention a bit too much on human factors and on the cultural context which conditioned the sacred authors in their work of composition. We run the risk of forgetting that when we read Scripture, through this historic data we are placed before a Word that has mastery over time and that creates history, the history of a people that listens to it and of each believer personally, beginning with the most lowly. The Word leads them to an encounter with the living God. Certainly we should carefully take into account the historical and human envelope of Scripture, but this should not prevent us from seeing that in its substance it is formed by a Word that surpasses words, ideas, categories, and sentiments. When God wishes to speak to us, who can hinder it, what reasonings of Scripture scholar or theologian?

We perceive here the higher source of theology and Christian ethics. As the account of Pentecost shows, this Word transcends differences of languages and cultures and, with the perspicacity of wisdom, lights up the depths and details of human action in order to work its discernment in the human heart. With regard to the problem of abortion, for example, the light of the Spirit shows us, in the littleness and weakness of the child hidden in its mother's womb, the work and the image of God, the very figure of Christ identifying himself with the least of the little ones. Where shall we find the criteria of judgment about this interior Word? Quite simply, we shall find them in the conformity to the writings of the evangelists and apostles.

I should like to add two important clarifications. First of all, the Gospel has been entrusted to the Church and should therefore be read and interpreted in accordance with the Church's teaching, within the framework of liturgical prayer, as well as in personal prayer and meditation. Secondly, all this is useless unless the Word is put into practice; this alone wins us the experience of the realities of the life of faith with spiritual wisdom. It is by practice that a judgment of connaturality is formed within us, a judgment which is the characteristic of the virtuous man and which bears fruit in prudential judgment.

We have distinguished three levels in the complexity of the human act: the material level of the external act; the directly moral level of the interior act; and the level relating us to God, which we may call theological. In a concrete action, however, which is always personal, these three levels converge and compenetrate each other, beginning from the dynamic interiority which conceives our acts and which is our very selves, in our freedom received from God. The theological dimension raises us above the level of the moral life by inviting us to imitate the perfection of the "heavenly Father"; yet it also inclines us toward what is most concrete, toward helping our brother in need, toward forgiveness, and toward love even of our enemy.

The reproach we might offer to "consequentialism" is that it has narrowed moral theory by reducing judgment to a pre-moral level, to a kind of technical calculation of consequences in view of an end, and by limiting the moral plane to an option between good and bad intention. At the same time, this system has practically severed the bonds between moral theology and Scripture with its distinction between the transcendental and categorical levels. Morality or ethics being confined to the categorical level, the system was permitted to be developed with the aid of reason alone, having no further need of Scripture.

Such rational, if not rationalistic, truncations impoverish moral theology and are contrary to the perspective and language of Scripture, which proceed directly from concrete experience in all its richness, considered in terms of the heart, where man stands before God and before his neighbor. The preaching of Jesus to which the Sermon on the Mount bears witness, with its parables and examples drawn from everyday life, is characteristic in this connection, and is at the opposite pole from abstract divisions and theories.

Scripture unites all the dimensions of the human act in the experience in which wisdom is formed: experience first of the Word of God who is the source of Scripture; experience then of personal action in docility to this Word; experience too of the ecclesial communion in which charity and the accompanying virtues place us; experience, finally, of the world as the work of God, wrought through God's creative Word who governs it. Such is the loving Word revealed in Jesus Christ, which unites moral teaching intimately with Scripture and presides over their relationship. The Word, received in the faith that justifies, engenders Christian morality through the grace of the Spirit, who sanctifies us in charity.

4 ∾ The Place of Philosophy in Moral Theology (1999)

Does moral theology need philosophy? What place does it have? What role does it play? In a word, what is the relationship between philosophy and theology in Christian moral doctrine? We could discuss these questions in a variety of ways. The simplest and most instructive is to examine a fully developed theological synthesis on these questions, such as St. Thomas Aquinas's, which can be taken as a model and is considered a classic: it is the direct heir to the theology of the Church Fathers and serves as a reference point for modern theological currents.

We can reduce the components of Thomistic moral teaching to four structural elements:

1. Morality is essentially a response to the question of happiness and the ultimate end of human conduct, according to the general way morality was conceived by ancient philosophers and the Fathers. It is *the treatise on beatitude and the ultimate end.*[1]

2. Humans move toward beatitude through their actions on the basis of two kinds of principles corresponding to the two parts of each human act: the internal act and the external. First there are the internal principles or personal sources of action, which are *the virtues.*

Originally published as "The Place of Philosophy in Moral Theology," *L'Osservatore Romano,* June 16, 1999, 14–15. Translated by Michael Sherwin, O.P. [A longer version of this essay appears in Timothy L. Smith, ed., *Faith and Reason* (South Bend, Ind.: St. Augustine Press, 2001), *10–20.*]. Edited for publication in *The Pinkaers Reader.*

1. [Editors' note: The editors have chosen to translate *"bonheur"* as "beatitude" rather than "happiness," both to remind the reader of Aquinas's particular understanding of the end or goal

3. Then the external or superior principles of action come into play: *law and grace.*

4. This structure presupposes an analysis of the human being as made in God's own image, endowed with different faculties that together make up a specifically human act: *free choice.* All the work of moral doctrine is aimed at informing, on the basis of universal principles, the choice that produces concrete action.

Let us note that, from the study of principles to the making of a choice, St. Thomas's thought appears "conjunctive," in the sense that it aims at the cooperation of all the human faculties under the aegis of the partnership between reason and will. Thus, the decision to act consists of a practical judgment and a free choice inseparably joined. This conjunctive character will also be seen in the composition of the treatises on the particular virtues, where the virtue or internal principle, along with the gift resulting from grace and the precept of the Decalogue, as external principles, will be studied in each case.

On each of these four points we will examine the place and role of philosophy in St. Thomas's moral theology.

The Treatise on Beatitude

In the five questions which make up the treatise on beatitude, the role of philosophy, represented primarily by Aristotle and Boethius, appears so substantial that certain interpreters have regarded these questions as purely philosophical. They have not seen, first of all, that the study of the ultimate end and of the different goods offered to humans form a threefold way—comparable to the five ways leading to the existence of God—bringing us to the Christian response: the call to the vision of God beyond this life, for "God alone" can fully satisfy the human longing for beatitude. In dealing with this high point of his reasoning, Thomas no longer relies on the philosopher, but on a theologian, on Augustine, who himself explains Catholic morality by starting with the question of beatitude that every person asks himself, he says, even before expressing it. The One who can satisfy this longing is really the Trinitarian God, revealed and accessible in Jesus Christ. Nor did they consider that the expla-

---

of human life, and to avoid the senses of "happiness" which are more psychic and transient that what Aquinas understood by *"beatitudo."*]

nation of the Beatitudes in the commentary on St. Matthew was an underlying source of the *Summa theologiae*'s treatise, that it was already following the plan of the progressive search for the true good,[2] and was showing that only Christ revealed the complete beatitude which the philosophers, including Aristotle, were unable to discover. Moreover, the treatise on beatitude will only be completed in the explanation of the Gospel Beatitudes,[3] which St. Thomas reserves for his exposition, with the aid of the virtues and gifts, of the Christian's beatitude here below.

Philosophy and theology, then, each play a large part in the treatise on beatitude, but they are not simply juxtaposed; they are connected by what we could call a natural relationship. Together, in fact, they answer a question which arises from man's spiritual nature: what is the true good or genuine beatitude? Enlightened by Revelation, the theologian perceives that this spontaneous desire can be fulfilled only by the vision of God because of the openness of the human intellect and will to the infinite. Hence the famous argument about the natural desire to see God, which is the mainspring of St. Thomas's reasoning on this subject.[4] Regarding this vocation, philosophy is both necessary and inadequate. It can neither attain nor even consider such a totally gratuitous and truly supernatural beatitude. But although the theologian knows of the call to beatitude in God by faith, he still cannot show the paths leading to it without the work of reason, without a philosophical reflection on acts and virtues.

Organized in this way, the treatise on beatitude provides the overall structure for the moral part of theology. We will thus find the connection we have just seen between philosophy and theology in each treatise of the *secunda pars*.

Finally, we should note that this treatise on beatitude will disappear from the post-Tridentine manuals of moral theology, as well as from the modern ethics of Kantian influence, following the critique of eudaemonism. It will only survive as the search for a material, empirical happiness advocated by utilitarianism. The *Catechism of the Catholic Church* has fortunately reintroduced the consideration of beatitude at the start of its treatment of Christian morality as a vocation to beatitude in the light of the Gospel Beatitudes.[5]

2. *ST* I-II 2.   3. *ST* I-II 69.

4. [Editors' note: For more on this argument, see "Aquinas on Nature and the Supernatural," essay #18 in *The Pinckaers Reader*.]

5. *CCC*, n. 1716–29.

The Virtues and the Gifts

The extensive treatise on *habitus* and virtues is a masterpiece of Thomistic moral teaching. There we find the heritage of ancient philosophy and the reflection of the patristic authors, every one of whom saw virtue as the very essence of human and Christian perfection. Here again the role of philosophy is so substantial as to be considered preponderant. But in fact St. Thomas's teaching on the virtues is the result of the patient search of medieval theologians guided by the gradually rediscovered works of Aristotle. Thomas uses the Stagirite's precise analyses even in their details, as in the treatise on prudence. In order to define and divide the related virtues, he will follow the lists drawn up by Cicero and Macrobius, which will make it difficult to find a place for Christian virtues such as humility, obedience, and vigilance. The impression that the teaching on the virtues is mostly philosophical is even stronger, the more accustomed we are to thinking of virtue as being essentially the result of human effort, of repeated acts.

However, when the treatise on the virtues is read as a whole, we see that it is mainly a theological construction. The virtues actually form a living organism comparable to the human body and its organs. They neither exist nor act separately, as one might suppose from an analytical study of the *Summa*. They are united by dynamic links forged by charity and prudence, and act together, like the limbs of our body.

This consideration particularly applies to the relationship between the theological and moral virtues. Faith, hope, and charity constitute the head of the Christian organism of the virtues and impart life from within, like a vital impulse, to the human virtues so that they can be ordered to divine beatitude, but not without transforming them to some extent. St. Thomas will have such a strong sense of this influence that he will consider it necessary for the infused moral virtues to be added in order to perfect the acquired virtues. In each treatise on the moral virtues, we will see the changes he makes with respect to Aristotle. Thus martyrdom will become the supreme act of the virtue of fortitude instead of courage in warfare, and virginity for Christ will be the perfection of chastity. Thomas will even maintain that there can be no true patience without charity and, thus, without grace.[6]

6. *ST* II-II 136.3.

Moreover, St. Thomas links the virtues with the gifts of the Holy Spirit, which thus enter the organism of the virtues in order to perfect them. The gifts are an integral part of Thomas's moral teaching, in accordance with the definition of the New Law as the grace of the Spirit, and are necessary for all Christians. They add a receptivity to the virtues, a docility to spiritual impulses. In this way the Holy Spirit's action, like the virtues, can affect all that the Christian does. Morality truly becomes "life in the Holy Spirit," as the *Catechism* calls it (n. 1699). Here we see no separation between morality and mysticism, to which the gifts will be reserved by later theology.

In fact, under the influence of Revelation and Christian experience, the very idea of virtue is transformed: to the acquired virtues are added the infused virtues that originate in the grace of Christ and no longer in human effort alone. These virtues, beginning with the theological ones, are so vitally linked to the human virtues that their action will be the work of God and the human person together, united in charity.

Finally, we should note that the apostolic catechesis,[7] particularly St. Paul's teaching on virtue and vice in the Letter to the Romans, Aquinas's commentary on which prepared the way for this part of the *Summa,* represents the source, the principal "authority," for St. Thomas's doctrine, together with the explanations of the Fathers, particularly St. Augustine, St. Gregory the Great, etc. The Thomistic study of the virtues thus combines the leading scriptural, philosophical, and theological currents.

Once again we find philosophy joined to Revelation within theology according to the Pauline command: "Your thoughts should be wholly directed to all that is . . . virtuous or worthy of praise" (Phil 4:8); but also in the idea that the Word of God deepens philosophical knowledge and develops it beyond human thoughts and hopes.

Laws and Precepts

In Christian teaching the Decalogue has always been considered a basic foundation, and Scholastic theology related it to the natural law inscribed in every human heart. Post-Tridentine theology made the Decalogue the cornerstone of moral teaching to the point of dividing its material, no longer accord-

7. Cf. *CCC*, n. 1971.

ing to the virtues as St. Thomas did, but according to the Ten Commandments, interpreted as the expression of obligations and prohibitions imposed on humans by God's will.

St. Thomas likewise assigned an essential place to the Decalogue and the natural law; but he puts them in a broader legislative context that makes them dependent on Christian Revelation. In his view, laws form a true organism that has its origin in God and his eternal law. The latter is known to humans in the natural law, which will serve as the basis of human laws. Revelation will clarify, corroborate, and perfect this legislation in the form of the Old Law, concentrated in the Decalogue, and of the New or Gospel Law, taught chiefly in the Lord's Sermon on the Mount. The New Law represents the apex of the moral law and brings the divine law to its perfection here below. The Decalogue and the natural law are thus taken up into the legislative dynamic which has its source in God and returns to God through the New Law. This results in a reinterpretation of the Decalogue in the sense of an interiorization and a higher perfection. For St. Thomas, the Decalogue sets out the rules for external acts which the New Law brings to perfection by governing the internal acts that inspire them, with the help of the virtues beginning with faith and charity. Thus the Decalogue is made to serve the virtues. It plays a particular role in the first stage of the divine pedagogy, in the training of beginners who must struggle against their sins and eradicate their vices.

The philosophical part of Christian moral teaching mainly concerns its foundations, the natural law and the Decalogue that expresses it, by putting it in the context of the covenant. Its task will continue in the establishment of civil law by way of deduction or addition, which will be specifically the work of reason. Added to this is reflection on the virtues, which calls for experience and maturity.

Let us note that the natural law does not appear as a barrier to freedom but, in St. Thomas, possesses a basically dynamic nature: it proceeds from the natural inclinations and yearnings for the preservation of being, the gift of life, the good, truth, and life in society, which are already found in Cicero's *De officiis*.[8] These inclinations will be developed through the virtues. As for the negative commandments, they forbid actions incompatible with the formation of the virtues and thus lay the groundwork for them. In this way, the natural

---

8. Cicero, *De officiis* Bk. I, ch. IV.

law and the Decalogue can be ordered to the Gospel Law as to a higher perfection, a total fulfillment. Here as well, theology takes up and completes the philosophical quest.

Lastly, we should mention the sapiential nature of law in St. Thomas: it is the organizing function of reason on the part of the divine or human lawgiver, and not a mere act of will by one who holds authority, as will generally be the case in the modern conception. This results in an equally sapiential obedience, combining reason and will. The coordination of the different philosophical and theological levels of moral legislation will be the work of this wisdom.

Prudential Judgment

The principal task of practical reason in the moral realm consists in applying precepts to personal action in concrete circumstances. We can think of this operation as a deduction starting from the first principles of the moral order, on condition that they are linked to the natural inclinations which form the basis of the law and the first source of human action. These principles, then, are not theoretical and abstract, even if their foundation is universal and appears impersonal. They correspond to the meaning of truth and goodness, to love of self and others, which are natural to human persons and derive from that spiritual spark which St. Thomas calls *synderesis*. The task of applying the principles of practical reason is the work of prudence integrating the data of moral science and of conscience, the interior witness of the law. It is not limited to determining what is permitted or forbidden, but searches for excellence, a certain perfection of action in the existing situation, as an artisan seeks to make something good by plying his or her trade. Such work calls for intelligence, experience, effort, and attentiveness. This is why moral action requires the involvement of all the subject's faculties and the use of the external abilities acquired, among other things, by education.

Prudential judgment is different because it goes beyond ideas, however beautiful they may be, beyond intentions, counsels, and commandments, however judicious they can be, to a decision to act, which gives rise to action and transforms the acting subject: it makes one a better person and enables one to grow. This is why true prudence needs the other virtues which particularly govern affectivity. We can say that prudential judgment or choice is all-encompassing; it engages the human person with his whole being, the past he has inherited, even his unconscious. A person's character is judged by his actions, as a tree is known by its fruits. The all-encompassing nature of concrete action requires the joint intervention of philosophy and theology, of reason and faith, in the Christian moral judgment. The study of "cases," in particular, cannot be limited to a rational analysis or a material application of revealed principles. It requires the exercise of faith, which receives the light of the Spirit, and of reason, which reflects and seeks to discover in concrete terms what is good, what is the best thing to do. Therefore the Christian moralist should assimilate the teachings of the Gospel, which is often so concrete in its very formulation of principles, and reflect with her philosophical and scientific sources, all the while knowing that this work will be incomplete and even useless, if she does not take pains to put her personal prudence into action, which alone will enable her to experience and enjoy good results.

In the First Letter to the Corinthians, Paul offers us an excellent example of what could be called apostolic casuistry. In his examination of the different cases submitted to him, his method is always the same. It could be characterized by the compenetration of two levels: first, criteria of the rational order such as can be found in the philosophers and rabbis. In the case of fornication, for example, Paul writes: "Every other sin which a man commits is outside the body; but the immoral man sins against his own body."[9] But criteria drawn from faith also come into play: "Do you not know that your bodies are members of Christ? . . . Do you not know that your body is a temple of the Holy Spirit?"[10] Thus we can see that in Paul's discernment there is a close connection between the meaning of what is human and the meaning that stems from Christ, each assuming the other and reinforcing it. But the Christian criteria will predominate, particularly through the action of charity uniting believers as brothers and sisters, as members of one body under the impulse of the Holy Spirit.

Conclusion

As we can see, there is a very close association between philosophy and theology in the moral teaching of St. Thomas. Far from being separate, much less in competition, these sciences work together through what we could call a

9. 1 Cor. 6:18.
10. 1 Cor. 6:15, 19.

vital integration of philosophy and theology. At the prompting of the theologian, the philosopher comes to reflect on the fundamental questions about the purpose and meaning of life, about good and evil, about beatitude and suffering, about death and the afterlife, and he no longer thinks that only he can offer a complete answer to these problems. The theologian, for her part, needs the philosopher in order to learn how to use her reason with rigor and insight as she investigates the human dimensions of action, and to provide her with the necessary categories and language for a sound explanation of the riches of the Gospel and Christian experience.

This sort of association between philosophy and theology is based on St. Thomas's maxim: *"Gratia non tollit, sed perficit naturam,"* which could be rephrased: theology does not destroy, but perfects philosophy. In our opinion, however, the principle should not be understood in the sense that philosophy, as a work of reason, must first be constructed while saying to oneself that in any case it will be confirmed by grace, but rather in the opposite sense: we must have the boldness to believe in the Word of God and to abandon ourselves to grace, in the assurance that, far from destroying whatever is true, good, and reasonable in philosophy, grace will teach us how to make it our own, to develop it and to perfect it, while revealing to us a broader and more profound wisdom than any human thought, the wisdom given by the Holy Spirit who unites us with the person of Christ and his Cross by teaching us to "live in Christ."

5 ✍ Dominican Moral Theology in the 20th Century   (1993)

This text will be a testimony of gratitude to the *Revue Thomiste,* which published my first articles. In 1955, I wrote "A Study of the Structure of the Human Act According to St. Thomas."[1] In it, I critiqued the interpretation of the study of the human act in questions 6–17 of the *prima secundae* as a psychological succession "in twelve stages," which has become a classic since Billuart. I proposed rather to see in the text an analysis of the structure of the human act. This publication was accompanied in the *Bulletin Thomiste*[2] by a review essay that led me in the direction of Fribourg. It was about the controversial exchange of articles by Father Deman and Father Gauthier on the distinction between the prudential precept and the command in the analysis of the human act.[3] In these articles, the concept of freedom of action was involved. Then came the publication of my doctoral thesis, "The Virtuous Nature of Hope, from Peter Lombard to St. Thomas," in 1958.[4] This was the beginning of a collaboration that is still going on.

Having made this acknowledgment, I should like to make it clear that my

Originally published as "L'Enseignement de la théologie morale à Fribourg," in *RTh* 93 (1993): 430–42. Translated by Sr. Mary Thomas Noble, O.P. Edited for publication in *The Pinckaers Reader* by Craig Steven Titus.

1. S.-Th. Pinckaers, "La structure de l'acte humain suivant S. Thomas," *RTh* 55 (1955): 393–412.

2. *Bulletin thomiste* 9 (1954–56): 345–52. My review of Th. Deman, *Le précepte de la prudence chez saint Thomas d'Aquin, RTAM* 20 (1953): 40–59; and R. A. Gauthier, *S. Maxime le Confesseur et la psychologie de l'acte humain,* ibidem.

3. *ST* I-II 17.

4. S.-Th. Pinckaers, "La nature vertueuse de l'espérance, de Pierre Lombard à saint Thomas," *RTh* 58 (1958): 405–42, 623–44.

paper is not exclusively about Fribourg, as the original title might lead one to think, but it also touches on the faculty of theology at the University of Fribourg in its relation to other French-speaking Dominican Houses of Study through exchanges at the level of professors, students, and publications. I shall even mention the youngest and humblest of these houses, La Sarte at Huy in Belgium, where I did my theological studies and taught for twelve years. I choose it for this historical reason and for the great debt of gratitude I owe it; because it was fairly representative, thanks to its regular communication with other Houses of Study; and finally, because there is a danger of its remaining unknown, for unfortunately it was never able to celebrate its centenary. It was at La Sarte, in fact, that I patiently prepared my material, practiced methods, and developed those ideas regarding moral theology that I have taught at Fribourg.

My presentation is divided into three parts. I shall first give an overview of the historical setting of our Dominican Houses of Study in regard to moral theology. Next I shall develop the substance of my subject: the question of the method applied to the study of St. Thomas and its consequences for moral theology. In closing, I shall take a look at the future.

Overview of the Historical Setting: Dominican Houses of Study, from La Sarte to Fribourg

The theological studium of La Sarte was founded at Easter 1942 as the result of its separation from the studium at Louvain for linguistic reasons. The intellectual leader of the group of young professors who took over the new center of studies was Father Louis Charlier. A dogmatician with a systematic turn of mind, he tended to use the historic method in theology, beginning with Scripture and the Fathers. This question of method bonded him in friendship with Professor R. Draguet, who was teaching patristics at the University of Louvain. The latter put him in touch with Father Chenu, who published his booklet *Le Saulchoir, a School of Theology* in 1937, while Father Charlier brought out his *Essay on the Theological Problem* in 1938 and Draguet his *History of Catholic Dogma* in 1941.

After the Roman sanctions of 1942,[5] Father Charlier had to discontinue his

---

5. Cf. R. Guelluy, "Les antécédents de l'encyclique *Humani generis* dans les sanctions

teaching at La Sarte, which he had just begun. (Thanks to the intervention of Father Suarez, Master of the Order, he was able to take it up again in 1952.) It was necessary to replace him and reconstruct the professorial group with young priests whom he had formed and who had adopted his method: Father Hamer for dogma and Father Augustine Leonard for apologetics and spirituality. At the end of the war, both were sent to Fribourg to earn their doctorates in theology. Father Leonard did his thesis with Father Deman on mystical experience, and got into trouble with him because he favored a proof for the existence of God based on mystical experience. Excerpts of his French thesis, entitled "A Study of the Apologetic Value of the Testimony of Christian Mystics," were published under the title "Phenomenological Research on Mystical Experience" in 1952.[6] This led to his later writing the article "Spiritual Experience" (1961).[7] For teaching on morality, we had Father B. Olivier, who went to the Saulchoir with several other brethren to get his degree.

After the war, the studium at La Sarte thus provided a team of philosophers and theologians who were young, enterprising, competent, and relatively innovative in orientation. Collaboration with the Province of Toulouse and the studium of Saint-Maximin, both considered more traditional, became less frequent, although there was no antagonism. The geographical distance should be taken into account as well, because people traveled less at that time than they do today. Thus, between the French-speaking Houses of Study, including Saint-Alban-Lesse and later Arbresle—still more classical—regular, intellectual bonds were formed that were favorable to the work of serious theological renewal.

As witness to this intellectual dynamism, I mention the founding of a book series entitled *Cahiers de l'Actualité Religieuse [Series on the Current State of Religion].* The contents of the first volumes come from the exchanges in the lecture series *Rencontres doctrinales de La Sarte [Doctrinal Discussions at La Sarte],* which begin in 1951. The first published volumes in the book series were entitled *Tolérance et communauté humaine [Tolerance and the Human*

---

romaines de 1942: Chenu, Charlier, Draguet" ["The antecedents of the encyclical *Humani generis* in the Roman sanctions of 1942: Chenu, Charlier, Draguet"] *Revue d'histoire ecclésiastique* 81 (1986): 421–97.

6. "Recherches phénoménologiques autour de l'expérience mystique," supplement to *La Vie spirituelle,* 1952, 430–94.

7. "Expérience spirituelle," *Dictionnaire de Spiritualité,* 4/2 (1961).

Community] and *Morale chrétienne et requêtes contemporaines [Christian Morality and Contemporary Research]* (Tournai, 1954). Contributors to the second volume were Jacques Leclercq, with an essay on "La présentation classique de la morale chrétienne et les tendances actuelles" ["The Classical Presentation of Christian Morality and Current Tendencies"]; Father Spicq, who discussed Pauline morality; and Father B. Olivier, who introduced the collection and gave a presentation entitled "Pour une théologie morale renouvelée" ["For a Renewed Moral Theology"]. Father Leonard, in his conclusion, summed up the thrust of this latter paper with the words: "Moral catechesis . . . constitutes the pre-critical stage of theology, but cannot itself be an autonomous branch of theology" (p. 271). The volume also contained essays on the contribution of psychology by Father Delville and of sociology by the Franciscan Father Driessen.

Beneath these personal questions and exchanges between our Houses of Study and Fribourg, one can perceive a certain situation in moral theology that had been inherited from the past. It developed at Fribourg through the division of the teaching of morality into two courses: a major course on speculative morality and a minor course on practical morality. This second course was exemplified by Father Prümmer and his *Manuale theologiae moralis [Manual of Moral Theology]* in three volumes—a classic with us—which was condensed in a *"vademecum"* usually referred to as "the short Prümmer," to facilitate its use and the preparation of examinations for confessors. Recall that Father Prümmer taught at Fribourg from 1908 to 1930.

Prümmer was a fine, solid representative of the moral teaching of the manuals of the period, generally thought of as "Catholic morality." With J. Leclerq we can say that the authors who presented it felt that "morality as taught from the 16th century on reaches the peak of the entire movement of Christian thought and represents a maturity of thought whose main lines will never change."[8] Actually, Father Prümmer, in an effort to return to St. Thomas, had undertaken a renewed presentation of this classic morality, centering it on the virtues rather than the commandments. But the virtues never furnished him with anything more than a different framework; the material itself was still oriented to obligations and sins.

Along with Father Prümmer, Father J. de Langen-Wendels taught specula-

---

8. *Morale chrétienne et requêtes contemporaines* (Tournai, 1954), 13.

tive moral theology from 1902 to 1923. He remained nostalgic for Fribourg when called to Nymegen, where, doubtless, moral theology did not attain the same level.[9] Among de Langen-Wendels's publications was a review of a book by Dr. J. V. de Groot *(Les penseurs du notre temps [Thinkers of our Times]*, 1910), which was written in such a pleasing style that it makes us regret the fewness of his works.[10] Then came Father Ramirez, from 1923 to 1945. We can say of him that he was a redoubtable champion of the speculative commentary on St. Thomas, particularly on the questions on beatitude, of which an edition was made in Madrid from 1941 to 1947, and then of his complete works, at Salamanca in 1971. Father Ramirez pondered deeply and speculatively on a vast amount of material including, besides the works of St. Thomas, ancient and modern philosophers, Scripture, the Fathers, Church documents, theologians, mystics, and literature concerning them.

Father Deman, who succeeded Father Ramirez from 1945 to 1954, is of special interest to us because of his lengthy and excellent article on probabilism, which appeared in 1936.[11] There he makes a penetrating critical and systematic study of moral casuistry. He describes the controversy which had centered on probabilism since the seventeenth century in response to the problem of a doubtful conscience in the application of the law, and which ended in the recommendation of the teachings of St. Alphonsus Liguori. The latter became the patron saint of moral theologians because of his balance, which avoids the laxity of the casuists and the rigor of the Jansenists. However, Father Deman concludes his study on St. Alphonsus and on the concept of moral theology, of which he is the eminent representative, in these words:

Between St. Alphonsus and St. Thomas there remains the lack of harmony of two irreconcilable systems. Every attempt at reconciliation is doomed to concordism, that is to say, to artifice, that is to say, to failure. The historical reality of their misunderstanding cannot be denied.[12]

This judgment seems to me entirely justified. Between St. Thomas and St. Alphonsus and the authors of the manuals, even when they follow the Tho-

---

9. Cf. C. E. M. Struyker Boudier, "Wijsgerig leven in Nederland en Belgie 1880–1980," *De Dominicanen*, 235.

10. Review of Dr. J. V. de Groot, *Les penseurs du notre temps*, in *RTh* 10 (1910): 657–60.

11. "Probabilisme," *Dictionnaire de la théologie catholique*, vol. 13 (1936), col. 417–619.

12. Ibid., col. 590.

mistic school, it is certainly possible to find some partial agreements, but there is always a fundamental lack of harmony at the level of systematization, all the more difficult to resolve when it is not perceived. In St. Thomas we are dealing with a morality of beatitude and the virtues, centering around charity and prudence, and with our modern moralists, with commandments and legal obligations, focusing on conscience and sins.

Another controversy united Father Ramirez and Father Deman. They had a similar reaction to the reading of Jacques Maritain's *Degrees of Knowledge,*[13] and critiqued his distinction between a knowledge or science that is speculatively practical, of which St. Thomas furnishes the most accomplished example, and a moral knowledge or practical science, which Maritain finds in St. John of the Cross and in other spiritual authors. The division was based on the difference in the mode of defining and conceptualizing the real, and led Maritain to explain, for example, that St. Thomas defined contemplation as the highest human activity, while St. John defined it as a non-acting, or an emptying of the faculties, without the definitions contradicting each other in reality. The one expressed reality as the object of a speculative gaze, while the other viewed it as something seen in a spiritual experience. Our colleagues rejected the proposed distinction between two different levels existing at the heart of moral theology in order to safeguard its scientific character, which an expression closer to spiritual or pastoral experience would diminish.

Behind this reaction there could be seen on the Thomistic side a rejection of the distinction between moral theology and ascetical and mystical theology, a distinction that goes hand in hand with a morality of obligation of which St. Thomas was obviously not aware. It was also a refusal to distinguish between moral theology and spirituality—the names in use since the beginning of the twentieth century—even if its most esteemed representatives, such as the Spanish mystics, had made such a distinction. This doubtless explains the fact that a regular, required course in spirituality has never been included in the program of our faculty, nor did we ever dream of creating a chair of spirituality, as is done at other centers of theological study.

We had, therefore, on the one hand, a moral theology of a high caliber, based directly on the *Summa* of St. Thomas and claiming a properly scientific

13. Jacques Maritain, *Distinguish to Unite, or The Degrees of Knowledge,* trans. Gerald B. Phelan (New York: Charles Scriber's Sons, 1959).

status, and on the other hand a morality with a practical goal, dispensed in the manuals used in seminaries and actually representing the notion of Catholic morality generally held in public opinion. This last included, like an annexed science, the fields of ascetical and mystical theology, later called spirituality or spiritual theology.

The Method of Studying St. Thomas's Moral Theology

The method we followed in our teaching had two components. One was traditional and consisted in a direct reading of the text of St. Thomas and the commentaries on it. The other component was new, positive, and historical. It included the study of Scripture and the Fathers, particularly as sources of St. Thomas's teaching.

Commentary on the Text of St. Thomas

At La Sarte, as at Louvain and in our tradition, the course in moral theology had as its foundation the reading of the text of the *Summa,* which was explained and commented on, question by question, as far as possible, while using breadth and freedom in the teaching of the course and the explanations. This method may not be the best for all students pedagogically, but it provided an excellent formation above all for the professor, who had to work with such rich and solid material and could draw upon recent relevant publications for help. Since the four years of theology formed a cycle, the professor covered the entire moral synthesis of the *Summa* during this time. This permitted him to deepen his study each time he repeated the cycle, if he was willing to make the effort.

This kind of teaching had a very important and decisive advantage for me. I received directly from St. Thomas, and not from manuals as in the seminaries, my first formation in moral theology, with all that that implies: the principal ideas, basic categories, and overall organization. I quickly perceived that there were profound differences between the morality of St. Thomas, which he had himself largely inherited from the Fathers, and that which was currently being taught, moving from the manuals, as catechesis, into everyday preaching.

Beyond partial problems, such as where to situate St. Thomas's teaching on conscience, I noted that, as Father Deman had ably demonstrated, we were dealing with very different systems, included in works drawn up "according to the thought of St. Thomas." A simple comparison between the contents of the *secunda pars* on the one hand and that of the manuals on the other bore witness to this. St. Thomas, like Aristotle and Augustine, conceived moral theology as a response to the question of beatitude; that was his point of departure. He responded to it by organizing morality on the foundation of the virtues, beginning with faith, and the two centers of charity and prudence. In the course of my teaching, I discovered the gifts of the Holy Spirit along with the virtues, and above all the primary place occupied by the questions on the New Law, which had never been taught me, for lack of time, and which introduced the study of grace. In this regard, the table of contents in the manuals proposed only four pillars for fundamental moral theology: firstly the law, that is, natural law, identified with the Decalogue, which, since the commandments replaced the virtues, served to organize special moral theology; and then conscience, human acts, and sins. At the center of this morality, not explicitly mentioned but everywhere present as taken for granted, was the concept and sense of obligation. In this presentation of moral theology the treatises on beatitude, the New Law, and grace had disappeared, while the virtues got the smallest share of attention. We were dealing with a morality that could be qualified by different names: a morality of law, of obligations, of conscience, or of sins, a morality of actions or casuistry. For the manuals had made morality the domain of cases of conscience, to the point of devoting volumes to the examination of these. In contrast, there was practically no study of such cases in the *Summa theologiae*; we had to go to the *Quaestiones quodlibetales* to find them.

Furthermore, in reading the modern authors, whether philosophers or theologians, I could see that the composers of the manuals were not unique. In addition to their pastoral preoccupation with the sacrament of Penance, they took care to adapt morality to their times. They seemed to have more similarities than one might suspect with the philosophies of obligations and imperatives that still dominated moral thought. Thus, the problem grew deeper. In justice I should add that these moralists had basically carried out the task entrusted to them by the Council of Trent, to give a moral foundation to the faithful through their parish priests according to the intention of the *Roman Catechism*. But, aiming at simplification, they had narrowed the field of morality, thereby limiting the horizon of the Christian life too much.

In seeking the source of these profound differences in the concept, organization, and teaching of moral theology I was led, by a study at once systematic and historical, to the idea of freedom undergirding the two systems. On the one hand was the freedom of indifference, which brought Ockham into opposition with St. Thomas, while its concept went back to two compatriots, Gauthier of Bruges and Henry of Ghent, contemporaries of St. Thomas but outliving him. On the other hand, in Aquinas we find a freedom rooted in the intellect and will according to their natural inclinations to the true and the good, and this is what we call a freedom of excellence or of perfection. This I explained in the second volume of *La somme de La Revue des jeunes,* on human acts.[14]

The Application of the Positive Method to the Study of St. Thomas

The second aspect of our method of studying St. Thomas was actually presented first. It consisted in interpreting his text, no longer by material that came after him in time, but rather by what came before; not so much by consulting his commentators, in a chiefly speculative reflection, but rather by reading his sources, beginning with Scripture, thus using the historical method.

Our courses in both moral and dogmatic theology were usually designed according to this scheme: a scriptural part, an exposition of the teaching of the Fathers, and finally the systematic study of St. Thomas, taking into account the chronological order of his works. This method was actually not far from that of St. Thomas himself. We see him commenting on Scripture as his first source and studying it in the light of the Fathers as his second source. Needless to say, we did not overlook the philosophical sources, especially Aristotle, as well as modern problematics, exegetical or philosophical.

The application of the historical method could have been done in a material way by studying St. Thomas in the university context of his day, in the setting of the development of doctrines in the twelfth and thirteenth centuries, and by trying to retrace the progress of his own thought through his successive works. In this type of research, Dom Lottin, with his *Psychology and Moral Theology in the 12th and 13th Centuries,*[15] was a model, and furnished us

---

14. *ST* I-II 18–21. [Editor's note: *Somme de La Revue des Jeunes* is a multivolume Latin-French edition of the *Summa.* S.-Th. Pinckaers translated and provided extensive notes and technical apparatus for three of these volumes, including the one he refers to here on human acts.]

15. Odon Lottin, *Psychologie et morale aux XIIe et XIIIe siècles,* 8 vols. (Louvain: Abbaye Mont César, 1942–60).

with vast documentation. I had noticed, however, that when he set out to make his personal synthesis by way of a conclusion, Dom Lottin reverted spontaneously to a systematization and to positions like those in the manuals, and began to restrict St. Thomas in their cramped manner. Thus, in his *Morale fondamentale [Fundamental Moral Theology]*, he adopted the basic framework of the manuals and discarded the teaching on the gifts of the Holy Spirit and the infused moral virtues, which he had carefully studied in his historical section, as useless complications imposed by the Scholastic tradition of the thirteenth century.

For our part, we tried to combine the two methods in such a way that history would serve theological reflection and would help us to trace the genesis of St. Thomas's teaching, so as to better understand it in its broad lines and actualize it for ourselves and our contemporaries.

The Evangelical Dimension of the Moral Theology of St. Thomas

Studying St. Thomas through his sources was fruitful, and produced an important development in the interpretation of his thought. At first, our attention and teaching had focused primarily on the rational and philosophical dimension of St. Thomas's moral theology: the systematization ordered to the ultimate end, resting on the theologal and human virtues, particularly justice and prudence, and based on the natural law. It was a vast edifice, solid, intelligent, well structured, and capable of playing a useful role in meeting the demands of contemporary thought. It was at the service of faith, to which it gave a broader and more satisfying basis than did the voluntarist moralities of obligation.

But soon, moving back and forth between reflection on revelation, St. Thomas, and the reality of thought and life, I perceived the evangelical and Christian aspect of his teaching progressively emerging in the *secunda pars* of the *Summa*. Behind the treatise on beatitude, which we had presented as purely philosophical, I saw the Beatitudes of the Gospel of St. Matthew, which, according to St. Thomas, provide the true answer to the question of beatitude. Among the virtues, I recognized more clearly the preeminence of faith as the root of moral action and not merely as the acceptance of dogmas. I then became more aware of what had been right in front of me all the time, but which I had not seen: that to each virtue St. Thomas linked a gift of the Holy Spirit. This gave a spiritual, even mystical aspect to Christian action in relation to charity. Among these gifts, I could see which ones were most necessary for theologians: wisdom, understanding, and knowledge; and for moral theologians: the gift of counsel. Finally, and most importantly, I saw behind the natural law the treatise on the New or Evangelical Law, that brief masterpiece composed by St. Thomas as the capstone in the vault of his edifice. To its definition all the lines in the *Summa* converged: the New Law understood as an interior law, as the grace of the Holy Spirit received through faith in Christ and working through charity. The Sermon on the Mount provides the text of the law, like a summary of the apostolic catechesis. It is purveyed through the sacraments.

The moral theology of St. Thomas stood out therefore as fundamentally Christian and theological, while at the same time profoundly human and solidly philosophical. It harmonized well with the apostolic and Dominican vocation of preaching the Gospel to all people, as well as with the charism of teaching the faith, which Thomas attributed principally to Christ,[16] and with the gift of teaching, *"docere,"* to which he gave priority in his explanation of the charisms enumerated by St. Paul in First Corinthians.[17] Without taking away from the rational rigor of his construction, this highlighting of its evangelical dimension restored to moral theology a spiritual breath and vitality sadly lacking in the moral teaching of recent centuries.

At the same time, the question of Christian morality, which remains the central focus of contemporary discussions, was revealed in a new light. It offered the possibility of reestablishing a profound connection between Catholic morality and the Gospel, and of giving the Holy Spirit a direct role in the forming of Christian action.

A New Historical Connection between the Gospel and St. Thomas

However, this highlighting of the Gospel in Thomas's moral theology led to an important transformation in how we represent the link between our Doctor's teaching and Scripture.

If we consider the history of moral theology from the viewpoint of its rational systematization, for which St. Thomas provides one of the most successful models, we spontaneously picture it to ourselves as a development fol-

16. Cf. *ST* III 7.7.
17. Cf. *ST* I-II 3.4.

lowing an ascending line. It starts with the Gospel and progresses through the lengthy work of reflection, systematization, and the elaboration of a certain technique of thought and language, culminating, at its summit, in the Scholasticism of the thirteenth century, after having profited by the successive contributions of Ambrose, Augustine, Anselm, Albert the Great, and many others. It is thus that Father Deman could write in his book *Aux origines de la théologie morale [At the Sources of Moral Theology]:* "With the *secunda pars* of the *Summa,* the goal toward which history has moved is reached. Henceforth moral theology becomes a distinct branch of theology."[18] But in the following pages Father Deman has to guard against the prolongation of this trajectory. The representatives of casuist morality believe that the ascending movement continued after St. Thomas, with the development of a sharper distinction in regard to the other parts of theology, which made moral theology an autonomous and specialized science from that time on, with its own casuistic method.

Father Deman's view of things is certainly not false, and I support his description of the progressive formation of moral theology, at the scientific level, as solid. But it is not complete, and could cause us to miss an essential point.

Theology, in fact, is not merely the result of the work of reason elaborating science on the basis of the documents of revelation—which our condition as intellectuals inclines us to think. Beyond the discursive reason, theology finds its principal source, as St. Thomas himself says, in the light of the Word of God received in faith. From faith and charity proceed a certain knowledge through connaturality and a certain experience of divine realities capable of enlightening, with the wisdom of the Spirit, the learned as well as the little ones, to whom this light is equally promised. This light of faith, the *lumen fidei,* is not sporadic. It accompanies and directs the lives of believers and of the Church all along the way, notably in the reflection of theologians.

Consequently, we had to amend our schema of evolution. We could no longer place the Word of the Lord transmitted through the Gospels at the bottom of our picture. We were obliged, on the contrary, to place it at the top of the historical picture, dominating the whole, like a source of higher and permanent light, whose rays descend upon Augustine, upon Thomas Aquinas, and upon us, each catching the light according to his capacity, with the help of

18. Thomas Deman, *Aux origines de la théologie morale* (Paris, 1951), 110.

the others, in a communion of faith and understanding, with the variations due to personalities, times, and gifts.

The Sermon on the Mount, in what we might call its popular or prescientific language, contains more spiritual power and richness than all the commentaries that have been made on it, learned though they may be, and therefore more than the *secunda pars* itself. It is the direct vehicle of the Word of Christ addressed to those who receive it with faith and who, putting it into practice, experience its truth. All the spiritual renewals that feed upon the Sermon bear witness to this, and St. Thomas himself was persuaded of it, as he says at the beginning of his commentary on the Beatitudes in Matthew: *"Notandum autem quod . . . numquam aliquis in verbis Domini posset ita subtiliter loqui, quod pertingeret ad propositum Domini,"*[19] which I translate as: "No one can ever speak of the words of the Lord with a delicacy and a penetration to equal that of the Lord himself."

The scientific elaboration of theology is obviously necessary; improvements always have to be made in the work. But we should never forget that the principal source of this science lies in something higher, in a Word far loftier than our reasonings, and that it is ordinarily expressed in a simpler language than ours, adapted to the humility of the faith it wishes to teach us, so as to introduce us to the realities that are the objects of theology.

A Look at the Future

This last consideration brings me to my third part, a look at the future. It is a delicate thing to talk about the future, because it looks as if one were trying to play the prophet. All the same, let me essay a rough sketch of the future we are called to build, modest though my contribution may be.

I am convinced that the virtue-based moral system of St. Thomas has a future, if we know how to actualize it. A presage of this is the rediscovery of the Aristotelian morality of the virtues in the United States, especially with Alasdair MacIntyre's book *After Virtue,* and the repercussions it has had.[20] At the theological level the future seems even more promising to me, if we succeed in turning to good account the evangelical dimension of St. Thomas's work. His

19. *Super Mat.* lect. V, n. 404.
20. Alasdair MacIntyre, *After Virtue: A Study in Moral Theory* (Notre Dame, Ind.: University of Notre Dame Press, 1981; 2nd ed. 1984).

teaching on beatitude can help us to resolve the split that reached its height in post-Tridentine and Kantian morality. It can bridge the gap between the desire for beatitude and morality, and remedy the break at the very core of morality between the good and beatitude, inseparably reunited in the *"bonum"* of a St. Augustine or a St. Thomas. We need the teaching on the virtues and gifts, on the Evangelical Law and grace, if we are to restore to Catholic morality its spiritual richness and vitality, to the moral law its dynamic interiority, and to the action of the Holy Spirit its primacy—and all this within the framework of a vigorous systematization. Thus we can heal the breach that has existed for several centuries between morality and spiritual experience—now assigned to mysticism—leading to the impoverishment of both. Dare I say that St. Thomas thus understood could help us to escape from the prison of the Kantian imperative and the straitjacket of moral juridicism, and bring us to recapture the fresh air of the spirit?

In any case, it is encouraging and promising to note that the *Catechism of the Catholic Church* has reintegrated in its moral section the consideration of beatitude and the Beatitudes, the virtues and the gifts of the Holy Spirit, and the New Law and grace, no longer mentioned in catechisms modeled on that of the Council of Trent.

Toward New Connections between St. Thomas, St. John of the Cross, and St. Paul

In this task, however, St. Thomas alone is not enough. Here we are dealing with progress in the reading and interpretation of his moral work, the better to relate it first of all to spiritual authors who explain theological material more directly related to experience, such as the mystics, and then and chiefly in its connection with its scriptural sources, particularly St. Matthew and St. Paul.

In my opinion, Jacques Maritain has put his finger on a very real and important problem when he demonstrates, in *The Degrees of Knowledge,* the difference between the viewpoints of St. Thomas and St. John of the Cross, between speculative theology and theology at the level of experience. I believe we have to admit at the core of theological science and in its elaboration the existence of different modalities of thought and expression. St. Thomas moves at the speculative, ontological level, exposing things according to their nature, from a basically analytical viewpoint that reminds one of an anatomical dissection. He expresses himself in technical and abstract language. St. John of the

Cross moves at the experiential level, with a more directly practical aim and a more global view, using more ordinary language, by preference symbolic and poetic. It would be good, therefore, to reestablish in theological thought a regular movement back and forth between experience and speculation, as St. Thomas did, in fact, when making use of St. Gregory the Great and Cassian, St. Benedict and many others, according to the problems being discussed. In this way theology could guard against the dryness of a too-rational science and rediscover the vigor and freshness of a living science. And I think that in saying this I am in agreement with the excellent posthumous article of Father Labourdette, published in the issue devoted to him, "What is Spiritual Theology?" where he explains the characteristics distinguishing spiritual theology from speculative theology.[21]

But we need to go a step further and prolong our reflection on the differences in modalities and expressions of thought, looking at St. Thomas's relationship to his New Testament sources. Here, I shall take as an example St. Paul, Aquinas's principal source, and his teaching on the virtues. The apostle uses the word "virtue" only once, in a text, moreover, that is very significant (Phil 4:8). But he cites and recommends numerous virtues, beginning with the trilogy of faith, hope, and charity. He does not refer to the four cardinal virtues, but he enumerates and emphasizes other virtues, although without any apparent ordering. Is this the result of a theology still at the stage of a rough draft?

When we take a close look at this and are sensitive to the material behind the words, we perceive that there are important differences between St. Paul and St. Thomas, which do not signify the technical imperfection of the one or the inaccuracy of the other, but rather, a diversity of perspectives and expressions in thought and language. Paul speaks at the level of spiritual experience in its first outpouring. His doctrine is like molten metal. Thomas looks at things from the level of a reflection that analyzes, distinguishes, and organizes, like an engraver who gives us metal that has been carved and is hardened. Paul exhorts to virtue. He teaches it and infuses it with the ardor of his word and example. Thomas studies virtue and describes it with the care and precision of a professor. One has the charism of an apostle, the other of a teacher of theology.

21. M.-Michel Labourdette, "Qu'est-ce que la théologie spirituelle?" *RTh* 92 (1992): 355–72.

An entire conference would be needed to show these differences with the nuances they deserve. It is enough for me to indicate two characteristic traits of St. Paul's teaching on the virtues.

While St. Thomas's first concern is to distinguish the virtues among themselves and to classify them as theologal, moral, or intellectual, in St. Paul *agape* is so central that the other virtues appear as qualities and aspects of the one charity. The formula is clear in First Corinthians: "Love is patient and kind; it is not jealous . . ." and one may continue, it is prudent, courageous, just, temperate, and then conclude: "it believes all things, hopes all things, endures all things" (1 Cor 13).

Again, and this is a second characteristic, for St. Paul the association of charity with the other virtues becomes so close that he transcends the distinction between the theologal and moral virtues, in this sense, that patience, humility, kindness, constancy, and vigilance acquire a truly theologal value. This seems to me particularly clear in the hymn in Philippians where, to describe "the mind which was in Christ Jesus," that is to say, the greatness of his love for us, Paul chose the two traits of humility and obedience even to the cross, in extreme contrast with being "in the form of God" and possessing "equality with God." This humility and obedience show the divine splendor of the love of Christ; thus we can say that these two virtues possess a truly theologal dimension, as forms of charity.

The contrast with the analytical and speculative view of St. Thomas is patent in this case. In the *Summa,* humility and obedience are ranked among the moral virtues and are classified with the help of lists borrowed from philosophers who were chiefly Stoics and gave them scant attention. The position of these two virtues seems very modest in the classification established: humility comes under modesty in the framework of temperance[22] and obedience comes under observance, according to Cicero, in the treatise on justice, regulating relationships with superiors.[23] In fact, in the questions he devotes to them, St. Thomas makes up for it, if I may say so, and takes into account to the best of his ability the riches accumulated around these virtues by Christian spirituality. But the difference in perspective and classification persists.

The conclusion I draw from this is not a reproach to St. Thomas, but the

22. Cf. *ST* II-II 161.
23. Cf. *ST* II-II 104.

recognition of the existence, within theological work and science, of different modalities and manners of expression that oblige us to follow, once again, a regular movement back and forth as we reflect on our two doctors, between the sources of revelation and the theological work. Thus we will be following the very procedure of St. Thomas himself, who commented on the letters of St. Paul as a preparation for his *Summa theologiae*. Like him, we need to plunge regularly into the source of the Word of God, but on the other hand his teaching is necessary to explain the content of revelation and to give a firm and broad structure to our theological research, in the face of the problems of our time.

There is work for the future for us, moral theologians and historians as well. To me, it looks promising.

SECTION II   Beatitude and

Christian Anthropology

6 ❧ Aquinas's Pursuit of Beatitude

From the *Commentary on the Sentences* to the *Summa Theologiae* (1993)

When we study Aquinas's successive treatments of "beatitude," from the *Commentary on the Sentences* to the *Summa theologiae,* we are deeply impressed on two scores. First, we marvel at the breadth, penetration, and originality of the research; and next, we are astonished to note how far this teaching, so essential for Aquinas, has been neglected by many of his disciples and by later theology. This essay will examine Aquinas's successive analyses of "beatitude" in order to assess their import, and above all to discover their evangelical dimension and spiritual impact.[1]

Outline of the Treatise on Beatitude in St. Thomas's *Commentary on the Sentences*

In his *Commentary on the Sentences,* St. Thomas, being obliged to follow the plan of Peter Lombard, first takes up the question of beatitude in connection with the Gospel Beatitudes.[2] Treating the question of the relationship between the virtues, the gifts of the Holy Spirit, and the Beatitudes, which had

Originally published as "La voie spirituelle du bonheur," in *Ordo sapientiae et amoris* (1993): 267–84. Translated by Sister Mary Thomas Noble, O.P., with the assistance of Craig Steven Titus. Edited for publication in *The Pinckaers Reader* by John Berkman.

1. [Editors' note: The editors have chosen to translate *"bonheur"* as "beatitude" rather than "happiness," both to remind the reader of Aquinas's particular understanding of the end or goal of human life, and to avoid the senses of "happiness" which are more psychic and transient that what Aquinas understood by *"beatitudo."*]

2. III *Sent.* dist. 34.

become a classic following the anonymous *Gloss on St. Matthew,* St. Thomas defines the Beatitudes as perfect works emanating from virtues perfected by the gifts, or more precisely as acts accomplished by means of the gifts. Aquinas follows St. Augustine in ordering the seven gifts and the seven Beatitudes as a progression from exterior to interior goods and from the active to the contemplative life.

This is only a preliminary step. Commenting on Lombard's discussion of the beatitude of the saints after the judgment and the desire for beatitude that animates human beings,[3] St. Thomas introduces his first draft of the treatise on beatitude. Thomas's treatise on beatitude is much vaster in scope than the few questions presented by his contemporaries, for example, by St. Bonaventure. Here Aquinas already sets forth the key concepts that he will develop more freely in his later and more mature works. Let us simply run through the table of contents.

The first question is devoted to a study of beatitude itself. Its first article, quite brief, shows that beatitude lies in goods of the soul and not of the body. The second article defines beatitude as an act of the intellect brought to completion by the "delectation" of the will.[4] St. Thomas next explains that he is speaking of an act of the speculative intellect, the vision of God, which cannot be attained in this life. In the following article Aquinas shows the complexity of beatitude, uncreated from the viewpoint of its object and created from the viewpoint of the human person, whose most perfect act it is. It is identified with eternal life, with peace, and is attained in the Kingdom of God. Thomas next considers the question from the aspect of the desire for beatitude implanted by the Creator in the human soul so as to lead it to Himself. Present in every person, this desire is at the source of all our willing. Finally, Thomas examines Lombard's treatment of the beatitude of the saints after the judgment.

The second question examines the vision of God under its various aspects: the possibility of a human being's seeing God; the realization of this possibility in the saints in heaven; and its extent. St. Thomas shows that it is supernatural and cannot be enjoyed in this life.

---

3. See IV *Sent.* dist. 49.

4. We will retain the term "delectation" *(delectatio),* which signifies equally both pleasure and joy, and is thus applied to both the physical and the spiritual levels in the language of St. Thomas. As such, it has no equivalent in English (or in French), for "pleasure" is too heavy a word to describe unequivocal spiritual joy.

In the third question, "delectation" is the object of a study whose length attests the great interest the subject held for St. Thomas. He clarifies the difference between pleasure and joy in the face of sadness, and their moral quality; he establishes the superiority of spiritual joys. Thus "delectation," which is at first a passion, can serve in the very definition of beatitude. Here we find Thomas's contribution to the debates between philosophical schools on the subject of pleasure.[5]

God's Plan and Human Beatitude, according to the *Summa contra Gentiles*

In the *Summa contra Gentiles,* St. Thomas's genius can at last spread its wings. He places the treatise on beatitude at the very center of this work, as a hinge which insures communication between the action of God and human life and action. Here Thomas discusses beatitude from a perspective proper to this work: the providential action of God which perfectly regulates all things— particularly human beings—and does so with a view to their perfection, through the communication of the fullness of goodness as far as they are capable of receiving it. Because God is the ultimate end of creation and in particular the plenitude of human beatitude, God exercises His governance by giving it the special form of law and grace in regard to intelligent and free creatures, who can from this fact direct themselves by ordering their actions toward the end that suits them.[6] In this setting the study of beatitude dominates the entire third book, which we may consider the "moral section" of the *Summa contra Gentiles.* The work no longer reaches the term of the theological considera-

---

5. St. Thomas concludes his treatise with a very interesting interpretation of the traditional teaching on the dowries and haloes attributed to the saints. The dowries are explained in connection with the Letter to the Ephesians 5:32, in which the marriage between Christ and the Church is discussed, and their study introduces a teaching on spiritual marriage that merits a comparison between medieval and modern mysticism. The question of haloes leads to a discussion of the three great spiritual ideals that animate the Church under the action of the Holy Spirit: virgins, martyrs, and doctors, who impart the wisdom of the Gospel and lead the combat against the devil. Here the symbolic language of Scripture, liturgy, and spiritual writers converges with the rational language of the Scholastics. Unfortunately, St. Thomas was never able to return to this subject, which was to be discussed in the unfinished *tertia pars* of the *Summa theologiae.*

6. *SCG* III prologue.

A CRUCIAL

tion at the end of salvation history, as was the case with Peter Lombard, but unfolds within the context of the divine action, the intention of God who communicates Himself to us in the measure in which we exercise control over our actions and participate in God's plans.

Finality in God's Work and Human Action

Although St. Thomas clearly demonstrates his profound interest in the topic of beatitude by the sheer number of questions he devotes to the topic— sixty-three chapters in *Summa contra Gentiles* III—what most significantly displays their importance to St. Thomas is their position in the overall plan of the *Summa contra Gentiles.* Their placement in this *Summa* is meant to illustrate the guiding intention of God and of human beings at the source of their respective actions.

Aquinas begins with an analysis of the finality that inspires and determines every action, in all creatures as well as in God. He devotes twenty-five chapters to this. Every being acts in view of an end, more precisely in view of goodness and not of evil, thus tending spontaneously toward God, toward assimilation with the sovereign Good. This intentionality is universal. It is natural, for it sets in motion the inclination to the good that St. Thomas will place at the source of the natural law in the *Summa theologiae.*[7] It functions in a special way in intelligent beings capable of knowing and accepting this finality and becomes spiritual in them, ordering them to God as the end of their knowledge and love.

Here we need to note Aquinas's analogical use of the term "nature." This enables him to indicate, in light of the Genesis account he has pondered under the guidance of patristic authors, what was primordial in the human being created by God in His image to act freely under God's impulse and in imitation of God. It is through finality engendered by the attraction to the good that human action combines with divine action and orders itself thereto. Thus this study of finality concludes by showing that the end of every intellectual substance consists in the knowledge of God.[8]

7. *ST* I-II 94.2.
8. *SCG* III 25.

The Ascent to God by Way of Beatitude

The question of the finality of action prepares the way for the more concrete question of beatitude or felicity,[9] which is discussed in chapters 26 to 63. This study is a veritable journey, an ascent to God, bringing into play the desire for beatitude natural to every human being in its noblest form, which is the desire to know the truth. Throughout this lengthy analysis the spiritual thrust of St. Thomas's theology comes to the fore, discreetly but unmistakably: the loving desire for God as the fullness and source of truth and goodness. We can see in these pages a veritable passion for truth, developing in the intellect's research and effacing itself in the humility of the contemplative pursuit.

The journey comprises two stages. The first stage (chapters 27–36) seeks to answer the question, "What is true human beatitude; in what human good or activity does it consist?" This section closes with the affirmation that human beatitude lies in the contemplation of God. The second stage of the journey is divided into two parts: the first part of the second stage (chapters 37–50) seeks to answer "What is this beatific knowledge as contrasted with other forms of knowledge accessible to both human beings and angels?" The second part of the second stage (chapters 51–63) addresses the question of the possibility of seeing God, and of the means and modalities of this vision.

The search begins with a preliminary affirmation which we would not have expected here, but which nevertheless orientates the entire journey. St. Thomas shows that beatitude does not consist in an act of the will, but rather of the intellect, which grasps the desired and beloved object (chapter 26). In this way Thomas insures the objectivity of the search for beatitude and the primacy of contemplation in beatitude. The first question is, therefore, "What good can render the human being happy?" It cannot be the will itself, under the form of desire or "delectation," for these remain subjective.

Thomas's analysis unfolds through a series of demonstrations suited to negative theology. It proceeds by induction, reviewing all the goods that arouse human desire, arranged in progressive categories. Complete human beatitude cannot consist in external goods such as pleasures, honors, glory,

9. See Pinckaers, *La Beatitude* (Paris: Cerf, 2000), explanatory note no. 40 (233–34) and 318–22.

wealth, and power (chapters 27–31). Nor can it be attained in goods of the body (chapter 32). It is not to be found in the order of sensibility, and does not lie in the exercise of the moral virtues or intellectual virtues such as art and prudence (chapters 33–36). These successive eliminations lead us to the following conclusion: human beatitude consists in the contemplation of truth (chapter 37).

In a discussion that anticipates the study of the contemplative life in the *Summa theologiae*, Aquinas notes why human beatitude or felicity is to be found in the contemplation of truth. It is that which is most proper to human beings, it is done for its own sake, and it is closest to divine action. Other significant human endeavors—efforts to generate a healthy body, the quieting of passions by the moral virtues, and providing a tranquil political society—all prepare the way for the contemplation of truth. Furthermore, the contemplation of which Aquinas speaks is not merely contemplation of first principles and/or the sciences. It is in the contemplation of God and divine realities that the human person finds beatitude.

It remains to determine the character of this "contemplation" (chapters 37–50). St. Thomas's analysis again proceeds in a negative mode. Contemplation that leads to beatitude cannot consist in an ordinary knowledge of God, which remains confused and uncertain. Nor does it lie in knowledge gained through demonstration, such as that of the theologian, or through faith during this life, which is, however, superior. It also cannot consist in the knowledge of separate substances, in which philosophers like Alexander the Aphrodite and Averroes placed beatitude, nor in any knowledge of God, however lofty, that the soul may possess in this life.

Thomas then comes to his ultimate conclusion: human beatitude lies in the vision of the divine essence. No creature can attain this vision through natural intellectual powers. It is the work of a special divine light, which alone is adequate. The vision of God is a participation in eternal life and it alone responds fully to the human desire for beatitude. Primarily it fulfills the desire for truth, but it also satisfies all other aspirations: the thirst for virtue in the active life—including civil life—and the desire for honors, glory, even wealth and pleasure. All this is to be enjoyed in security and forever.

The Experience of the Contemplative Life

To adequately understand St. Thomas's conviction that nothing in this world comes closer to perfect beatitude than the contemplative life, it is important to acknowledge Thomas's cultural context and personal experience, which help us understand his teaching more deeply. According to Gregory the Great, the Gospel gives us the model for the ideal of contemplation in the person of Mary of Bethany, seated at the feet of Jesus and listening to him. Thomas's ideal—that contemplation of the truth is the beginning of our future life—was one he lived out in the "springtime" of his Dominican religious order. In the previous century St. Dominic had founded the order for the contemplation and preaching of evangelical Truth. All the power—better, all the fire—of Thomas's efforts for spiritual renewal in the thirteenth century is contained in these pages. In reasoning that is exquisitely ordered and rigorously elaborated, St. Thomas reveals the soul of his theology and the heart of his personal experience in communion with his brothers.

Two Observations: Union of Intellect and Heart, and the Natural Desire to See God

First, to understand St. Thomas's claim that beatitude lies in the contemplation of truth, we must realize that Aquinas does not separate the contemplative intellect (or demonstrative reason) from the will that loves and desires. For Aquinas, contemplative knowledge and loving desire are united. They collaborate, if we may put it this way, each for the other and each in the other. They join together in making a free choice and ordering it to an ultimate end that has become personal through the intervention of Christian revelation. The fruitful ground of Thomas's lengthy analytical discourse is a spiritual experience closely linked with the human experience of love of truth that makes for beatitude. We are not speaking of the kind of contemplation that rises gradually into the realm of abstractions, at the risk of drifting away altogether. The separation of the contemplative intellect from loving desire was established by nominalism and modern rationalism. Rather, Aquinas speaks of a life that lays hold of all of a person's desires in their totality and grows in intensity, depth, and richness in the measure in which that person moves toward the one Object capable of fulfilling both mind and heart.

Second, it is clear that St. Thomas's thought and argument continually evoke desire, that strongest and best desire which is the desire for truth and which outstrips all other desires since it can be satisfied by God alone.[10] Hence in this third book of the *Summa contra Gentiles,* the famous argument from natural desire is brought out forcefully more than once: it is impossible that our natural desires should exist in vain, which would be the case if it were impossible for us to attain that knowledge of the divine substance which all minds naturally desire.[11] Caught in the toils of a different problematic, modern Thomists have feared basing their arguments on natural desire, since this would seem to them to compromise the supernatural character of the vision of God. So they have tried to reduce it to a velleity, proceeding simply from an obediential power. We cannot go any further into the subject here, but for anyone who dares to read the texts, such as they are, it will be clear that St. Thomas's thought was quite different. In the definitive debates in which he engaged with pagan Arab and Jewish philosophers, St. Thomas, eager to demonstrate that it is possible for human beings to see God—a possibility that conditions the entire orientation of Christian morality—made natural desire the spearhead of his demonstration. It was as if he said to his adversaries: "You need not travel across the world in search of a proof that we can see God. The proof lies within you, in your mind and in your heart, in the longing for truth and beatitude that impel you to seek wisdom. Is this not our most characteristic desire, springing from the depths of our human nature?" Yet at the same time St. Thomas reveals himself as a lover of truth, to which he is drawn by a veritable but spiritual "instinct," the instinct for God. In the *Summa theologiae* Aquinas will speak of "reason's instinct," which the "instinct of the Holy Spirit" *(instinctus Spiritus Sancti)* perfects through the gifts.[12]

The Double Ladder that Leads to the Vision of God in the *Summa Theologiae*

The *Summa theologiae* offers us a solidly constructed treatise on beatitude in five questions: a little masterpiece. It comes at the beginning of the section

10. *SCG* III 50.9.

11. *SCG* III 51.1.

12. *ST* I-II 68.2. [Editor's note: For a detailed discussion of "instinct" in Aquinas, see "Morality and the Movement of the Holy Spirit: Aquinas's Doctrine of *Instinctus*," essay #20 in *The Pinckaers Reader.*]

on morality in the form of an answer to the question of beatitude that dominates the whole of ethics. Here Thomas takes up and sets in order to the best of his ability the ample material found in his earlier works.

Let us note first of all that, since the writing of the *Summa contra Gentiles,* the perspective has changed. The study on finality and beatitude in the *Summa theologiae* is not considered from the viewpoint of God and His governance of things (found in the *prima pars* of the *Summa theologiae*) but is situated at the level of human action (the subject of the *secunda pars*). This perspective is presented in the prologue of the *prima secundae:* "Now that we have treated of the exemplar, i.e., God, and of those things which came forth from the power of God in accordance with His will; it remains for us to treat of His image, i.e., man, inasmuch as he too is the principle of his actions, as having free-will and control of his actions."[13] The exemplar/image relationship points to an active correspondence and at the same time to a difference of levels. The finality and beatitude studied in the *Summa theologiae* are precisely human although they proceed from God and return to Him.

The Double Ladder

In considering this powerful construction, I shall focus especially on the structure of the two central questions that complete and clarify the ascending path to God.[14]

After the study of finality that concludes that human action postulates an ultimate end not only for each person but for all of humanity and all creatures, St. Thomas divides the search for beatitude, which fulfills this end, into a twofold dimension. First he considers the objective aspect: in what good does human beatitude consist?[15] Then he studies the subjective aspect: in what human action does beatitude consist?[16] These two complementary questions suggest a reasoned approach that progresses through a negative path toward its summit. We might say they form a double ladder leading to God, the human person's true beatitude.

Let us take a look at the rungs of the ladders. On the objective side, human beatitude does not consist in external goods such as wealth, honors, reputation and glory, or the exercise of power, political or of other kinds. It does not lie in the more interior goods of the body, such as health and pleasure, or of

13. *ST* I-II prologue.   14. *ST* I-II 2 and 3.

15. *ST* I-II 2.   16. *ST* I-II 3.

the soul, such as knowledge and virtue. Nor can it be found in any other created good, but in God alone. On the subjective side, beatitude cannot be obtained through any action in the sensible order, or through a sheer act of the will, but only by the grasp of the intellect. Still, beatitude is not the work of the practical but rather of the speculative or contemplative intellect. Yet it cannot result from the contemplation of sciences, philosophical and so forth, or even of angels, but only from the vision of the divine essence. We reach the answer to the search for beatitude, therefore, at the summit of this double ladder. The complete beatitude of the human person, able to fulfill all our desires for truth and goodness, can lie nowhere but in the vision of the divine essence. St. John expresses this in more concrete terms: "When he appears we shall be like him, for we shall see him as he is."[17]

It is well to note that in these two articles, at the decisive point at the summit of the double ladder,[18] St. Thomas takes his stand on the natural human desire for beatitude, a desire so broad and deep that only God can fulfill it. He does this by revealing Himself in His very essence and uniting Himself to us in the intimacy of love.

These articles will be completed in a more positive perspective in the next question, where St. Thomas shows the contributions made by various goods such as pleasure, external goods, and human friendship to beatitude thus defined.[19] Finally, he treats of the possibility of attaining beatitude and ends with the very human question: does everyone desire beatitude?[20]

Remarkable in this study is the fact that in each question, and for each good being examined, St. Thomas gives us profound and pertinent reasons that penetrate to the nature of things. His reasons serve us as criteria for appreciating and utilizing goods that though insufficient are yet necessary in our search for beatitude.

The Human and Christian Dimension of the Treatise on Beatitude

On reading these questions on beatitude—condensed, framed in rigorous and at times technical language, and Scholastic in outlook—we may think (and many have made the comment) that we are dealing with purely philosophical

17. 1 Jn 3:2 (RSV).   18. *ST* I-II 2.8 and 3.8.
19. *ST* I-II 4.   20. *ST* I-II 5.

and fairly abstract research. We may also consider that the interest attached to this kind of study is in our day and age merely historical, since the manuals of the seventeenth century eliminated the question of beatitude and Kant banished eudaemonism from moral theology. On the contrary, I would like to argue that these questions—seemingly reduced to a rational, skeletal network reminiscent of arches in some Gothic chapel—express in their own way and describe in a remarkable manner a rich spiritual experience whose roots plunge deep into the Gospel and the teaching of the Fathers.

First of all, let us note the profoundly human character of these questions. That everyone is intimately concerned with the question of beatitude is no surprise and requires no proof, especially when we are tested by an encounter with suffering. What is more surprising is that most moral theologians over the last four centuries have ignored this question. Passing in review the problems St. Thomas brings up, it is not too difficult to see in them examples of human experience through the ages, both individual and social. There is the attraction of money (e.g., capitalism), of honors, glory, and power (e.g., the class struggle), and an attachment to sense pleasures and consumer goods (e.g., luxurious living, the consumer society). There is also the higher attraction of the theoretical and practical sciences and the power conferred by the technology they spawn. Nor can we forget the will to power in the depths of every human heart, as well as the need for love and friendship. Finally, underlying all these is the desire for God that is natural to the soul and takes the form of a longing for truth and goodness. This is the hidden mover behind the search for beatitude, the most radical, primitive desire at the heart of all the others; but it is also the most elevated, spiritual, and powerful thrust when it reaches full development. Emanating from God, it can be satisfied by God alone.

Human experience is Christian experience. Because of St. Thomas's discretion, people were not sufficiently aware of the spiritual and evangelical dimension of the treatise on beatitude, which nonetheless was clearly indicated by numerous quotations from Sts. John, Paul, Matthew, the prophets and the Psalms, as well as from St. Augustine, Pseudo-Dionysius, etc. These are found particularly in the *sed contras* that ordinarily provide the sources for his arguments.

This dimension becomes apparent when we compare our five questions with the lengthy explanation of the Gospel Beatitudes found in St. Thomas's *Commentary on St. Matthew*. This was very probably composed during St.

Thomas's second stay in Paris, 1269–70, and thus slightly preceded question 69, *prima secundae,* which is devoted to the Beatitudes in connection with the gifts of the Holy Spirit, studied in question 68.[21] Here we can already find the principal ideas underlying the *secunda pars.* I shall mention some of these that will be useful for our purpose.

The Christ of the Beatitudes as the Teacher of Wisdom in the Commentary on St. Matthew

St. Thomas explains St. Matthew with the help of St. Augustine's *Commentary on the Sermon on the Mount,* taking up some of its main ideas. In the first place, the Sermon on the Mount "contains all the perfection of our life," and this leads St. Thomas to make the Sermon the specific text of the New Law.[22] Then comes St. Augustine's stroke of inspiration: that the gifts of the Holy Spirit enumerated in chapter 11 of the prophet Isaiah correspond to the Beatitudes. St. Thomas will adopt the correspondence established by Augustine (from poverty linked with the gift of fear of the Lord to peace linked with the gift of wisdom) for the *Summa theologiae,* where he will associate a particular gift and Beatitude with different specific virtues. From this we can see the major role of the study of the Beatitudes in the very organization of the *Summa.*

Of particular interest is St. Thomas's general explanation of the Beatitudes, where he takes liberties with St. Augustine. For example, Augustine had explained the Beatitudes as a description of the seven stages of the Christian journey, from conversion in humility and fear of God up to the peace and wisdom given by the Spirit. Although St. Thomas retains the idea of a journey, he sees it in a different way. According to Aquinas, the Beatitudes give us the Lord's response to our chief desire, our longing for beatitude. This is the question the philosophers tried to answer in their search for wisdom. For St. Thomas, the Lord presents himself as a teacher of wisdom, the Doctor par excellence, who communicates to us the knowledge of God concerning true beatitude.

Christ's answer is progressive. It discards one after another the four prin-

---

21. [Editor's note: For a discussion of the dating and text of the commentary on St. Matthew, see J.-P. Torrell, *Saint Thomas Aquinas: The Person and His Work* (Washington, D.C.: The Catholic University of America Press, 1996), 55–57, 339.]

22. *ST* I-II 108.3.

cipal human responses, made chiefly by the philosophers, and rises by degrees to true beatitude.

The Lord begins by correcting the opinion of those who place beatitude in the possession of external goods. This is the Beatitude of the poor.

Christ next shows the error of those who think beatitude lies in self-satisfaction, whether of the irascible appetite in a desire for vengeance (Beatitude of the meek) or of the concupiscible appetite in pleasure-seeking (happy are those who mourn). Others search in the area of the will, preferring their own will to the constraint of a higher law (happy those who hunger and thirst for justice) or by dominating others (happy are the merciful).

In the third place, the Lord rejects the answer of those who seek beatitude in the active life, in the exercise of the moral virtues. Yet He does not say it is erroneous, like the preceding opinions, but shows how it points out a path to beatitude for us, but is not itself beatitude. This is the case with those who think beatitude lies in the human perfection achieved through virtues such as temperance, courage, or chastity. The end of these virtues is purity of heart which rules the passions and is the object of the sixth Beatitude. There remains justice, which regulates our human relationships with others and has as its end the establishment of peace.

Finally the Lord comes to the opinion of those who, like Aristotle, maintain that beatitude is to be found in the contemplation of divine realities. Christ does not reject this in itself, for beatitude does indeed consist in the vision of what is best and most intelligible, that is, God Himself. But these philosophers were mistaken in their timing, for they looked for beatitude in this life.

Note that this consideration comes after the seventh Beatitude, the last according to St. Augustine's count since he put that of the persecuted outside of the series, seeing in it the confirmation and perfection of all the others.[23] Actually, this response goes back to the sixth Beatitude, which is more fitting for the contemplative life with its promise of the vision of God for the pure of

---

23. *Super Mat.* lect. V, n. 443. "*Item rationi: quia beatitudo hominis est ultimum hominis, in quo quietatur desiderium ejus. Naturale autem desiderium est quod homo videns effectus inquirat de cause: unde etiam admiratio philosophorum fuit origo Philosophiae, quia videntes effectus, admirabantur et quaerebant causam. Istud ergo desiderium non quietabitur donec perveniat ad primam causam, quae Deus est, scilicet ad ipsam divinam essentiam. Videtur ergo per essentiam.*"

heart. These inconsistencies in the matter of placement in a *reportatio* should cause no surprise; in fact, they sometimes have the advantage of making the "veins" of the thought structure clearer to us.

The rest of Thomas's *Commentary on St. Matthew* makes important clarifications about the Beatitude of the vision of God, which we encounter again in the *Summa theologiae.* There is the secondary quality of enjoyment in beatitude that comes with achievement, as beauty in youth for instance, which is added to the substance of beatitude constituted by the full knowledge of God. Further on in his explanation of purity of heart St. Thomas discusses the major objection that claims it is impossible to see God. In addition to the authority of Scripture, he answers with the argument from natural desire set out in good and proper form: "[This opinion] is contrary to reason because human beatitude is the ultimate good that fulfills human desire. Now it is a natural human desire for a person who sees an effect [produced] to seek its cause. Thus in the beginning philosophers, admiring the effects [of things produced in the world] sought their cause. This desire will not be fulfilled so long as human beings do not arrive at the first cause, which is God, that is to say, at the divine essence itself. [God] will therefore be seen in His essence."[24]

This vision requires the purification of the heart, as we cleanse our eyes, and this is accomplished by faith according to St. Peter: "[he] cleansed their hearts by faith."[25] Here the commentator has apparently forgotten to mention the gift of understanding which accompanies the Beatitude and which St. Thomas will associate with faith. Purity of heart is also effected by the moral virtues, objects of the preceding Beatitudes, and particularly by chastity.[26]

The Question of the Relationship between Faith in Christ and the Wisdom of the Philosophers

If we consider this explanation of the Beatitudes as a whole, it takes on the aspect of a dialogue on beatitude initiated by Christ and carried on first with every person seeking beatitude and then with the main schools of philosophy that have formulated answers. If St. Thomas quotes only Aristotle by name,

24. *Super Mat.* lect. V, n. 434.
25. Acts 15:9.
26. *Super Mat.* lect. V, n. 435.

we can clearly see behind the various opinions he critiques the profiles of Epicureans who place beatitude in "the life of pleasure" and Stoics who place it in the virtues of the active life, self-control, and political action.

Here a basic question comes to mind. In this discussion of the Gospel Beatitudes, which is ultimately more important: the teaching of Christ or the contribution of philosophers from whom we borrow the categories that facilitate the interpretation? And how do these two contributing elements find expression in the dialogue on beatitude?

Or again: St. Thomas's argumentation reveals two intersecting lines in the works we have been considering. I shall call the first line that which rises by way of transcending and detachment and ends in the affirmation that God alone, in the vision of His essence, gives complete beatitude to the human person. This is Christ's response expressed in philosophical terms; it is no less supernatural for all that. It is not limited to a doctrine, for it includes a demand for detachment bearing on the most intimate human desire. In order to ascend to God we must break away not only from material goods and evil pleasures but must relinquish—which is more difficult—attachment to our own virtues and ideas, even the loftiest, in order to open ourselves to the sole desire for the divine Transcendent One. This is indeed the Gospel renunciation pushed to its completion. It reminds us of the "Nothing, nothing, nothing" of St. John of the Cross.

The second line is also clearly marked. We might call it the line of the integration of philosophical wisdom focused on the question of beatitude. The first response of external goods and pleasures is discarded here as an error.[27] But if the first response is discarded as an error, St. Thomas admits that the virtues of the active life are a necessary path toward beatitude. As for the study of the contemplative life, so precisely analyzed and praised by Aristotle, we get the impression that St. Thomas experiences real difficulty in moving away from it, so true and useful does he find it for his own reflection.

To transcend and to integrate philosophy, this is how the question of the Christian character of St. Thomas's theology, and even of his interpretation of the Gospel, is posed. What, then, is the relationship between human wisdom,

---

27. This is recovered in a sense later on when, for example, the study of "delectation" will lead us to joy and will supply one of the terms in the definition of beatitude as "delight in truth," which has to be understood in the context of Book X of Augustine's *Confessions* ("This is the happy life, to experience joy in Thee, for Thee, because of Thee").

so largely exploited, and the evangelical wisdom dispensed by Christ in the Gospel?

The Predominance of Faith in the Cross of Christ over the Wisdom of the Philosophers, according to the *Commentary on First Corinthians*

We find a remarkable answer to this important question in St. Thomas's *Commentary on First Corinthians*.[28] It is an *expositio* written or dictated by St. Thomas himself.[29] Here the apostle is treating specifically of the opposition between the wisdom of God that he is preaching in the name of Christ, and the wisdom of men who reject the Gospel. "Christ did not send me to baptize but to preach the gospel, and not with eloquent wisdom, lest the cross of Christ be emptied of its power. For the word of the cross is folly to those who are perishing, but to us who are being saved it is the power of God. For it is written, 'I will destroy the wisdom of the wise, and the cleverness of the clever I will thwart.'"[30]

Basing his thought on the fact that *logos* in Greek means reason or word, St. Thomas interprets the wisdom of the word as that of human reason, the wisdom of philosophers. He thus is backed into a corner. Is he not forced to renounce the use of philosophy if he wants to be faithful to St. Paul and the Gospel? We might apply such a conclusion to the *Gloss* of Peter Lombard.[31] Nevertheless, in his *sed contra* Aquinas invokes the authority of St. Jerome, who sings the praises of "teachers of the faith who have disseminated the teachings of philosophy and the sciences to such a point that we know not which to admire more, their secular erudition or their knowledge of the Scriptures."[32] Is it not in this approach that St. Thomas will position himself, as did St. Augustine, in the use of the philosophers to build up theology?

28. *I ad Cor.* ch. 1, lect. III. Thomas's commentary on First Corinthians was composed at the end of his life, probably during his second stay in Paris in 1270–72. [Editor's note: For a recent discussion of the dating of the commentary on First Corinthians, see Torrell, *Saint Thomas Aquinas,* 250–57, 340.]

29. Cf. James A. Weisheipl, O.P., *Friar Thomas D'Aquino* (Garden City, N.J.: Doubleday, 1974).

30. 1 Cor 1:17–19 (RSV).

31. Peter Lombard. *PL* 191, col.1541. See Marie Hendrickx, "Sapienza della croce o sapienza della parola?" in *Annunciare Cristo a l'Europa* (Milan, 1991), 93–117.

32. *I ad Cor.* ch. 1, lect. III sc. "Doctores (fidei Dei) in ornatu Philosophiae doctrinis atque scientiis suos refarserunt libros, ut nescias quid in illis primum admirari debeas, efuditionem saeculi, an scientiam Scripturarum."

Aquinas's response lies in a distinction so penetrating that it goes to the very roots of the act of teaching and to the source of theology. It shows us St. Thomas's concept of his role as a teacher. Here it is: "It is one thing to teach with the wisdom of the word (that is, with human wisdom), and another to use the wisdom of the word to teach." And he explains: "He teaches with the wisdom of the word who takes this wisdom as the taproot of his teaching in such a way that he approves only what this wisdom includes and rejects whatever is outside of this wisdom. Such a method," Aquinas concludes, "corrupts faith."[33]

"On the contrary, [that teacher] uses the wisdom of the word who presupposes the foundations of the true faith and who puts at the service of faith whatever he finds of truth in the teachings of the philosophers."[34]

The question bears on the root of teaching that supplies the decisive criteria for judging: is it faith or human reason? At this level the opposition is radical. It led the wise men of this world to refuse the Gospel Paul preached. In fact, St. Thomas explains, the preaching of the Cross of Christ, the object of faith, contains truths that seem impossible to the eyes of human wisdom, for example, that God should die, that the all-powerful One should be subjected to human violence. Further on he will say that the wise men of this world think it impossible for God to become man and suffer death in His human nature. Preaching the Cross of Christ also seems contrary to human prudence: that a man should not avoid shame when he could, like Christ, of whom it is said that "for the joy that was set before him endured the cross, despising the shame."[35] It was thus that the Jews, expecting Christ to show power through His miracles, were scandalized to see Him suffer on the cross out of weakness. In the same way it was quite contrary to reason for the Greeks to think that God could die and that a just and wise man could willingly expose himself to the most infamous death.[36]

St. Thomas adds a complementary explanation at the level of reason itself:

33. *I ad Cor.* ch. 1, lect. III sc. *"Aliud est docere in sapientia verbi, quocumque modo intelligatur, et aliud uti sapientia verbi docendo. Ille in sapientia verbi docet qui sapientiam verbi accipit pro principali radice suae doctrinae, ita scilicet quod ea solum approbet quae verbi sapientiam continent, reprobet autem ea quae sapientiam verbi non habent; et hoc fidei est corruptivum."*

34. *I ad Cor.* ch. 1, lect. III, n. 43. *"Utitur autem sapientia verbi qui suppositis verae fidei fundamentis, si qua vera in doctrinis Philosophorum inveniat, in obsequium fidei assumat."*

35. Heb 12:2 (RSV); *I ad Cor.* ch. 1, lect. III, n. 50.

36. *I ad Cor.* ch. 1, lect. III, n. 58.

it was their corrupt hearts that prevented the wise men of this world from recognizing the wisdom of God shown in the works of creation. The works of
God are in fact comparable to the words of a master who leads a student to
wisdom by stages. Creatures are like a lesson given by God that makes Him
known, according to the saying of St. Paul: "his invisible nature . . . has been
clearly perceived in the things that have been made."[37] Since this manner of
teaching failed because of the hardness of human hearts, God had to use another method, revealing Himself through the "folly" of preaching that ap-
pealed to faith.[38] This faith brings us into a relationship with God of disciples
to a teacher since, as St. Thomas will say in the *Summa theologiae*, "In order
that a person come to the full, beatific vision, the first requisite is that he believe God, as a learner believing the master teaching him."[39]

Philosophical Wisdom at the Service of Faith

We now come to the second method, which befits the wisdom of God and
proceeds from faith in Christ. It is not described here at any great length but is
clearly indicated.

The teaching method St. Thomas proposes to us, like that of the Fathers
of the Church, includes two moments. The first consists in planting faith in
the disciple as the root of the wisdom of God, placing it in mind and heart as a
foundation and source of divine truth. Faith is the acceptance of the preaching
of the Cross of Christ as a mystery hidden from human eyes. It is not contrary
to reason but rises far above it and summons us to abandon our human reasoning in order to receive this higher wisdom as a sheer gift of the Holy Spirit.
Through faith, we become true disciples of Christ, disciples of God. In this
sense we have only one Master and one Teacher, Christ, as the Gospel tells
us.[40] In Thomas's view this is how the Christ of the Beatitudes appears.

But then comes the second moment. When faith and even love of the
Cross have been firmly anchored in the disciple of Christ, above all if he has
received the gift and charge of teaching from the Spirit and the Church, he
may and indeed should return to human wisdom and the teaching of the
philosophers to discern the truth and goodness they contain and subject it to

---

37. Rom 1:20 (RSV). 38. *I ad Cor.* ch. 1, lect. III, n. 55.

39. *ST* II-II 2.3. *"Unde ad hoc quod homo perveniat ad perfectam visionem beatitudinis prae-
exigitur quod credat Deo tamquam discipulus magistro docenti."*

40. Mt 23:8.

the wisdom of God for the service of evangelical preaching. Such a procedure takes its inspiration from St. Paul himself. After having presented to his readers the mystery of the Cross of Christ in all its starkness—Christ "who, though he was in the form of God . . . emptied himself . . . and . . . humbled himself and became obedient unto death, even death on a cross"[41]—he gives them the following advice as a consequence of their faith. "Finally, brethren, whatever is true, whatever is honorable, whatever is just, whatever is pure, whatever is lovely, whatever is gracious, if there is any excellence, if there is anything worthy of praise, think about these things."[42] This is the example the apostle gave them and invited them to imitate, that the peace of God might be with them.

This was indeed Paul's method in studying moral problems and the cases of conscience he discusses in his letters. We see him habitually beginning with human reasoning dictated by common sense as any philosopher would do. Then he rises with one swift motion to relate the question to Christ, and this gives him criteria for decisive judgments in harmony with the words and actions of the Lord.[43]

Two Aspects of St. Thomas's Meditation on the Beatitudes

It is now time to return to St. Thomas's explanation of the Beatitudes. In light of St. Paul's understanding of the relationship between faith and philosophical wisdom, we can discern more clearly the spine of Aquinas's account. Behind the philosophical terminology and categories it is indeed evangelical. Thomas's explanation is made up of what we called the line of progressive transcendence and detachment which ends in the specifically Christian affirmation that complete human beatitude lies in God alone, in the vision of God promised to the pure of heart, beyond the sentiments and ideas of human and angelic beings, beyond every creature.

This is a contemplative way; it is also a way of spiritual ascent through detachment of mind and heart. It is close to that way to God through the speech and silence of creatures that St. Augustine describes in the vision of Ostia on a more personal level as a mystical experience.[44]

The Cross of Christ is present in the Gospel Beatitudes through the re-

---

41. Phil 2:6–8 (RSV).   42. Phil 4:8-9 (RSV).

43. See the exposition of St. Paul's moral theology in S. Pinckaers, *The Sources of Christian Ethics* (Washington, D.C.: The Catholic University of America Press, 1995), 104–33.

44. Augustine, *Conf.,* Book X.

nunciations and purifications indicated. It will be clearer in the explanation of the Beatitudes in the *Summa theologiae,* where St. Thomas introduces the gifts with the virtues. He shows the radicality of the Holy Spirit's work according to each one's vocation through the despoilment of poverty, the renouncement of pleasures to bear the "grief" of Christ's Cross, through a more generous justice and a boundless mercy. Such a presence would perhaps have been still more apparent, had St. Thomas integrated within his series the eighth Beatitude of the persecuted, which expresses the ideal of martyrdom as a reproduction of the Passion of the Lord.

However we look at it, an ascent by the way of the Beatitudes is neither conceivable nor practicable without faith in Christ and the help of the Holy Spirit.

The second aspect of this theological meditation, the utilization of philosophy, is more visible in the explanation of the Beatitudes; it could even block our view. It is no less pertinent and rich as a teaching. To expose the contents of the Beatitudes and to describe the path they propose to us, St. Thomas uses the categories provided by Aristotle: the distinction, clearer in the *Summa theologiae,* between the types of life, pleasure-seeking, active, and contemplative, determined by the three concepts of beatitude; the division of the faculties: concupiscible, irascible, the will, the intellect with the practical and speculative reason. Such an application of philosophical categories to a Gospel text might seem contrived but rests nonetheless on a profound insight: the Beatitudes fulfill and perfect human nature as God created it. Now Aristotle is a good witness, a remarkable analyst of human nature. It is fitting therefore to use his study of the human person to explain God's work in us, for there is a profound harmony between creation and redemption, between nature and grace, signified notably by the desire for beatitude, the natural desire to see God. Behind and beyond Aristotle, it is human nature that interests St. Thomas, as the basis for the work of grace. Yet we always have to remember that grace surpasses nature, that the Word of God transcends the intelligence even of theologians, as our Doctor acknowledged at the beginning of his section on the Beatitudes in his *Commentary on St. Matthew:* "Many things will be found here on the Beatitudes. Yet no one could ever comment on the words of the Lord with sufficient penetration to express perfectly all that He said."[45] We

---

45. *Super Mat.* lect. V, n. 404. "*Notandum autem, quod hic ponuntur plura de beatitu-*

need to use the philosophical categories with discernment, therefore, and the necessary flexibility, in order to adapt them to a reality and an experience that surpass human reason.

This is how St. Thomas makes use of Aristotle to trace the principal stages of the spiritual life of the Christian, marked out by the Beatitudes. They correspond perfectly to the three stages of growth in charity.[46] Beginners in charity, the "little children," have as their principal task to fight against sin and the evil desires that lead to the "pleasure-seeking life." Progressives—we might call them the adolescents—are concerned with making progress in the virtues and this brings them into the "active life" with the practice of justice, generosity, and mercy. Finally, those whom St. Thomas calls the perfect—and we could also call them adults in the life of charity—aspire to "depart and be with Christ," but they are equally ready to serve all in the name of Christ.[47] These are the "contemplatives" who aspire to the vision of God, while being disposed to give to others the fruits of their contemplation in the apostolic life through preaching and teaching.[48]

In his study of the active and contemplative life,[49] St. Thomas will again initiate a dialogue between philosophy and the Christian experience, notably between Aristotle and St. Gregory the Great, meditating on the Gospel account of Martha and Mary and comparing these two ways of life.[50] Here Aristotle supplies the human base and St. Gregory, with St. Augustine and others, witnesses to the richness and dynamism of the Christian life oriented to the vision of God. St. Paul's rapture[51] is the nearest approximation to it in this world.[52]

Here we will close our survey of the successive drafts of the treatise on beatitude. It has shown us the prime importance of the question of beatitude throughout the work of the Angelic Doctor, manifested by the important place he gives it. Going beyond the philosophical façade, we have laid bare the evangelical foundation and the spiritual content of this teaching. We have also tried to throw light on the astonishing dialogue initiated by St. Thomas between

---

dinibus; sed nunquam aliquis in verbis Domini posset ita subtiliter loqui, quod pertingeret ad propositum Domini."

46. *ST* II-II 24.9.
47. Phil 1:23–25.
48. *ST* II-II 188.6.
49. *ST* II-II 179–82.
50. *ST* II-II 182.1.
51. Cf. 2 Cor 12.
52. *ST* II-II 180.6.

Aristotle's philosophy and the theology which finds its source in faith and in the Cross of Christ. Folly for the wise of this world, it is an instrument of the very wisdom of God for those whom the Spirit enlightens and to whom the Spirit entrusts the task of preaching and teaching the Beatitudes in the footsteps of Christ, as did St. Thomas.

7 ❧ Beatitude and the Beatitudes in Aquinas's *Summa Theologiae* (1998)

The Sources, Composition, and Situation of the Treatise on Beatitude

The opening questions of the *prima secundae* of St. Thomas's *Summa theologiae* are remarkable, considering the sources and materials they bring together, the care taken in their lengthy elaboration, and the place they occupy in St. Thomas's grand theological synthesis. The sources of these five questions on beatitude are clearly indicated, being quoted therein.[1] Of the theological sources, Scripture is cited sixty times and the commentaries of the Church Fathers receive sixty-one citations (forty-two citations from Augustine, eleven citations from Dionysius the Areopagite, and three citations from Ambrose and Gregory the Great). Of the philosophical sources, Aristotle is cited sixty-six times, Boethius is cited thirteen times, and there are two references to the *Liber de Causis*.

One can argue that St. Thomas's citations are more significant than those in modern works. In conformity with the *lectio* (i.e., the first stage of the Scholastic method, the "reading" of works known for their intellectual caliber), these citations indicate "authorities" in the order of erudition, all of which are accepted sources of enlightenment and knowledge. Aquinas's treatment of beatitude brings together authoritative texts of the Christian tradition

---

Originally published as "The Desire for Happiness as a Way to God," in the *Maynooth University Record,* 1998. Edited for publication in *The Pinckaers Reader* by John Berkman.

1. [Editors' note: The editors have chosen to translate *"bonheur"* as "beatitude" rather than "happiness," both to remind the reader of Aquinas's particular understanding of the end or goal of human life, and to avoid the senses of "happiness" which are more psychic and transient that what Aquinas understood by *"beatitudo."*]

and philosophical traditions, especially the Aristotelian tradition. Further-more, St. Thomas's citations are sometimes merely the tip of the iceberg, re-ferring as they sometimes do to lengthy studies such as Boethius's *Consolation of Philosophy,* the reading of which is practically a necessity to understand the depths and nuances of Thomas's treatment of beatitude.

As for Thomas's treatments of the subject of beatitude, he worked on them all his life. He made three principal redactions. The first one is found at the end of his *Commentary on the Sentences.*[2] The second and third are in the *Summa contra Gentiles* and the *Summa theologiae.*

In addition, Thomas treats the subject of beatitude in several other places. His *Commentary on Aristotle's Nicomachean Ethics* was probably done in preparation for the *secunda pars* of the *Summa theologiae.*[3] It clarifies first the definition of beatitude (Book I), then the nature of beatitude as an operation of the highest virtue in the order of speculative wisdom (Book X). The unfin-ished second book of the *Compendium theologiae* (1272) connects the ques-tion of beatitude with the virtue of hope, which is expressed in the Our Father, just as faith is expressed in the Creed.[4] Here we have a sketch of our treatise. Finally, *Sermon 12, for the Feast of All Saints* (which is in the process of being published in the Leonine edition),[5] contains a summary of our treatise in con-nection with the Gospel Beatitudes.

It is well to note especially the central and fundamental place given to the

2. [Editor's note: For St. Thomas's treatment of beatitude in his commentary on the *Sentences* of Peter Lombard, see "Aquinas's Pursuit of Beatitude: From the *Commentary on the Sentences* to the *Summa Theologiae,*" essay #6 in *The Pinckaers Reader.*]

3. [Editor's note: An English translation is St. Thomas Aquinas, *Commentary on Aristotle's Nicomachean Ethics,* trans. C. I. Litzinger, O.P. (Notre Dame, Ind.: Dumb Ox Books, 1993). Torrell argues that this commentary was composed in Paris in 1271–72, and that it was contem-poraneous with the composition of the *secunda secundae* of the *Summa theologiae,* for which it was a preparation. Torrell also notes the existence of a "tabula" or index of the principal themes of the *Nicomachean Ethics,* an unfinished work composed in 1270, when Thomas was preparing to write the *secunda pars.*]

4. [Editor's note: An English translation is St. Thomas Aquinas, *Compendium of Theology,* trans. Cyril Vollert, S.J. (St. Louis: B. Herder, 1947).]

5. [Editor's note: Here Pinckaers is referring to St. Thomas's sermon *Homo quidam fecit ce-nam magnam,* established as one of nineteen authentic sermons in Aquinas's Opera Omnia by L.-J. Bataillon in "Les sermons attribués à saint Thomas: questions d'authenticité," *MM* 19 (1988): 325–41. Pinckaers translates this sermon in "Un sermon inédit de saint Thomas," *Sources* 12 (1986): 9–22.]

questions on beatitude in the *Summa.* Freed from the constraints of Peter Lombard's plan, Thomas shifts the treatise on beatitude from the last place to the first, in conformity with Aristotle's *Nicomachean Ethics,* the thought of St. Augustine, and the method of the Lord himself (in the Sermon on the Mount). Placed at the pivotal juncture between the *prima pars* and the *secunda pars,* these questions are not merely a simple preamble to the moral section of the work, but form a veritable keystone which supports the whole. Beatitude, seen as the last end, will furnish higher criteria governing the principal treatises: the treatise on human acts;[6] the virtues, especially the theological virtues;[7] sin, chiefly mortal sin;[8] law;[9] and the grace of the Spirit in the New Law.[10]

This threefold consideration shows us the importance and interest of the treatise on beatitude. It is the centerpiece in the construction of the *Summa theologiae,* to such an extent that the *secunda pars* may accurately be described as the morality of beatitude.

In view of this, we cannot help regretting that the treatise on beatitude has enjoyed so little success, even in the Thomist tradition, and that it was definitely excluded from fundamental moral theology by the authors of the manuals. For example, Juan Azor, the Spanish Jesuit who at the beginning of the seventeenth century offered the earliest example of the method of the manuals, while claiming that he followed St. Thomas's order, never in fact mentions the treatise on beatitude, and begins his elucidation of fundamental morality with human acts. Post-Tridentine moralists were capable of setting forth an entire exposition of moral theology, as did St. Alphonsus in his voluminous *Moral Theology,* without seeing any need to speak of beatitude. In fact, the mention of beatitude was actually suspect, as if it implied a self-interested, egotistical desire. The result was a veritable divorce between morality and beatitude, something which still obtains—the implication being that a person must sacrifice beatitude in order to be faithful to the moral law. The same crucial problem also turns up in philosophy with the Kantian critique of eudaemonism in the name of the categorical imperative and of a duty-oriented morality.[11]

6. *ST* I-II 6, prologue.   7. *ST* I-II 62.1.
8. *ST* I-II 72.5.   9. *ST* I-II 90.2.
10. *ST* I-II 107.1; 108.3.

11. [Editor's note: For a lengthier narration of this historical development, see Pinckaers, *Sources of Christian Ethics* (Washington, D.C.: The Catholic University of America Press, 1995).]

In order to demonstrate the current significance of the problem of the relationship between beatitude and morality, let us now examine the structure of St. Thomas's treatise on beatitude.

The Question of True Beatitude

St. Thomas was not in the habit of leaving his readers with unanswered questions, nor of guiding them along roads which led nowhere. After having acknowledged, in the prologue to the second part, that God created humans in His image, conferring on them mastery of their actions through free will, St. Thomas at once takes up the question which God had inscribed in the human heart, a spontaneous, natural, and universal question. As St. Augustine wrote, in a text of the *De Trinitate* cited by St. Thomas: "If the comedian [who promised to tell the audience what each person wanted] had said, 'You all want to be happy, you do not want to be wretched,' no one at all would fail to recognize this desire at the root of their will. Whatever else a man might want in the secret depths of his heart he never forgets this desire, which is well known to all, and is in all."[12]

Philosophers, and people in general, have given many different and contradictory answers to this natural question. The decisive question would therefore be: what is man's true beatitude? Thomas responds by making a joint appeal to the wisdom of the philosophers, who are the interpreters of human experience, and to the teaching of the Gospel, commented upon by the Fathers of the Church who are the authorized interpreters of the Christian experience. Drawing upon these rich traditions, Thomas constructs a path, one which is built as solidly as a Roman road. It will lead to the twin affirmations that God alone can fulfill the human longing for beatitude, and that ultimate beatitude can lie only in the vision of the Divine essence, according to the Divine promise: "When he appears we shall be like him, for we shall see him as he is."[13]

Thus, in the light of the Gospel, and with the help of philosophy, Thomas traces for us, beginning with the desire of beatitude, a path which rises toward God, a path comparable to the ways of demonstrating the existence of God.

12. Augustine, *De Trin.*, Book XIII, ch. 3; cited in *ST* I-II 5.8.
13. 1 Jn 3:2 (RSV); cited in *ST* I-II 3.8.

This description takes up, principally, the first three questions, and evokes the image of a highway. At the center, a long white line extends indicating the direction; this is the first question, on finality. On either side of the line lie the two aspects of the problem. To the right is the objective side: in what good does human beatitude consist?[14] On the left is the subjective side: from a human point of view, what actions will make a person blessed?[15] The remaining two questions bring out, first, the subjective elements of beatitude[16] and then the powers and means a person uses to attain to the promised beatitude.[17]

Beatitude is both objective and subjective. It is objective, because it is caused by a good reality, one which renders person good and blessed. It is subjective, because it corresponds to the desire of man, which carries him toward the good and beatitude. The avowal of a lover, "*You* are *my* beatitude," well expresses this constitutive duality. On the one hand, it is formed by the person who is the object of love. On the other hand, it is the sentiment of beatitude which the person who is the object of love causes in the lover. Let me add that for Thomas, as for Augustine, the term *bonum* combines inseparably the ideas of the good and of beatitude: what is good is what makes one blessed; what is evil is what makes one wretched. One of the tragedies of modern ethics lies in the separation imposed between the good, conceived of a pure obedience to law (something which renders ethics tedious), and beatitude, which is suspected of egoism.

The Way of Beatitude

Let me briefly outline the path to beatitude, according to St. Thomas.

The Finality of Acts

At the center there runs the line of finality. Like a spinal column it controls the structure of morality. Thanks to a person's reason, it is proper to her to act in view of an end,[18] which specifies the quality of her acts,[19] and joins them to an ultimate finality which orders her whole life, as well as all her acts.[20] This ultimate end transcends individual action, and works as the chief unifying

14. *ST* I-II 2.
15. *ST* I-II 3.
16. *ST* I-II 4.
17. *ST* I-II 5.
18. *ST* I-II 1.1–2.
19. *ST* I-II 1.3.
20. *ST* I-II 1.4–6.

principle with regard to all person, through the societies which they form.[21] The ultimate end even creates an active solidarity between human persons and all other creatures.[22] Thus we rise from the finality that informs our particular acts to an ultimate finality which rejoins the Divine finality operating in the government of the universe, and particularly in human beings.[23]

I should like to note two points here. Firstly, we are dealing with a kind of continuous finality, in contrast to the more brief and occasional finality of casuistry, which is limited to individual actions and cases of conscience, and forms not a line but a series of disconnected dots without any order. On the one hand, then, we have a fundamental finality in morality, and on the other a subjective finality which has become a component of the action itself.

Secondly, we need to avoid confusing the finality which Thomas is considering with the modern, technical finality which has become increasingly commonplace with the development of the natural and social sciences. In the *Summa* we are dealing, not with a technical finality related to some external work, mechanically realizable according to its relation to intermediate ends, but with a moral finality which unfolds within a human being and bears on his or her personal acts, such as desire and love, as well as on intention, deliberation, and choice, which are the sources of human action. The great difference between these two finalities consists in the fact that personal acts may have as their object human qualities and persons lovable in themselves, that is, as ends. Examples of these personal acts (e.g., charity, truth, or friendship), however, are ordered by us and for us in virtue of one single and ultimate end, thereby granting us access to this end, and are not given as mere means or instruments to be discarded after their use. In this way, Christ himself, as Thomas says, "has shown us in his own person the path of truth which, in rising again, we can follow to the blessedness of eternal life."[24] It is by loving Christ as a person, and not merely as a means to beatitude, that Christ becomes for us a path to our ultimate end, namely blessedness in God. It is at the heart of our personal experience that we discover this finality.

Since Thomas had no knowledge of technical finality in the modern sense, he did not make all the clarifications which are now necessary in a discussion of this subject. However, Thomas does bring out the finality inscribed in the

---

21. *ST* I-II 1.7.
23. *ST* I 103.

22. *ST* I-II 1.8.
24. *ST* III prologue.

nature of various realities, such as riches, power, virtue, and, indeed, in the human person. It is not, therefore, a question of a finality fabricated by human beings, or of a technology. It is this singling out of a natural finality that gives to Thomas's reflections a solidity which guarantees their permanent worth.

The Objective Aspect of Beatitude

Returning to our analogy of the highway: the right side of the path of beatitude is more concrete, in conformity with the itinerary toward God mapped out by St. Augustine in his contemplation at Ostia,[25] by Aristotle in his *Nicomachean Ethics,* and by Boethius in his *Consolation of Philosophy.* Its form is negative: the ultimate end and complete beatitude of the human person does not consist in riches (whether natural or monetary), nor in honors, nor in reputation and glory in the eyes of others, nor in the possession of power. It is easy to see the timeliness of these issues for our society, dominated as it is by political and economic questions. The search then deepens, penetrating into human nature itself: the ultimate end cannot reside in the goods of the body, such as health (valuable though this is), nor in pleasures, nor in goods of the soul such as knowledge and virtue, nor in any other created good, but in God alone, who, according to Psalm 102, "satisfies you with good as long as you live." This path directs the natural desire toward the good and toward beatitude. The ordering to God alone as sovereign Good therefore constitutes both the ultimate end and the supreme criterion of human acts, both at the personal and at the social level.

Note that this account, while it describes an intellectual search, indicates at the same time (though perhaps a little too subtly) a spiritual journey beginning with ascetical detachment from external goods, continuing with detachment from interior goods, and culminating in a summit which could be called mystical, namely a union with God lived above all else as the Unique One, as the Ultimate End, and as Perfect Blessedness. We are reminded of Teresa of Avila's words, "God alone suffices." God is indeed the universal Good, the source of all good. This lengthy undertaking begins in the human heart with its faculty of loving and desiring, and is rounded off by an indication of the positive contribution of goods, even of corporeal ones and of those external to us, to the search, carried on in this world, for beatitude in God.[26]

25. Augustine, *Conf.* IX.10.23–26.
26. *ST* I-II 4.

The Subjective Aspect of Beatitude

The second path, on the left side of the road to beatitude, is concerned with the action of the person who is following it, and principally in the intellect, which grasps the good and presents it to the will. Here, likewise, progress is made through negation: complete beatitude cannot be the work of sense perception,[27] but rather of our spiritual faculties, and primarily of our intellect.[28] It is not, however, the work of the practical intellect but of the speculative intellect, which seizes upon truth and goodness in themselves as the perfection of contemplation.[29] This knowledge cannot be limited to the speculative sciences such as the various branches of philosophy;[30] it must even surpass the knowledge of angelic intellects which are superior to ours,[31] in order to open itself out mysteriously to the measure of the vision of the Divine essence.[32]

Here, then, is a new aspect of Christian asceticism: that intellectual and spiritual detachment produced by the desire for truth, which urges us firstly to transcend sensible perceptions, then to transcend the ideas formed by our reason, then finally to transcend the intuitions of our mind, in order to allow the development within us of that contemplation, at once obscure and luminous, intelligent and unknowing, which is proper to faith in this life.

When we reflect on these texts of the *Summa* we can read between the lines to discern the spiritual experience of the Angelic Doctor, an experience animated by the ardent love of truth which spurred Thomas on to seek God before all other realities, as his biographer William of Tocco tells us. We are not in his case dealing with a purely intellectual search, one which might become so abstract in its series of transcendent moves that it might risk vanishing like a rocket into the space of concepts, and even beyond that. From beginning to end, Thomas's venture remains linked with the desire for beatitude and that love of goodness which moves the will. In his very succinct and sober style he describes for us the progress of our spiritual appetite, which unites the desire for truth with the love of the good, thus directing all the movements of the human mind and heart toward God. The pathway built by Thomas is in-

27. *ST* I-II 3.3.
28. *ST* I-II 3.4.
29. *ST* I-II 3.5.
30. *ST* I-II 3.6.
31. *ST* I-II 3.7.
32. *ST* I-II 3.8.

deed predominantly intellectual and sapiential, just like the teaching of the Fathers of the Church; but it is at the same time unitive through the love of God, which is strengthened by charity and the desire for beatitude, and lifted higher by the virtue of hope.

We can therefore compare our treatise on beatitude with the works of those spiritual writers and mystics who describe the stages of the human person's ascent to God. In his rigorous and sparse language, Thomas describes the theological structure of that search for God which is capable of touching the human heart: without God there is no perfect beatitude for the human person, nor any adequate response to his or her deepest longing for truth and goodness. For Thomas, God is the very source, the object and the cause of true beatitude. As Augustine said, "You have made us for yourself O Lord, and our hearts are restless until they rest in you."[33]

Two Difficulties

However powerful and rich these texts which St. Thomas devotes to beatitude may be, they still leave the reader with two questions:

1. Why is it that in the *Summa* Thomas cites the Gospel Beatitudes only once (the Beatitude of the pure of heart in connection with the rectitude required in the will: *ST* I-II 4.4), whereas in his *Commentary on St. Matthew* he presents the Christ of the Beatitudes as the sage *par excellence,* who gives the perfect answer to the question of true beatitude of which philosophers could never adequately treat? Is he standing aloof from the Beatitudes in this regard?

2. Furthermore, when he treats of the incomplete nature of the beatitude which is attainable in this life, St. Thomas always refers, in our questions, to Aristotle, without ever including Christian insights drawn from the Gospel or from patristic teaching concerning, for example, the usefulness of bodily health,[34] of external goods,[35] of the contributions of friends,[36] or, again, of the attainment or loss of beatitude in this life.[37] We get the impression that he systematically avoids all mention of the Beatitudes in the treatise on beatitude, and omits the contributions of the Gospel and of Christian experience from his description of the beatitude attainable in this life.

33. Augustine, *Conf.* I.1.1.   34. *ST* I-II 4.6.
35. *ST* I-II 4.7.   36. *ST* I-II 4.8.
37. *ST* I-II 5.3–4.

The Explanation of the Beatitudes, the Culmination of the Treatise on Beatitude

The *lacunae* we have just mentioned find their explanation, I believe, in the structural demands of a rigorously systematized work like the *Summa theologiae*. The treatise on beatitude is not finished; it awaits a completion foreseen in the overall plan of the work. This completion is the question in the *prima secundae* devoted to the evangelical Beatitudes.[38] There we are given a detailed description of the Christian beatitude which can already be experienced in this life, as a preparation for, and a prefiguring of, future blessedness.

The separation between the treatise on beatitude and the question on the evangelical Beatitudes is explicable on historical and methodological grounds. These studies created different problematics in theology in the thirteenth century. In his *Commentary on the Sentences,* St. Thomas studies the Beatitudes after the gifts of the Holy Spirit.[39] The question is: how are the Beatitudes to be distinguished from the virtues and gifts, with which they are connected by St. Augustine? This was the problem debated by the "Masters." Thomas, therefore, would not deal with the Beatitudes in the treatise on beatitude placed at the end of his *Commentary* on the fourth book, but rather discussed the Beatitudes in conjunction with the virtues and gifts which underpinned his entire moral construction. In the *Summa* the order is reversed and the study on beatitude comes first. It is followed by the Beatitudes, which are grafted on to the analysis of the virtues and gifts; but the distance separating them in the plan is such that the connection is lost on many readers.

This historical reason overlays a more systematic one which is of particular interest to us. St. Thomas refuses to define the Beatitudes as *habitus,* and presents them instead as perfect acts. They designate the work of the virtues, and more especially of those gifts which enable us to act more perfectly through the grace of the Spirit. In this way Thomas puts into our hands all the elements needed to describe Christian beatitude in this life. Beatitude issues from the exercise of the virtues animated by charity, the "heart of perfection," under the inspiration of the gifts which cause us to act with excellence and render us more docile to the Holy Spirit. Thus, through the virtues and gifts

38. *ST* I-II 69.
39. III *Sent.*, dist. 34.

the most finished spiritual work is achieved, the fulfillment of the Beatitudes. It is like a fruit which has come to full maturity.

The relation of the Beatitudes to the virtues and gifts is so important in St. Thomas's view that he introduces it into the structure of the *secunda secundae*. To each virtue he relates a gift, and in the question discussing it he indicates the Beatitude which corresponds to this gift. We are dealing, therefore, with a morality of beatitude which begins to be realized in this life in the practice of the Beatitudes, through the work of the virtues and gifts.

The Description of Christian Beatitude in This Life in the Light of the Beatitudes

An attentive reading of the four articles devoted to the Beatitudes in the *Summa* shows that St. Thomas considered his question on the Beatitudes to be very important.[40] In it he described what for him is the perfection of the Christian life, the summit of Gospel spirituality. These few pages are so full and so richly delineated that they remind us of a vast tapestry, worked out down to the finest lace-like detail. Thomas takes consummate care in his explanation of the Beatitudes, because he saw in them both the response of the Lord himself to the question of beatitude, and a precise description of the paths leading to the promised blessedness. With St. Augustine, he held that the Beatitudes are inchoate in this life and are a preparation for future beatitude, or even an imperfect but real beginning of blessedness, as can be seen in the lives of the saints.[41]

I should like to point out here that St. Thomas did not know, and would certainly have rejected, the modern distinction between morality and spirituality, or between asceticism and mysticism, which has removed the gifts and the Beatitudes from moral theology. For him the moral life, ordered to the perfection of charity with the help of the virtues, attains its fullness in the action of the Holy Spirit working through the gifts, and reaches its summit through the practice of the Beatitudes. As the organization of the *secunda pars* shows, the gifts and the Beatitudes, as well as the virtues and precepts, are not reserved for a chosen few but concern all Christians. With the Beatitudes we reach that

40. *ST* I-II 69.
41. *ST* I-II 69.2.

level in the moral life which is rendered accessible through the grace of the Spirit.

The Sources for Thomas's Treatment of the Question on the Evangelical Beatitudes

I should like to show in a few words the importance of the question on the Beatitudes from the consideration of its sources.[42] Let us take the theological sources first. Obviously, St. Matthew's statement of the Beatitudes at the beginning of the Sermon on the Mount is most important. Concerning this, St. Thomas notes that all the Beatitudes contained in Scripture should be referred to this key text.[43] Now the Sermon on the Mount is the specific text of the New Law, which is defined as the grace of the Holy Spirit received through faith in Christ.[44] The realization of the Beatitudes in the Christian life should therefore be accomplished through faith in the Christ who spoke them, and with the help of the Spirit from whom flows all the energy of this interior law. In this light, the Christological and spiritual character of St. Thomas's moral theology becomes evident.

To demonstrate more precisely how the action of the Spirit works, our Doctor takes up and interprets in his own way the tradition created by St. Augustine in his preaching on the Sermon on the Mount, where Augustine had the idea of relating the Beatitudes to the gifts of the Spirit enumerated in Isaiah 11. For Augustine, the Beatitudes describe the Christian journey from conversion in humility to purity of heart and the attainment of peace in God. According to the teaching of St. Paul, however, the Christian cannot follow this path without the help of the Holy Spirit. This intervention of the Spirit manifests itself in the correspondence between the seven Beatitudes and the seven gifts which St. Thomas takes up in all his works, basing it on the relationship to the seven principal virtues. In this way he organizes to the best advantage the moral heritage both of the Gospel and of the Fathers of the Church.

Nevertheless, in order to explain the Beatitudes, St. Thomas does not hesitate to make use of philosophical categories borrowed from Aristotle, notably the distinction between the three kinds of life corresponding to the three types

42. *ST* I-II 69.
43. *ST* I-II 69.3 ad.4.
44. *ST* I-II 106.1.

of response to the question of beatitude: the life of pleasure, which is rejected by the first three Beatitudes; the active life, with which the fourth Beatitude on justice and the fifth on mercy both deal; and finally, the contemplative life, related to the Beatitudes of the pure of heart who shall see God, and the peacemakers.[45] This distinction shows that the Beatitudes are concerned with human life in its entirety, and characterize it according to the kind of beatitude which is sought. These categories can also be applied to societies.

The division of the human faculties likewise contributes to the interpretation of the Beatitudes, as does the distinction between the irascible passions, regulated by the Beatitudes of the meek, and the concupiscible passions, the concern of the Beatitudes of those who mourn. This shows the human rootedness of the teaching.

As with the treatise on beatitude, the question on the Beatitudes combines the riches of the traditions of the Gospel, the Fathers of the Church, and the philosophers, but with a definite emphasis on the Gospel.

A Brief Look at the Question on the Beatitudes

Obviously we cannot engage in an in-depth study of this question here.[46] I shall simply give a general outline, to whet your appetite. St. Thomas begins by distinguishing the Beatitudes from the virtues and the gifts, while showing their coordination. We can move toward beatitude through the acts of the virtues and gifts: these acts are the Beatitudes.[47] The analysis of the Beatitudes which follows is based on the relationship, fundamental in moral theology, between merit and reward—it being understood that merit proceeds essentially from charity and the Holy Spirit. The rewards promised in the Beatitudes come to us already in this life, as both a beginning of blessedness and a preparation for it.[48] The detailed explanation of the Beatitudes describes the actions which they either disparage or recommend, ordered according to the distinction of the three kinds of life: the life of pleasure, the active life, and the contemplative life, depending on the kind of beatitude which is sought. It shows the different ways in which the Beatitudes may be accomplished, whether according to the rational measure of virtue or according to the inspiration of the

45. *ST* I-II 69.3.
47. *ST* I-II 69.1.

46. *ST* I-II 69.
48. *ST* I-II 69.2.

gifts.[49] Finally, Thomas explains the rewards of the Beatitudes by showing how each one fulfills, on a higher plane, those desires which urge humans toward false or imperfect forms of beatitude. Thus, for example, when the poor realize the spiritual riches to be found in God, this discovery sublimates their desire for earthly goods.

We might say that St. Thomas really wanted to include his entire moral teaching in this question on the Beatitudes, in order to show that it reaches its summit in the fulfillment of the Beatitudes, so as to place everything under the aegis of the Word of the Lord, which he considers to be the Teacher par excellence.[50]

The Beatitudes, Fruits of the Virtues and Gifts

In closing, I should like to draw your attention to the comparison St. Thomas makes, in the accomplishment of the Beatitudes, between what virtue commands in accordance with the measure of reason, and what the gifts inspire in accordance with the higher measure of the Holy Spirit. Through the first Beatitude virtue teaches us to use external goods in moderation, according to our need of them, but the gift of the Spirit goes further and would have us scorn material goods entirely, so as to detach our heart from them without reserve. Such was the evangelical poverty actually practiced by St. Dominic and St. Francis. As the second Beatitude, virtue moves us to control the irascible appetites (anger and fear) with due reason. The gift of the Spirit keeps the soul tranquil in the face of even the greatest danger, as happened in the case of the martyrs. Regarding the concupiscible appetites with which the third Beatitude deals, virtue would lead us to use these movements of sensibility with due measure, while the gift detaches us from them altogether, giving us a spirit of compunction and penance in union with the Passion of the Lord, according to the monastic tradition. Likewise, the Spirit causes us to "give each one his due" in justice, with a fervent desire which is like hunger and thirst, in the way that St. Louis, the contemporary of Aquinas, administered justice in the kingdom of France. It also moves us to practice mercy by giving generously to all in need, beyond the bounds of friendship or kinship, as did so many saints, such as St. Vincent de Paul.

49. *ST* I-II 69.3.   50. *ST* III 7.7.

These brief indications of St. Thomas concerning the practice of the Beat-itudes could be extended by reference to his study of the particular virtues and gifts. They show clearly the nature of the beatitude which the Christian can have in this life. Its source is within the person, in the place where virtue is formed in the light of reason illumined by the Word of Christ, and where the Holy Spirit is at work in its depths, inspiring the most personal and noble acts.

Finally, in order to recount all the riches of life lived according to the Spir-it, St. Thomas thought it appropriate to add to the Beatitudes the fruits of the Holy Spirit as enumerated by St. Paul in his Letter to the Galatians:[51] charity first, as the prime source of beatitude; then joy, which serves to define beati-tude as "joy in the truth"; and peace, which renders it perfect.[52] Is not "fruit" the best image of beatitude—a fruit that has acquired its full perfection and beauty? It is the image of a life's work which has reached its maturity.

We can say that St. Thomas's teaching on beatitude and the Beatitudes is one of the most beautiful fruits of his theological genius, nourished by the Gospel and the reflections of the Fathers of the Church. Is it not a cause for re-gret that for four centuries, and even still in our own day, the treatise on beati-tude and the questions on the gifts and Beatitudes have been omitted from the handbooks of moral theology? Surely we should extol the *Catechism* for hav-ing reintroduced them into the teaching of fundamental moral theology.[53] Let us hope that the Holy Spirit will lead moralists to grasp the importance of this innovation, which bears within it a principle of the renewal and rejuvenation of moral theology.

This is the path to beatitude proposed by the moral and spiritual teaching of St. Thomas, a central path directing our entire life to God as to our blessed-ness. It is built on solid foundations: Christian experience, founded on the Rock of the Word of Christ (as the patristics testified) and human experience, interpreted and witnessed to by the most lucid of the philosophers. This, it seems to me, is the best and most enlightening gift, the most joyful message that St. Thomas could give to us today.

51. Gal 5:22–23.   52. *ST* I-II 70.
53. *CCC*, 1716–24; 1830–32.

8 ∾ Ethics and the Image of God   (1989)

When we explore the history of the theme of the image of God in the human person in a very fine article such as the one in the *Dictionnaire de la spiritualité* on the subject, for example,[1] we are led to make a general observation: the theme is present almost everywhere; it occupies an important place in the theology of both Greek and Latin Church Fathers and among medieval theologians. In the modern period, however, it becomes marginal and often even disappears from view for theologians, at least when they do not follow directly in the path of ancient tradition. Among the Church Fathers, it is a living and vital theme. For moderns, it is more like a showpiece. I shall try to throw some light on this historical phenomenon, paying special heed to anthropology, which includes or presupposes the theme of man created in the image of God, a subject with which we are particularly preoccupied. Moreover, I believe that a certain concept of man and of freedom favors the development of the theme of the image of God, while another, the modern concept of freedom of indifference, is an obstacle to it. I can touch on these problems only briefly and schematically, but I hope it will provide sufficient matter for our discussions.

First, I shall explain in broad outline the theme of the creation of man in the image and likeness of God, as presented by the Fathers and especially by St. Thomas, who is their interpreter, both faithful and original. This will be the main part of my contribution. I shall then say a few words about my hy-

Originally published as "Le théme de l'image de Dieu en l'homme et l'anthropologie," in *Humain à l'image de Dieu* (Geneva, 1989), 147–63. Translated by Sr. Mary Thomas Noble, O.P., with the assistance of Craig Steven Titus. Edited for publication in *The Pinckaers Reader* by Craig Steven Titus.

1. "Image et ressemblance," *Dictionnaire de Spiritualité* (Paris: Beauchesne), vol. 7/2, col. 1401–72, 1971.

pothesis regarding the two concepts of freedom, one favoring, the other impeding, the theological development of our theme.

I approach the theme as a moralist, it is true, but one whose concern is to reestablish close bonds between Scripture, dogmatic theology, and the Christian experience, each of which expresses itself in its own way, converging in our theme.

The Image of God in the Human Person according to the Fathers

One of the characteristics of the teaching of the Fathers on the image of God in humans is on the one hand its general presence in the Greek tradition, as in the Latin, and on the other hand the variety of interpretations. The differences bear on the location of the image. Does it reside in a person taken as a whole, body and soul, including the distinction between man and woman, or only in one's spiritual nature? Is it in the faculties that reflect the Trinitarian relationships, and in what way, or does it lie principally in the acts of knowing and loving God? Should we distinguish between image and likeness? If so, is the likeness less than the image or does it signify the perfection of the image? What is the relationship of the image in the human person to the three Persons, and in particular to the Word, the perfect Image of the Father, and is it in the order of creation, restoration, and glorification? Is the image of God proper to humans alone, or is it found to some degree in nonrational beings and in nature? Is it superior in the angels? And so forth.

To all these questions the Fathers give different answers, which we can enumerate in detail.[2] But this variety, which could be discouraging, should not hide from us the immense convergence of patristic and medieval theology in the exploitation of the theme of man created in the image of God, as well as the central place accorded to it in theology.

To give an example, Dom Jacques Leclercq wrote in his introduction to the Sermons of St. Leo: "All of St. Leo's anthropology is based on the idea that man was created in the image of God; this image was corrupted in Adam, but restored by Christ. Each of us should therefore come into contact with Christ, unite himself to him, participate in his grace, imitate his life."[3] Here we

2. Ibid.

3. Leo the Great, *Sermons,* introduction by Jacques Leclercq, trans. René Dolle, *Sources chrétiennes,* vol. 22 (Paris: Cerf, 1949), 44.

can distinguish four stages in the evolution of the image: formation through creation, deformation by Adam's sin, reformation by Christ, and conformation through imitation of Christ and the Father. We might add, the perfection of the image in glory. St. Leo is still at the meeting place of Greek and Latin theology. But we will find the same anthropology of the image in a spiritual writer of the twelfth century, William of St. Thierry, who evidences rich and original thought and experience.[4] We cannot help but ascertain that the theme of human beings in the image of God is a common bond between patristic and medieval theology.

Among the Fathers, the theme of the image of God is a living tree that puts forth branches in every sense, in all the areas of theology and Christian life. The very proliferation of interpretations bears witness to its vitality.

The Image of God according to St. Thomas

Let us now take a brief look at the presentation of the theme of the image of God according to St. Thomas.

We first note the position of question 93—treating this topic—in the *prima pars* and in the overall architecture of the *Summa theologiae.* "That man is made in the image of God" comes at the end of the study on the six days of creation. It marks the end, goal, and achievement of the production of human beings. The work of creation is then followed by the divine government, the work of providence, where a human being plays an active role with her free will. The latter confers on a human being mastery over her actions and enables her to collaborate in the work of providence, for herself and for others. Following St. John Damascene, St. Thomas believes that the image of God in human beings lies precisely in their free will. This is why Thomas places the theme of the image of God as the hinge between his study of the work of God, in the *prima pars,* and of human action, in the *secunda pars.* The famous Prologue of the *prima secundae*[5] is not simply a threshold. It shows God laying a foun-

---

4. Cf. Yves-Anselme Baudelet, *L'expérience spirituelle selon Guillaume de Saint-Thierry* (Paris: Cerf, 1985).

5. *ST* I-II, prologue: "Since, as Damascene states (*De Fide Orthod.* II, 12), man is said to be made to God's image, insofar as the image implies an intelligent being endowed with free will and self-movement: now that we have treated of the exemplar, i.e., God, and of those things which came forth from the power of God in accordance with His will; it remains for us to treat of

dation, free will, which will support all that follows: morality viewed as man's return to God. Nor should we forget that finally, in the *tertia pars*, St. Thomas will study Christ who, in his humanity, is the necessary way to God, while in his divine personality Christ is the Word of God, the perfect Image of the Father.

Let us note, further, that question 93 is supported from beginning to end by Scripture—obviously the text of Genesis 1:26, cited in the first article, but also Paul in the Letters to the Ephesians and Colossians, where the spiritual character of the image of God is established. Paul says in Colossians 3:10: "You have put off the old nature with its practices and have put on the new nature, which is being renewed in knowledge after the image of its creator. . . . Christ is all, and in all." Here the *Jerusalem Bible* adds a note connecting this text with Genesis 1:26. This demonstrates how, as for the Fathers, the Genesis text is not the only one to support the theological theme of the image of God. Paul also contributes to it. Yet St. Thomas never reads Scripture in isolation. He always reads with the help of those Fathers who are particularly competent in treating the topic he is considering. Here, he makes use of the works of St. Augustine—among them his *De trinitate*—and of St. Gregory the Great, the "spiritual authority" of the Middle Ages. St. Thomas adds some of the Greek Fathers, notably St. John Damascene, who is an Aristotelian like himself and has given him the definition of the image: a human being is made in the image of God insofar as she is "an intelligent being endowed with free will and self-movement."[6] St. Thomas therefore does not work out his teaching on the image from the starting point of philosophy, but in the light of Scripture, read and commented on in the Church in the tradition of the principal theological and spiritual currents of his time.

Here is a brief summary of St. Thomas's teaching on the image of God in humans:

1. His study begins with an analysis of terms. "Image" adds to simple likeness a relationship of origin. An image comes from another *(est ex alio expressum)*. An egg resembles an egg but is not its image; but a son is the image of

---

His image, i.e., man, inasmuch as he too is the principle of his actions, as having free will and control of his actions."

6. *"Intellectuale et arbitrio liberum et per se potestativum."* This definition was borrowed from Nemesius of Emesa, cf. *Bulletin Thomiste* 11 (1962): 101.

his father. Equality with the model is not necessary, however. Thus, humans may be made by God in God's image, despite the distance that separates them. Here is another striking comparison: Christ is the image of God as a son resembles his father, while a human being is an image in the same way in which a coin reproduces the head of an emperor (I 93.1).

2. To be perfectly accurate, only intellectual or spiritual creatures, capable of knowing God and of receiving God's wisdom, are made in the image of God. Consequently, the angels are better images than humans, contrary to the opinion of the Franciscans, because of their higher spiritual nature (I 93.2 and I 93.3).[7]

3. A clarification: humans resemble God in the measure in which they imitate God's knowing and loving, and therefore in the degree to which they progress in the knowledge and love of God. The image is realized at three levels corresponding to the three stages of the history of salvation:

a) through the natural capacity to know and love God which belongs to everyone as a creature of God;

b) through the actual or habitual knowledge and love found in the just here below, that is, in those who are Christians but still in an imperfect state; this is the work of grace and the theologal virtues;

c) through the perfect knowledge and love of the blessed (I 93.4).

4. The image of God in human beings is established not only in relation to the divine nature, but also in relation to the Trinity of Persons. In fact, in the movement of the human spirit toward knowledge and love we can see a specific enough resemblance to the procession of the Word uttered by the Father, and the procession of Love issuing from both, to be able to speak of an image of the Trinity, imperfect though it may be.

The entire search for God discussed in St. Augustine's *De Trinitate* is integrated here, but there are differences. I shall return to this point. Other aspects of the human person, the body with its sexuality and particularly the human face, cannot properly be considered as being images of God, but rather traces or reflections of God (I 93.5 and I 93.6).

---

7. Let us remember that St. Thomas has a very strong sense of the unity of the human composite. For him, the intellect never functions without the body. He will show how sensibility participates in the spiritual life in the order of knowledge and love. Nevertheless it is necessary to distinguish what is proper to the life of the spirit.

5. The image of God in the soul is dynamic. It resides directly and principally in the acts of knowing and loving God and the Trinity, in loving contemplation and active charity.

It is only by way of consequence that the image of God resides in our faculties, insofar as they are the principles of the knowledge and love of God.

We can also see an image of the Trinity—indirect, however—in the actions by which we know and love ourselves, in the manner of the Trinity (I 93.7 and I 93.8).

6. Finally, St. Thomas clarifies the meaning of "likeness" in its relation to "image" in the text of Genesis and distinguishes between the two. Likeness can be understood in two ways: either as the forerunner of the image or as its perfection. As the forerunner of the image, likeness designates sensibility and the body, which share in the preparation for spiritual knowledge and love. But likeness can also designate the expressiveness and perfection of the image of God in man, as St. John Damascene in particular thought, according to the progress of the virtues, owing to love (I 93.9). Here we are dealing above all with an interpretation of the texts of St. Augustine, but we run into a broader problem: the twofold interpretation of "likeness" according as one gives it a weaker or a stronger meaning than one gives to "image."

This schematic overview, which shows the various layers of Scholastic analysis, should not obscure the dynamic power of the concept. As I have said, the theme of the human person as the image of God is a cardinal point throughout St. Thomas's theology. God's work in creation was to form human beings in his image, by giving them the capacity to know and love God. The end of this work was to lead humans to the perfection of an image through full knowledge and love of the Father, Son, and Holy Spirit. This is the end that orientates the entire moral life of the Christian, even as it was the end of the creation of human beings. Finally, this work of sanctification finds its principal source in the grace of Christ, who is both Son of God, perfect Image of the Father, and son of Mary, truly human like us. But this grace requires human collaboration, above all through faith, hope, and charity.

The theme of the image of God therefore involves dogmatic theology with the study of God, the Trinity, creation, and then Christology and the sacraments. It is concerned with the whole branch of moral theology which, governed by the theologal virtues and the gifts of the Holy Spirit, possesses a spiritual, contemplative, and even mystical dimension, as is indicated in St. Thomas's principal source, the *De trinitate* of St. Augustine.

There is a striking contrast here with modern theology manuals, especially in the field of moral theology. The latter separates dogma from morality with great determination, and then separates asceticism from mysticism or spirituality. The result is that we absolutely cannot see any connection now between the theme of the image of God and moral theology with its preoccupation with obligations. The ancient teaching is relegated to a corner of dogmatic theology for specialists or historians who may still take an interest in it.

The Underlying Anthropology: St. Augustine and St. Thomas

We shall now try to bring out the anthropology underlying the theme of the image of God according to St. Thomas. When we study him closely and compare texts, we see that St. Thomas made an important change in regard to the outlook of St. Augustine. He indicates it very discreetly in objection 3 of article 7 (I 93), where he mentions as an objection the teaching of *De trinitate*, that the image of the Trinity is found in the human soul in its three principal faculties: memory, intellect, and will. This teaching created a powerful tradition and influenced spiritual and mystical writers. We come across it in St. Ignatius of Loyola and St. John of the Cross. We can situate it in the Platonic tradition, which assigned a primary role to reminiscence and thus to memory. But it also corresponds to a personal experience, shown by St. Augustine's wondrous admiration as he explores the riches hidden in the caverns of the memory in Book X of the *Confessions*: "The power of memory is great, O Lord. It is awe-inspiring in its profound and incalculable complexity. Yet it is my mind: it is my self."[8] Memory is for him the mysterious reservoir of ideas and emotions, and thus, the source of the life of the Spirit. This is why it can be compared to the Father in the Trinity. For St. Augustine, in contrast with Aristotle and even Plotinus, the nature of the memory is intellectual.

Furthermore, St. Augustine's teaching implies a certain approach to human beings: guided by his personal experience, St. Augustine looks at the human person from the vantage point of God, of the Trinity which reveals to us

8. Saint Augustine, *Confessions,* trans. R. S. Pine-Coffin (London: Penguin, 1980), bk. X, ch. 17. See also A. Solignac's note 14 on "La mémoire selon saint Augustin" ("Memory according to St. Augustine") in *Confessions* (Bibliothéque Augustinienne, vol. 14), 557–67.

the intimacy of God as creator and redeemer. His search for God, too, takes the form of a seeking after images and reflections of the Trinity in creation: in humans first, with their three spiritual faculties—and this will be the image properly so-called—then in sentient and even inanimate creatures in harmony with the trinity of measure, number, and weight.

As for St. Thomas, he looks at humans from his own point of view, in terms of human nature as it appears in the light of Aristotle's penetrating analyses of human faculties. Actually, it seems that the Aristotelian concept tends to diminish the intellectual memory, reducing the remembrance of concepts to a new action of the intellect upon the images retained by the sensible memory.[9] St. Thomas's view remains nuanced: there is indeed an intellectual memory, but its function is purely retentive.[10] The intellectual life, therefore, focuses on reason and will. This leads to a shift in the image of God in man. Firstly there is the relation to the act of the intellect, which utters the word and forms ideas, and then to the will, whose specific action is to love; finally, in relation to free will, which has the advantage of uniting reason and will, knowledge and love, in the act of choice. This places the image of God in the power humans have to act on their own, in mastery and moral responsibility.

Freedom for Excellence, Supporting the Image of God in the Human Person

Here we should pause for a moment. For we have come to a point in the history of theology that will be decisive for the future, particularly for the future of the theme of the image of God and for anthropology. What precisely is St. Thomas's concept of freedom, in which he sees the image of God in humans, following St. John Damascene?

St. Thomas describes freedom beginning with the definition supplied by Peter Lombard in the second book of the *Sentences:* "True free will is the faculty of reason and will, through which good is chosen with grace assisting, or evil with grace desisting."[11] For St. Thomas, free will is the faculty of reason

---

9. Cf. A. Solignac's note 14 in *Confessions,* 558.

10. Cf. *ST* I 79.6. In *De veritate* (10.1–3), he considers memory a sensitive faculty, and in a certain measure intellectual, but without being really distinct from the intellect.

11. *"Liberum verum arbitrium est facultas rationis et voluntatis, qua bonum eligitur gratia assistente, vel malum eadem desistente."* Peter Lombard, *In Sent.* II 24. 3 (Grottaferrata-Rome: Ed. Colleghi S. Bonaventurae, 1971), 452.

and of will in this sense, that it proceeds from both in such a way that choice, its proper act, is the joint work of the two faculties and includes a practical judgment and an act of the will that cannot be disassociated from one another.

That the knowledge and the will precede free will means that they are its source. The free choice will be inspired by natural inclinations or spontaneous aspirations toward truth and goodness that constitute these faculties and flow from the spiritual nature of the human person, ordering her to beatitude and in fact to God as her ultimate end. The work of free choice is to place acts which possess the quality of truth and goodness, and which thus lead the human person toward her perfection and beatitude. Free will is therefore a power, progressively formed in us, to produce moral acts of excellence. Therefore this concept can be called freedom for excellence or for perfection. Without doubt, the free will can sin. Sin is a weakness, the possibility of which is inherent in the condition of a creature. But this possibility is not connected to the very nature of free will. Creative freedom is total in God; it is also perfect in the blessed, who cannot sin. Our freedom is without doubt an imperfect participation, but it is a real participation, in the freedom of God, in such a way that the more it conforms to God through knowledge and love and grace, the more it grows as a power to perform works of excellence.

In this concept of the freedom of the human person and his faculties, St. Thomas remains faithful to ancient, philosophical, and Christian thought, and continues to provide a solid and fitting foundation to support the theme of the image of God in the human person. He firmly maintains the basic principles that were the pillars of ancient philosophy, admitted by all schools and always referred to by them, as can be seen in the philosophical dialogues of Cicero, among others. The first principle is that morality, and even philosophy in its entirety, begins with the question of beatitude and is an attempt to answer this question. Schools vary enormously as to their responses; they are unanimous as to the question. Such is, in fact, the constitutive inclination of the will: the desire for beatitude, subsuming all human desires. It should develop together with the demands of the inclination to truth. The main question therefore will be, What is true beatitude or true good? The Fathers had no difficulty in relating the desire for beatitude with the Beatitudes and promises of God. For St. Thomas, for example, the Beatitudes were the response of Christ, teacher of wisdom, to the question of beatitude to which the philosophers had not been able to find an adequate answer.

The second principle is the famous *sequi naturam* which we find so difficult to understand and which we easily calumniate. For us, "nature" stands for the physical or biological universe, or again the ontological world, that is to say, one dimension, one part of things, radically distinct from freedom and conscience, and belonging to the order of the necessary and irrational. In our minds, nature and freedom are necessarily opposed. This was not the concept of nature held by the ancients, among them Christian authors. St. Thomas does not hesitate to place nature at the origin and source of freedom. For him, we are free not in spite of but because of our natural inclinations. He means by this, however, a spiritual nature that manifests itself by the aspiration to truth, goodness, and beatitude, and by a sense of the other, expressed in a natural inclination to live in a society ordered by justice and friendship.

For St. Thomas as for his predecessors, both philosophers and theologians, nature designates a basis for man's spiritual spontaneity. It is at this level, for example, that Aristotle, thinking of Alexander, places the genius that through intuition outstrips the slow steps of reason. St. Thomas situates the gifts of the Holy Spirit similarly. To the perplexity of his modern translators, he does not hesitate to call them *"instinctus Spiritus Sancti"* sixteen times in question 68 of the *prima secundae*. St. Thomas obviously does not mean inferior instincts, but inspirations of loftier quality that enable the Christian to act with excellence under the motion of the Spirit of God.

Nevertheless, the principal action of the Holy Spirit, working in humanity on this foundation of spiritual nature which constitutes the person, does not reside in the gifts but in the chief elements of the Evangelical Law, as Thomas defines it. This Law consists primarily in the grace of the Holy Spirit received through faith in Christ and working through charity, which obviously implies hope. With the spiritual interiority of human beings as its point of departure, the action of the Holy Spirit penetrates and forms with its freedom what we might call the Christian head of the organism of the virtues: faith, hope, and charity. These receive the gifts of the Holy Spirit, but they also assume the human virtues, chief of which are prudential discernment, the will to practice justice, courage, and mastery over one's sensibility and body (or temperance). Thus is formed a vital and dynamic organism of virtues and gifts that renders man capable of collaborating with the grace of Christ in the work of sanctification.

This concept of humanity, of human nature and freedom and of the moral life and action they produce, harmonizes almost as well with the patristic theme of the image of God as with the Augustinian perspective.

The image is in the spiritual faculties God has given humans in order to render us *capax Dei,* capable of knowing and loving God and thus resembling God in the Trinitarian relationships. But the image, properly speaking, is found in the free will, which according to God's will confers upon us through the virtues and gifts mastery over our actions and other faculties, including our bodies. Thus all of our parts coordinate and converge progressively in actions of the greatest excellence, in the knowledge and love of God who conforms us directly to God's very self. Understood in this way, the theme of the image does not remain static, like a mirror reflecting a face. It is essentially dynamic: the theme of imitation necessarily completes that of image, tending to perfect the resemblance and effect the conformation.

Two Observations

1. The participation of the intellect in the image and imitation, with its acts in the order of contemplation such as wisdom or prudence, is essential here. One could simply say that imitation fulfills the image, that conformation is realized by the eyes, by the interior gaze, as much as by the heart, the one supporting and profiting by the other moreover. Also, one would seriously diminish the theme of the image if one excluded from the Christian life and from theology the contemplative dimension, that eager quest of the heart that seeks to behold the face of God with all the resources of mind and faith.

2. Again, when we speak of the free will and the virtues in order to explain the image of God, we must never forget that the very idea of the image—like the concept of free will as we have just seen—refers us back to its Exemplar and Source, to the creator God of Genesis and to the Word, Light, and Life, of John's Prologue, that is to say, to the Trinity. It is precisely this Origin, ever present and active, that produces in the human heart a hunger for beatitude and truth which cannot be satisfied without the work of the grace of Christ in the redemption and of the Holy Spirit in sanctification. The study of the image of God in the *Summa theologiae* moves from grace to grace, in the manner of St. John's Prologue, which St. Thomas has studied with particular depth, and it cannot be understood outside of this context.

Freedom of Indifference and the Decline of the Theme of the Image of God

We might stop here, or take time to clarify our description and make it more nuanced, had not a certain event occurred scarcely a generation after St. Thomas, one with incalculable effects on Western thought. We might well call it the explosion of the first atomic bomb of history, granted that the atom which exploded at this moment was not physical but psychic. With the introduction of a new concept of freedom, nominalism shattered the harmony of the human faculties, separating them from one another to give birth to a new concept of man, which would lead to the formation of a new idea and organization of morality. The freedom of indifference that William of Ockham set up in opposition to St. Thomas's analysis of freedom would determine, like a tap root, the birth of the moralities of obligation which would, generally speaking, take over and characterize the modern period, in Christian teaching as well as in philosophy.[12]

A new anthropology, with a new systematization of moral theology, began to take shape in the fourteenth century. It would not enhance the theme of the image of God; it would remove its supporting points and no longer provide a sufficient basis for it to unfold in theology. I have described it elsewhere.[13]

The time has come to assess the effects of these new views on the theme of the image of God in the human person. The idea of the image of God presupposes a certain link that we might call natural between humans and God. This link can be seen from the viewpoint of the creator of human beings in the image and likeness of God, and through natural inclinations to truth and goodness that come from God and render humans *capax Dei*. It can also be envisioned from the viewpoint of beatitude, through the actualization of this capacity under the action of grace, faith, and charity, principally by way of imitation and a growing likeness.

12. As George de Lagarde writes: "For Ockham, there is absolute separation between God and the world. God created the world, but he remains a stranger to it. There is no symbiosis between the world and God. The two realities are isolated in their respective existence. Moreover, this is nothing but the consequence of the radical insularity of all beings." (*La naissance de l'esprit laïque au déclin du Moyen Age,* vol. 6 [1942], 56). This radical insularity is the direct effect of freedom of indifference.

13. For more details, see my book, *Sources of Christian Ethics* (Washington, D.C.: Catholic University of America Press, 1995).

The theme of the image of God also presupposes harmony between our faculties, especially the spiritual faculties, and between our actions. This harmony allows them to represent, however imperfectly, the Trinitarian relationships, and to collaborate through knowledge and love in the perfection of the image.

These are the fundamental conditions for the development of the theme of the image. They are broken, destroyed, by the introduction of freedom of indifference and the concept of morality to which it leads. Division and tension are set up between a person's faculties. Their relationship will henceforth be governed by a kind of accompanying dialectic expressed by the disjunctive formula, either/or: either freedom or law with its imperatives; either freedom or reason and its determinations; either freedom or grace; and finally, either humanity or God. Here we have one of the roots of modern atheism, which opposes humans and God in an irreducible conflict.[14] This disjunctive movement will lead to a growing separation between morality—which is no longer a morality of attraction but one of voluntary pressure in the form of obligation—and the other branches of theology (i.e., dogmatic, ascetical, mystical, and biblical theology).

One can no longer speak of the image of God in connection with freedom. The image of God in humanity now consists in the sheer self-determined voluntarism that characterizes freedom of indifference. Like God and confronting God, this man takes his stance by his own will in a free act. But this independent stance is precisely what isolates human freedom from the freedom of God, and from every other freedom, leaving him in isolation. We still have an image, if you will, but one closed in on itself. It no longer seeks to expand in likeness; quite simply it either is or is not like. As for its origin, it faces a dilemma: either it is its own origin, and the only origin of its free action, like God—but then how can God be its origin? Or it recognizes God as its origin—but in this case, how is it still true freedom in the image of God? It is a question of autonomy and theonomy or heteronomy.[15]

Finally, this concept shrinks the image of God. It consists only in free will. It no longer involves the intellect or receives its support. We are dealing now with a blind image that no longer seeks to know and to see the One whom it

---

14. Cf. E. Borne, *Dieu n'est pas mort* (Paris, 1974), 36.

15. [Editor's note: See the article essay #10 in this volume, "Aquinas and Agency: Beyond Autonomy and Heteronomy?"]

images. The theme of image is robbed of its entire contemplative dimension, as is morality, which focuses on the will and on the obedience of obligation. We can truly wonder if we can still speak of an image. In any case, the theme of the image is far too diminished and anemic to be able to play a significant role in theological thought.

In my opinion this is a basic cause of the decline of the theme of the image of God in modern theology. It is due to an anthropology determined by the concept of freedom, for freedom is what human beings are, as Aristotle has already told us. But perhaps in this period of change that we are now living through, a period of crisis and of new hope, the time has come to rediscover this theme and restore it to its place. This could be very important for the much-debated issue of human rights and dignity, in keeping with the challenge of St. Leo the Great: "Awake, O man, and recognize the dignity of your nature! Remember that you were created in the image of God."[16] It is always wise to realize that such a renewal calls for theological and anthropological reflection on many things, and notably on our concept of freedom and morality.

16. Seventh Christmas Homily, n. 6; op. cit. (cf. note 3 above), 145.

9 ◌ Aquinas on the Dignity of the Human Person (1987)

Studying St. Thomas on the dignity of the human person is not a matter of mere historical interest. It can lead us to a deep penetration of our subject and the discovery of its multiple dimensions, while giving us a certain concept of the human person that is a model of outstanding quality and an authoritative witness to Christian thought.

The Context of Our Thinking

Let us briefly situate St. Thomas's reflection on the human person historically and speculatively. His teaching comes at the close of an already lengthy history. Christian theology and Greek philosophy had confronted each other throughout the patristic period; St. Thomas brings them face to face with fresh insight. Incontestably, Christian reflection had sharpened awareness and intellectual perception of the quality of the human person. The cause of this progress was, on the negative side, the defense of the faith against the great heresies inspired by Gnostic philosophy. On the positive side, it was the effort to grasp, with reason and in adequate terms, the principal Christian mysteries that directly involved the notion of person. These were the mystery of the Trinity, with its distinction of Persons, Father, Son, and Holy Spirit, and the mystery of Christ himself, in whom faith recognized one unique Person and a twofold nature. The human person, associated in the Gospel with the divinity

Originally published as "La dignité de l'homme selon Saint Thomas d'Aquin," in *De dignitate hominis* (Fribourg: Editions Universitaires, 1987), 89–106. Translated by Sr. Mary Thomas Noble, O.P., with the assistance of Craig Steven Titus. Edited for publication in *The Pinckaers Reader* by Craig Steven Titus.

of Jesus Christ, was the starting point of Christian research on the nature and quality of the person. The undertaking encountered one major difficulty: Scripture never uses the word "person." St. Thomas, following the Fathers, noticed this, and gives us his response, which clearly indicates the context to which we refer:

The word "person" cannot be found in the text of the Old or the New Testament as referring to God. Nevertheless that which is meant by the word occurs many times in Holy Scripture, namely that he is the acme of self-existence and most perfect in knowledge. Were we bound only to say of God what the holy Scripture says in so many words, it would follow that no one could ever speak of God in any language other than that in which the Old and the New Testaments were delivered. We have to look for new words about God which express the old faith because we have to argue with heretics. Nor need we avoid such innovation as profane, that is, as out of harmony with the sense of the Scriptures; what St. Paul instructs us to avoid are *profane verbal innovations* (1 Tm, last chapter).[1]

The tradition of the Fathers on our subject reached St. Thomas chiefly through St. Augustine's *De trinitate,* by way of Peter Lombard, whose *Sentences*—especially in Book I, distinction 23—furnished the basis of very active Scholastic reflection in this connection in the twelfth and thirteenth centuries. Opinions about the distinction between the terms essence, nature, substance, subsistence, hypostasis, and person proliferated. St. Thomas's own accounts testify to this.

The new contribution of Aristotle would of course be of prime importance for St. Thomas, not concerning the term "person," but rather the concept of human nature that constitutes the person, with the faculties and virtues that govern moral action, as well as relationships with other persons through justice and friendship.

It was to this vast material, still very unsettled and shifting in his day, that St. Thomas applied his genius. He drew from it a clear, precise, and perfectly ordered teaching that would serve as a foundation and point of reference for all later Catholic theology. Without doubt profound changes in the concept of man would still evolve, beginning in the fourteenth century; new and complicated discussions of the human person surfaced among theologians in the modern period. But like all great classics, St. Thomas remains a source, neces-

---

1. *ST* I 29.3 ad 1.

sary and enlightening, for Christian thinking about the human person and the dignity that enhances personhood.

My Plan

As a point of departure for our study, I have chosen the term "dignity," which is central to our subject, and have looked the word up in the Thomist Index of Father R. Busa. The harvest was more abundant than I anticipated. The Index gives 1,455 references to *"dignitas"* in various Latin cases, to which we can add 25 references to *"dignitas + Christus."*[2] A perusal of this list shows the whole range of meanings for the term *"dignitas"* and, in particular, its special application to the human person.

The Dignity of the Person

St. Thomas did not study the concept of dignity; we can only discern the idea through the variety of uses of the word in his works. But happily for us, the most remarkable and most fully developed use of the term has to do precisely with "person."

Texts from the Commentary on the Sentences

The principal texts are in Book I of the *Sentences* (23.1.1 with, 10.1.5 and 26.1.1) and in the *prima pars* of the *Summa theologiae* (I 23.3, especially ad 2, with I 40.1 ad 1). All these deal with the question of the divine Persons, and more precisely with the distinction between the apposite terms of person, essence, substance or subsistence, and hypostasis, which allows for a clear application of these notions to God and to the mystery of the Trinity. But in order to define these terms we need to begin with their meaning in our language, which is based on human experience. Person, therefore, will be defined in connection with humankind before being applied to God analogically. Our texts will thus provide us first of all with a definition of the human person.

The definition of "person" used in the *Sentences* interests us directly. It is

2. The index mentions 1,760 uses of the term "dignity," chiefly in the *Sentences* (73+ 49+76+99 times), in the *Summa theologiae* (62+34+124+124 times), in the *Summa contra Gentiles* (41 times), in the scriptural *Commentaries* on St. Matthew (70 times), on St. John (90 times), on the Letters of St. Paul, etc.

current among the Masters; we find it again in St. Bonaventure in the same place, with the same explanations. Its origin has not yet been identified. Here it is, as cited at the end of *I Sent.* 23.1.1:

Hoc nomen "persona" significat substantiam particularem, prout subjicitur proprietati quae sonat dignitatem, et similiter "prosopon" apud Graecos; et ideo "persona" non est nisi in natura intellectuali.

The beginning of this same article provides us with a variant of this definition in the course of the exposition of different opinions:

quia vel significatur ("persona") ut distinctum aliqua proprietate determinata ad nobilitatem pertinente, et sic est nomen "persona"...[3]

Person, therefore, is distinguished from other singular substances by this property that constitutes the essential characteristic in its definition: its dignity or nobility. And St. Thomas clarifies this in two words: this is why persons exist only where there is a rational nature, which is precisely the dignity of the human being.

We have here an important first consequence: person is defined by its dignity, which results from its rational nature.

St. Thomas adds an etymological explanation of the term *persona* that he has borrowed from Boethius. It is of interest to us inasmuch as it gives us an initial explanation of the association between person and dignity. *Persona* comes from *personare* (to cause to resound), because tragedians and comedians wore masks representing the characters they were portraying in their recitations and songs. You truly had to be someone prominent in society (we, too, speak of "personages") to be so represented in the theater. Actually, for the ancients the theater was a mirror, sometimes a distorting one, of society and its dignitaries. We shall find this explanation again in the *Summa,* with an addition.

---

3. Further on, in I *Sent.* 26.1.1, the two terms of "dignity" and "nobility" are joined: *"Nomen personae specialem includit distinctionem quae ad dignitatem pertinet, prout dicit quid subsistens in natura nobili, scilicet intellectuali."* In I *Sent.* 10.1.5, the affirmation *"persona est nomen dignitatis"* is used as a sort of principle.

Texts in the Summa

Treating of the divine Persons in the *prima pars* of the *Summa,* question 29, St. Thomas revisits his Commentary on the *Sentences,* clarifying and amplifying it. Yet he begins by deferring to Boethius's definition of person: "A person is an individual substance of a rational nature," cited at the beginning of Article 1 devoted to this definition. This is not to say that Aquinas abandons the definition of the Masters based on "dignity," which he had mentioned in the course of the question in I 29.3 ad 2, and in I 40.3 ad 1. On the contrary, he makes the quality of dignity a predominant element of the person.

The Definition of Person

Let us follow the line of Aquinas's exposition. Article 1 establishes the definition of person by beginning with substances which are individual in themselves and as such merit a special name, that of hypostases or first substances. However, St. Thomas adds, particularity and individuality are found in a still more special and perfect way in rational substances, which have control *(dominium)* over their actions, and are not only acted upon as other beings are, but act on their own initiative. For to act is proper to singular substances. This is why singular substances with a rational nature are given a special name, that of "person," which accords perfectly with the definition of Boethius given above.[4]

It is well to note that this reflection is undergirded by the concept of the higher perfection of a rational nature, specified and characterized by control over its actions. It acts of its own accord, demonstrating that it has being in itself and is a special kind of substance.

This way of characterizing person by control over actions refers directly to the analysis of the will, in *ST* I-II 6.1, where St. Thomas establishes the hierarchy of beings according to the power they possess over their actions, and concludes: "[m]an sets himself to do something and knows what he is about. Ac-

---

4. *"Sed adhuc quodam speciaiori et perfectiori modo invenitur particulare et individuum in substantiis rationalibus, quae habent dominium sui actus, et non solum aguntur, sicut alia, sed per se agunt; actiones autem in singularibus sunt. Et ideo etiam inter ceteras substantias etiam quoddam speciale nomen habent singularia rationalis naturae. Et hoc nomen est persona. Et ideo in praedicta definitione personae ponitur substantia individua, inquamtum significat singulare in genere substantiae; additur autem rationalis naturae, inquantum significat singulare in rationalibus substantiis." (ST* I 29.1).

cordingly voluntariness in its full sense is a quality of human acts."[5] With this power of reason and will governing his actions, we are at the source of all morality. It is precisely this control that constitutes the perfection of the person and underlies his definition.

Person, Hypostasis, etc.

When we compare the notion of person with the concepts of hypostasis, subsistence, and essence in I 29.2, once more that property of person emerges that points to what the [other] three terms designate, but in the order of rational substances. In order to explain a citation of Boethius, the response to the first objection adds that the use of the term *hypostasis* among the Greeks goes beyond the proper meaning of the term, making it designate an individual so excellent that it possesses a rational nature.[6] This is what the term "person" properly signifies for St. Thomas; again we see it characterized by the excellence of a rational nature.

Personhood in God

The study concludes, in article 3, with the application of the term "person" to God. The reasoning begins with a very significant premise: "person" signifies the height of perfection in all of nature, namely, the individual with a rational nature. If it is true that every perfection should be attributed to God, from the fact that his essence contains all perfection, then it is fitting that this name of "person" should be applied to God. Yet this attribution is not made in the same way as it is made for creatures, but in a more excellent way, as with the other divine names.[7]

The superiority of the attribution of the name of "person" to God is clari-

---

5. "*Unde, cum homo maxime cognoscat finem sui operis et moveat seipsum, in eius actibus maxime voluntarium invenitur.*" (*ST* I-II 6.1).

6. "*Ad primum ergo, dicendum quod hypostasis apud Graecos ex propria significatione nominis habet quod significet quodcumque individuum substantiae; sed ex usu loquendi habet quod sumatur pro individuo rationalis naturae, ratione suae excellentiae.*" (*ST* I 29.2).

7. "*Respondeo dicendum quod persona significat id quod est perfectissimum in tota natura, scilicet subsistens in rationali natura. Unde cum omne illud quod est perfectionis, Deo sit attribuendum, eo quod eius essentia continet in se omnem perfectionem, conveniens est ut hoc nomen persona de Deo dicatur. Non tamen eodem modo quo dicitur de creaturis, sed excellentiori modo; sicut et alia nomina, quae creaturis a nobis imposita, Deo attribuuntur, sicut supra ostensum est, cum de divinis nominibus ageretur.*" (*ST* I 29.3).

fied in ad 4, on the basis of Boethius's definition, which may cause difficulty. "Rational nature" designates, in God, his intellectual nature, beyond the limitations of the rational discourse proper to human nature. Individuality, in God, designates the incommunicability of his nature and not individuation caused by matter. Finally, substance is fitting to God since he exists of himself.[8]

It is clear that for St. Thomas the idea of perfection and of excellence is the backbone of the notion of "person." Owing to this, personhood can and should be attributed to God. Because of this, a certain hierarchy is established in personal nature, at least between humankind and God: personhood befits God in the most perfect sense. This is manifested by the supreme perfection of intelligence and will in God, that assures his full mastery over his works.

The Development of the Meaning of "Person"

The response to the second objection establishes equivalence between the terms of perfection and excellence with that of dignity used in the current definition of the Masters we have considered. The objection is based on the text of Boethius that situates the origin of the name "person" in the "personages" of the theater.[9] Clearly, this original sense would in no way be fitting to be used of God, except metaphorically.

St. Thomas begins by conceding that obviously the name of "person" does not befit God in its original sense, which was noted above. But he immediately adds that the meaning can be very well extended to its current use in theology. And he undertakes to show how we have passed from one connota-

---

8. *"Ad quartum, dicendum quod Deus potest dici rationalis naturae secundum quod ratio non importat discursum, sed communiter intelligibilem naturam. Individuum autem Deo competere non potest quantum ad hoc quod individuationis principium est materia, sed solum secundum quod importat incommunicabilitatem. Substantia vero convenit Deo secundum quod significat existere per se. Quidam tamen dicunt quod definitio superius a Boethio data, non est definitio personae secundum quod personas in Deo dicimus. Propter quod Ricardus de Sancto Victore, corrigere volens hanc definitionem, dixit quod persona, secundum quod de Deo dicitur, est 'divinae naturae incommunicabilis existentia.'"* (*ST* I 29.3 ad 4).

9. The etymological dictionary of Oscar Bloch and Walter von Wartburg *(Dictionnaire étymologique de la langue français)* connects the Latin term *persona* with an Etruscan origin meaning "a theatrical mask." It means "personage" and, from the classical period, simply "person." In ecclesiastical and juridical Latin it has taken on various meanings that have passed into the romance languages. In the thirteenth century, the derivation "personage" had the sense of an ecclesiastical office. Cf. the English "parsonage" (cure) and "parson" (curate)—at first the holder of a benefice. This often occurs in old French, preserved in the Breton *"person."*

tion to the other. Since in comedies and tragedies famous men were represented, the word "person" came to be used of men of high rank in the city. He adds that it then became customary in the ecclesiastical world, a thing already mentioned by St. Bonaventure (*I Sent.* 23.1.1): this is how persons of rank and dignity in the Church were referred to. This is why, he adds, some theologians define "person" by saying that a person is "a hypostasis distinguished by dignity."[10] And he concludes: because to subsist in rational nature is a characteristic implying dignity, every individual with rational nature is called "person." Of course the dignity of divine nature surpasses all other, and so it is completely fitting to use "person" of God.[11]

The thought process is very interesting. It shows us the principal stages, historical and speculative, of the evolution of the meaning of the term "person." From the level of the theater, the mirror of society for the Greeks, we pass on to the level of civil, and then ecclesiastical, society in the Middle Ages. In the works of St. Thomas we find many uses of the term "dignity" to designate lofty personages or dignitaries in civil society—chief among them the king—and in ecclesiastical society, where bishops ranked highest. You may recall that in the Middle Ages only nobles had names.

But the evolution does not stop there. Influenced by philosophical, and above all theological, reflection, the term "person" came to designate everyone, since everyone possesses the dignity of human nature. And from that point it rose to qualify, in the light of faith, the divine nature, precisely because of the excellence of its dignity as the source of all dignity.

Here the powerful influence of Christian thought on language is apparent. The term "person" is given a real impetus to transcend its original and then its

10. The Canadian edition of the *Summa theologiae* gives, for this definition, a reference to Alain de Lille, *Theologiae Regulae,* regula 32 (*PL* v. 210, col. 637), but unfortunately I could not find it. Let me add that the definition is also quoted in the *"Contra errores Graecorum"* of 1263, and in the question *"De unione Verbi incarnatis,"* probably written in 1272.

11. *"Ad secundum, dicendum quod, quamvis hoc nomen persona non conveniat Deo quantum ad id a quo impositum est nomen, tamen quantum ad id ad quod significandum imponitur, maxime Deo convenit. Quia enim in comoediis et tragoediis repraesentabantur aliqui homines famosi, impositum est hoc nomen persona ad significandum aliquos dignitatem habentes. Unde consueverunt dici personae in ecclesiis, quae habent aliquam dignitatem. Propter quod quidam definiunt personam, dicentes quod 'persona est hypostasis proprietate distincta ad dignitatem pertinente'. Et quia magnae dignitatis est in rationali natura subsistere, ideo omne individuum rationalis naturae dicitur persona, ut dictum est. Sed dignitas divinae naturae excedit omnem dignitatem, et secundum hoc maxime competit Deo nomen personae."* (*ST* I 29.3 ad 2).

social meaning, to rise to a universal level, and finally to be applied to the God of Revelation in his most intimate mystery, to the Persons of the Trinity. This is a unique destiny for a term not found in Scripture but forged by the most authentic tradition, beginning with the great Councils, to signify, beyond words, the most profound reality, the most secret place where God encounters us, speaks with us, and manifests God's own self to us.

Personal Relationships between God and Humans

I should like to add a clarification about the relationships between God and humans that are established by the qualification of "person." The differences between personality in human beings and in God, which enable us to speak of a hierarchy, still do not establish any breach or opposition, as would be the case in modern thought, where a person is in some sort defined by a difference and opposition in regard to other persons. In St. Thomas's exposition, the passage from the human person to the Person in God is made quite naturally, without any notion of concurrence, as a passage from a natural excellence or dignity to the supreme excellence. The limitations of the human realization of the person simply do not exist in God. The possibility of communication between man and God is not diminished by these differences, but rather reinforced. We already perceive that for St. Thomas the human person is not closed in upon himself but open to God; his dignity increases because of his resemblance to the divine personality.

Thomas's *Commentary on the Sentences* (Book 1) shows clearly how communication with the divine infinity increases the dignity of the person: the closer the union with God, the greater is the human person's excellence. Regarding distinction 44, question 1, St. Thomas wonders, in connection with the power of God, whether God could have created better things than he did, and especially the humanity of Christ. St. Thomas answers by distinguishing two points of view: 1) the creature taken in itself, and from this aspect it is complete and can always receive greater perfection; 2) the creature in relation to the uncreated good, and from this aspect the dignity of the creature receives a certain infinity of the infinite with which it is bonded, as in these four instances: the human nature united to God in Christ; the Blessed Virgin, as Mother of God; the grace that unites us to God; and everything insofar as it is ordered to God. From this a certain order results, according to which greater nobility follows upon greater union with God: human nature is at its noblest in Christ because of his unique union with God; next comes the Blessed Virgin because the Word became flesh in her womb, and so forth.[12] Personal union with God, therefore, gives to human nature a participation in the infinity of the divine dignity. Thus we are led to study another instance in which a person receives a particular dignity, that of Christ through the hypostatic union.

The Person in Christ

The case of Christ poses a new theological problem, which touches directly on the notion of person. According to the teaching of Chalcedon, in Christ human nature is united to the divine nature in the very Person of the Word. This article of the Creed spurred theology on to a new deepening of the notion of person, defined according to Boethius by the rational nature of man. The problem is treated in the form of a question: Was human nature more capable of being assumed by the Son of God than any other nature? We find it at the beginning of Book III of the *Sentences* (2.1), and at the beginning of the *tertia pars* of the *Summa* (III 4.1). I shall speak only of the text of the *Summa*, where the teaching is fuller and where we can better verify the notion of person and its dignity.

St. Thomas clarifies the position of the question by a distinction: the personal union of a creature with God obviously surpasses all passive power in the order of nature; but the problem can be posed in the form of fittingness *(congruentia)* between human nature and such a union. St. Thomas recognizes two indications of the fittingness of human nature having personal union with God, a dignity and a need. The dignity proper to human nature: because it is rational and intelligent, human nature can by its operation reach the Word himself in a certain measure, by knowing and loving him. The argument is

12. "*Respondeo dicendum, quod sicut quolibet bono creato, eo quod finitum est, potest aliquid melius esse, ita bono increato, eo quod infinitum est, nihil melius esse potest. Et ideo bonitas creaturae dupliciter considerari potest. Aut quae est ipsius in se absolute, et sic qualibet creatura potest esse aliquid melius; aut per comparationem ad bonum increatum, et sic dignitas creaturae recipit quadam infinitatem ex infinito cui comparatur, sicut humana natura in quantum est unita Deo, et beata Virgo inquantum est Mater Dei, et gratia inquantum conjungit Deo, et universum inquantum est ordinatum in Deum. Sed tamen in istis comparationibus est etiam ordo duplex: primo, quia quanto nobiliori comparatione in Deum refertur, nobilius est; et sic humana natura in Christo nobilissima est: quia per unionem comparatur ad Deum, et post beata Virgo, de cujus utero caro divinitati unita, assumpta est, et sic deinceps . . .*" (I Sent. 44.1.4).

based on the dignity proper to a rational nature, according to the definition of the Masters mentioned above in question 2, article 2, argument 2, referring to the *prima pars*. St. Thomas here clarifies this dignity by affirming the capacity to know and love God that is at the origin of moral action and that we find once more in the theme of the image of God in man. It is this capacity that distinguishes human beings from nonrational creatures. It is the foundation for the special fittingness of his personal union with God of which we are speaking.

As to need as an indication of this fittingness: it flows from human nature's need of redemption since being burdened with original sin. For angels, in contrast, the appropriateness based on need is lacking.[13]

This last reason is of interest in our study because it evokes the historical condition of the dignity of man with its variations in salvation history: the degradation of this dignity by the original fall and its unexpected restoration and increase through the redemption of Christ.

The Dignity of the Person of Christ

Before reaching this point, however, St. Thomas answers a major objection in *ST* III 2.2 ad 2: if the person is defined by his dignity, would it not be fitting that Christ, even more than we, should have a human personality? The answer shows on the contrary that human nature receives a greater dignity and perfection through its union with the Person of the Word than through a simply human personhood. It is more perfect for man to exist in a nobler being, as is the Word of God, than to exist in himself. Here again the notion of person is as it were expanded in order to be adapted to the mystery of Christ, for in itself "person" signifies existence by itself.[14]

13. "*Respondeo dicendum quod aliquid assumptibile dicitur quasi aptum assumi a divina persona. Quae quidem aptitudo non potest intelligi secundum potentiam passivam naturalem, quae non se extendit ad id quod transcendit ordinem naturalem, quem transcendit unio personalis creaturae ad Deum. Unde relinquitur quod assumptibile aliquid dicatur secundum congruentiam ad unionem praedictam. Quae quidem congruentia attenditur secundum duo in humana natura, scilicet secundum eius dignitatem et necessitatem. Secundum dignitatem quidem quia humana natura, inquantum est rationalis et intellectualis, nata est contingere aliqualiter ipsum Verbum per suam operationem, cognoscendo scilicet et amando ipsum. Secundum necessitatem autem, quia indigebat reparatione, cum subiaceret originali peccato. Haec autem duo soli humanae naturae conveniunt, nam creaturae irrationali deest congruitas; naturae autem angelicae deest congruitas praedictae necessitatis. Unde relinquitur quod sola natura humana sit assumptibilis.*" (*ST* III 4.1).

14. *ST* III 2.2, obj.2: "*Praeterea: Natura humana non est minoris dignitatis in Christo quam*

The hypostatic union confers on the human person, therefore, a new, incomparable dignity. This will be shown in the study of the mystery of the Incarnation and Redemption.

One of the reasons for the Incarnation given in *ST* III 1.2 is "to teach us about the great dignity of human nature, so that we will avoid marring it by sin." This argument had been used in Book IV, chapter 54 of the *Summa contra Gentiles,* in a different way that points up the moral dimension:

This dignity of humanity—namely, that in the immediate vision of God true beatitude is to be found—was most suitably manifested by God's own immediate assumption of human nature. And we look upon this consequence of God's Incarnation: a large part of humankind passing beyond the cult of the angels, of demons, and all creatures whatsoever, spurning, indeed, the pleasures of the flesh and all things bodily, have dedicated themselves to the worship of God alone, and in God only they look for the fulfillment of this beatitude.[15]

The argument from the dignity of humanity is among the reasons given for the Passion of Christ: just as a human was conquered and deceived by the devil, so it was a human who conquered the devil; and as a human had deserved death, a human also triumphed over death by accepting death (ST III 46.3).

From the dignity of a human nature personally united to the Word flow the prerogatives of Christ: the fullness of grace which he possesses, due notably to "the nobility of his soul, whose operations attain to God in the greatest proximity through knowledge and love" (ST III 7.1), the dignity of being the head of the mystical body, which is comparable to royal dignity (ST III 8.1 and *Super evangelium s. Ioannis,* ch. 1, lect. 8.3), and the power to judge all things (ST III 59.4). The ascension of Christ likewise flows from the dignity of his personal union with God, which surpasses the dignity of all spiritual sub-

---

in nobis. Personalitas autem ad dignitatem pertinet, ut in Primo habitum est. Cur ergo natura humana in nobis propriam personalitatem habeat, multo magis habuit propriam personalitatem in Christo." ST III 2.2 ad 2: *"Ad secundum dicendum quod personalitas intantum pertinet ad dignitatem alicuius rei et perfectionem, inquantum ad dignitatem alicuius rei et perfectionem eius pertinet quod per se existat; quod in nomine personae intelligitur. Dignius autem est alicui quod existat in aliquo, se digniori, quam quod existat per se. Et ideo ex hoc ipso humana natura dignior est in Christo quam in nobis, quia in nobis quasi per se existens propriam personalitatem habet, in Christo autem existit in persona Verbi . . ."*

15. See also *De rationibus fidei,* c. 5, and *Compendium theologiae,* vol. I, c. 201.

stances (ST III 57.5). It is also because of this personal dignity that the gift of his life won our salvation, because of its infinite value (III 48.2).

We cannot linger over this point, which is the principle of all of Christology and salvation history. I shall only mention a text from the *Commentary on the Letter to the Hebrews* (ch. I, lect. 2) which, in connection with the eminent dignity of Christ, describes the components of dignity. Three things are needed to confer dignity: wisdom—the wisdom of Christ was Wisdom itself, "the splendor of glory"; nobility—Christ is "the figure of the substance of God"; might and power—Christ sustains all things by the power of his Word.

The Dignity of the Human Person Created in the Image of God

A final theme, that of the human person created in the image of God according to his rational nature, will permit us to perceive the richness and the implications of human dignity in St. Thomas.

The theme, of Augustinian origin, is broached in the *Sentences,* distinction 16. In article 2, St. Thomas shows how the image of God is properly found in rational creatures. Among all creatures that bear a resemblance to God, the last and the loftiest is the one that shares in intellectual dignity, because this presupposes all the other forms of participation. Also, an intellectual nature attains to an imitation of God that could, in a certain way, be called specific. This is why we place in the same operation the ultimate beatitude of the intellectual nature and the beatitude of God, that is, in intellectual contemplation. The intellectual creature alone can be said to be in the image of God.[16] The human being therefore possesses personal dignity because of this intellectual or rational nature, and personal dignity also confers the privilege of being in the image of God.

The theme is clarified in I 93. "Image" designates an expressive resem-

---

16. "*Respondeo dicendum, quod, ut dictum est, illa imitatio rationem imaginis constituit quae est in aliquo ad speciem pertinente. Ex primo autem et communi nihil sortitur speciem, sed ex ultimo et proprio, sicut est differentia constitutiva. Consideratis autem divinae bonitatis processibus in creaturis, quibus naturae creatae constituuntur in similitudinem naturae increatae, ultima invenityr intellectualis dignitatis participatio, et quae omnes alias praesupponat et ideo intellectualis natura attingit ad imitationem divinam, in qua quodammodo consistit species naturae ejus; et inde est quod in eadem operatione ponimus ultimam felicitatem intellectualis creaturae, in qua est felicitas Dei, scilicet in contemplatione intellective; et ideo sola intellectualis creatura rationabiliter ad imaginem Dei dicitur esse.*"

blance to someone; but it can be imperfect. Such is the case with the image of God in the human person. Because of this imperfection, Scripture simply says that the human person was made "in the image of God" (a. 1). It is because of their ultimate resemblance among all creatures, insofar as they share not only being and life, but wisdom and knowledge, that human persons are properly called the image of God, as rational creatures (a. 2). Herein lies the dignity of human nature (ad 2).

The theme will be brought up again in III 4.1, which we have looked at, in regard to Christ's assumption of human nature:

> The likeness of image is found in humans insofar as they have a capacity for God, i.e., for attaining God by the distinctive activities of knowledge and love . . . But union with God in personal union is far greater and more perfect than union through activity.[17]

A comparison throws light on the degrees of the image of God: the image of a king in his son (this would be the case of Christ who is, properly speaking, "the Image") is one thing; quite another is his representation on an engraving (an imperfect image, as in the human person).

The Dynamism of the Image of God in the Human Person

Although the image of God in the human person is imperfect, it can grow and perfect itself. This is what the rest of question 93 shows us. The image of God in us is not static, as we might think judging from the images we make through engraving, painting, or photography. It is dynamic, because human nature is the principle of personal action, capable of moving toward God and conforming itself to God through the intellect and a loving will. The image of God in the human person is therefore destined to change, to pass from imperfection to perfection through personal action.

Similarly, and as an exact parallel, the dignity of the human person is not static, something acquired once and for all. It too is destined to grow precisely as we grow in resemblance to God through knowledge and love.

Let us recall the main points of St. Thomas's explanation of the growth of the image of God in the human person. It will take place according to the progress of the imitation of God through knowledge and love, bearing on both

17. See also *ST* II-II 175.1 ad 1.

the divine nature and the Persons of the Trinity. We can distinguish three stages in the resemblance to God (a. 4). The first is given to us by reason of our rational nature and consists in its aptitude for knowing and loving God. This pertains to every human person. This point could be developed in connection with the natural inclinations to the truth, goodness, and social life, which are proper to a rational nature (I-II 94.2). This is the fundamental, indestructible image; it is also our highest dignity, which cannot be lost. Our rational nature and natural inclinations underlie the quality of being a human person.

The second stage lies in the conformity to God that a person acquires in this life under the action of grace, through actions and virtues. This progressive conformation to God through grace has its source in the substance of the soul and unfolds actively through faith, hope, and charity principally. It is the entire work of the Christian moral life.

The third stage lies in perfect knowledge and love of God reserved for the beatitude to which we aspire. This will be the perfect image, the resemblance in glory.

The dignity of *the just* and of *the saints* corresponds to the second and third stages. In this connection I quote a beautiful text from the *Commentary on Psalm 32,* which dates from the end of St. Thomas's life:

After having exhorted the just to rejoice [the psalmist] shows their dignity . . . The dignity of the saints is the highest because they alone have arrived at the point that human beings naturally long to reach . . . If one or two persons were to arrive where all wish to be (we may think of the summit of a mountain), this would be a great honor *(dignitas)*. Now, all wish to tend toward that beatitude which, however, only some have reached: they will obtain it perfectly in the future, and now only an inchoate manner and in hope.

The dynamism of the theme of the image of God reaches its culminating point at the end of the analysis, in I 93.7 and 93.8. The image of God in us is strongest in our actions, even more than in our virtues, because thus our resemblance to the Persons of the Trinity is greatest, to the Word who proceeds from the Father and to Love who is the Holy Spirit. And this likeness is most perfect when our acts of knowledge and love focus directly upon God and the divine Persons.

Thus the perfection of resemblance to God corresponds to the highest exercise of our most personal faculties, in actions that unite us most intimately to the divine Persons. Herein lies precisely the highest human dignity, in direct participation in the dignity of God through the power of grace.

The Loss of Dignity

Human dignity is dynamic. It tends to grow, but it can also diminish and be lost, and then regained through penitence.

The basis of teaching on this subject is furnished by the study of the effects of sin, in *ST* I-II 85. St. Thomas distinguishes three kinds of natural goods:

1. the very principles of human nature with its properties, that is, our rational nature with its faculties. This is the first and principal foundation of human dignity. These goods cannot be destroyed, nor even diminished by sin. Natural human dignity therefore subsists beneath sin.

2. the natural inclination to virtue constituted by the natural inclinations to truth and goodness. It is a question of the dynamism that tends to develop human dignity by ordering and conforming it to its ultimate end, beatitude in God. Sin, which is directly opposed to virtue, diminishes this natural good. We can even measure the gravity of sins and the degradation they produce, by the excellence and dignity of the virtues to which they are opposed (I-II 73.4). Nevertheless, sin cannot entirely destroy the natural inclination to virtue, for it is firmly attached to reason itself. Now, with reason, the very capacity to sin will be lifted (I-II 73.2).

3. the gift of original justice given to the first man. This natural good was completely lost through original sin. We rediscover here the evoking of salvation history that will achieve the restitution of a higher dignity through the Incarnation, Redemption, and the gift of grace.

Sin, therefore, however grave, does not destroy the dignity of the human person, but diminishes it by blocking its dynamism in some way and preventing it from developing itself through virtue in the sense of truth and goodness.[18]

Again, we can connect the dignity of the human person with what St. Tho-

---

18. Among the sins especially related to dignity, we could mention acceptance of persons, which consists in attaching undue importance to some quality or dignity of a person and is contrary to distributive justice (ST II-II 63).

mas says of the stain *(macula peccati)* which is the effect of sin (I-II 86). This stain deprives a person of the beauty and brilliance provided by the light of reason that directs actions, and the reflection of the divine light, that is, of the wisdom and grace that perfect conduct. The stain impedes a certain delicacy of soul that love produces.

The Dignity of the Human Person and the Death Penalty

We need to say a word now about a vigorous and delicate text related to the sinner's loss of dignity. It is the question of the death penalty: is it lawful to put sinners to death? We need not treat the problem from the sinner's own point of view. St. Thomas is obviously thinking of crimes punished by death by civil law in the society of his own day, where this penalty was commonly applied. The third objection holds that to put a human being to death is an evil in itself, which can never be done even for a good end.

At a first reading, St. Thomas's answer shocks us:

When a man sins he cuts himself off from the order of reason and loses his human dignity in this sense, that being naturally free and existing for himself, he falls in a certain way into the slavery of animals, so that one may dispose of him as is required for the utility (good) of others . . . Therefore, although it is evil to kill a man possessed of human dignity, it may yet be good to kill a sinner as it is to kill an animal. Actually, an evil man may be worse and more harmful than a beast, as the Philosopher says.[19]

Obviously, this text does not harmonize with our times. It has to be understood in light of a different social situation and sensibilities. St. Thomas goes on to clarify his point by saying that only legitimate civil authority may impose the death penalty.

But there is still a problem for us. Does not St. Thomas admit here that a sin, a crime, can deprive some humans of their dignity as human persons and lower them to the level of an animal, which seems to run counter to what we have just seen: that sin can never destroy reason, nor a person's natural incli-

---

19. *"Homo peccando ab ordine rationis recedit: et ideo decidit a dignitate humana, prout scilicet homo est naturaliter liber et propter seipsum existens, et incidit quodammodo in servitutem bestiarum, ut scilicet de ipso ordinetur secundum quod est utile aliis; [. . .] Et ideo quamvis hominem in sua dignitate manentem occidere sit secundum se malum, tamen hominem peccatorem occidere potest esse bonum, sicut occidere bestiam: peior enim est malus homo bestia, et plus nocet, ut Philosophus dicit."* (*ST* II-II 64.2 ad 3).

nation to virtue, and thus cannot rob persons of their fundamental human dignity?

At first sight, the contradiction between the texts is flagrant. However, when we look closely we see that they are moving at different levels. Our text, like the whole question of the death penalty, is situated clearly on the social level evoked by the state of freedom, which St. Thomas declares to be natural—let us note it well—and the state of servitude. It is, therefore, precisely a question of dignity, we shall say of the rights, at the core of society. This is properly speaking the dignity or the right that the criminal loses.

On the contrary, the teaching that we have exposed on the dignity of the human person and on sin is situated precisely on the anthropological and moral planes at the level of universal human nature.

This difference of levels explains, in my opinion, the difference in the expressions used by St. Thomas. However, it does not completely resolve the problem at hand; for we cannot totally separate these two levels, in any case not for St. Thomas, and we may well wonder whether the personal dignity recognized on the moral plane does not lead us to recognize a fundamental social dignity, crime notwithstanding. But we do not have to solve this problem here. Let us note, all the same, that for St. Thomas human dignity includes the obligation to conform to reason in moral action and on the social level. Crime runs counter to this and explains his severity in regard to the death penalty.

The Restoration of Dignity through the Sacrament of Reconciliation

Let me mention, finally, the restoration of dignity offered to us in the sacrament of Reconciliation. Shortly before breaking off the *Summa* (III 89), St. Thomas shows how Penance can give us a twofold dignity, in both the moral and ecclesial order. In the moral order, we need to distinguish between the dignity of the children of God that confers grace on us and raises us up from sin, and the dignity of innocence. The first is given us in the sacrament of Reconciliation, but the second cannot be. However, reconciliation can give us something more than innocence, in keeping with the Gospel saying that there is more joy in heaven over the finding of the sheep that was lost than over the other hundred [*sic*]. As for ecclesial dignity, this consists in the ability to assume charges and positions of dignity in the Church. This is of less concern to us.

Conclusion

Our study of the uses of the term "dignity" in St. Thomas has provided us with rich and interesting material. Its principal use has to do with the person: "dignity" is a part of the very definition of person as a quality proper to a rational nature. This dignity takes on a higher dimension in the case of the divine Persons and the person of Christ, the study of which contributes greatly to theological progress in reflecting on the person. A person's dignity flows from his being made in the image of God and this resemblance is developed through virtue and acts conforming to reason and grace, particularly when their object is God himself and the divine Persons. This dignity, however, is also diminished by sin and can be restored through the sacrament of Reconciliation. The principal stages of salvation history have to do with human dignity: the loss of original justice in Adam with its harmful consequences, then restoration through Christ, and the gift of a higher dignity in the Incarnation and Redemption.

The term "dignity" has many other additional uses: in civil society it designates noble personages, especially kings, and this is doubtless its first meaning historically; in the Church it designates those appointed to offices, especially bishops, but also the just and saints.

The Characteristics of Dignity According to St. Thomas

Having considered this vast panorama, I shall in closing point out those characteristics of the concept of dignity as applied to the human person which I find in St. Thomas.

1. The depth of the study. It passes beyond the social level to the philosophical and theological plane where the essence of the human being before God is treated, where we come to the moral responsibility of the person, properly speaking, face to face with the Word of God. It transcends, therefore, the level of law, as well as that of the human sciences dealing with external relations between persons, in which the very notion of "person" risks being lost.

2. The open-endedness of the concept of the person and his dignity. The human person is naturally open to God and to the divine Persons, thanks to the Person of Christ, and shares in their higher dignity. This open-endedness extends to other persons, who share a rational nature, and particularly to the just and to saints through communion in Christ. We are in no sense dealing

here with a concept of personhood closed in upon itself, claiming its own dignity as over against God, society, and other persons.

3. The dynamic character of personal dignity. The dignity of the human person naturally tends to unfold and develop through action conformed to reason and virtue, in view of its ultimate end: blessedness in God. This is compromised by sin. Human dignity thus includes profound moral demands that are constant and precise, in the sense of truth and goodness. It is not limited to a static quality maintained throughout.

4. Finally, according to St. Thomas, dignity includes in all its uses an essential note of high quality, nobility, perfection, and excellence. This is in accord with his concept of the human person, and more precisely, of freedom: being based on the natural inclinations to truth and goodness, human freedom tends spontaneously toward quality, perfection, and excellence and is diminished by evil. We could say that human freedom achieves its own dignity through the quality of its actions.

Modern concepts based on freedom of indifference are totally different. Freedom of indifference establishes itself above every natural inclination, even the rational order, and as its name suggests, claims to be indifferent to quality, since it has absolute power to choose between contraries. In this case, personal dignity is constricted within the sheer claim to freedom.

According to St. Thomas, dignity contributes to establishing a certain hierarchy among the faculties and virtues, as among the functions at the heart of society, but this is so in view of the good of the human person or of the common good, of the harmony and progress of the whole, that is, of the judicious development of equal dignity recognized in all persons.

From the viewpoint of freedom of indifference, all hierarchy is perceived as a contradiction, an offense against equality and dignity based on the sole claim of personal freedom.

Clearly, the thought of St. Thomas can help us to discuss very timely problems by giving us new insights, causing us to reflect on the precious gifts we risk neglecting. But above all it makes us aware of these fundamental contributions of the great Christian tradition: a sense of the irreducible and basic dignity of the human person, exalted in Christ and called to communion with the divine Persons and with all human persons, through the theologal and moral virtues and under the impulse of grace.

SECTION III   Moral Agency

10 ❧ Aquinas and Agency

Beyond Autonomy and Heteronomy?   (1978)

The question of autonomy and heteronomy in moral theology is a contemporary one with vast implications. It is connected with the question of Christian morality, its existence and specificity, and with the correlative problem of the constitution of an autonomous rational morality of universal relevance that would provide criteria for regulating action in a pluralistic society like ours, where believers must live and work with nonbelievers.

I propose in these few pages to look into the question of autonomy and heteronomy in St. Thomas, since he is considered to be one of the principal representatives of Christian moral tradition. At the least, I would like to offer some reflections and useful comments to aid such research, a work obviously too extensive to be contained within the present limits of space.

I think we need to reflect first of all on the actual question we wish to present to St. Thomas: autonomy or heteronomy? This is a modern question. As defined in the Kantian tradition, it seems to take the form of a dilemma: *either* autonomy *or* heteronomy, with a leaning toward autonomy. I wonder whether the question, formulated in this way, is suitable for St. Thomas, or if he would have put it this way. As a matter of fact, interpreters of Aquinas have been able to find in his teaching elements favorable to the autonomy of morality, such as his insistence on the legislative function of the human reason, and others of a heteronomic nature, such as his placing outside of the human person, in God,

Originally published as "Autonomie et hétéronomie selon saint Thomas d'Aquin," in *Dimensions éthiques de la liberté* (Fribourg: Editions Universitaires, 1978), 104–23. Translated by Sr. Mary Thomas Noble, O.P., with the assistance of Craig Steven Titus. Edited for publication in *The Pinckaers Reader* by Craig Steven Titus.

the ultimate end considered as the supreme criterion of morality, and his declaration that all legislation derives from the eternal law.

Furthermore, we need to take into account the question posed in the overall organization of moral theology established by our author. For example, the meaning and function of justice are not the same in Plato or Aristotle, in St. Augustine or St. Thomas, and in Kant, Hegel, or Marx, because their systematizations differ. The system of morality proposed by Thomas is vastly different from that of Kant, or of modern Catholic moralists, and this naturally has repercussions for the question of autonomy and heteronomy.

Although it is not possible to go into detail, I should like to indicate in Part I of this essay three historical events in Catholic tradition intervening between Aquinas's day and ours that had direct consequences for the systematization of morality and for our question. We need to consider these if we want to interpret St. Thomas correctly and align ourselves with him, as well as with the patristic tradition he represents so well. We shall then see, in Part II, what answer is given to us in the treatise on the Evangelical Law, which is one of the high points, too often neglected, of the moral exposition in the *Summa theologiae*.

I. The Changes in Moral Theology from St. Thomas to Our Day

Nominalism

Nominalism instigated a veritable revolution in the structuring of moral theology in the fourteenth century, to such a point that it created a real break between the preceding centuries and our own. Here we will consider two main characteristics of nominalism as it affected moral theology.

Two Concepts of Freedom. Nominalism produced a new concept of freedom as a choice between contraries that emanated from the will alone, known as freedom of indifference. It removed from the realm of freedom every natural inclination, including the desire for beatitude as our ultimate end, so essential in St. Thomas. Henceforth this inclination was to be subject to choice between contraries. Nominalism also broke the bonds between freedom and what could, outside of itself, be based on natural inclinations: reason, law, sensitivity, and other people, even God. Freedom became an enclosed atom, an isolated island, a monad. From that time on, it best affirmed itself by claiming independence of everything other than itself. It was in constant tension, if not opposition, in regard to everything outside itself, particularly the law.

This concept of freedom had direct consequences for our subject: it created a dilemma in regard to the two terms, autonomy and heteronomy. Either a moral system was autonomous, centered on the human person, and precisely on his freedom to claim radical independence in his choice of external things, or it was heteronomous and subjected his freedom, in one way or another, to a rule, a law, to alien obligations. No middle way or compromise was possible; one had to choose between autonomy and heteronomy.

Like the ancients, St. Thomas knew no such concept of freedom as that of nominalism, even though the latter had its forerunners in some of the current opinions of his day, particularly those of the Franciscans. For Aquinas, freedom was rooted in the natural inclinations which animate the spiritual human faculties: the inclination to truth for the intellect, to beatitude and goodness for the will, the inclination to live in the society of other persons, the natural desire for God, and so forth. According to Thomas, the human person was not free in spite of these natural inclinations, needing to resist them in order to rule them, but was free precisely because of the natural inclinations to truth, beatitude, and goodness, which opened the mind and heart to infinite dimensions and conferred the ability to freely transcend every limited good.

From this perspective, nature—and here we are speaking of spiritual nature—is not opposed to freedom like something alien and threatening; on the contrary, it lends it its own vital power. Thus freedom is affirmed and developed through its conformity to truth, beatitude, and goodness. Proceeding from this interior guiding light and the love that inspires it, freedom is ordered to outward reality—whether it be the neighbor, God, nature, or the body—in a relationship of harmony and collaboration. Morality proceeding from this kind of concept will have at its foundation, thanks to the natural inclinations—whose first expression will be the natural law—and as its end, the ideal of harmony and active convergence, whatever divisions and contrarieties may arise at the heart of the moral life and in the inevitable spiritual combat. Here we have, therefore, an "open" concept of freedom that establishes a natural joining of the will to the other faculties of the human person and to the outer world.

As a result of this, the dilemma between autonomy and heteronomy loses its radicality. The fact that the first origin and ultimate end of morality transcend the human person and lie in God in no way hinders morality from having its source within the person, who having a spiritual nature is capable of sharing directly in the legislative action of God. The more one submits to God in accordance with one's natural inclinations to truth and goodness, the more capable one becomes of self-direction and the freer one becomes also as a person, sharing in the divine freedom. Here we have a direct application of the biblical concept of the human person made in the image of God, mentioned in the prologue of the *secunda pars*.

We have to admit, however paradoxical it may sound, that the more one submits to the divine heteronomy, the more autonomous one becomes. That is to say, the more one follows the natural sense of truth and goodness that carries one toward God, and the more one opens oneself to God, the greater will be one's self-fulfillment and one's ability through wisdom and love to be one's own legislator and provider, and to exercise these roles in regard to other persons as well. This also seems to me to be the meaning of the Thomistic saying, "Grace does not destroy nature, but perfects it."[1] The more one surrenders to grace the more one is fulfilled, even on the natural level; the more fully one gives oneself to God, the more fully one becomes oneself.

Therefore, if we look for St. Thomas's answer to the question of autonomy and heteronomy in moral theology, we cannot express it in terms of a clear-cut dilemma: either autonomy or heteronomy. Rather, we need to give an open form to the question—*both* autonomy *and* heteronomy, without a necessary opposition between them—and to look for the harmony Thomas establishes between these two terms, that is, between divine legislative action and that of human reason.

Two Concepts of Morality. A second important result of nominalism has had repercussions throughout our entire moral tradition. It has made the sentiment of obligation central for morality and has reconstructed morality around this center, erecting as poles human freedom with its actions on one side and on the other absolute and sovereign divine freedom, whose moral law expresses sheer will with the force of obligation. Henceforth, morality will be defined by its relation to obligation. An action is good if it conforms to obligation and, according to Ockham, if it is performed for the sake of this conformity itself. An action is evil if it is contrary to obligation. With nominalism, we have the first appearance and propagation of a morality of obligation in history.

This concept of morality would become classic in moral theology textbooks from the seventeenth century on. Their subject matter would be organ-

1. Cf. *ST* I 1.8 ad 2; I 2.2 ad 1.

ized chiefly according to the laws and commandments (of God, the Church, and canon law) that detailed obligations. It would cover obligations but stop there, omitting from moral theology properly so-called, for example, spirituality and mystical theology, which went beyond obligations.

Moral questions from then on would focus on laws, norms, commandments, or obligatory precepts. The question of autonomy and heteronomy would affect the foundations and criteria of moral norms and obligations. The problem of Christian morality would be viewed, from within, as dealing with the precepts contained in the New Testament as compared with those of the Old Law and non-Christian or philosophical systems.

Now, strange as it may seem to us today—accustomed as we are to thinking of morality in terms of obligations—such a concept was completely foreign to Aquinas, just as it was to the patristic tradition, whether theological or philosophical, that preceded him. For St. Thomas, as for Aristotle and St. Augustine among others, the first and central question in moral theology was the question of beatitude, true beatitude, expressive of the natural inclinations to goodness and truth that are at the source of free human action. Moral theology therefore extended to all human actions as they were ordered to truth, goodness, and beatitude, and included as one of its principal parts the spirituality that seeks moral perfection. The subject matter of moral theology would be divided according to the virtues, seen as the interior and personal principles of action that develop the natural human inclinations so as to render them capable of acting with perfection—with spontaneity, ease, and freedom. Precepts and obligations would drop to a second level and would be placed at the service of the virtues as particularly useful elements in the first stages of training in virtue. We could almost say that obligations were viewed here as props or crutches for the virtues. The precepts would chiefly indicate what was necessary to virtue and its progress, that without which it could not exist, but they were destined to be surpassed by virtue and would not provide an overall view of what made up moral value. Morality would no longer be defined in terms of obligation, but by true goodness and true beatitude, established by the joining of reason to will, the latter always being understood as the faculty of love and desire.

St. Thomas's moral theology is therefore based on beatitude and the virtues, the latter being grouped around faith, charity, and the cardinal virtues. This explains the minimal space given to moral obligation in the *Summa*.

When we question Thomas about morality, and especially about Christian morality, we cannot therefore limit ourselves to what he teaches on the precepts and obligations, which it notably includes. For him, precepts and obligations are elements of moral theology entirely subordinated to the virtues. We even have to say that from his point of view the more virtue increases, the less need there is for precepts and obligations. In the Evangelical Law, which is in his eyes the most perfect law and which confers the most virtue through the action of the Holy Spirit, he will also reduce to the necessary minimum the number of precepts (*ST* I-II 108.2 ad 1). But it would be a grave misunderstanding to conclude from this that for him Gospel morality is limited to these precepts and in practice to the natural law, which they express. It is at the level of the virtues that we should look for the Christian contribution in his moral system; it appears at the level of the cardinal and theologal virtues, as well as in the organic structure they form together.

It is good to recall as well the interior note of virtue as it encounters the external character always implied by obligation and the precepts. For Aquinas, virtue is interior to freedom itself, because it develops the spiritual spontaneity that carries it toward truth and goodness in order to confer upon the will the power to act with perfection. In the human person, therefore, self-control, correct judgment, and effective action increase with virtue, enabling her to be her own legislator and that of others as well.

The Protestant Crisis and Catholic Moral Theology

The Protestant crisis had a profound impact on the Catholic moral theology of the Counter-Reformation. The latter grew partially out of a reaction to the major positions of Protestantism, among them those that had to do with the place and role of faith and grace in the moral life.

On the Protestant side, the affirmation of justification by faith alone and not by works created a breach between the order of faith, which alone has value in the eyes of God, and the order of works, where ethics was ranged along with criteria for action regulated by reason.

In contrast to this, Catholic moral theology wanted to safeguard the value of works performed according to right reason and the law. It firmly maintained a reasonable morality based particularly on natural law as expressed in the Decalogue, whose commandments provided the principal division of subject matter in textbooks of moral theology.

While Protestant thought began with faith and exalted it, at the same time rejecting all ethical teaching that attributed direct value to works, and notably the teaching on the natural law, post-Tridentine Catholic morality grew accustomed to following an inverse route, exposing and establishing the natural data of morality in the first place and assigning to a lower level the return to faith, at the risk of lingering beyond due measure over the natural level and its problems. In fact, in moral theology textbooks the treatise on faith was reduced to an exposition of what one must believe in order to be saved and sins contrary to faith. Faith became a preeminently speculative virtue assigned principally to dogmatics without any great stress on its practice. As for the treatise on grace, it was simply removed from moral theology.

Thus on both sides, Catholic and Protestant, a separation was made between faith and morality that made it very difficult to answer the question of Christian morality and that of the relationship between faith and reason in moral theology. Christian thought would oscillate between a life of faith that was wholly interior and personal without any observable impact on concrete action, and a morality or ethical system based on the resources of reason that tended to claim a broad if not complete autonomy in regard to faith. We are thus faced with the dilemma: either the autonomy of a purely rational morality or heteronomy if faith is to intervene from a higher plane than reason.

The separation between faith and morality was totally foreign to the teaching of St. Thomas and to patristic thought. In contrast, the Thomist system presupposes harmony and a close and constant collaboration between faith and reason at the very heart of morality. Here again, we do well to bypass the dilemma of either faith or reason and accept a close linking of the two in the building of a moral system.

If we want to discover St. Thomas's thought on Christian morality we need to give faith a preponderant role in the system, since it is the first theologal virtue and possesses a practical power affecting all the actions of a believer even down to the slightest acts of particular virtues. The treatise on faith should recover its position of prime importance in moral theology, as also should that on grace. Certain other treatises that treat directly of faith's contribution to morality and that were neglected later on, such as the treatise on the New or Gospel Law and the study of the gifts of the Holy Spirit, should also be reevaluated. To remove these expositions from the moral theology of St. Thomas is truly like beheading it.[2]

2. Cf. my articles "Existe-t-il une morale chrétienne?" in *Sources* 1 (1975): 11–22, 49–59, and "La morale de S. Thomas est-elle chrétienne?" in *NV* (1976): 93–107.

Being so bold as to begin once more with faith and to believe in its profound accord with right reason and with the natural desire for beatitude, we can see how morality unfolds under the action of these two bonded luminaries throughout the entire organism of the virtues. We can discern better how faith acts in the realm of the particular human virtues. We will also recognize that if the moral theology of St. Thomas should be called heteronomous because of the prime importance it attaches to faith (which is faith in "another," in Jesus Christ), it still attributes to reason, more than did the Augustinianism of his day and the nominalism that followed, a principal role that gives it a very marked character of autonomy.

The Universalism of Reason

Finally, we should like to say a word about one of the principal components of the current problem in moral theology. In a pluralistic world and in societies where the Christian faith is often in the minority, it seems impossible to find a common ground between persons in the establishment of necessary rules or in the area of human reason. One of the present tasks of moral theologians is to build up a rational moral autonomy, essentially independent of the Christian faith as of all particular beliefs, which all persons of good will could accept as a common foundation. The autonomy of such a human morality seems to be the condition of its universal value.

The problem is not new. It goes back to the Renaissance, the discovery of the New World, and the division of Western Christianity. It crops up in humanistic and rationalistic movements. This universalist perspective has prompted Catholic moral theologians to emphasize natural law, which is valid for all and enjoys a determining role today in the post-conciliar scene, where openness to the world is a prominent value.

St. Thomas's moral theology answers to this need for universalism on the one hand by the importance it attaches to reason and even to its pagan representatives, especially Aristotle. It would be quite possible to draw from the *Summa* a moral system conceived at the purely philosophical level. This fact is so obvious that it has occasioned arguments against the Christian character of St. Thomas, declaring him to be more Aristotelian than Christian. But this would be a serious betrayal of St. Thomas, both historical and theoretical. The Thomistic moral system, as well as right reason, brings into play the universalism of faith issuing from the action of the Holy Spirit, which actually defines the Evangelical Law at the summit of the moral system, and operates directly through the theologal virtues and the gifts to attain and transform even the moral virtues. This is true to such a degree that it led St. Thomas to elaborate his teaching on the infused moral virtues. In his eyes, these were necessary for the purpose of ordering all of human action to the supernatural end of the vision of God, that is, to the only true and adequate end of the human person, in accord with the natural human desire for beatitude. From this viewpoint, the Christian faith is not simply one belief among many in a pluralistic world where Christians ought to have the generosity and selflessness to put their efforts and even their faith at the service of some one human moral system which alone would be valid for all, without in any way imposing on others what is proper to them alone. This would lead, actually, to eliminating any claim on the part of faith to intervene directly in a concrete moral system.

The moral structure that St. Thomas gives us is at once fully rational and fully Christian, based on the correspondence between the universalism of reason and the power of universalism contained in faith through the work of the Holy Spirit. According to this morality, only the action of God through faith in Jesus Christ answers fully to those natural aspirations of the human person to beatitude and truth that reason strives to govern. Faith is not opposed to right reason and does not limit its sway by forming an elite group of persons apart from the rest. It answers to the aspirations hidden in the heart of every person, even beyond what reason can grasp, while at the same time remaining in harmony with reason.

Again, faced with the moral problem we do not have to make a choice: either faith or reason, either a moral system without faith, heteronomous in nature and reserved to believers, or a rational moral system, autonomous and universal.

Obviously, the universalism of Christian morality calls for what we might call "faith in faith," precisely, faith in the action of the Holy Spirit that works through faith and charity. Consequently, it requires us to transcend our too-human and limited views of faith and the Church and their function in our life and in the world. It may be that we Catholics will need to make a special effort to rise above certain habits of thought formed over the past centuries and characterized by an anti-Protestant reflex as well as by a humanism and rationalism that have made us overly timid in the face of the intellectual and spiritual leap faith demands of us. Particularly in the moral domain, we must dare to believe that the Christian faith is more "reasonable" than a certain reason. We must place this faith once more at the source and heart of moral action as well as of theology. This is the price of our discovery of the rational and universal dimension of faith and our power to bear witness to it as St. Thomas did in his day. In order to discuss Christian morality properly, therefore, we must go straight to the point and begin with the Gospel teaching that harmonizes with the moral aspirations inscribed in the heart and mind of every human person.

II. The Evangelical Law and the Autonomy of Morality

In our study of the question of the autonomy of Christian morality, it may seem paradoxical to begin with St. Thomas's treatise on the evangelical or New Law. In addition to the fact that it has to all practical purposes been ignored by modern Catholic moralists, this treatise would appear at first sight to give a profoundly heteronomous character to Christian morality, since it draws on revelation for its material. If we want to demonstrate the factors of autonomy contained in Thomas's moral system, would it not be better to refer to those texts in the *Summa theologiae* that treat of the role of reason in morality and in the establishment of laws, and that show how reason renders the human person capable of self-direction and the direction of others by making laws?

Clearly, there is something of the truth in this last question, but it only addresses one aspect of the problem. Within the limited space of this paper, it seems preferable to draw attention to that treatise of St. Thomas that has been far too neglected—could it be because it is too Christian?—the treatise on the Evangelical Law, because it is at the summit where all the themes of his moral theology converge, and because it shows so clearly the "autonomy" of action enjoyed by the Christian. I believe it is impossible to interpret Aquinas's moral teaching perfectly and give its multiple elements their due proportion unless we place the Evangelical Law at the center of the entire perspective. Here, a few main characteristics will have to suffice.

A Clarification about the Term "Law"

A preliminary remark is called for. In the time of Thomas the term "law" did not have the harsh connotation of our modern usage, expressing as it does the juridical nature of an external will restricting freedom by force. Nor did it carry the pejorative nuance that a Protestant reading of St. Paul has given it. To repeat once more, Aquinas wrote before the age of nominalism with its legalistic and voluntaristic morality, before Protestantism with its distrust of all law in the name of faith. He lived within the more serene ambience of the patristic and ancient philosophical tradition, which saw in law the expression of the dynamic wisdom of the lawmaker, eliciting as far as possible the collaboration of mind and the spontaneous, willing assent of those subject to him. He conformed to the usage of Scripture, which ordinarily sees in God's law a source of light and a way of love. With him, we are not in a context dominated by the confrontation of freedom and law; law is seen as supporting freedom in its aspirations to truth, goodness, love, and beatitude.

Furthermore, St. Thomas will give a definition of the Evangelical Law, which will ascribe to it a particular nature and will win for it the title of the New Law, different from all other laws. Here we realize the inevitable inadequacy of our human terms to express the realities that come from God. We should not reproach Thomas for having used a term such as "law," which sounds harsher to our ears than to his and which cannot manage to convey its full meaning to us because of the weakness of ordinary words. It is up to us to strive to grasp his teaching exactly; since it emanates from the richest Christian tradition, it will be well worth the effort.

The Definition of the New Law

Let us recall briefly how Thomas defines the evangelical or New Law, taking his inspiration from St. Paul in the Letter to the Romans and from St. Augustine. He distinguishes two elements in the New Law, a principal element and a secondary one. The absolutely principal element *(principalissimum)* of Law in the New Testament is the grace of the Holy Spirit given through faith in Christ. In this lies all its power (ST I-II 106.1). Further on he clarifies this: "the grace of the Holy Spirit shown in faith, working through love" (ST I-II 108.1). Hence the New Law has a unique nature: it is not a law that remains external but becomes interior, being inserted in the heart of believers by the presence and action of the Holy Spirit *(lex indita)*. The New Law also has the power to justify the human person before God like the faith that it contains (ST I-II 106.2).

The various things that dispose a person to receive the grace of the Holy Spirit or to make use of it fittingly form the second element of the New Law.

This means especially the Gospel text itself, and particularly the Sermon on the Mount. In this sense the New Law is a written law *(lex scripta)*. In its character of a written text or letter external to the human person the New Law cannot justify. The letter of the Gospel can even "kill" like that of the Old Law without the intervention and interior action of the faith that heals from sin (ST I-II 106.2). Nevertheless, the Gospel text is the work of the Holy Spirit and corresponds precisely to his action. In the Sermon on the Mount we can see a summary of the entire teaching on the Christian life *(tota informatio christianae vitae,* I-II 108.3).

The New Law, Crowning Point of St. Thomas's Moral System

As we have demonstrated elsewhere,[3] the treatise on the New Law is not isolated in St. Thomas's *Summa.* Beyond its connection with the treatise on beatitude, inspired by the Beatitudes at the beginning of the Sermon on the Mount, the New Law forms the crowning point of all other laws, natural, human, and Old, and draws them together, carrying them to a point of perfection that cannot be surpassed in this world (ST I-II 106.4). Through the action of the Holy Spirit coming to the aid of faith and charity, the New Law becomes the source and inspiration of all the virtues and gifts, that is, the human virtues that it animates and transforms from within so as to order them to their higher end.

The treatise on the New Law thus connects directly with the entire treatise on law and the organism of the virtues and gifts, and relates equally to the study of the Trinity, through the Holy Spirit, and of Christ and the sacraments that give us grace. So it seems, as we said above, that we cannot make an adequate study of St. Thomas's moral theology without turning our attention to the treatise on the New Law that crowns it and stamps it with a clearly evangelical character.

Let us note in passing that here we come upon a remarkable answer to the major difficulty that has often given modern exegetes and moralists pause in regard to the Sermon on the Mount: is not the teaching presented here an inaccessible mountain, a moral "impossibility," something in reality impracticable?

This would indeed be the case if the New Law were simply a legal text handed to us like the Decalogue or any human law. But if the New Law con-

3. See previous note.

sists principally in the action of the Holy Spirit working through faith and charity, then we should not view the Sermon on the Mount as a legislative text listing a number of obligations that we must carry out more or less well according to our ability. Rather, we should see it above all as a series of promises describing what the Holy Spirit wishes to accomplish in the lives of those who believe in Christ and who try to correspond to this faith according to the attraction and impulse of grace, being all the while aware of their own weakness. What seems impossible to the human person is possible to the Holy Spirit working through faith. The Sermon on the Mount is first of all an object of faith, hope, and prayer at the origin of our effort. Hence it is the model of all Christian morality.

The Dynamic Interiority of Christian Morality

In Aquinas's treatise, the New Law possesses two principal characteristics that confer on the Christian a real and growing moral autonomy, if indeed we understand the term "autonomy" in a way that is open to the action of God. These characteristics are interiority and freedom.

Interiority is one of the major traits of the New Law, particularly as compared with the Old Law. St. Thomas's position is clear: in regard to external acts that are the objects of precept or prohibition, and needful for the exercise of virtue, the New Law adds nothing to the Old (ST I-II 108.2). The entire contribution of the New Law focuses on interior acts: love and longing for God as our ultimate end, love of self and neighbor in conformity with the teaching of the Sermon on the Mount (ST I-II 108.3).

This interiority, however, would remain material and would lead to an excessively demanding morality if we continued to think of the New Law as a collection of precepts imposed on the human person from without. The deeper the Gospel teaching with its effect on our intimate feelings, the more difficult it would seem in practice, were we to consider it from the perspective of the distance that separates the free will from moral obligations.

The interiority of the doctrine of the Sermon on the Mount is the prolongation of a more essential interiority: it is created in the heart of the believer by the action of the Holy Spirit through charity. By means of charity the Holy Spirit does away with the distance that exists between our free will and the moral law expressed in the Gospel, inclining our heart to love God and neighbor in Christ by its own movement, with a personal thrust, to such a point that we recognize in the Gospel teaching the desires and exigencies of our own love as well as Christ's.

We are not dealing here with a psychological interiorization realized by a subject of good will in regard to an external law, but with the spontaneous recognition of an intimate correspondence between our heart and the New Law, which causes us from now on to love it as our own law, the law of the progress of our love. In this way the New Law becomes interior for us with the very inwardness of love. Too, as believers we seek to fulfill this Law personally, desiring to carry it out to the utmost and as perfectly as possible, in spite of our many imperfections. We are no longer dealing with an external, minimalist law made up of constraining precepts, but an interior and "maximalist" law, carrying us far beyond precepts.

In a very beautiful text of the *Summa contra Gentiles* (Book IV, ch. 21–22), St. Thomas compares the action of the Holy Spirit in the soul of the believer to the life of friendship, which he uses to define charity and which he considers to be the most complete form of love. Here he shows especially how interiority and spontaneity, of which we were just speaking, make up the freedom of a Christian: "Because the Holy Spirit inclines the will by a movement of love to the true good to which it is ordered by a natural spontaneity, the actions of the human person avoid these two slaveries: slavery to passion and sin which is contrary to the natural order of the will and slavery to the law that compels us to observe the law against our will, like slaves rather than friends of the law." And the apostle says: "Where the Spirit of God is, there is freedom" (1 Cor 3:7), and again, "If you are led by the Spirit you are not under the law" (Gal 5:18).[4]

Let us note that such interiority cannot be integrated within the settings of a morality of obligation or of duty, such as we have inherited from nominalism and from Kantianism. As soon as we place obligation at the center of morality and make it the very essence of morality we are necessarily led to subordinate love, and even charity, to it, along with every spontaneous inclination or desire, even spiritual ones. Charity will then consist in acquitting ourselves of our obligations to God and neighbor with great precision. We are also familiar with the daring assertion of Ockham that so clearly reveals the priority of obligation over love in his view: if God commanded a person to hate him, this ha-

4. Cf. Servais Pinckaers "L'Esprit-Saint et l'amitié," *Sources* 2 (1976): 105–10.

tred would become good, since goodness consists in doing what God commands as obligatory.

To understand St. Thomas's teaching on the New Law, we need to break away altogether from the perspective of moral obligation so as to enter into that of true beatitude and the virtues that belong to this teaching. Virtue is defined precisely as a dynamic interiority that causes us to act in a personal way with ease and joy. The New Law, which consists in the action of the Holy Spirit through faith, touches our deepest interiority through charity that makes us sharers in the very love of God and impels us to act according to his will in all things. Thus through charity the New Law is situated at the very root of the virtues, at the source of their acts, in our will whose first and principal act is to love. The New Law can also be called "a law of love," since it causes us to act through love and to exercise the virtues according to the movement of love. "Those who have moral virtue are drawn to the exercise of virtuous actions for the love of virtue, not on account of some external penalty or reward. And so the New Law, consisting primarily in grace itself implanted in men's hearts, is called *the law of love*" (ST I-II 107.1 ad 2).[5]

Let us note what a mistake it would have been to use St. Thomas's affirmation that the New Law adds no external precept to the Old Law to argue against the specificity of Christian morality. Such an argument might have been valid if morality consisted principally in external precepts; but the essence of morality resides precisely in the interior principles of action, the virtues. We must therefore understand what Thomas is saying when he notes that virtue predominates over precept, and interiority over exteriority. Its effectiveness will in consequence be more perfect: the person who acts out of true love will advance much further, interiorly and exteriorly, than the one who acts out of obligation or even in a spirit of dutifulness.

The interiority of the New Law will communicate itself to all the virtues and to every action of the believer by means of charity, the "form" of the virtues operating within each of them. Even on the natural level, the actions of the Christian will be taken up and perfected by the New Law.

---

5. "*Illi autem qui habent virtutem, inclinantur ad virtutis opera agenda propter amorem virtutis, non propter aliquam poenam aut remunerationem extrinsecam. Et ideo lex nova, cuius principalitas consistit in ipsa spirituali gratia indita cordibus, dicitur lex amoris.*" *ST* I-II 107.1 ad 2.

The Law of Freedom

According to St. Thomas, an essential characteristic of the New Law is that it is a law of freedom. The expression is classic; yet it is nonetheless surprising when we weigh the words. How are we to associate law and freedom? Is it not a paradox, a play on words, like speaking of the squareness of a circle? For in the realm of morality we are used to thinking of law and freedom as opposite, irreducible poles.

Once again, in order to understand this teaching we have to relinquish a nominalist concept of law and freedom and acknowledge that freedom rooted in the inclinations to truth, goodness, and beatitude can grow in us with the help, among other things, of the law that directs it in its progress. Harmony and collaboration, therefore, can be established between freedom and law: law should foster the growth of freedom.

The New Law deserves the name of "a law of freedom" by special right, according to St. Thomas. All law is composed of precepts and terminates with an obligation born of a command. Here, however, we are dealing with a law that proceeds from an interior principle of love and that therefore possesses a power and thrust spontaneously transcending the limits of a precept. This is why the New Law will include as one of its essential parts—and this is a unique instance—a number of counsels mentioned in the Gospel which contribute in their own way, by the detachment they produce—in the sense of bonds one breaks—to rendering the human person more and more capable of self-direction according to the movement of charity. The counsels of the New Law show the moral autonomy of the Christian who through the interior impulse of the Holy Spirit has become capable of making free choices of paths beyond the necessary precepts that will lead to God.

Thus the evangelical counsels form an integral part, precious and characteristic, of Christian morality. They are signs of the freedom of the Christian in contrast to the slavery of the Old Law (ST I-II 108.4). They are useful means of assuring the human person the greatest spiritual autonomy.

Let us note that this viewpoint is very different from and even opposed to the tendency of more recent moralists to distinguish precepts and counsels within the framework of morality of obligation. Having placed obligation at the center of morality, they define the moral domain by the precepts, decide that whatever falls under the counsels is outside of the moral system properly speaking, and allocate it to ascetics or mysticism. Working out of such a perspective, it is normal that they should no longer understand the treatise on the New Law, and should omit it from their system.

For St. Thomas on the other hand, the New Law, and consequently Christian morality, is defined notably by the evangelical counsels and by the interior freedom that the grace of the Holy Spirit brings through faith, a freedom that will communicate itself to the exercise of all the virtues.

A Moral System Contrasted with Casuistry

In closing I should like to mention a general characteristic of St. Thomas's moral system, which is explained specifically by interiority and freedom, that is, by the autonomy that it recognizes in the human person and the Christian in the moral domain. Although he maintains moral theology's orientation to particular action and divides his *secunda pars* into a general and particular part (prologue of the *secunda secundae*), St. Thomas stops with the study of the virtues and never descends to particular cases, which later was to become the favorite subject matter of moralists in the seventeenth century. The *secunda pars,* which contains 303 questions or about 1,500 articles, includes practically no case of conscience. To find the study of such a case in the works of St. Thomas one would have to read the *Quaestiones quodlibetales,* which brought theological disputes to the attention of the public. One can frankly say that Thomas would have been anti-casuist, had there been casuists in his day.

I think we can explain this general trait as follows. For Aquinas, the task of the moral theologian consists in forming the human person to virtue (which implies the establishment of precepts necessary for virtue), it being understood that the one who possesses virtue, and through it love of truth and goodness according to their diverse species, is most fit to make concrete judgments about the conformity of actions to virtue, and to carry them out. Aristotle had already said this, and it is again verified for the Christian and the spiritual person by St. Paul (1 Cor 2:15), thanks to the interior action of the Holy Spirit. This would be equally true for the moral as well as the theologal virtues. The moral theologian cannot take the place of a human person endowed with virtue in the forming of a judgment and in a moral action; indeed, her work is for the sake of the human person, whom she serves.

Such a concept in no wise leads to arbitrariness of individual freedom in the forming of moral judgments, as might be feared from the viewpoint of morality of obligation, which can never act freely except under the external pressure of a command. For St. Thomas the principal light and power in the moral order reside within the human person in the virtues, beginning with the "virtue" of the Holy Spirit. They contribute to the development of a freedom that tends naturally to truth and goodness, and waxes strong in the measure in which it responds better and better to their attractions and exigencies. The more moral freedom grows in this sense, thanks to the virtues, the more it is protected from the arbitrary, rejecting it so as to move toward what it loves in truth. Spiritual freedom is thus directly opposed to arbitrary or carnal freedom, as St. Paul would say. The autonomy it engenders is based on love of true goodness, of which the moral judgment is the concrete manifestation.

11 ⟶ A Historical Perspective on Intrinsically Evil Acts (1986)

The Problem

The question of intrinsically evil moral actions is a central preoccupation and topic of discussion for Catholic moral theologians today. It determines the positions they take on concrete problems being debated currently by the world at large: contraception, abortion, torture, etc. If actions such as these are intrinsically evil, one may never perform them under any circumstances. If they are not, then we can imagine exceptional situations providing sufficient reasons to allow us to perform them without incurring any moral guilt.

The debate surfaced in recent years after the appearance of the encyclical *Humanae vitae* and the divergences of Catholic moral theologians in regard to Paul VI's stand on contraception. Discussion extended to other difficult cases such as abortion. From concrete problems the debate has been extended to the reasons and principles that underlie solutions, and to the conception of moral agency that supports them. In the end the debate came face to face with the classic teaching on intrinsically evil actions. Thus the problem became generalized to the point where it challenged the traditional moral system based on natural law, whose precepts were held to be universal and unchangeable. For if there are no intrinsically evil actions, no law can be truly and perfectly universal and unchangeable, always applicable and admitting of no exceptions of space, time, historical period, or culture.

Originally published in Servais Pinckaers, *Ce qu'on ne peut jamais faire* (1986): 20–66. An abbreviated version was previously published as "Le problème de l'Intrinsece Malum. Esquisse historique," *Freiburger Zeitschrift für Philosophie und Theologie* 29 (1982): 373–88. Translated by Sr. Mary Thomas Noble, O.P., with the assistance of Craig Steven Titus. Edited for publication in *The Pinckaers Reader* by John Berkman.

Not least among the difficulties of our problem is the multiplicity of its dimensions. When we listen to the discussions of moralists on the question of intrinsically evil actions, we initially have the impression that we are moving in a very specialized area where the problem, by dint of excessive refining, appears to focus on the head of a pin, and where differences of opinion seem trivial. Yet when we look at the theories that have been elaborated in regard to these questions, when we follow their logic from principles to applications, we realize that the entire Catholic moral tradition has been shaken by recent challenges. Even those who are not moral theologians sense this and sometimes wonder whether morality, Christian morality, still exists.

The Usefulness and Difficulty of Having Recourse to History

Recourse to the history of morality can throw far more light on the treatment of our moral problems than we often suppose. There are several reasons for this, one being that historical study that is carefully done reveals the existence of various models, concepts, and systems of morality throughout the long Christian tradition, which lead to different methods of dealing with moral problems. This confrontation with our cultural past also opens up new horizons for us and helps to broaden our perspective, liberating us from short-sightedness. There is no real breadth of mind without an understanding of the past that has formed us and is still active within us, as youth lives on in mature age. Knowledge of the past is equally necessary if we are to adequately assess our present ideas, get a better measure of them, and make needed corrections.

The historical study of the doctrine of intrinsically evil actions presents several special difficulties, however. To my knowledge, the very expression of an action *intrinsece malum* does not occur before the sixteenth century. Outstanding theologians of the modern period consider the theme itself as a kind of corollary of their treatises on morality, and the authors of the manuals are content to summarize the results of their study, when they deal with it. It is impossible therefore to follow the theme of intrinsically evil actions through texts extending from the Church Fathers to contemporary moral theologians, as can be done for example with the question of lying or the death penalty.

Yet when we go beyond the formulation of the question in the manuals of moral theology in order to deal with the problem in itself, we see that it is so basic that it is constantly raised in one form or another. From the time of St. Thomas, for example, the question was formulated as follows. Are some actions evil in themselves, and thus forbidden by the moral law since they are evil, as contrasted with others that are evil only because the law forbids them, being indifferent in themselves? In the former cases the malice of the action precedes the law that expresses it, while in the latter it results from the law that is its basis.

This question is of utmost importance. It is not simply a matter of finding one or another exceptional action that would be evil in itself and at all times, but of laying the first foundation regarding the moral quality of acts. Does this moral quality flow from the nature of actions in conjunction with a truly natural law or does it depend essentially on an external law with its precepts and prohibitions? What we are concerned with here is the intrinsic or extrinsic character of morality, as well as the objectivity of moral judgments in general.

Thus understood and broadened, the question of intrinsically evil actions surfaces again and again as fundamental throughout the entire course of the history of moral theology. While not always treated explicitly and theoretically, it inevitably elicits a response which a historian of moral theology should know how to discover.

Another difficulty arises from the delay in the development of historical studies of moral theology. The historical method has been fully applied to Scripture and dogma but far less to Christian morality. It seemed as if significant results were not expected a priori. The undertaking was extremely difficult because, in order to be worth the effort, one had to penetrate to the depths where moral concepts originate and are worked out and shaped into a system. But once this had been done, one realized that such a study was well worth the effort.

The present study traces the chief historical lines of the question of intrinsically evil actions as approached by theologians from the Church Fathers up to our own time. It makes no claim to being complete, even in regard to the authors studied; the material is vast and as yet scarcely explored. My purpose is to sketch the main lines of the evolution of the question and draw out certain models of solutions that may be helpful for current reflection.

The Fathers of the Church

In the Greek and Latin Church Fathers we find, based upon the Scriptures, the first systematic elaborations of Christian morality. Without mentioning particular authors, I shall describe some of the chief characteristics of their approach to our subject.

The teaching of the Church Fathers is fed by two great sources, Scripture and philosophy:

1. Scripture is the first and ever-present source of moral teaching. The Church Fathers emphasize the law of Moses and the Wisdom books of the Old Testament and especially the Sermon on the Mount in the New Testament. Their Christian rereading of the Old Testament confers on all of Scripture a moral dimension centered on Christ as the Teacher of Christian Wisdom.

2. The great philosophical trends of the period are Platonism and Neoplatonism (with St. Augustine, for example), Aristotelianism (with St. John Damascene), and Greek and Latin Stoicism (notably Cicero taken up by St. Ambrose).

The combination of these two sources, Gospel and philosophy, originates with the Church Fathers and is quite different from what modern thinkers make of it. When all is said and done, the teaching of the Gospel always predominates for them, and subjects the adopted philosophical categories to profound changes. It is true that the latter are taken up and exploited, but not without undergoing a basic critique that makes it possible to integrate them in a new concept of the moral life, centered henceforth on faith in Christ and charity given by the Holy Spirit.

Two major characteristics mark the Christian morality taught by the Church Fathers:

1. They always approach morality from the vantage point of the question of beatitude. They conceive it basically as a response to this question, which is so natural that every human being wonders about it even before putting it into words, as St. Augustine will remark. This idea of morality is obvious to them as to the philosophers of their time, but they bring to it a response that is incomparably better because it has been given to them by God in the Scriptures with their promises.

The answer to the moral question will be developed by the Church Fathers in an exposition of the ways leading to the promised beatitude, chiefly the interior ways of the virtues underlying good actions, as proposed particularly in the New Testament. In doing this, the Fathers will not hesitate to treat of the classic virtues of prudence, justice, courage, and temperance, and of other ordinary categories such as actions that are upright *(honestum),* appropriate *(decorum),* and useful *(utile).*[1] But they make substantial changes in these in order to put them at the service of the properly Christian virtues of faith, hope, and charity, which are of another nature with their receptive dimension in regard to divine action.

Thus, the moral teaching of the Church Fathers, whether Greek or Latin, and whatever their other differences, is always a morality based on beatitude and virtue. As for the precepts, commandments, and positive or negative laws contained in Scripture, they view them as teachings about virtues to be acquired rather than as the imposition of obligations and duties by an external law or will. For them the precepts serve the virtues and the spiritual interiority they form, and this is the heart of morality. We never find in them the modern concept of a morality centered on the idea of obligation or duty, which transforms the idea of virtue into conformity to obligations and ends by excluding the study of beatitude from morality. We have here two profoundly different concepts of Christian morality. This is a first lesson from a historical study of morality, and one that can have significant consequences: to recognize that the morality of the Fathers reaches these horizons that are not simply different from ours, but in my judgment, are far broader and more humane.

2. If the Church Fathers see Christian morality as essentially a response to the question of beatitude, we may wonder two things. First, are they bound to the philosophy and culture of their times? Second, are they being led into the subjectivism that so often affects the idea of beatitude?

However, according to the authoritative observations of Gilson and Holte,[2] two key characteristics of Christian thought that distinguish it from the ancient philosophers are a) the objectivity of its position on the problem of beatitude and the end of the human person, and b) the realism of its response to this question that dominates morality.

---

1. For example, St. Ambrose, *De offic.*

2. For example, E. Gilson, *The Spirit of Medieval Philosophy,* trans. by A. H. C. Downes (New York: Charles Scribner's Sons, 1936); K. Ragnar Holte, *Béatitude et sagesse, saint Augustin et le problème de la fin de l'homme dans la philosophie ancienne* (Worcester, Mass.: Augustinian Studies, Assumption College, 1962).

For the philosophers, and this is particularly clear with the Stoics, beatitude, the *telos* or end of the human person, consists essentially in the perfection of virtue in the highest faculties where wisdom dwells, that is, in the most elevated and lofty human activity, notably in contemplation. In this sense the end of the human person is wholly within the person, it is immanent. It is the work of the person according to his natural powers, even if he aims, through contemplation, at beings higher than himself.

For Christian theology, beatitude, the ultimate end of the human person and of human activity, resides rather in the effective attainment of the divine object. This is exterior to us and so superior that we can never hope to reach it without the gracious initiative of God himself.

We can express the difference by using a comparison proposed by Aristotle. It is the example of the archer who must do everything in his power to attain his end, the target, and yet it is to do all that is fitting in this aim which would be for him his last end, which corresponds to what we call the sovereign good. As for hitting the target successfully, this is something that deserves to be chosen, not sought for its own sake, for it does not depend on us alone, but also on external happenings beyond our control.[3] Thus the end of Greek morality is immanent to life itself and resides precisely in human virtue. Beatitude and the end tend to be identified with virtue to the point of neglecting the reality and the attraction of external goods even while one seeks them.

If we apply this comparison to Christian theology, we shall say that its principle is very precisely to attain successfully the target aimed at, the end which is God in his own reality as the source of all good and all beatitude. Thus the Christian concept of beatitude and morality will be deeply objective. For it, virtue cannot be an ultimate end, although we cannot say either that it is simply a means. It is a path to beatitude. There can be no beatitude without virtue, but beatitude is not identical with virtue, for Christian virtue opens out and attaches itself to a good which surpasses the human person and which alone can fully respond to our desire for beatitude.

Thus the question of beatitude and of the *telos* or end that dominates the morality of the ancients is profoundly transformed by Christian thought in the sense of objectivity and realism in the yearning for the God of revelation.

We can cite the passage from Cicero's *De finibus bonorum et malorum*

---

3. Gilson, *Spirit of Medieval Philosophy.*

where he declares, "Wisdom does not resemble the art of the pilot and physician but rather a role in the theatre or a dance; for the height of art and its fulfillment lies in itself and is not at the beck and call of anything external to it."[4] And he adds that Wisdom is even more independent of external happenings than the arts.

For Christian theology, according to St. Paul, the source of wisdom will be in God and will be communicated through the events of salvation history thanks to faith in Christ. Wisdom comes to the human person from without, but this does not hinder it from penetrating to the ultimate depths of the person. Wisdom, the supreme moral quality, thus acquires an objectivity and reality that are specific characteristics of Christian thought.

The same movement toward realism and objectivity can be noted in the concept of love, which is however by far the most profoundly subjective of sentiments. Holte observed this very clearly in St. Augustine:

In his definitions of love Augustine has a strong tendency to turn his attention from the subject in order to see different objects capable of being objects of love. This is related to his general tendency in speculating on the *telos* to shift the emphasis a little from the question posed by the ancient philosophers, who had the *telos* derive from a human function. Thus in his *De doctrina christiana* all reasoning is dominated by the various categories of *res* that Augustine draws from the teaching of the Christian faith to serve as points of orientation for all of morality. "Ordered love" will therefore be defined as "an integral appreciation of things."[5]

The objectivity and realism about the fundamental notions of beatitude, the end of the human person, wisdom, and love that we observe as a characteristic trait of Christian thought among the Church Fathers will be communicated to morality as a whole by means of the virtues that dominate it and whose concept will also be modified. In particular, the organism of the principal virtues will be ordered and inspired by virtues of a new type that we might call virtues of openness. These are faith, hope, and charity, which open the human mind and heart to the God of Jesus Christ. God, whose reality surpasses every creature, thus becomes in a most radical and powerful sense the object of these virtues.

Clearly such a transformation, affecting all of morality beginning with its

4. Cicero, De *finibus*, VII, 23.
5. Holte, *Béatitude et sagesse*, 258.

fundamental notions, has as its direct cause a phenomenon proper to Judaeo-Christian revelation: the divine initiative, its intervention in human history through the Word and Scripture, promises and laws, wisdom and prophecy, through the life and teaching of Christ and through the Holy Spirit working in the Church. Such is the action that manifests to the ecclesial community and to each believer, both exteriorly and interiorly, what we might call the objectivity and reality of God.

Let us add that a similar modification is at work in the representation of the neighbor at the heart of Christian theology. Our neighbor will no longer appear as a virtuous companion, an associate in an enterprise undertaken in justice or friendship. In light of the Gospel, the Church Fathers teach us to see in every person an image of God, a brother or sister in Christ, destined for the Kingdom of Heaven. The objectivity and realism of God are in a sense communicated to our neighbor. To love or to wound our neighbor is henceforth to love God or to sin against God. Christian morality will strive to take into account this profound modification of the virtues of which the philosophers speak, that bind us to one another.

In dealing with the Church Fathers, we have touched on the problem of intrinsically evil actions in a fairly general way, beginning with the objectivity of their view of Christian morality. This enables us to see clearly the various dimensions of a problem that we shall now study in a more restricted sense.

From our exposition we can draw a twofold conclusion:

1. Objectivity in our judgments about beatitude, our end as human beings, as well as about particular virtues and goods, has a decisive importance for Christian morality. It is this very characteristic and dimension that most markedly distinguishes it from the pagan schools of morality in antiquity. This observation can certainly be applied equally well to modern philosophy, far more tempted as it is by subjectivism and the desire to make man the only end of man.

2. The objectivity envisioned here is something far deeper, broader, and richer than that material objectivity often implied when dealing with cases of conscience. Without overlooking those physical realities that relate people to each other, moral objectivity refers primarily to persons in their own reality, whether related to God or to other persons. In order to understand this we first need to overcome an almost inveterate sense of opposition between the

personal subject and the object, the latter of which has become impersonal and wholly material. The objectivity of love, however, consists in loving others for their own sake, for what they are in themselves, in their *res* or personal reality. Such is the righteous love of St. Augustine, such also the love of friendship which St. Thomas uses to define charity.

Without losing sight of the precise and particular moral problems that challenge the objectivity of moral judgment, we need to know how to situate them in a global vision of Christian morality. We cannot isolate concrete actions as we do ideas; each act inscribed in reality by an action inevitably reverberates throughout the life and in the personality of the one who performs it. This is the logic of objective reality that must unify and order moral judgment if it is to be right and true as far as is humanly possible.

The study of the teaching of the Church Fathers could be pursued by beginning with studies of cases dealing with acts recognized as being evil in themselves and always reprehensible. Examples would be St. Augustine's two brief works on lying, *About Lying (De mendacio)* and *Against Lying (Contra mendacium),* in which he maintains and demonstrates how one may never lie under any circumstance. This teaching became classic after his time and has been discussed extensively by moralists. Here we have a typical instance of an action that is considered to be intrinsically evil.

I shall simply note that we need to avoid narrowing the dimensions of the Augustinian problematic by limiting it to the proportions of a particular and exceptional case of conscience. What moves St. Augustine in the position he takes is the sense that in the question of lying the Christian understanding and love of truth are at stake. Lying is absolutely repulsive to such an understanding and love of truth, especially when it becomes a tactic to win over heretics, as the Spanish bishop Consentius had proposed when he consulted Augustine.

We can observe further how powerfully Augustine maintains the objective demands of truthfulness in human speech, beyond all considerations of self-service or usefulness to another which can be brought forward in favor of lying in certain cases. Jean-Jacques Rousseau will do this later, for example, in the fourth step of his *Reveries of the Solitary Walker,* where truth is said to be separated from the reality of things, from justice and from sincerity, and is supplanted by sentiments of utility.

Peter Abelard and the Primacy of Intention

Current discussions on morality have sparked a renewed interest among moralists in the thought of Abelard, chiefly because of the primacy he attributes to moral intention.[6] With Abelard, in fact, a new period in the history of theology opens, the Scholastic period characterized among other things by its use of dialectic. Abelard renews both methods and theological positions with an audacity that does not fear extremes. In his *Ethics*,[7] Abelard basically maintains this thesis: evil does not consist in an external action, or even in a desire, but essentially and uniquely in voluntary consent. He takes as an example the precept "Thou shalt not covet" (Dt 5:21) and remarks that one can often perform actions that fall under this prohibition without committing sin, as when one acts in ignorance or by constraint. Abelard's examples include a) a woman forced to yield to a man's advances, b) a man who makes sexual advances upon a woman he erroneously thinks is his wife, and c) the case of a court error whereby an innocent person is condemned to death. From all this Abelard concludes that sin does not consist in the desire for another man's wife, nor in the fact of intercourse with her, but only in consent to the desire or the action. This is how we are to understand the Gospel interpretation of the precept "He who looks upon a woman to desire her, etc. . . ."

Abelard thus establishes a general principle: wherever actions are objects of a moral precept or prohibition, we must relate the latter to consent rather than to the actions themselves. This is the case with the precepts "Thou shalt not kill, thou shalt not bear false witness." The one who does what is forbidden by the precept is not to be considered a transgressor; rather, it is the one who consents to what he knows is forbidden.[8]

If moral quality is thus determined by the intention, one same action can be either good or evil according to the varying intentions of those performing

6. See, for example, R. Van Den Berge, "La qualification morale de l'acte humain: ébauche d'une réinterprétation de la pensée abélardienne" [Editor's note: "The moral qualification of the human act: sketch of a reinterpretation of Abelard's thought"], *Studia moralia* 13 (1975): 143–73.

7. Peter Abelard, *Ethical Writings: His Ethics or "Know yourself" and His Dialogue between a Philosopher, a Jew, and a Christian,* trans. Paul Vincent Spade (Indianapolis: Hackett, 1995), 10–11.

8. "*Sicut ergo transgressor non est dicendus, qui facit quod prohibetur, sed qui consentit in hoc quod constat esse prohibitum: ita nec prohibitio de opere, sed de consensu est accipienda.*"

it. This was the case with the act of handing over Christ. It was a sin on Judas's part but not on the part of the Father nor of Christ who willingly delivered Himself up. From this we can conclude that God considers not what is done but the disposition of soul of the one who acts. Merit and praise, like blame, accrue to the good or evil intention, not to the action itself.[9]

Good dialectician that he is, Abelard even finds a precept of Christ that it was good to transgress with a good intention. When Jesus forbade certain sick people to speak of their miraculous cure, the Gospel recounts that the more He bade them to be silent, the more they spread the story.

To conclude, for Abelard sin consists solely in free consent; action adds nothing.

Abelard's opinion is interesting because it represents a fairly simple position in regard to the problem of morality. It gives complete pride of place to the intention or voluntary consent as compared with the action itself and even the desire. We can conclude from this that for Abelard there are no intrinsically evil actions, that actions are indifferent in themselves and become morally significant solely through one's intention. This is how many moralists have understood Abelard and why they have often condemned him. He is at the opposite pole from the morality of the modern manuals, which give priority to the object of the action and consider the intention as a circumstantial factor in forming a moral judgment.

Yet in fairness to Abelard, if we want to gain from reading him we must avoid situating him improperly in a casuistical setting and interpret him rather in the context of the problematics of his own era. Abelard's position belongs in the setting of the Augustinian analysis of sin borrowed from Genesis, with its distinction between temptation in the form of a serpent, sensible desire represented by Eve, and rational consent signified by Adam. Abelard clearly reacts against a concept of sin that comprises solely external actions forbidden by law. The penitentiaries of his time favored this rather legalistic attitude, which has remained a frequent temptation throughout history. Abelard, on the contrary, wants to reestablish St. Augustine's teaching, placing the essence of sin beyond external action and beyond sensibility and desire, in reason and will. As long as the will has not consented, there is no sin.

Yet Abelard is a dialectician at heart. He must deny in order to affirm, as in

9. The example was probably taken from Augustine, *In Ioan. Evang.*, Tract. VII, n. 7.

his famous *Sic et non*. By preference, he establishes his opinions by demolishing those of his adversaries, and in his passion for dialectic he risks carrying negation too far. He is so enamored of manipulating ideas that he does not always notice their failure to reflect all the aspects of reality.

Abelard's position looks in two directions. His main thrust is positive: the essence of morality lies in free consent, in the intention that produces the act. In this Abelard is a disciple of St. Augustine. St. Thomas will follow the same tradition in giving priority to the interior act and to the end when considering the elements contributing to the morality of actions.

Abelard's second thrust is negative. There is no moral value in the external action, none even in desire. In themselves, these add nothing to morality. Since an action can be either good or evil according to one's intention, it is morally indifferent in itself. Here Abelard immediately draws criticism; his opinion appears exaggerated. Against him are St. Augustine's well-known texts in his treatise *Against Lying:* "As to those actions that are sinful in themselves *(cum iam opera ipsa peccata sunt),* such as theft, fornication, blasphemy, who would dare to say that in performing them for a good motive *(causis bonis)* they are no longer sins, or what is still more ridiculous, they are just sins?"[10] In the ardor of dialectical combat against those who situated morality in actions, Abelard has not been able to find a position firm and balanced enough to be credible. This defect should not make us forget the service he rendered to theology in his day by strongly emphasizing the importance of consent and voluntary intention in moral action.

From Abelard's position one could conclude that he denies the existence of actions that are intrinsically evil in themselves; this will be discussed further on. It is only partially true, for having situated the essence of morality in the voluntary intention, Abelard will recognize that at the level of interiority many things exist that are in themselves good or evil. These are the virtues and vices which form, for him as for the Fathers, the framework of moral theology. He clearly affirms this in his *Dialogue:*

For certain things are called goods or evils properly and so to speak substantially. For instance, the virtues and vices themselves. But certain things are so called by accident and through something else *[per accidens et per aliquid],* like actions that are our deeds *[operum nostrorum actiones].* Although they are indifferent in themselves, nev-

10. Augustine, *Contra mendacium,* VII, 18.

ertheless they are called good or evil from the intention from which they proceed. Frequently, therefore, when the same thing is done by different people, or by the same person at different times, the same deed is nevertheless called both "good" and "evil" because of the difference in the intentions. On the other hand, things that are called goods or evils substantially and from their own nature remain so permanently unmixed that what is good once can never become evil, or conversely. And so the discernment of these things, both the goods and the evils, is called prudence.[11]

The interesting thing about the discussion raised by Abelard is the fact that it provided the essential data of the morality of acts from the beginning of the period of the systematization of theology. On the one hand we have the will with consent and intention, and on the other the work, the external act (to which he added the desire preceding consent) which is directly touched by the law of Scripture. We shall encounter these two dimensions throughout the history of theology as well as philosophy. Opinions oscillate from one pole to the other, favoring either the interiority of the intention or the exteriority of the act.

St. Bernard: The Stability of Moral Precepts

We cannot leave Abelard without quoting one of his outstanding adversaries, St. Bernard, in an interesting text that throws light on the context of moral ideas of the period. It is the distinction made between three kinds of precepts or laws according to the possibility of obtaining dispensation from them.[12] First, there are *stable precepts,* from which prelates can dispense, for example those concerning the fast, ecclesiastical laws, the rule of religious, etc. Then there are *inviolable precepts,* promulgated by God, who alone can dispense from them, such as the precept "Thou shalt not kill" (on the second tablet of the Law). Finally, there are *unchangeable precepts,* from which even God can never dispense: these are the precepts of the Sermon on the Mount that concern the essence of virtues such as love, humility, meekness, etc.

For St. Bernard too, the firmest essential morality is located at the level of the virtues and interiority. It is equally interesting to see the position of first place assigned to the Sermon on the Mount, neglected by too many modern theologians in their teaching of Christian morality.

11. Abelard, *Ethical Writings,* 112.
12. St. Bernard of Clairvaux, *praecepto et dispensatione.*

As for what St. Bernard has to say about the inviolable precepts, might we conclude that these have to do with actions not evil in themselves, since God can dispense from them, and that they would therefore be indifferent in themselves and would only become evil by divine promulgation? St. Bernard would doubtless have answered rather that actions such as killing, stealing, etc., are evil in themselves, unless God in His omnipotence should by exception eliminate their malice as in certain Scriptural examples. But St. Bernard is not devoted to systematization as is Abelard; his outlook is above all religious and practical, not Scholastic.

Peter Lombard: The First Scholastic Balancing of Intention and Action

Peter Lombard devotes distinction 40 of Book II of the *Sentences* to the question of the morality of actions according to intention or external act. He presents the followers of Abelard and their adversaries attempting to give a balanced response to the problem, based on St. Augustine.

The framing of the question is Abelardian: should all actions be judged simply *(simpliciter)* good or evil according to their end, according to a person's intention and will?

Lombard first gives the opinion of the Abelardian school: all acts are indifferent, in such wise that in themselves they are neither good nor evil. But each act becomes good through a good intention and evil through an evil intention. Abelard's position, which began as a reflection, has thus become a general theory about morality.

Lombard next lets Abelard's adversaries speak. The most radical of them maintain that certain works are good in such a way that they cannot be evil, whatever the manner in which they are performed. On the other hand, certain works are evil in such wise that they cannot be good, whatever the reason *(causa)* behind them. Other works, finally, are good or evil according to their end or reason *(causa)*.

In this discussion, which is already carried on in the form of Scholastic questions, Lombard will try to find a balanced response which will take into account the truth of the opposing opinions. He begins by quoting at length from the text of Augustine's *On Lying (De mendacio)*, an extract from which we gave above. This certainly served as a battering ram for Abelard's opponents, making a breach in Abelard's position. From it Lombard draws the conclusion that all human acts are judged good or evil according to their intention or voluntary cause, except those that are evil in themselves *(per se mala)*, according to the examples cited by St. Augustine: stealing to help a poor person, falsification of a will in favor of a generous heir, adultery to save a man from death, all actions that remain evil in spite of the goodness of the intention inspiring them.

Lombard then takes Abelard's side when he maintains that the voluntary intention is the cause of the morality of actions, but he stands apart from him in admitting exceptions to this principle. It does not apply in the case of an act that is in itself evil. Here we have the solution of compromise and research, which safeguards the principal elements of the morality of actions but does not succeed in establishing their reciprocal contribution clearly and solidly.

However, the position is firm enough to cause the Abelardians to combat it. They observe that intrinsically evil actions that counter the thesis of morality based on intention have, in reality, neither a cause nor a good intention. The person who steals to give to the poor, for example, does not really do this for the sake of the good, since it is not good to give the poor things that belong to others. So in practice the positions coincide. This is actually a retreat on the part of the Abelardians, seeking to evade the line of argument of *On Lying (De mendacio),* wherein a firm and constant position of Christian moral teaching is expressed.

St. Thomas Aquinas: The Great Classical Analysis of Moral Action

St. Thomas is at the center of the history of theological teaching on the morality of human acts. While assuming the Augustinian theological tradition of which Peter Lombard is the official interpreter, he transforms and perfects the doctrine received from his predecessors thanks to the precise analyses that come to him from Aristotle and his commentators as well as the Latin authors Cicero and Boethius. His study on moral action is an extraordinary synthesis of preceding works which he draws together, despite their diversity, into an ordered whole at once faithful and profoundly original. The analyses of St. Thomas on the elements of morality will become classic and will serve as the foundation for all later theology, in spite of the changes in the concept of morality that will intervene. Up to our day, the heirs of casuistry, but also their opponents, will refer to St. Thomas as a prime authority from whom they will draw their arguments.

The problem of the existence of intrinsically evil actions and the importance of intention will henceforth be approached in the new setting of the Thomistic analysis of moral action. Later, the problem will take on a new form that had already appeared in the time of St. Thomas. In the *Summa contra Gentiles* he had to oppose the opinion, undoubtedly Franciscan, that human acts are just and good solely because of the "position taken by the law," by the will of the divine legislator.[13] St. Thomas himself firmly maintained that actions prescribed by the divine law are right not only because of this positive ordinance but also because of their very nature. Obviously it would be the same for evil actions. The entire Thomistic conception of morality based on the nature of acts and on the natural law as their interior rule is involved here. But the debate will only come to its height with nominalism, which will separate freedom from nature and make the law external to the moral act.

In order to grasp the historical thought of St. Thomas on the problem of the intrinsic morality of acts we need to take a brief look at the analysis of morality that he elaborated so as to situate his position with precision. In doing this, we obviously cannot go into all the details of the necessary studies. We will be content to use those already done, even though it may mean filling them in later.[14] I believe that in order to interpret St. Thomas's thought in the treatise on human acts with precision, a historical examination completing speculative reflection is indispensable. We will assume this here and utilize the results.

Our exposition will be divided into three parts: first, St. Thomas's precise determination of the elements that make up moral action; next, their contribution to moral quality in accordance with the action they compose. Finally, we shall note the characteristics of St. Thomas's thought on morality.

---

13. *SCG* III 129.

14. See Odon Lottin, "Le problème de la moralité intrinsique d'Abélard à saint Thomas d'Aquin," in *Psychologie et morale aux XIIe et XIIIe siècles* Volume 2 (Louvain: Abbaye du Mont César, 1948), 421–65; Lottin, "La place du *finis operantis* dans la pensée de saint Thomas d'Aquin," in *Psychologie et morale aux XIIe et XIIIe siècles* Volume 4 (Louvain: Abbaye du Mont César, 1957), 489–517. See also S. Pinckaers, "Le rôle de la fin dans l'action morale selon saint Thomas d'Aquin," in *Le renouveau de la morale* (Tournai: Casterman, 1964), 114–43.

The Elements of Moral Action: Definition of "Circumstances"

St. Thomas makes use of several sources for his study of circumstances: Aristotle, Cicero, the pseudo-Gregory of Nyssa (Nemesius), and Boethius. They provide him with several lists of circumstances that are the foundation for the Latin enumeration in the Middle Ages: who, what, where, with what helps, why, how, and when. But we should note that these are understood as the enumeration of the elements of action that a philosopher or lawyer would take into consideration when analyzing and studying a case, and a distinction is not made between essential and secondary elements. All are placed on the same footing even though they vary in importance. The term "circumstance" itself *(peristasis)* is first used in the singular to designate the concrete situation, singular case, object of the appeal. Boethius will be the first to use it in the plural to designate all these elements.

St. Thomas will take up as faithfully as possible these precious contributions of the philosophical tradition;[15] but he will make an important elaboration revealing the historical comparison, so as to adapt them to the needs and perspectives of theology. In his thought, the point of view of the theologian includes three convergent lines that determine his analysis of moral action: the orientation of the action to beatitude as to man's end; the quality of the action in itself, good or evil and more or less so; the effect of this quality, whether merit or demerit.[16]

St. Thomas's constructive work will cover two points:

1. Following the authority of the pseudo-Gregory of Nyssa, according to whom the principal circumstances are the *cuius gratia* or the end, and the *quid est quod agitur* or that which is done, St. Thomas makes of the end and the matter of the act the elements of the action. For him, the end is the principal *(principalissima)* element of the action, that which moves the agent to action and which directly involves the will. The second element is what is done, the matter of the action, which forms its substance. These two elements are essential to the action and around them the other elements will be ordered and will gravitate.

2. The term "circumstances" is given a more precise meaning. Taking his

15. *ST* I-II 7.3.
16. *ST* I-II 7.2.

stand on the etymology of the word *circum-stare,* or that which surrounds something, St. Thomas distinguishes the circumstances from the essence of the act which is formed by its end and matter: henceforth circumstances will designate those elements of the action that are added like accidents to its substance, in this sense, that they contribute to increasing or diminishing the moral quality of the action already essentially established by its end and matter; but they cannot of themselves render an act good or evil.

It should be observed that this division between essential elements and secondary ones, or circumstances properly so-called, leaves a few elements on the traditional lists that are without interest or indifferent as far as moralists are concerned, such as the fact that a theft was committed on such and such a day, at such and such an hour *(quando).* Yet this fact could be of great importance to a lawyer or policeman who might eventually find in it a proof of guilt or innocence.

Let us note that this definition of circumstances and of the essential elements of moral action is in reality new and obliges St. Thomas to make a "courteous" interpretation of his sources, for these in fact include the end and matter of the act in the list from which St. Thomas draws circumstances or accidental elements. St. Thomas acquits himself of this obligation by distinguishing between an end that pertains to the essence of the action—that chiefly motivates the one who acts—and a secondary end that may be added and that is properly speaking a circumstance. Likewise, in every act there will be matter of secondary importance that increases or diminishes the moral quality of the action.[17] The distinction thus established is in no sense artificial, for it adds a useful complement to the analysis of the components of a moral action.

Two zones are thus formed for the elements of a moral act, that is, the essential elements or the principal end and matter, and the secondary elements or circumstances. It is well to add here the indifferent elements, without importance for the moralist but still part of the concrete action.

This teaching on circumstances, with the distinctions it establishes between the elements of an action, is of prime importance. It allows the moralist to withdraw his attention from the almost infinite number of factors that enter

17. *ST* I-II 7.3 ad 3.

into every particular action so as to build a science extending to the universal, which can form universal rules based on experience and apply them to concrete actions with as much verity as possible. In order to apply a moral law to an action, it is enough, essentially, to ascertain the action's principal end and matter.

In regard to the problem of "intrinsically evil" acts, it will suffice to consider the essential end and matter to be able to determine that such an action is evil in itself.

Remark

The reader may have noticed that until now I have avoided using the term "object" when speaking of the elements of a moral action. My reason is that St. Thomas's vocabulary is more supple and richer than what was to follow later. For him, the term "object" does not signify a material thing as contrasted with a person, but the reality placed before the reason or will as its matter, and this could easily be God or another person when one is talking about the object of love. Nor is the object opposed to the end, for he will say that the end is the proper object of the will and designates the reality that the will seeks through desire and love. With St. Thomas therefore there is no identification between the object and the matter of the act, as there is with modern moralists.

Matter signifies not only what is material as opposed to what is spiritual, but also that on which an act has bearing. Thus, a person can be the matter of an act without prejudice to his dignity, as in the case of knowledge and love.

It is good to note also that the term *res* does not particularly signify a material "thing" but should rather be translated "a reality," and can therefore designate personal beings as in the Augustinian distinction between *res* and *signum,* which leads to the Trinitarian Persons as to the only "reality" absolutely worthy of love.

Finally, the term *substance* can also designate a person and should be understood in a special way when it is applied to a moral action, for this is a reality with a dynamic nature that accordingly includes an ordering to the end that is essential to the person.

Clearly, a correct interpretation of St. Thomas demands continual critical prudence on our part in regard to the moral vocabulary we ordinarily use. But this effort, required for that matter in studying any author of the past, can be very fruitful and enriching for the one who is willing to make it.

The Structure of a Moral Action

After the lengthy structural analysis of a human act in questions 11–17 in the *prima secundae,* dominated by the will to attain the end, and by the intention which is centered in choice and ends with *fruitio,*[18] St. Thomas explains the essential structure of a moral action in a remarkable article that contains the totality of his study of morality, an article which gives us the Thomist model of moral action.[19]

Moral action is divided into two parts: the interior act and the external act. These are not two separate acts but two parts or dimensions of a concrete action. We can distinguish them and study their respective contributions to the moral quality of the action, but we then must reunite them and show their coordination, their collaboration in forming the reality that is the total action. The terms used indicate this coordination: the act of the will is interior to the external act, and this through a dynamic interiority that inspires and moves. The external act is the outward manifestation of the interior act that produces it.

The interior act is constituted by the movement of the will which has its source in a simple wanting or determined by an end, unfolding in an intention to form the choice and ends finally in the *fruitio.* It is determined by the end as by the proper object of the will.

The external act begins in the choice and is directly determined by its matter with the circumstances. The work of choice will be to order this matter to the end willed to the point of executing the action to culminate in its *fruitio.*

These two parts of the action bring to morality their own proper and essential contribution: the contribution of the interior act which proceeds directly from the will is the formal principle of the morality of the action, for an act is properly speaking moral insofar as it proceeds from the will. The contribution of the external act is the material principle of its morality owing to the matter that is its object, to which the circumstances are added.

The interior and external act, the intention directed to the end and the

18. ST I-II *11–17*. See also my commentary on the Thomistic structure of the human act annexed to the two volumes on human acts in the 1962–66 *Somme de La Revue des Jeunes* edition (i.e., a French translation) of Aquinas's *Summa theologiae.* (*Les actes humains,* v. I, ch. III., *414–37*).

19. *ST* I-II 18.6.

choice of the matter, are ordered to each other therefore as form and matter, we might say as soul and body, to constitute the morality of the action. Let us recall that in his *Commentary on the Sentences*,[20] St. Thomas began by maintaining that the external act had moral value only *per accidens,* through the action of the will which came to it from without. But in his *De malo*,[21] he expressly abandons this opinion, which links him with Abelard, in order to coordinate the two parts of moral action no longer as substance and accident but as form and matter.[22]

The model of moral action that St. Thomas gives us can be shown in the following schema:

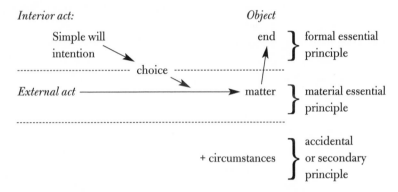

Interior act: *Object*

Simple will   end ⎱ formal essential
intention   ⎰ principle

-------------------------------- choice --------------------------------

External act ⟶ matter ⎱ material essential
                                                              ⎰ principle

                                                                    ⎱ accidental
+ circumstances ⎰ or secondary
                                                                    ⎰ principle

This analysis is the result of the Scholastic research on moral action initiated by Abelard and Peter Lombard. Moreover it is profoundly original, as is shown by comparing it with St. Albert or St. Bonaventure.[23] St. Thomas maintains the prime importance of the intention and the end in the establishment of morality and establishes this far more firmly and broadly in his theology than do his contemporaries. But he is no longer content to restrict the contribution of the external act to certain exceptions, certain cases of actions evil in themselves that no intention can legitimize. For him the external act is an essential composite in every moral action, good or evil.

St. Thomas completes his analysis of morality with a precise study of the

20. I *Sent.,* 40, 1.
21. *De malo,* q. 2, a. 2, ad 5.
22. See *Les actes humains,* v. II, n. 17, 184–85.
23. *Les actes humains,* v. II, n. 15, 177, and n. 17, 184.

proper contribution of the interior and external acts,[24] showing how the goodness or malice of the one communicates itself to the other and depends on it. We can thus study the moral quality of the interior and external acts in succession, one after the other, on condition that we then reunite them to show their interdependence, since it is together that they form the concrete action as well as the complete moral judgment, both of which are incumbent upon the moralist and any person of prudence. Despite some remaining difficulties of interpretation, we can without bias view this analysis as a masterpiece, even if we do not share the Thomistic concept of morality.

It is useful to note that the division of moral actions into an interior and an external act will be encountered again throughout the *secunda pars* of the *Summa theologiae.* In the *prima secundae,* virtue, as the interior principle of action, corresponds to the interior act, and then to the New Law, defined by the action of the Holy Spirit and exposed in the Sermon on the Mount, which regulates interior acts. In the *secunda secundae,* the study of each virtue in relation to a gift of the Spirit again points to the correspondence. Law corresponds to the external act as the external principle of action, expressed chiefly in the Decalogue and regulating external actions. The commandments of the Law are taken up once more in the detailed study of the precepts associated with each virtue. Clearly, St. Thomas's entire moral system is based on the twofold dimensions of the interiority and external quality of moral action. We cannot modify his study without jeopardizing the entire edifice.

Some Observations

I should like to add a few brief remarks on St. Thomas's teaching on the contribution made to morality by finality and by the external act.

a) The Primacy of Finality. For one who takes an unbiased view of St. Thomas, finality obviously plays an essential and preponderant role in his study of moral action, as we have seen in question 18, article 6 and throughout his moral theology. The latter begins with a study of the ultimate end and develops the supreme criterion to which St. Thomas will refer in all later treatises.

This point of view was novel in his day and reversed traditional positions. St. Albert and St. Bonaventure, for example, looked at moral action from the

24. *ST* I-II 19 and 20.

perspective provided by the Augustinian problematic of God's participation in evil action, and distinguished a threefold goodness in all His action: first, a goodness *secundum genus,* insofar as it is an action and God can intervene in it actively; next, a goodness *secundum speciem,* which comes to it from a fitting object; finally, a goodness caused by circumstances, of the end, which is accidental.

From the time of the *Sentences,*[25] St. Thomas reverses perspectives and considers moral action beginning with the will which causes it and the end seen as the object of the will. This is the moral goodness which he will qualify as formal beginning with *De malo.*[26] When, in the *Summa,* St. Thomas takes up the authoritative list of the threefold goodness of the human act, he will explain it in his own way. Notably, he modifies it by adding a fourth goodness "that results from the end as from its relationship with the cause of the goodness,"[27] which is, in reality, the first for him, as the context shows.

One can notice the same kind of change in the very definition of the voluntary. The classic definition that St. Thomas read in Aristotle and St. John Damascene was practically this: *"Cuius principium est intra cum scientia singularium in quibus est actus."* Now when St. Thomas cites this definition he always stops after *"cum scientia"* without mentioning the circumstances, and when he explains the nature of the voluntary he bases his whole explanation on knowledge of the end, which is plenary in the human person and which confers upon the person moral control of his acts as contrasted with those of other living beings.[28] The Thomist definition of the voluntary is: *"Cuius principium est intra cum cognitione finis,"* linking free spontaneity and knowledge of the end to form the essence of moral action.

b) A Finality Linked to Beatitude and End. Modern interpreters referring to St. Thomas often seem afraid to say this and even to see it, but it is clear that for the Angelic Doctor finality is inseparably linked to the question of beatitude, of which it is one aspect: the ultimate end of the human person is beatitude. Following Aristotle and the Sermon on the Mount, St. Thomas has reversed the order followed by Peter Lombard. He studies beatitude at the

---

25. I *Sent.,* 40, 1.
26. *ST* I-II 2.2 ad 1 and ad 5.
27. See *Les actes humains,* v. II, n. 14, pp. 175.
28. *ST* I-II 6.1.

beginning of theology, in his moral section, and not at the end, as in the fourth book of the *Sentences*. It is clear that in his eyes the question of the ultimate end and of beatitude is the centerpiece of moral theology. We are dealing therefore with a finality which touches the profound being of the human person in his love and desire for beatitude. It is not possible to linger over this extremely important point. I can merely observe that it would be a serious infidelity to St. Thomas to separate his teaching on finality from his study of beatitude, to accept the one and neglect the other, as has too often been done.

We have already remarked in connection with the Fathers that one might think the importance given to the question of beatitude would lead St. Thomas's morality to subjectivism. This is not true, any more than is the case with the Fathers who, as we saw above, were distinguished from the philosophers precisely by the objectivity of their concept of beatitude, love, virtue, and consequently, morality. St. Thomas is strictly in the patristic tradition when he begins his treatise on beatitude with the question: What is the true object of beatitude? He then progressively passes in review all external and interior, material and spiritual goods that could furnish a response to this fundamental question. He describes a human path to God in the moral order comparable to the five ways of the *prima pars*.[29] Paradoxical as it may seem to modern minds, the objectivity of the concept of beatitude in St. Thomas determines the objectivity of desire and love and through them the need for objectivity in every moral action.

Consequently the finality, intentionality, and interiority of a moral act likewise possess a dimension of objectivity that is primary and places them in the order of truth and goodness. For St. Thomas there can be no question of opposing a finality that would be subjective to the moral objectivity that would pertain to the act uniquely through its matter or its object.

c) A Finality That Is Moral and Not Technical. I should also like to indicate briefly a profound difference that separates St. Thomas's concept of finality from that of modern authors.

The finality of which St. Thomas speaks is properly moral; it is quite different from finality in the order of usefulness, or the technical finality we generally think of. The latter, based on the relation of means to end, abstracts from

29. *ST* I-II 2.

the nature of the things to which it is applied in such a way that everything can become a means or an end depending on how we view it in the order of utility. Moral finality, on the contrary, is based on the nature of things and discerns certain realities that can only be considered as ends and not as means. Notable among these are persons and moral qualities such as virtues. One cannot effectively attain virtues, become just, courageous, or truthful, if one does not know how to renounce direct utility and immediate pleasure out of love for justice or truth. Likewise, one does not truly love another person if one is not ready to sacrifice one's own interest or the pleasure of that person's presence out of love when the need arises. Such is the love of friendship, which surpasses interested love and is of another order. These personal realities are thus ends by nature and lead us into the properly moral order or the order of the *honestum,* as the ancients called it, which differs radically from the order of utility, where everything ends up by becoming a means or tool.

These realities, which are ends by nature, still do not constitute the ultimate end, but are for us the necessary paths by which to reach it. They are not means, but secondary ends. We can apply to them the very broad expression of St. Thomas, *"ea quae sunt ad finem ultimum,"* on condition that we do not understand them as simply means, which is all too easy to do. As persons and by our virtues, such as faith and charity, we order ourselves to God as *"ad finem ultimum,"* and yet it is precisely these virtues that render us capable of transcending the order of utility and self-interest most radically through sacrifice and gift, so as to raise ourselves to the level of "final realities."

This clarification was necessary in order to avoid interpreting the primacy of finality in St. Thomas's moral theology as a certain form of utilitarianism or as the principle of a kind of broad moral technique. What we have just said is opposed, for example, to the support that is sought in St. Thomas by current moralists, "proportionalists" or "consequentialists," for whom moral judgment consists basically in balancing the good and evil effects of each action according to the end that is sought. Utilitarianism is the danger that logically lies in wait for them and deludes them, because they can conceive of no finality save the technical in the order of utility. As a consequence of this they will be led to deny, at least theoretically, the existence of intrinsically evil actions.

d) **The Division between *Finis Operis* and *Finis Operantis*.** As we shall see further on, the separation between the *finis operis,* which designates the end inherent to the act and is identified practically with its object, and the *finis* *operantis,* or end added by the one who acts, will become in later Scholasticism a key to the interpretation of St. Thomas's teaching on morality.

Now when we study the texts of St. Thomas we perceive that he is well aware of this distinction and uses it sometimes in the *Sentences* in different connections;[30] but we do not find it anywhere in the *prima secundae* and therefore never in the study of morality and its foundations. We have to wait until the *secunda secundae,* in the treatise on temperance,[31] to see this division appear once more.

The conclusion is obvious: from a simply historical viewpoint it is clear that St. Thomas did not believe the distinction between *finis operis* and *finis operantis* necessary for the analysis of the composite parts of morality. As he himself says, moreover, at the beginning of the *Sentences: ". . . finis operis semper reducitur ad finem operantis."*[32] The end being the proper object of the will, all finality, even external, is led to the voluntary finality and integrated with it when it is taken up into the voluntary action. But later on, a new concept of morality and of action will lead interpreters of St. Thomas to consider this separation essential to moral finality. It will enable them to discard with ease those texts of Thomas which prevent them from focusing the moral judgment on the object of the act (its matter) and reducing the end sought by the acting subject to the rank of a circumstance.

e) Conclusion regarding the Problem of Intrinsically Evil Acts. For St. Thomas, the moral quality of an action depends on two essential components: the ordering of the interior act, will or intention, to the end, and the ordering of the external act to its proper matter. Some acts are intrinsically evil in themselves by nature at these two levels, such as hating another and killing or torturing an innocent person. But in a single action, it suffices that the end willed or the matter of the act be evil by nature, to make the entire act evil, according to the principle *"bonum ex integra causa, malum ex quocumque defectu,"* the deficiency being essential here. St. Thomas, following St. Augustine, will therefore admit that certain actions, even considered externally, are evil in themselves and can never be legitimized by a good end. It makes no difference that the evil cannot be fully explained without reference to the will and to the order of ends that determine and move it.

30. II *Sent.* 1.2.1 and 12.4, especially IV *Sent.* 16.3.1[2 and 3]; also *De malo,* 2.4, ad 9.
31. *ST* II-II 141.6 ad 1.
32. II *Sent.* 1.2.1.

We wonder only whether St. Thomas would have accepted the expression "an intrinsically evil" act, since for him "intrinsic" normally designates an interior act, voluntary interiority, while for modern moralists "intrinsic" actually signifies the external act in its opposition to, and inability to be reduced to the voluntary intention, owing to its object.

Ockham and Nominalism: The Radical Challenge to Intrinsic Morality

With Ockham and nominalism, the end of the Middle Ages is truly a revolutionary period for moral theology. A profound breach, not yet fully gauged, was created between the age of the Fathers or great Scholastics, and modern moralists. Under cover of classical vocabulary and teaching, Ockham inaugurates a new concept of morality that gives an unaccustomed meaning and role to words and to the elements of a moral act, within a novel structure and organization. Even though he was preceded by a Franciscan tradition, Ockham was truly an *"Inceptor,"* or beginner, if I may be allowed a pun on his traditional title. The problematic of morality was to receive new foundations, entrenched to the point of becoming classical and indisputable, as evidences. Historically, Ockham would elaborate his ideas on moral theology in direct opposition to St. Thomas, who had become the theologian of his great adversary, Pope John XXII. It was this pope who canonized the Angelic Doctor and who was the principal target of Franciscan criticism.

Two Concepts of Morality and Two Kinds of Freedom

I shall summarize here the chief differences between St. Thomas and Ockham concerning the concept of morality, in order to show subsequently their effect on the question of intrinsically evil acts.[33]

As we have seen, for St. Thomas the first and principal moral question is that of true beatitude, understood as an ultimate end ordering all moral acts to itself and thus unifying all action. Moral theology will be organized on the foundation of the virtues, recognized as interior principles of acts and as dy-

---

33. Cf. Pinckaers, *The Sources of Christian Ethics* (Washington, D.C.: The Catholic University of America Press, 1995); also L. Vereeke, "L'obligation morale selon Guillaume d'Ockham," *Supplément de la Vie Spirituelle* 45 (1958): 123–43; and A. Garvens, "Grundlagen der Ethik von Wilhelms von Ockham," *Franziskanische Studien* 21 (1934): 243–73.

namic qualities and capacities for producing quality actions in view of beatitude. First will be the theologal virtues, to which are joined the gifts of the Holy Spirit, the Beatitudes, and the acquired and infused moral virtues. We thus have a morality of beatitude, finality, virtues.

For Ockham, the first and fundamental notion regarding morality becomes the idea of obligation imposed by law, which expresses the omnipotent will of God limiting human freedom. The domain of morality will be circumscribed by obligations while the question of beatitude will become marginal. Moral theology will no longer be ordered according to virtues but according to the commandments of God which determine and impose obligations upon each free act. We will therefore have a morality of obligation, of law, of individual acts.

While St. Thomas's morality was, like that of the Fathers, a morality of interior attraction developed by the virtues, with Ockham there appears for the first time a morality of obligation properly so-called. It is not that the role of obligation had been unrecognized or neglected before his time, but it had never been placed at the center of the moral universe.

At the source of these two systematizations of morality lie two radically different concepts of freedom, expressed in two opposite interpretations of the definition of free will provided by Peter Lombard: *"Liberum arbitrium est facultas rationis et voluntatis."*[34]

For St. Thomas, reason (or intelligence) and will precede and engender free will and its act, choice. The source of freedom lies in the natural inclinations to truth and to goodness or beatitude, which constitute our spiritual nature and confer on us an opening onto infinite truth and goodness, rendering us free in regard to all limited good. We are free, *not in spite of, but because of* our natural inclination to truth and beatitude. The attraction of the true and the good are the foundation of our freedom and orientate it. We can therefore call it a freedom for excellence. It is developed through the virtues that enable us to act with excellence, ease, and joy. The natural law is the expression of God's wisdom and benevolence, revealing to us our spiritual nature orientated to truth and beatitude and prescribing the paths leading thereto.

For Ockham, on the contrary, free will precedes reason and will, since it can command their acts and choose whether or not to perform them. Freedom

34. "Free will is the faculty of reason and will." *In Sent.* II 24.

is defined, in fact, as the radical and absolute power we possess to choose between contraries solely in accordance with our will. Freedom is thus characterized by its indifference in regard to the contraries presented for choice. It will manifest itself most radically in this character when Ockham will demonstrate that we are free even in regard to the natural inclinations to beatitude and to being, for I can will to be happy or not to be happy; I can will to live or reject life by means of suicide. Freedom, in thus subjecting the natural inclinations to itself, casts them outside of itself and banishes them from the center of morality together with all that derives from them, the natural law and the virtues.

We find the same concepts and logic in regard to God, considered as the origin of the moral law. The moral law is no longer based on any nature whatsoever, divine or human, but draws its origin from the sole, all-powerful freedom of God, likewise understood as a power of choice between contraries, like a sheer, limitless will. The divine will is therefore the unique source of the moral law; but in itself it remains entirely indifferent and free in respect to law, in all its precepts. If and when God wills, God can change the precepts of morality, including the first precepts of the Decalogue.

The only foundation of morality, then, will be the law, seen as an expression of the divine will imposing itself upon human beings with the force of obligation, issuing from the divine omnipotence in regard to God's creatures. An act will therefore be moral only through its relation to the law. In itself it is indifferent, but becomes good or evil through conformity or contrariety to the commandments, as obedience or disobedience to obligation.

The moral universe thus swings between two poles: human freedom, the source of free acts, on the one hand, and the law, the expression of the divine will and source of obligation, on the other. The entire moral problem revolves around assessing the relation of each free act with the law, and this is done primarily through a consideration of the object of the act which harmonizes best with the law as it is verbally expressed.

Thus morality is no longer based on even a spiritual nature, which would assume a relationship and harmony between us and God, but on a struggle between two freedoms or wills that would keep all of morality in a state of perpetual tension, for obligation would always seem to us, from this perspective, like a restriction and obstacle to our freedom.

A New Position regarding the Question of Intrinsically Evil Acts

As we have seen, the traditional question was: Are there acts that are intrinsically evil in themselves and which one may never perform, even for a good intention? There was also a more general formula: Are there acts commanded or forbidden by law because they are good or evil in themselves by their very nature, or are all acts good or evil simply because they are commanded or forbidden by law?[35]

St. Thomas responded that obviously certain acts were good or evil in themselves and he based this quality on the natural law, issuing from natural inclinations and being the foundation of the structure of moral theology that the New Law would perfect. For him the positive law, human or divine, is added to the natural law in the same sense, in harmony with it, in order to clarify and perfect it. The quality of moral actions flows therefore first from their nature; after this a supplementary quality may be added through the positive intervention of a law.

For Ockham, the picture changes completely. All acts are indifferent in themselves, like the freedom from which they issue. This indifference affects not only external acts, *opera*, as Abelard called them, but in fact extends to interior acts, to love and the desire for beatitude. Pushing his thought to its logical conclusion, Ockham will actually go so far as to maintain that God could command a person to hate God and that in this case the hatred would be a good act.

Only through the intervention of law do acts lose their indifference and become good or evil. It is the positing of the law, therefore, or the imposition of obligation, that produces the moral quality of acts.

In the tradition of the theologians cited by St. Thomas, who had already said, *"quod justa et recta sunt solum lege posita,"* Ockham replied that human acts have no moral quality outside of the law that commands or forbids them. Ockham's position becomes still more radical when he makes natural law, which he continues to speak of, a positive law, a simple statement of the omnipotent will of God. Thus every law is in reality a positive law; natural law in St. Thomas's sense no longer exists. Although Ockham still refers to natural law, he places it entirely at the free disposition of God, who can always command the contrary.

35. Cf. *SCG* III 129.

We are thus confronted with the radicalization and generalization of the question of the existence of intrinsically evil actions. For Ockham there are not, and can never be, actions evil in themselves or by nature, for only law, which is always dependent upon the divine freedom, can render an action morally evil. Beginning with nominalism, therefore, the question of the intrinsic character of morality will broaden and involve the entire concept of morality.

Some Nuances

I have attempted to describe the position of Ockham and of nominalism by following the logic of the system. A few important nuances should be added in order to round out the picture fairly.

Ockham recognized the existence of what could still, in line with theological tradition, be called natural law. Natural law regulates the ordinary course of things as we know them and thus possesses a certain stability for us. But God can at will modify the ordinary course of things, as well as the natural law and its precepts. Herein lies the basis for saying that certain acts are evil in themselves, before any intervention occurs on the part of human reason and conscience. Nonetheless, this law is always dependent upon the freedom of God. It is like a bridge of snow over a bottomless ravine.

When cornered, nominalism will end by admitting that there is an absolute in morality, an act that is intrinsically good or evil, but only one: to obey or disobey the will of God, an obligation in itself, or a sheer duty. This is the supreme law for Ockham, and it leads him to designate God by only one name: the Norm. This basic act of obedience or disobedience remains formal and independent of its content, for everything else is relative. Every other act can be indifferent, either good or bad, including the most personal acts such as loving and hating.

The Effects of Nominalism on the Study of Moral Action
in the Setting of a Later Problematic

The extraordinary success of nominalism from the fourteenth century on has profoundly transformed moral concepts in the West, even among its adversaries. These will often unconsciously accept a nominalist position on moral questions which they should first have critiqued. The following three areas of influence have a general bearing on the subject.

1. One of the first characteristics of nominalism is the breaking up of action into atoms. Every human act, being the work of a freedom which could at each instant choose the contrary, becomes a separate atom. Consequently, the moralist will focus his consideration on individual acts, on cases of conscience. This is the logical origin of casuistry, of moral theology viewed as a study of cases.

Nominalism breaks all the bonds that unite human acts by their interiority and duration in time, that is, by finality, habits, and virtues. The last play only a secondary role and the concept of them will shrink and grow impoverished. The virtues, for example, become psychological mechanisms, habits, or again categories serving to classify obligations. To see how this differs from St. Thomas we need merely note that in the whole of the *secunda pars,* which counts 303 questions and more than 1,300 articles, we do not find a single case of conscience. For him the entire moral field is occupied by the virtues, seen as the unifying sources of acts. Cases appear only in the disputed questions posed by the university public.

We shall say therefore that casuistry as such originates with nominalism. Obviously, this is not to say that it is false, but only that its perspectives differ from those of the morality of St. Thomas and the Fathers.

2. Henceforth morality will be understood basically as the relation of the free act to the law that determines obligation. Moralists debate the nature of this relation: nominalists will say it is predicamental and Thomists will think it transcendental; but for all, morality will be defined by the relation of the single act to the legal obligation.

The Decalogue will be considered as the typical moral law, offering with its Ten Commandments the principal division of morality in place of the virtues.

Because he is watching the trajectory of the legal obligation, the moralist will in fact fix his attention on what St. Thomas called the external act in its relation to its matter or object, insofar as it can be directly touched by the law in its imperative or prohibitive expression.

The intention and the end will be curtailed and will lose their essential importance. Finality no longer signifies an interior principle of coordination of a group of human actions moving hierarchically and dynamically to an ultimate end. The end now under consideration is solely that which the subject proposes in the single act and which is added to the act externally, like a circumstance. The intention itself is reduced, concerning what is morally essential, to the willing of good or evil causing the single act faced with the prescriptions of the law.

It is already possible to describe the new model of moral action which will gain the ascendancy more and more:

Freedom

    The intention

        ↘

           The single act⟶ the object (or matter) ⟶ ◄— law

                          + the circumstances, whose

                           end is sought by the subject

3. Many moralists, notably of the Thomist school, will react against nominalism and will fight it, particularly on the point of the existence of actions in themselves evil, and they will attempt above all to maintain the natural law as the first foundation of morality, guaranteeing the intrinsic morality of actions that are conformed to it or contrary to it. They will also define morality as an intrinsic relation of acts to the moral law.

Nevertheless, these theologians will not succeed in avoiding the nominalist influence on some essential points. In general, they will adopt the concept of freedom of indifference. As a result they will not be able to escape the irreducible opposition it establishes between the subject on the one hand, with its radical demand for freedom, and on the other hand the object, law, nature, other subjects as well, and society, which oppose the subject by restricting its freedom. The function of classical moralists is to interpret and defend the moral law. They will therefore attempt to base it as objectively as possible on a natural foundation. But they will always be tempted to harden and materialize the object and the law in order to set up solid barriers to freedom and subjectivity. Thus they will be suspicious of "subjective" elements, intentionality, finality, affectivity, etc., and trust only in the imperative rigor of reason to establish the moral relation between the act and law. The moralist's objectivity will assume an aspect of anti-subjectivity at the risk of arousing an anti-objective reaction in the moral subject. Today we are witnessing a dialectical return toward the subject on the part of moralists themselves.

Francisco Suarez (1548–1617)

The theology of Suarez, a Spanish Jesuit who claims to be a commentator on St. Thomas, has exerted a profound influence particularly on the moralists who produced the modern manuals from the seventeenth century on. Suarez becomes the principal authority for the interpretation of St. Thomas in the Society of Jesus, which opted, at the end of the sixteenth century, in favor of the teaching of Aquinas. The influence of Suarez will be great especially in moral theology, for he will provide the speculative elaboration of the foundations of morality needed by Jesuit authors to work out a moral system destined for practical teaching, such as we find in the Suarez's *Institutiones morales* and the manuals of moral theology which take it as their model. Thus the Suarezian concept of fundamental morality, and particularly his analysis of morality, will be all the more influential in casuistry, to the point where the authors of the manuals, totally preoccupied with cases of conscience, are no longer concerned about the foundations they are building on. These appear to them to introduce a speculative reflection that is beyond their competence. As for Suarez, he provides us with a rereading of St. Thomas in the spirit of Renaissance humanism and joins the Scholasticism of the university, in its Thomistic renewal of the period, to the moral theology that has evolved since the Council of Trent in a pastoral perspective and is oriented to teaching priests in the seminaries about the administration of the sacrament of Penance and the solution of moral cases.

The work of Suarez is vast and complex. Although in general he follows the exposition of St. Thomas's *Summa theologiae,* he inserts later controversial principles into his commentary, notably those of the nominalists, and in the course of his lengthy questions Suarez adroitly slips in his personal thinking, which is original and open to contemporary ideas. It is sometimes difficult to distinguish it from the thought of Aquinas, whose language he uses and whose ideas he is explaining.

The Problem of Intrinsically Evil Acts

Suarez approaches the problem of intrinsically evil actions explicitly. We can therefore focus our exposition on disputation VII of his treatise on the goodness and malice of human acts.[36]

---

36. Suarez, *Tractatus* III, disp. VII, *Opera* v. IV (Paris: Vivès, 1856).

The fact that Suarez approaches the problem directly shows the importance it has acquired. Furthermore, though Suarez uses the expression *actus intrinsece mali,* it does not appear again in the wording of the question, which seems to indicate that the formulation, which will become classic, is just beginning to come into its own. The title of section 1 is worded thus: *Utrum sit aliquis actus voluntatis ex se et natura sua malus, etiam seclusa extrinseca prohibitione.* The third corollary poses the question: *quo sensu dicantur aliqui actus intrinsece mali;* but the expression *intrinsece malum* was already found in the response to the principal question.

Suarez first explains the problem that gives rise to the *dubium.* No voluntary act can be evil in its positive entity but only by defect in regard to the rule of the will which is the law, that is, in regard to the obligation it imposes. Thus it seems that one can only explain the malice of the act by its relation to the external law that commands or forbids it.

In his response, Suarez gives three opinions disposed dialectically. They make up a *status quaestionis* that is actually more speculative than historical, in spite of the authors' references.

The first opinion is that of the nominalists. Suarez cites, among others, Ockham and Gerson; to these he adds Duns Scotus and even a text from St. Thomas carrying the same sense.[37] This opinion holds that no act of the will is evil in such a way that it cannot not be evil *(quin posset esse non malus).* In effect, moral evil depends entirely on an external prohibition, at least on the part of God, whose will is free in all its effects *ad extra.*

The second opinion is directly contrary to this. It is absurd to deny that there could be evil acts of such a kind that they cannot be separated from their malice, by God's omnipotent power. To put it plainly: there are some acts from which malice is inseparable, and these God must necessarily prohibit. This opinion seems to be constructed by Suarez for the sake of argument, for he admits he has never found it in any author. It constitutes an extreme in the problematic. Suarez adds that this position respects the freedom of God for it only imposes a conditional necessity on Him: if He wills to create man free and acting according to reason.

This second opinion can all the same lead to a third, thanks to a distinction found notably in Gabriel Biel. One must admit that there are, necessarily,

---

37. *ST* I-II 79.6 ad 4.

intrinsically evil acts, even of the *potentia Dei absoluta;* but it is fitting to distinguish two kinds of laws: the indicative law that says *hoc est faciendum, vel non,* and the law of precept that commands *fac hoc vel non facies.*

The indicative law is wholly in the reason and does not depend on the will. It forms a judgment indicating the thing *(rem ipsam prout est).* It does not depend on the power of a superior, but on the thing itself.

The law of precept depends on the will insofar as it wishes to impose such and such an obligation and thus claims the power and jurisdiction of a superior.

In conclusion, this opinion holds that every evil act requires an indicative law but not a law of precept.

In his study of natural law, Suarez had marked out a middle path, maintaining against Gregory of Rimini, whom he also cites here that this law is more than indicative and contains a command that leads to obligation. But referring to Gabriel Biel, he maintains against Ockham that good and evil found in law do not proceed only from the divine will but flow from the fitness or unfitness of actions in themselves, according to the relation of their object to right reason. If the object of an act is contrary to reason the act is already a sin or a fault, at least philosophically speaking.[38]

Suarez's answer to our question includes two assertions and three corollaries, which I shall summarize here.

The first assertion states that certain acts of the will are in themselves evil *(ex se)* before being forbidden by any will and independently of it. Proceeding first by induction, Suarez cites some instances of actions that are in themselves contrary to reason. Firstly, hatred of God (if it is a free act and not committed in ignorance). Likewise, willing to act against one's conscience, against reason, against the command of a superior. Included here could be acts that God cannot will: such as willing to lie; willing not to keep a promise, etc.

The reason for this assertion is that the will receives its goodness or malice from its object. Now there are objects that are of themselves contrary to reasonable nature as such, beyond the imperative will of a superior. Such a will is therefore evil in itself because of its tendency to such an object, before an external prohibition has been declared.

38. Suarez, *De legibus,* lib. II, cap. 6, n. 5. Cf. A. M. Meier, *Das Peccatum mortale ex toto genere suo* (Pustet: Regensburg: 1966), 298–99.

In the second assertion Suarez maintains that there is no evil act of the will that is not contrary to the dictates of reason judging the malice of the act, or of the object. This gives a general significance, in the order of evil wills, to the relation of the act to the judgment of reason about its object.

The schema of moral action that Suarez brings into play thus includes the following essential elements: the will that produces the act, the relation or inclination of the act to its object, the twofold relation of the act through its object to the reason that judges its goodness and malice and to the law that is the source of the obligation and that emanates from the external will of God or of the superior. For him, the whole problem is how to establish the relation of the act to reason, which is at the basis of the existence of intrinsically evil acts according to tradition, in such a way that the fact of an objective morality, and its relation to the external law, is the cause of the obligation properly so-called, where the essence of morality lies. The schema is as follows:

In his third corollary, Suarez shows in what sense acts are said to be intrinsically evil. This expression does not signify that the malice is inherent to the physical entity of the act, but that the act cannot be performed morally, with freedom and without ignorance of such an object, without malice being joined or innate *(innata)* to it. The idea that such acts are good or indifferent is repugnant to him.

There is, however, a certain variety among intrinsically evil acts:

—in some, the malice stems from their direct and physical inclination to their object, as with hatred of God, or from a directly willed condition that causes depravity, such as the will to lie, to steal, etc.

—in other acts, the malice stems indirectly from their inclination to the object, as when one wills to take something or to be united to a woman without considering the fact that these do not belong to us. This condition could be modified from the point of view of the object without changing the act since it does not tend directly to it.

In conclusion, when one says that all evil must be contrary to a prohibition or a debt, this affirmation is true if one understands by debt *(debitum)* something intrinsic to rational nature as such. From this *debitum* there follows a judgment of right reason which forbids the malice that is contrary to nature without imposing any new obligation. It is therefore not necessary for an external prohibition to intervene, although in fact such a prohibition is always present in consequence of the perfection of divine Providence.

Morality by Reason of the Object and the End

We then find an interesting clarification, and one which will be successful, in Suarez's response to the question: Is there such a thing as objective morality and what is it?[39]

Objective morality, also termed "honesty" by Suarez, derives from the object of the act according to its suitability to the rational nature as such. But in regard to the end, it is well to distinguish two kinds of relations it has with the object of the act:

—the object may coincide with the intrinsic end of the act, and this amounts to saying that the act receives its goodness from the object or the end, for example, giving alms to relieve the misery of another;

—but the will can also move toward a worthy object because of its intrinsic goodness while at the same time ordering the act to a lesser worthy end; for example, one can love God for the sake of obtaining merit. In this case, the act's goodness is essential and substantial because of its object, while the goodness flowing from the end is only accidental and is added by an extrinsic implication.

We apparently have here, in the analysis of morality, the first general separation between the end inherent to the act and leading to the object, which is essential, and the end pursued by the subject, which is called accidental. Without doubt, Suarez had not yet established a connection between this difference of ends and the distinction between *finis operis* and *finis operantis*, but the idea is clearly expressed and will at once be taken up. We should note that although certain texts of St. Thomas could lend themselves to Suarez's distinction, St. Thomas in no way gave them such a meaning, to the detriment of finality, in his analysis of the moral act.

In conclusion, it seems quite clear that Suarez's problematic concerning

39. Suarez, *Tractatus* III, disp. II.

the question of intrinsic acts, and more broadly of their intrinsic or objective morality, is very much determined by the nominalist position on the moral problem. Suarez responds to the nominalist opinion by taking a position in favor of intrinsic morality having at its center the obligation that issues from the law as God's external will, and also the reduction of the act, taken in its singularity, to its inclination to the object, with the rejection of the end among the circumstances.

All Scholastic moralists of the modern period, when they come to discuss the nature of morality, will be caught on the horns of the dilemma. On the one hand is the concept of morality issuing from nominalism, now become general but logically leading to the rejection of intrinsic morality; on the other is their concern to be faithful to St. Thomas and Church tradition, both maintaining the existence of intrinsically evil actions. They can only escape by distinctions like the one Suarez proposed between the relation of the act to reason and to obligatory law, but such distinctions will always appear too subtle and complicated to gain a real foothold.

I might add that this problematic is not as artificial as one might think today. It is logical and real in its own way. We can find similar problems in other terms among theologians who criticize casuistry and even among philosophers who are strangers to it. The problem remains serious.

The Salamancans

The *Cursus theologicus* of the Carmelites of Salamanca is a classic example of the seventeenth-century theology of the Thomist school. It approaches the problem of intrinsic morality at the end of the study of human acts in a *dubium* devoted to the question of objective morality: *"utrum in obiectis sit aliqua moralitas quae dici solet 'objectiva' et in quo consistat."*[40]

In their response, the Salamancans make use of a characteristic distinction between formal and objective morality.

Formal morality depends upon freedom in its relation to law and cannot precede the act of the will. Morality that issues from matter and circumstances, that is, from the object of the act, and which precedes the latter, is the

---

40. The Salamancans, *Cursus theologicus*, v. VI, Tract. XI, disp. I, Dubium VI (Brussels, 1870).

cause and root of the goodness of the interior act, or its foundation: it is objective morality. It consists in the ordering of the act to the object as to its term, which becomes properly speaking moral through the intervention of freedom in relation to the rule of customs.

Before the determination by law, the relation of the act to the object is not formally moral nor distinct from its physical being, but it nonetheless constitutes a basic objective morality. We can call it radically or virtually moral.

The propriety or impropriety of objective morality is necessary for the distinction between good and evil and is established according to the four natural inclinations exposed by St. Thomas: self-preservation, propagation of the species, political and social life, and knowledge of the truth, the last two being proper to a rational nature.[41]

Objective morality does not yet imply a relation to law. It is nothing more than an extrinsic indication coming from a precept or prohibition made by the law, although such an indication is necessary by way of condition. This is why sins will not receive their species from the precepts they act counter to, but from their objects. Objective morality is a quality inherent in the object, not really distinct from its entity, expressing the manner of being of the will, through propriety or impropriety according to its ordering to its term, to its object, and underlying the determination through the law from which it abstracts.

From the point of view of the object, we can distinguish:

—the physical object: the physical entity;

—the fundamental moral object capable in itself of being regulated by law: here we find objective morality;

—the object in relation to law: this is formal morality subject to the precept of the law.

Objective morality is therefore independent of law; it is anterior to it as a foundation and plays a specifying role in its regard. It constitutes an intrinsic morality that precedes the extrinsic morality issuing from relationship to a legal precept.

Further on, the Salamancans clarify the objective morality that belongs to the act through its object and end.[42] They take up once more the distinction

---

41. *ST* I-II 94.3.
42. The Salamancans, *Cursus theologicus,* disp. V, Dubium.

proposed by Suarez, but add to it the distinction between *finis operis* and *finis operantis,* remarking that one should always keep this in view—which means that for them it is a necessary key to interpretation. They explain the position which will become classic in the manuals and which seems moreover to have already become adopted by custom.

Goodness as to the object is absolute and essential to the act. Goodness as to the end is twofold. There is the end to which the act tends immediately by its very nature, such as giving alms to help a poor man. This is the *finis operis,* which they also call *finis proximus* or *finis intrinsecus.* This end coincides with the object of the act and is essential to objective morality. In addition to this there is the end to which the action is directed by the free will of the one who acts. This is the *finis operantis,* also called *finis remotus* and *finis extrinsecus;* for example, to give alms for the satisfaction of one's sins. This end is distinguished from the immediate object and is accidental to the act.

Conclusion

We find in the Salamancans as in Suarez a mixed concept of morality in this sense, that they join the nominalist concept, which formally establishes morality through the extrinsic relationship of freedom to law, with the classic concept of objective and fundamental morality which is based on the relation of act to object, allowing the affirmation of intrinsic morality.

It is noteworthy that the Salamancans begin their analysis of the moral act with its physical entity which is determined by the object, at a level prior to formal morality that would today be called pre-moral or ontic. This perspective is the exact opposite of that of St. Thomas, who begins his study of moral action with the interior act whose finality is the essential dimension. Clearly, it is a matter of finality moving the acting subject.

Filippo Grossi (+ 1704)

In passing we should note a seventeenth-century author who in fidelity to St. Thomas does not align himself with the common opinion concerning the intervention of the end in moral action. This is Filippo Grossi, an Italian Dominican, in his *Tractatus in universam theologiam.*[43]

43. Grossi, *Tractatus de actibus humanis,* q. 6, a. 3 (Modena, 1694).

When he discusses the contribution of the end to the moral quality of acts, Grossi makes a clear distinction between the *finis operis* and the *finis operantis;* but in speaking of the latter he maintains that the goodness or malice it confers on the action is essential and specifies the act in a way parallel to the specification conferred by the object. It is a matter, Grossi goes on to clarify, of the end to which the intention tends and which motivates the action, and not of the end which the act in fact attains, while being *praeter intentionem,* for this latter, called the *finis terminativus,* could only play an accidental role in morality.

Certainly, the specification by the object and the specification by the end could be different, but they are intimately connected, for the same act cannot be good in regard to its object and evil in regard to its end, or again, evil in regard to its object and good in regard to its end, if it is not materially good. The malice in the intention communicates itself to the external act, as when one gives alms out of vanity. Likewise, the malice of the external act is transmitted to the interior act, as with one who steals in order to give alms. In these two cases the act is a sin and is contrary to prudence.

Grossi then adds this distinction borrowed from Cajetan, which was subsequently abused: malice *ex fine operantis* is essential to the commanding act in relation to the intention; but if considered from the viewpoint of the act commanded, it seems to be accidental, for example the classic case of one who steals in order to commit adultery: it is accidental to the theft that it is ordered to adultery. This distinction becomes dangerous when the consideration of moralists focuses on the commanded act as something taken in itself, and considers it to be the main subject of morality.

Grossi's example shows us that a faithful reading of St. Thomas could very well maintain the essential role of the *finis operantis* in the morality of an act, which leads to an intimate compenetration of the intention and of the act commanded to form the concrete action that the moralist is engaged in studying in its totality. But Grossi is going against the current and moreover has to accept a problematic and categories too narrow to allow him to truly align himself with St. Thomas.

Billuart (+ 1757)

Billuart is a classic representative of eighteenth-century Scholastic theology. He is highly skilled in explaining difficult theological doctrines simply and clearly. He was just the author needed to take up the complicated theological discussions of the preceding centuries and to prepare the material for the manuals of moral theology of the nineteenth and twentieth centuries. Billuart gives us analyses and categories that seem obvious henceforth, and a teaching that deals only with limited and very localized controversies.

For Billuart,[44] the principles of morality are the object, the circumstances, and the end, which is without doubt a circumstance but which St. Thomas always treats in a special way because of its particular influence on human acts.

The respective contributions of object and end are:

1. The first and essential goodness (or malice) of the human act is derived from the object morally considered. This moral essence of the act undergirds the quality conferred by circumstances and the end; it remains invariable even though the circumstances and end should change. Without it, the act cannot be conceived.

The act is specified by its object as by the term to which it tends. The object qualifies the act morally by its own relation to the regulation of reason and to the law that commands or forbids. This relation makes it differ from the physical object.

The act receives its goodness (or malice) mediately through the law, immediately through its object, as its direct term placed in relation to the rule of reason and the law.

This is indeed the analysis of the essence of morality already formulated by Suarez and the Salamancans. It focuses on the tendency of the act to the object, the latter passing from the physical to the moral order through the twofold relation to reason (in line with the Thomistic and humanistic tradition) and to law, the source of obligation (in line with nominalist thought). Priority is given to the morality caused by the object, as with the Salamancans, which establishes an objective morality as a foundation and a mediation in regard to a morality caused by law. The teaching is henceforth disengaged from the complexity of controversies and presents itself as a common good.

44. Charles R. Billuart, *Tractatus de actibus humanis,* dissertatio IV, art. III (Lyon, 1874).

2. Since the essence of morality is determined by the object of the act, the end can add only an accidental qualification, whatever importance one may attribute to it. Obviously Billuart, like all St. Thomas's commentators, comes up against numerous and explicit texts in which Thomas gives finality a top-ranking role in moral action. The response is not difficult; it is already at hand. It is clearly based on the distinction between the *finis operis* and the *finis operantis.*

It is in the light of the *finis operis,* which is intrinsic to the act and coincides with its object, that one must interpret all the texts of St. Thomas which give a prominent role to the end and make of it an essential element of morality. The *finis operantis* or extrinsic end is ranked among the accidents or circumstances of the act, even if one might call it the chief one. From this point, Billuart will attempt to explain all the texts of St. Thomas that may be used in objection to his position in favor of an essential finality.

Historically, when one is aware of the problem and reads the texts of St. Thomas as objectively as possible, this interpretation seems surprising, so clear is the primacy of finality in the approach of St. Thomas. But Billuart is sincere and believes he is right, like all the others who preceded and followed him in this reading of it. It simply happens that the perspective on the moral act has lost depth and has narrowed since the time of St. Thomas. We can no longer see finality and morality as he saw them. The correction was all the more difficult as Billuart had neither the perspective nor the historic means of studying St. Thomas sufficiently.

Billuart concludes his exposition of the moral act by enumerating a fourfold goodness:

1. natural goodness, constituted by the physical being of the act, for it is good insofar as it has being;

2. moral and specific goodness because of the object considered morally (that is, in its relation to reason and faith);

3. goodness owing to the circumstances, which is accidental;

4. goodness owing to the end, equally accidental.

Here we can observe various views of the moral act. Billuart's view begins with the natural or physical goodness, centers on goodness owing to the object, and marginalizes goodness due to circumstances and to the end. St. Thomas's view, differing from that of his precursors, begins with the relation of the act to its end as to the object of the will, which leads him to add a fourth goodness to the classic list and to qualify it as a cause of moral goodness, without neglecting the importance of the relation of the act to its matter and circumstances.

Interior Act and External Act

As an assiduous reader of St. Thomas, Billuart clearly perceived the importance of the distinction between the interior act and the external act in the *Summa,* and the priority given to the former. He therefore tried to take this into account in his own analysis of moral action and to show how the interior act produces the essential morality.

However, when we read Billuart attentively we notice a shift in his concept of the interior and external act and a leaning toward exteriority, in contrast to St. Thomas. For Billuart, the interior act consists properly speaking in the will's moving the commanded act to its object, wherein the essence of its morality lies. The external act is then reduced to the mere execution of the will, already determined and qualified, so that it only has a *secundum quid* contribution to morality in relation to the accidental reward or penalty, that is, secondary effects. As for the interior act whose end is the object according to St. Thomas, it, too, is marginalized in morality along with the end of the one who acts, and becomes a mere accident.

Thus Billuart, without being fully aware of it, introduces what the Schools call a subtle equivocation. The interior act of which he is speaking is no longer in reality that of St. Thomas with its full dimension of interiority and its power of intentionality. From now on it consists in the will (intention and choice issuing from freedom of indifference) moving the act which is morally qualified by reason and the law according to its object. This will is obviously essential to morality, but its direct goal is the matter of the external act, such as St. Thomas conceived it.

Billuart's error is not accidental. It is a perfect portrayal of a concept of morality that had become current. The essence of morality lies in the will (or intention, which can again be qualified as an interior act) to perform an act determined according to its object (its matter) by reason or law. The heart of morality thus becomes the act in its objective exteriority as decreed by law. Moral interiority collapses before the intention and the choice to obey or disobey a rational or legal imperative. As for spiritual interiority, it is forced to abandon the field of morality and take refuge in spirituality and mysticism.

Intrinsic Morality

Billuart does not approach the problem of intrinsically evil acts explicitly, doubtless because he avoids getting into discussions that are too speculative and no longer of current interest. But it is easy to see how he could have upheld the intrinsic morality of acts. This rests on the tendency of an act to its object placed in relation to reason, as the rule for morals. This direct qualification is assumed by law, which qualifies acts mediately and adds to them the obligation issuing from a precept. Billuart thus takes his place among the modern defenders of intrinsic morality as opposed to nominalism, but accepts the same duality as his precursors in the definition of morality.

We can schematize Billuart's analysis in the following chart:

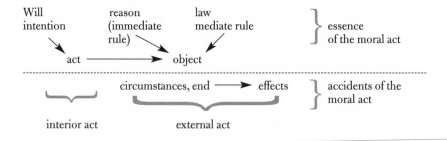

The Manuals of Moral Theology

We can complete our historical overview by glancing quickly at the manuals of moral theology of the last two centuries. The teaching on the *fontes moralitatis* that we have found in Billuart, already classic in his day, is taken up generally by all the authors of manuals without further discussion. It has become common property. When the teaching on intrinsic morality and intrinsically evil acts is treated, it is established on this basis and these categories. Present-day critics of the traditional positions express themselves with the ideas and categories inherited from this school. It is well to note, moreover, that the moralists of these two centuries deal mainly with practical problems and the solution of current difficult cases. They are no longer interested in questions of fundamental morality and are content, at this level, to adopt the ideas elaborated in the preceding centuries. Now, things are beginning to change. The structure of theology as well as its practice is shaken to its very foundations. It is time to take a look at this. In a recent doctoral thesis, J. Murtagh has studied the teaching on intrinsic malice among the moralists of the nineteenth century up to our time.[45] The author reveals two tendencies today in the concept of *intrinsece malum*. One conceives and defines it as that which is intrinsically evil because of its object, independently of circumstances and motivation. This is the position that has become classic in the manuals. The other tendency, presented as novel, holds that one cannot judge a moral act without including, in addition to its object, all the circumstances and especially the motivation or intention. Thus one cannot establish the existence of an intrinsically evil act without taking all these elements into account, which is, to say the least, difficult.

The author also notes the diversity of formulations of the teaching on *intrinsece malum* in the manuals. He rightly observes in current discussions the variety and imprecision of meanings given to the term "circumstance" and also "object," which is not always clearly distinguished from the physical object.

Yet everywhere the distinction between the *finis operis* and *finis operantis* is found ranked among the circumstances.

Regardless of the shifting vocabulary and a certain confusion of ideas, the basic categories that were used at the beginning are still to be found in the manuals for the most part, or if by chance new names appear, they can easily enough be traced back to the originals. In other words, the basic schema, always presupposed even by those who critique the manuals, remains as follows:

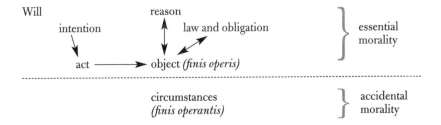

45. J. Murtagh, "Intrinsic evil. An examination of this concept and its place in current discussions on absolute moral norms" (doctoral thesis, Gregorian University, 1973).

We will close our historical overview here, having reached some present-day discussions which merit separate treatment. I should like to draw together a few teachings flowing from our study which may help to throw light on the present situation.

Conclusion

Our historical journey is obviously unfinished. We have chosen theologians representative of the moral teaching of their times. In consulting them, we have not limited ourselves to texts that address the problem of intrinsically evil acts explicitly, for this formulation apparently dates from the sixteenth century, while the problem of intrinsically evil acts was already recognized by Fathers of the Church such as St. Augustine and is logically related to the broader question of the intrinsic morality of human acts, or one's concept of morality itself. We should therefore note the insertion of the problem into the analysis of the moral act elaborated by various authors, whom we could only evoke rapidly. This was necessary, however, as is shown by current discussions during which the questioning of the existence of intrinsically evil acts has led numerous writers to the critique and revision of the entire treatment of the *fontes moralitatis.*

Despite its gaps and its sketchiness, our research still allows us to propose some conclusions.

1. In traversing the various periods of the history of Christian theology as we have done, it has become clear that the conviction that there are actions evil in themselves, things one may never do even for a good intention, was a constant conviction in the tradition, firmly established in the consciences of theologians and faithful alike even before the theological formulation and its systematization came into being. This conviction is closely related to the Christian perception of the objective dimension of moral action in the sense that it is intimately connected with the God of revelation and therefore with one's neighbor as well. This leads theologically to the affirmation of the intrinsic character of the fundamental morality of human acts.

Thus, it seems that—despite their limitations—modern Catholic moralists (i.e., the manualists) are rightly defending a constant and necessary given of Christian moral teaching when they uphold, with the Magisterium, the existence of intrinsically evil acts. The narrowness and eventual imperfection of views and reasons put forward in defense of this claim should not blind us to the inherent justice and importance of the cause. It is up to us to make the needed improvements. Yet this is not easy, for the problem cannot be circumscribed as one particular question; it has, in fact and logically, a general bearing on morality.

2. We can divide the history of our question into three periods forming a sort of dialectical movement. In the first period, extending from the Fathers to the thirteenth century, when morality is understood as a response to the question of beatitude attained through the theological and human virtues, the doctrine of the intrinsic morality of acts rests on the solid foundation of revealed law and natural law. The intrinsic quality of the virtues is communicated to our acts in conformity with our spiritual nature and the objectivity of the God of revelation.

The second period begins with the nominalist crisis. In opposing freedom to nature, as much from the human side as from the divine, Ockham robs moral theology of any criterion for judging the intrinsic quality of acts and is logically led to deny the intrinsic goodness or malice not only of external acts but even of interior ones. All acts depend on the absolute freedom of God, who has power over the very precepts of the natural law or the Decalogue. Nominalism thus introduces into moral theology a logic that if followed rigorously leads to the radical and general negation of the existence of any intrinsic quality, morally good or evil, in human acts. In the ordinary course of events, the theory whereby the law customarily called natural retains its value for us merely veils the consequences of this logic issuing from freedom of indifference, thus allowing the Christian conscience to accept the nominalist system. There is nothing now to prevent human acts from being indifferent in themselves and receiving their moral qualification from an external law alone.

The third period covers the reaction of Scholastic theology to nominalism, chiefly expressed by defending the intrinsic quality of certain evil acts in particular by the reestablishment of natural law and reason as foundations of the objectivity of moral judgment. Nevertheless, the systematization of moral theology being organized in the modern period accepts a duality and a compromise that render its construction fragile and complex. Although fundamental morality rests on reason and human nature, formal morality is nonetheless conceived as issuing from legal obligation, from the sheer will of God in accord with freedom of indifference. The seed of nominalism is thus still present, even though its development is opposed by a rational objectivity that tends to stiffen in order to ward off the subjectivism this seed conceals.

These historical stages are not buried in the past, as one might suppose. It is not difficult to see that they are present and active in the depths of the Christian conscience and experience. Current discussions about intrinsically evil acts have this advantage at least: they awaken and revive in us the remembrance of this history.

The patristic period in particular, drawing directly from the Gospel and culminating with the theology of St. Thomas, offers a model of Christian morality which could be enormously useful to us. Of course, there can be no question of making a copy of it to apply to our times. But the theology of the Fathers and St. Thomas describes a type of morality that helps us to evaluate the systems of recent centuries, so as to form a judicious critique that will prepare the way for a more solid and adequate reconstruction.

From this perspective, I offer a brief indication of two characteristics that seem to emerge from our study.

Modern Scholasticism has defended the teaching of intrinsically evil acts or of intrinsic morality by placing it in a setting that is too narrow. Within this framework the moral question focuses entirely on the tending of the individual act to the object, considered in its relation to the legal obligation, that is, at the level of the exteriority of the act, with an insistence at the same time on the objectivity that treats the moral act as a physical act.

It is indispensable that moral theology should rediscover the sense of dynamic interiority which is the primary source of human action, and that it should once more recognize the essential role of finality which penetrates and tends to unify the multiplicity of acts so as to dispose them according to progress in the virtues. This is of no little importance, for the reestablishment of interiority is the condition for the strengthening of the attenuated bonds between morality and the New Testament, where we find morality described as life in the Spirit, as the life of "the interior person." In other words, the wall of separation between morality and spirituality must be overthrown in order to reestablish the lines of communication between morality and the Gospel.

It is of the utmost importance to reestablish at the same time the demands of objectivity, of truth, we could say of reality, that dominate Christian moral interiority and the finality that inspires it. This is the primary source of the objective claims of truth and moral good which then move on, by way of the virtues, to the external acts whose own demands can thus be morally integrat-ed. We cannot establish the intrinsic morality of acts solidly unless we have properly based it on the moral quality of interior acts, where a discreet dia-logue unfolds between the human person and God, and unless we have firmly reestablished communication between these two constitutive dimensions of human persons and their acts: interiority and exteriority.

In closing, I should simply like to note that ultimately this entire problem-atic is controlled by two basic questions that determine the concept of morali-ty. Firstly, there is the problem of the primary question in moral theology: the question of beatitude and the question of obligation. And secondly, there fol-lows the problem of the nature of freedom: Is it the freedom of indifference as opposed to natural inclinations, or is it what we call the freedom for excel-lence, rooted in the inclinations of the human person's spiritual nature? I be-lieve it is impossible to go any deeper; but here we have as it were the root questions of the moral problematic.

12 ∿ Revisionist Understandings of Actions in the Wake of Vatican II (1982)

Catholic Moral Theology after the Council and after the Encyclical *Humanae Vitae*

Since the Second Vatican Council, numerous factors have contributed to enlivening Catholic moral theology, which had been stranded in the teaching of the manuals of recent centuries. There had already been (particularly Thomist) criticism of these manuals in the period following the Second World War, especially with regard to their narrowness and inadequacy in their treatment of Scripture and tradition.[1] It was inevitable that the innovative trends in the areas of Scripture, theology, and pastoral practice surfacing after the Council, with more or less fidelity to it, should have led like succeeding waves to progressive challenges in the realm of moral theology, the meeting place of the Church's theory and practice, thought and life. As elsewhere, questions were asked and changes introduced, particularly in the name of openness to the world, that is, to modern philosophies and human sciences, above all sociology, psychology, and history, regarding which theology had formerly often been on the defensive. This openness revealed new horizons, vast as the world itself and characterized by human solidarity. It held the attraction of novelty

Originally published as "La question des actes intrinsèquement mauvais," in *RTh* 82 (1982): 181–212, and reprinted in Servais Pinckaers, *Ce qu'on ne peut jamais faire* (1986): 67–110. Translated by Sr. Mary Thomas Noble, O.P., with the assistance of Craig Steven Titus. Edited for publication in *The Pinckaers Reader* by John Berkman.

1. See Jacques Leclercq, *L'enseignement de la morale chrétienne* (Paris: Editions du Vitrail, 1949); S. Pinckaers, *Renouveau de la morale; Études pour une morale fidèle à ses sources et à sa mission présente* (Tournai: Casterman, 1964); S. Pinckaers, "Notes and Appendices," in Thomas d'Aquin, *Somme théologique: Les actes humains. I-II 6–17, 18–21*, translated into French by H. D. Gardeil and S. Pinckaers (Paris: Editions du Cerf, 1962, 1966).

and in addition offered the enticement of shaking off the yoke of preceding generations. But it also had its dangers, particularly for minds too long sheltered and little accustomed to navigate the high seas of modern philosophical teachings and ideologies. The temptation was strong to favor the broad view of the world as contrasted with the narrow Gospel path, without the necessary discernment and foresight in regard to results.

The paramount catalyst, however, was not so much the call to renewal launched by the Council as the shock of the encyclical *Humanae vitae* in 1968 and the stand taken by Paul VI against artificial means of contraception. The reaction of moral theologians who did not share the view of the encyclical spread progressively, through reflection, from practical behavior to arguments, methods, and principles, and led to a reappraisal of the very authority of the Magisterium in matters of morality. Thus a critical and innovative trend came into being in regard to the traditional moral teaching of the manuals. It attempted to construct a theological and rational justification for broader opinions on concrete moral problems at the very heart of the classic moral edifice, with particular attention to the contributions and perspectives of current thinking.

The problem of essentials would thus be articulated and debated in the very terms and categories of Scholastic moral theology of recent centuries, but from a perspective of criticism and broadening.

Here as elsewhere, we need to avoid polarization between traditionalists and innovators, for this kind of division lacks nuance and too easily becomes polemical; there are other trends in moral theology today that use other categories and pose other problems. It is a fact, nonetheless, that what presents itself as new, and a break with tradition, is often a revival of old problems, if not an actual return to the past.

However this may be, I shall try to describe here the problematic that predominates in discussions between Catholic moral theologians today, and attempt to untangle and trace the profound logical thread that guides reflection, underlies the positions taken, and ends by forming a particular system of thought. I shall conclude with a critical assessment of the principal points found in the opinions discussed.[2]

---

2. [Editor's note: In the French edition, Pinckaers inserts a bibliography of more than fifty essays on this topic published between 1965 and 1985.]

I. The System of Proportionate Reason

Intrinsically Evil Acts and the Principle of Double Effect

At the center of the debates is the question of the existence of intrinsically evil acts, or acts evil in themselves, which one may never perform for any good end under any circumstances. The response to this question holds the solution to concrete problems under discussion: artificial means of contraception, abortion, sterilization, lying, etc., as well as torture and the death penalty. If certain acts are intrinsically evil, no motive can justify them and no exception is admissible in principle. In order to solve difficult cases and to open the way to exceptions that practice seems to require, "innovative" moralists set out to challenge the doctrine of intrinsically evil acts as it has been presented and taught by traditional moral theology, particularly in its application to difficult cases, which have always been the nerve centers and strongholds of the casuist in his discussions.

To solve these contentious cases, traditional moral theologians, in their concern to reconcile the demands of morality with their sense of human realities, have worked out the teaching on double effect. When an act produces two effects, one good and one evil, it is lawful to perform this act in spite of the evil effect, on four conditions.

1. The act must be good in itself or at least morally indifferent.

2. The intention of the one who acts must be upright, that is to say it must tend directly to the good effect, such that the evil effect is *praeter intentionem*.

3. The evil effect must follow after the good effect or at least be concomitant with it—this may be understood in the temporal, physical order or in the causal order—in such a way that the evil effect never becomes a means for attaining the good effect, according to the principle drawn from St. Paul: *Non sunt facienda mala ut eveniant bona* [It is not licit to do evil that good may come of it] (cf. Rom 3:8).

4. Finally, in performing the action there must be a motive proportionately grave in relation to the magnitude of the evil effect.

This principle has been applied in general to all doubtful and difficult cases, and has directly and principally occasioned the criticism of "revisionist" moralists. It is clearly based on the idea that there are acts and effects evil in themselves, which can never be the means to one's proposed end, however good it may be.

But make no mistake. Those who have not studied moral theology will feel that they are dealing here with technical and specialized considerations relating to some very esoteric problem. In reality, behind this question and starting with these foundations that suffer from the narrowness of casuistry, the entire concept of morality is at stake, notably in the form of the following question: is morality intrinsic to human acts in such a way that they are good or evil in themselves, or does this quality come to them from without, through their relationship to law, to reason, or through the relationship of means to a chosen end?

Universal Humanism and Natural Law. Furthermore, changes are going to be marked by a revival of humanism. Catholic morality after Trent had already been strongly influenced by Renaissance humanism. It was constructed mainly on the foundation of natural law expressed in the Decalogue and on a concept of human nature understood as practically self-sufficient in the field of morality properly speaking. The dominant intention was to build a strictly rational morality, valid for all people owing to the universality of reason.

"Revisionist" moralists will have the same rational perspective, but they will make it more radical under the influence of the Enlightenment and of current philosophies and sciences based on the autonomy of reason and often opposed to the intervention of revelation, the Magisterium, or any authority whatsoever. They will also have a revived concern for universalism in a world becoming more unified than ever before. Yet here they will again run into the problem of intrinsically evil acts: are there universal moral laws prohibiting certain acts as intrinsically evil and therefore as forbidden to all universally? Valid in time and space, these laws should be unchangeable and independent of cultures. Those who challenge the existence of intrinsically evil acts will thus be logically led to revise the teaching on universal and unchangeable moral laws and to critique the natural law that undergirds them. But then, on what foundations will they establish moral universalism?

Catholic morality of recent centuries thus finds itself challenged in its totality and its systematization. It is necessary to keep in mind these dimensions of the problem of intrinsically evil acts in order to discern its impact and to detect the internal logic that joins its parts, even unknown to the one who is working with it.

Peter Knauer's Approach. A publication highly representative of the new trend in the critique of the principle of double effect appeared shortly before *Humanae vitae.* It is an article of Knauer, "The determination of moral good and evil through the principle of double effect."[3] The mere wording of the title manifests the general importance the author gives to this principle in moral theology. Moreover, he faults the manuals for having treated it too briefly, not seeing its importance. This article is very significant because of its logical power. It already contains in essence all the elements that characterize the new approach to morality, to be completed by other authors in their various ways. We shall retrace Knauer's development of the theory as best we can, leaving to one side the critique of the manuals on which it is based, so as not to miss the forest for the trees.

For Knauer, the moral order is based on a preliminary assumption, the existence of ontological good and evil, which are defined on the basis of a metaphysical experience concerning the existence of a perfection appropriate to us or the privation of this perfection. The privation of such a perfection cannot be willed as such. Our acts therefore possess a primary goodness or evil in the ontological order, through what they produce. This is what other authors call ontic, pre-moral, or even physical good or evil.

The passage from the ontological to the moral order, which is also an extension, is made through the intervention of the will and precisely by the application of the principle of double effect to the matter of the act. Some fine-tune this further by saying that every act, in its concrete reality, inevitably has both good and bad effects, were it only because every choice deprives us of what we do not choose.[4] Thus the principle of double effect acquires a gener-

3. Peter Knauer, "The Hermeneutic Function of the Principle of Double Effect," *Natural Law Forum* 12 (1967): 132–62. Reprinted in Curran and McCormick, eds., *Readings in Moral Theology No. 1* (New York: Paulist, 1979), 1–39. [Editor's note: Pinckaers is citing Peter Knauer, "La détermination du bien et du mal moral par le principe du double effet," *NRT* 87 (1965): 356–76, which Knauer refers to as the "first form" of the essay. Knauer's "The Hermeneutic Function" is a translation from a later, German-language version of the essay.]

4. Thus, at the ontological level, Louis Janssens distinguishes two forms of ambiguity in our acts. They are due to our temporality and spatiality. Because of its insertion in time, every choice inevitably includes the sacrifice of another choice that cannot be attained at the same time; this loss constitutes a certain ontological evil. The external realities that our acts touch have their

al bearing on human acts because of these two effects or aspects that they necessarily possess. Without doubt, the application of the principle of double effect presupposes the estimation of ontological good and evil, but it precedes the moral judgment, which consists in the will to do such and such a determined good or evil act. Before the judgment about the effects of the act, there is not yet any moral evil properly speaking.

In Knauer's article, we encounter a complete reinterpretation of the principle of double effect that begins with the third condition of the classic theory. Traditional morality required a physical priority of the good effect over the evil effect in order to guarantee that the first should be a good willed directly and the second indirectly, in an objective way, which leads to an external splitting up of the action. For Knauer, the moral act forms a total structure wherein the motivation of the subject takes place in the *finis operis* itself, for this is none other than what is formally willed by the subject as the object of that person's will. It is therefore because it enters formally into the intention of the will that an evil thing becomes morally so. Whether it is physically mediate or immediate in the material unfolding of the action is of secondary importance to Knauer.

Having rid himself of this obstacle in his path, Knauer comes to the heart of his problem, how to establish the relationship in the order of priority between the good and evil effects, which will lead to the good or evil quality of the action as a whole? He at once gives us what he calls one of his key terms. This corresponds to the fourth condition of the traditional theory but receives an entirely new meaning here: it is the requirement of a proportionate reason.[5] Basing his argument on two examples, cooperation in another's sin and the difference between affirmative and negative laws, Knauer goes on to state that the existence or nonexistence of a proportionate reason is decisive and demands priority: an evil effect will be indirect, and the act will be legitimate, if there is a proportionate reason and the good effect is higher; the evil effect will be direct and the act will be evil if there is not a proportionate reason. Knauer

---

laws and always produce certain evil effects that we cannot separate from the good results sought; for example, industrialism produces pollution. See L. Janssens, "Ontic Evil and Moral Evil," *Louvain Studies* 4 (1972): 115–56 [Editor's note: Reprinted in Curran and McCormick, 40–93]; and Janssens, "Norms and Priorities in a Love Ethics," *Louvain Studies* 6 (1977): 207–38.

5. [Editor's note: In "Hermeneutic Function," Knauer uses the term "commensurate reason" rather than "proportionate reason."]

even takes the liberty of quoting a text from Pius XII in support of his theory. The proportionate reason thus serves as the essential criterion in forming a moral judgment. From this we can conclude that "the proportionate reason is none other than the actual direct object of an act,"[6] identified with its *finis operis*.

We now need to define a proportionate reason more precisely. The proportion involved here does not imply a comparison with other values, from which one must choose the highest[7] and which are often almost immeasurable; it is applied to one single object and considers it in the proportion of the act to its end. "There is a proportionate reason when the act is proportioned to the value it is pursuing,"[8] and this with a certain urgency, as being the necessary condition for obtaining this end. It is therefore the finality, that is, the relation of the proportionate means to the end or the value sought, which will dominate the moral judgment.

Moreover, and it is important to realize this, such a judgment of proportion includes, at the moral level, the consideration of the total reality that the act brings about, according to a metaphysical and universalizing reflection. The example given is enlightening: the thief appropriates a good in order to possess it, which is not evil at the pre-moral level; but in doing so he virtually denies the right to property in general, and so denies his own right to property. Thus in every evil act one denies, at the level of total reality, a condition of possibility for the very good one is seeking. Here, therefore, there is no pro-

---

6. Knauer, "La détermination du bien," 366. [Editor's note: "If a commensurate reason is present, the permission or causing of the evil becomes indirect and is *objectively no longer the object of moral intention.* The commensurate reason occupies the same area as what is directly willed and alone determines the entire moral content of the act. *If the reason of an act is commensurate, it alone determines the finis operis, so that the act is morally good.*" Knauer, "Hermeneutic Function," 10–11. (Italics in *Readings in Moral Theology No. 1* reprint, but not in *Natural Law Forum* original.)]

7. Knauer, "La détermination du bien," 367: "This solution is liable, at the very least, to the danger of rigorism. It does not admit the difference between the good and the best . . . This morality of charity aspires to the more perfect in response to a counsel and not to an obligation . . ." Note that this paragraph and this position are characteristic of the mentality of moralities of obligation, for which the search for perfection, not being of strict obligation, pertains not to morality, properly speaking, but to spirituality. An entire moral system can thus be erected without dealing with the search for perfection in charity. The latter would then be added as a superstructure; not as a logically necessary part of the edifice. [Editor's note: See also Knauer, "Hermeneutic Function," 17–18.]

8. Knauer, "La détermination du bien," 368.

portion between the end and the value sought, and the act is evil. On the other hand, one should not only permit, but "one ought to admit an evil if it is the only way of not directly contradicting the maximum value that opposes it,"[9] that is, if there is a proportionate reason.

We see here a mixture of a teleological perspective with a consideration of the universal along Kantian lines. But in fact the relation to the end predominates, as is shown by the application of the criterion of proportionate reason to the case of legitimate defense, of the death penalty, of theft in time of need, and of lying. Each time, the evil in question will be willed indirectly, and it will be acceptable to adapt oneself to it if there is a proportionate reason. Without that reason, these evils would be willed directly and the action would be evil.

Thus Knauer is able to conclude that to act with a proportionate reason is the key term in all moral theology. By means of such a reason one can determine what is willed directly or indirectly, what is the *finis operis* or object of the action that defines it morally, and thereby to pass from the ontological to the moral order in discerning goods and evils.

I have lingered over Knauer's article because of its systematic value. It constitutes the model for what has been called "the new morality" and yields up to us its essential features. This is indeed a new system of morality being proposed to us, and it will establish a new school. We find it again notably in the articles of Louis Janssens in *Louvain Studies*.

A Revolution in the Casuist System. Before taking a closer look at the chief trends in this systematization, let us note that it springs from the heart of casuist morality and even claims to remain with it, for Knauer believes that his exposition of the principle of double effect "provides an excellent explanation of the moral system of *probabilism*."[10] All the material, categories, and concepts, settings, and perspectives are taken from casuistry, however with the addition of elements borrowed from Kantian morality and values ethics, as in manuals that offer a philosophical reflection. But a profound transformation has taken place, a change of axis: the passage from a morality hinging on the relation of the act to its object, that confers upon it a moral quality in itself, independent of the subject's finality, to a morality that hinges on the subject's finality, which becomes a factor of the object itself by means of the proportion-

9. Ibid., 371.
10. Ibid., 375, italics mine.

ate reason. The principle of double effect, which had only a limited use in traditional casuistry for the solution of certain difficult cases, becomes a universal category in morality. It is no longer interpreted according to its first condition and the principle that one may never do what is evil in itself in order to attain a good, but according to its last condition, the proportionate reason, which serves henceforth to determine what is good or evil. So we are in the presence of a kind of revolution within post-Tridentine Catholic moral theology.

The consequences for the problem of intrinsically evil acts are direct: there are no intrinsically evil acts prior to the application of the judgment of proportionate reason to the end, as has been explained. Before this judgment, there are only ontological goods and evils. From the perspective of traditional morality (meaning that of St. Augustine and St. Thomas, whose approach is very different), this means that there exist neither intrinsically evil acts nor absolute evil in itself. Consequently there will be challenges to the universality and unchangeability of moral laws, as well as to the objectivity of moral judgments as heretofore understood. In fact, there has been an interaction here between the conclusions and the premises, between concrete cases and principles. The problem posed by *Humanae vitae* and discussed even before the appearance of the document has provoked a revision that goes back to the principles of moral judgment in casuistry, and this reflection, having transformed the very concept of judgment, returns to the cases of conscience to view them henceforth in a new light.

Developments in the System of Proportionate Reason

We shall now consider some later developments of what we might call the system of proportionate reason in view of the end.

Proportionalism and Consequentialism. The moral system elaborated by Knauer has received the name "proportionalism" because of the decisive importance it attaches to the criterion of proportionate reason. There are several moralists who situate themselves in this line of thought, and who have joined to constitute a group known as "revisionists" (e.g., Joseph Fuchs, Louis Janssens, Bruno Schüller, and Richard McCormick).

Another name that is used for a variant of the "proportionalist" approach is that of "consequentialism." The widespread use of the principle of double effect leads to the predominant consideration of the effects or consequences of the human act. Moral judgment will then consist in a comparison between the good and evil consequences of the action, a weighing or balancing that establishes which consequences prevail, and this always from the perspective of the end sought or the proportionate reason that characterizes the system. The act will be good if good consequences predominate; it will be evil if the contrary is true.

Obviously, judging the consequences of an act is difficult, for there are short-term and long-term consequences, some immediately foreseeable, others requiring practiced insight to perceive. A theft that is profitable to the individual at the moment may prove evil for him over time, because of the reaction of society or its eventual deterioration, to which the theft has contributed. Thus, <u>evaluations of consequences have social, political, and historical dimensions</u>. The insistence of Knauer (and others who take the same approach) regarding the need to consider an act in its totality, and not only in its object, makes it difficult for them to limit elements of judgment, which is necessary in order to avoid endless consideration of possible circumstances and consequences.[11]

However this may be, <u>the system remains clear</u>: moral judgment consists in an estimation of the good or evil consequences from the perspective of proportionate reason in view of the end. <u>This is consequentialism</u>. We can distinguish it from <u>proportionalism</u>, for the latter <u>does not limit its consideration to the consequences of the act. But in fact they are simply two variants</u> of the same basic approach, responding to the same internal logic.[12]

The Priority Given to Finality. One of the major characteristics of the proportionalist approach is the priority given to finality in moral judgment. While traditional moral theology determined the judgment solely by the object and subordinated finality to it so far as to make the subject's end a circumstance, the new system orders all the elements of the moral act in accordance with the ordering of means to end, and subordinates the very constitution of the object of the act to the finality that corresponds to the direct intention of the subject.

11. See Charles E. Curran, "Utilitarianism and Contemporary Moral Theology: Situating the Debates," in Curran and McCormick, 341–62 (342ff.).

12. See Richard A. McCormick, "Notes on Moral Theology," *Theological Studies* 36 (1975): 93–99. [Editor's note: Reprinted as "Reflections on the Literature," in Curran and McCormick, 301–9.] See also John Connery, "Catholic Ethics: Has the Norm for Rule-making Changed?" *TS* 42 (1981): 234.

This reevaluation of finality has claimed the authority of St. Thomas.[13] In considering the human act from the perspective of the interior act of the intentional will, St. Thomas considers the end, which is the proper object of the will, as an essential factor of morality. The end serves as an act's form, while the object of the external act serves as its moral matter. To raise this point is to put one's finger on an important infidelity that post-Tridentine morality has been guilty of in regard to St. Thomas, whom it claims nonetheless to follow. We can only wonder whether there is indeed any correspondence between St. Thomas and the proportionalists in the concept of finality and in the coordination between the interior and external act in the formation of morality. But I shall return to this question later.

In every way this priority given to finality effected a reversal and occasioned the passage to a morality that could be qualified as teleological, while the morality of the manuals was rather of a deontological type, according to a distinction that has become current today. Deontological moralities are characterized by the affirmation that certain acts, such as lying, are evil in themselves and therefore forbidden, regardless of the circumstances. Teleological moralists, on the contrary, determine the quality of acts precisely by the consideration of the consequences, which is regulated by the ordering to the end.[14] To be sure, there was no purely teleological or deontological morality, and it could be shown that the morality of the manuals often used teleological arguments. Even so, the fact remains that casuistic morality most often worked from a deontological perspective, centered on the relation of act to object determining a substantial morality, antecedent to the consideration of circumstances and consequences, to the point of making the contribution of finality accidental. The new morality, on the contrary, gives more importance to the teleological perspective, and we might wonder whether it will know how to maintain and legitimize the fundamental moral values of justice, truth, respect for life, etc., which traditional morality wished to safeguard.

The priority given to the end is equally the result of the necessity for taking into account the totality of the action and its elements in order to form a moral judgment. According to Knauer, in order to establish proportionate reason one must be at the level of total reality. Fuchs will take this up again, but at

13. See Janssens, "Ontic Evil and Moral Evil."
14. See Bruno Schüller, "Various Types of Grounding for Ethical Norms," in Curran and McCormick, 184–98 (184ff.).

the level of the elements of the act: to judge an action adequately one must reckon not only with its object, as did traditional casuistry, but also with its circumstances, end, and consequences. The action forms a concrete totality all of whose elements contribute to its morality and whose end plays the role of principal coordinator. We obviously encounter here the difficulty arising from the nearly infinite number of circumstances of a concrete action, which render every act in the end unique. Given this, how can we establish the existence of a universal law prohibiting an act as intrinsically evil, since we can never foresee all the cases or all the circumstances? Since no act is exactly like any other, can it elicit the same moral judgment?

Be this as it may, this need for totality also leads to giving primacy to finality, which coordinates the other elements. It is indeed legitimate, but we note that it disregards the distinction that St. Thomas established between essential elements and contingent ones, that is, circumstances properly so-called. Thus in practice the term "circumstances" comes to designate all the elements of an action and its situation, without distinction.

The Tendency to Utilitarianism. Ideas have their own logic and entail, so to speak, their own temptations. The current proportionalism will be inclined to judge and interpret everything from a finalist viewpoint, according to the relation of means to end, and from this fact it will inevitably approximate utilitarianism, for the useful is defined precisely as the adequate relation of means to end. The question then arises (even apart from the case of proportionalism, since we find it in St. Thomas): does not every teleological type of morality necessarily tend to utilitarianism, to the subjection of moral value to the consideration of the useful as its foundation? This is a basic question underlying all the nuances one may introduce into the notion of utility. It should come as no surprise, therefore, that this criticism has arisen and that it persists despite all responses and fine-tuning. It is well, in point of fact, to distinguish various forms of utilitarianism: act and rule, strict and mixed, leading to the designations of strict and mixed teleology and consequentialism.[15]

Rule utilitarianism, developed in response to objections to act utilitarianism, admits as the criterion of actions certain universal norms. These rules or norms must nevertheless be justified on a utilitarian basis as, for example, being the result of long experience that such and such behavior is always harm-

15. See Curran, "Utilitarianism and Contemporary Moral Theology," 346ff.

ful. Even from a strictly teleological viewpoint one could, according to Mc-Cormick, admit the existence of absolute practical norms. This would be the case if, after weighing all the consequences of acts, one reaches the conclusion that they are evil and that the admission of exceptions would in the end lead to evils greater than the good resulting from a single exception.[16] Knauer, for his part, appeals to the principle of universalizability to establish a weakness with proportionate reason in, for example, the case of traffic. If everyone were allowed complete and absolute freedom, travel would become impossible. So we are dealing with a mixed teleological system that is close to the mixed utilitarianism of Curran.[17] Curran breaks away from strict utilitarianism or consequentialism on the following three points: moral obligation arises from elements other than consequences; the good cannot be separated from the right; the way in which the good and evil are accomplished has a moral value.[18] Effectively, utility is a flexible and broad notion that can be applied to moral values recognized as universal, e.g., justice. Nevertheless, the primary and dominant perspective of the proportionalist approach consists in the relation of means to end which, as it is usually conceived, allies it with utilitarianism, whatever be the nuances and mitigations. This approach can provide arguments of utility for the existence of universal moral laws, practically without exception; but we can only wonder whether they are really sufficient, above all at the theoretical level, and whether the predominance of the useful does not lead necessarily to a certain relativity of the moral reality and the admission of certain exceptions to every law.

The Pre-moral Level of Good and Evil. Proportionalism is built on a very characteristic foundation, the distinction between two levels: goods and evils in the ontological order, as Knauer called it, or ontic, pre-moral, non-moral, or even physical order, as others call it, on the one hand, and on the other hand, moral goods and evils properly so-called. Ontic goods—let us use this term— are for example health, life, property, knowledge of truth, etc., while ontic evils consist in their privation. These are perfections in all orders, appropriate to the human person and contributing to human development; they do not as yet have, as such, any moral qualification. The moral order comes into being through the intervention of the will. Good and evil consist in willing (or reject-

16. Ibid., 344ff. 17. Ibid., 352.
18. Ibid., 352.

ing), for oneself or for another, by means of a direct intention, an ontic good or evil. A moral judgment is made of these ontic goods and evils, and consists in establishing the proportion between the good and evil connected with the act according to its elements, its effects or consequences, in accord with the ordering of means to the end that is sought. Up to the conclusion, the judgment can develop in the manner of a technical evaluation of the ontic goods and evils connected with the act. When the will accepts or rejects the conclusion of the practical judgment that such and such an act is well ordered in view of such and such an end by such and such means, or that it is badly ordered to it, we are in the moral order. This seems to be the outline of the structure of morality for the authors of the proportionalist trend. In any case, they all see the start of the moral order as a passage from the ontic to the moral order through the intervention of the will. So for Janssens the decisive question is: when and in what measure are we justified in causing or permitting an ontic evil?

We should note that in this the proportionalists do not oppose the moral teaching of the manuals. Rather, they inherit, with them, the teachings of the theologians of the seventeenth and eighteenth centuries such as the Salamancans, who distinguished between objective and fundamental morality established by the object, not yet distinct from its physical being, and formal morality instigated by the intervention of law, which sets freedom at odds with obligation. Billuart even prescinded from the physical reality of the act in order to establish, through the relation to reason, its subjective quality serving as mediation in regard to the legal obligation.

If there is some difference on this point between the authors of the manuals and the proportionalists, it lies in the latter's emphasis on the distinction between the ontic and moral levels, so that the entirety of the judgment about good and evil may and even should develop first at the ontic level, through the calculation of effects and consequences.

We simply note here that this way of forming a moral judgment is diametrically opposed to that of St. Thomas, although he is frequently invoked by the proportionalists in establishing the importance of finality in the moral judgment. St. Thomas, as Janssens has well shown, views the moral act no longer as rising from its generic goodness as an action, nor from its antecedents, but directly from the interior act of the will which has for its object the end. Now it seems very obvious to him that the interior act (willing, loving, desiring, hoping, choosing), together with the end that is its proper object, constitutes the primary essence of the morality that will then communicate itself to the external act and its object. Finality, the relation of the end to those things that are ordered to the end, *quae sunt ad finem,* is therefore wholly moral by nature, according to St. Thomas, and precedes, logically and structurally, the judgment about the external act and about its object with the circumstances, where the ontic or pre-moral order lies. Thus the treatise on the ultimate end and on beatitude comes before the treatises on the virtues and precepts. We shall have to return to this difference between a truly moral concept of finality, at the level of interiority, and a more technical concept adapted to exteriority in its calculation of consequences.

Formal and Concrete Norms. The separation between ontic and moral levels, very pronounced in proportionalist morality, helps us to understand how the "revisionists" pose the problem of intrinsically evil acts. Among the laws or norms that can define such acts, they distinguish on the one hand norms of a transcendental order (e.g., concerning faith and charity) or of a categorical order (e.g., concerning particular virtues such as justice), and on the other hand, concrete and material norms. The first norms obviously deal with intrinsically evil acts such as hatred, injustice, or intemperance. They are formal, including the moral qualification in the very formulation of the act, as when one speaks of murder or lying, and still remain on an abstract and general level, like references to justice or truth. In order to attain to the reality of a moral act, the norm must be concrete and material, must designate the act in its pre-moral or ontic essence (such as taking a man's life) and contribute an adequate moral qualification. It is precisely at this level that the actual problem arises of the existence of universally valid norms determining intrinsically evil acts and allowing of no exceptions. We can therefore leave aside all consideration of virtues at the transcendental or categorical level and focus our discussion exclusively on the concrete and material norms that correspond to the ontic or pre-moral level. Thus the debate, that in the end involves the entire realm of morality, will develop at this level, and no need will be felt to bring in the moral or theological virtues. Rather, owing to a certain concern for rational rigor, they will be excluded.

This is precisely where proportionalism's new categories of judgment will be applied. In order to establish a universal concrete norm, determining an act as intrinsically evil (i.e., always, everywhere, and without exception forbidden), one would have to take into account, in addition to the object, the end of the act and all the circumstances qualifying it. In other words, in order to provide an adequate basis for claiming a norm's universality, one would have to foresee all possible cases that might arise under other circumstances and in other cultures and periods. From this perspective, it is obviously impossible to establish theoretically the existence of a norm prohibiting, without exception, concrete acts that could be considered intrinsically evil. This does not prevent proportionalists from admitting that there are acts that are practically always evil, such as torture; but for proportionalists there will always be a gap between the theory and their practical concessions.

Consequently, the moral laws regarding concrete acts—the only effective ones—can no longer be called universal or unchangeable in an absolute sense but only relatively. They will be applied *ut in pluribus [for the most part]*, save for exceptions, which will be judged according to the criterion of proportionate reason.

Since the concrete norms necessarily serve as intermediaries between the transcendental or formal norms and concrete acts, the moral law as a whole will be affected by the indication of the relativity designated by the expression *ut in pluribus [for the most part]*, which is borrowed from St. Thomas but used in a moral context very different from his.

We see also that a practical separation is made between the order of concrete norms and the order of virtues, with its accompanying norms, transcendental values, and categories. I call it practical in the sense in which the whole problem of concrete norms and of the quality of acts is going to be treated without reference to the virtues, so that essentially the moral judgment will be formed at the level of ontic good and evil.

This separation is serious, for it markedly reduces the realm of operative morality and excludes the theological and even the moral virtues. Doubtless it will be acknowledged that these virtues contribute added and lofty inspiration, and their greatness will be lauded, but they cannot intervene directly in the concrete judgment of normativity, that is, in moral work properly understood. Reading the publications of current proportionalists confirms this and reveals their similarity moreover to casuist literature. We are still within the setting of a morality of obligations and laws of the same type as casuistry, which logically gave rise to the breach between morality and spirituality.

There is much at stake here, for this separation has a direct effect upon the relationship between Scripture and ethics. They all but close the door between, on the one hand, the doctrine of the New Testament centered on faith, charity, and the other Christian virtues and, on the other hand, this morality that gives all its attention to the analysis of norms, such that one can scarcely find any scriptural texts in harmony with its claims. Now what is at stake is the very heart of morality, the passage from universal teaching to the concrete act, from the Gospel to action. The problem of intrinsically evil acts will be set within so narrow a framework, so close to the modern morality of obligation, that neither Scripture nor the Fathers nor even St. Thomas, who used categories that were broad in quite another way, could address it with an appropriate response. The very formulation of the moral problem conditions the research and response so powerfully that it almost completely blocks communication of moral theology with Revelation and the larger theological tradition.

II. Critical Reflections

If we look at proportionalism from a *historical perspective* we can see clearly that it is situated at the time and in the setting of post-Tridentine morality of a casuistic type, always with the addition of elements borrowed from modern philosophy: from the Kantian school, whose morality of duty is fathered by the morality of obligation, from the philosophy of values, and also from current trends of the teleological and even utilitarian type. In brief, proportionalism is a kind of revolution within the casuistic system. Like the latter, it follows nominalism. But while the theology of the sixteenth century, which laid the foundations of casuistry, tried to erect against the basic relativism of nominalism a barrier of objective morality, intrinsic and based on reason and the natural law, proportionalism attacked precisely this protective barrier via the challenge of the theory of intrinsically evil acts. It thus inevitably revived the danger of relativism inherent in nominalism, however just the criticisms leveled at casuistic morality may have been. So we are witnessing the revival of the debate stirred up by nominalism at the heart of the moralities of obligation it had initiated, and this within the setting of the categories and problems it had imposed upon modern moral theology. The question of intrinsically evil acts is simply a point of focus for the wider problem of intrinsic or objective morality, which addresses to the entire field of morality questions about the universality and unchangeability of moral laws.

I believe that the only resolution of such a debate lies in transcending nominalism by critiquing the concept and system of morality it introduced into Catholic theology and modern thought.

In such an attempt to amend and renew morality, recourse to St. Thomas and the teaching of the Fathers can be a tremendous help, for their works give us profoundly different models and organizations of moral theology, far more closely linked to Scripture and tradition and also, I believe, far more promising for the future.

The study of St. Thomas is all the more necessary here since the proportionalist moralists relied on him for their critique of the morality of the traditional manuals and particularly their reestablishment of finality in morality, and in this they certainly were not wrong. But their reading was too limited; they did not take into account the entirety of St. Thomas's moral system and its proper structure, which alone allows one to take its proper measure and grasp the nature of its elements. They did not perceive that in a morality of the ultimate end and of beatitude, virtues, and gifts, where the interior act prevails over the external act while assuming it, finality in particular had a nature, a dimension, and a function different from what it could have in a morality of obligation and commandments, laws, or norms, and the single act, where the external act in St. Thomas's sense is inevitably brought to the fore and favored. In this, the vision of the proportionalists is not much more perceptive or faithful than that of the traditional moralists, their adversaries, who referred just as often to St. Thomas in laying the foundations of casuistry.

We cannot treat so vast and complex a problem here, but will confine ourselves to three essential clarifications concerning finality, objectivity, and the relation to revelation.

The Concept of Finality: Finality of the Technical Type and Moral Finality

As we have seen, we can characterize the proportionalist approach by the predominance given to the relation of an act to its end over its relation to its object. This is why it ranks among the teleological moralities and consequently has similarities to moralities of utility. In fact, the modern concept of finality based on the strict ordering of means to end unites the idea of finality to that of utility inseparably, for the means, by its essence, is what one uses to attain the end and as such should be as exactly proportioned to the end as possible. This is the idea of finality that has been applied in modern technology with such success and that has attained such a powerful grip on our minds that we can now hardly imagine any other concept of finality.

If we apply this idea of finality to human action, morality appears as a construct of higher utility, a certain technique for achieving human flourishing and perfection, which can include all human values but only as means relative to the end pursued. Even the moral system of St. Thomas, dominated by the pursuit of the ultimate end, could thus be faulted for being, in brief, a technique for gaining beatitude, secretly vitiated by the interested character that affects such a search when it becomes predominant. All teleological morality will be liable to this suspicion of being utilitarian and interested, and should be prepared to counter this fundamental objection.

Proportionalist moralists have of course not escaped these criticisms and they have been accused of becoming utilitarian. They certainly remain far from strict utilitarianism, which reduces everything to the useful, but regardless of clarifications, corrections, and nuances it remains true that the logic of the principle of finality that they have adopted contains an inbuilt, permanent risk of reducing moral values to the useful and is consequently open to the threat of relativism. Their adversaries are well aware of this, and many people perceive it in a confused way when observing their manner of treating concrete cases. It could be said that for them there are no longer any stable, intangible values that can stand independently and that every value, however important it is said to be, is relative to the end pursued.

Rediscovering Moral Finality

However, when we have spent some time with St. Thomas and the Fathers, and when in addition we try to plumb the depths of our own moral experience, we perceive that they had a concept of finality and of the ordering to beatitude different from what a consideration of the useful has to offer us.

In very clear texts, St. Thomas and the Fathers oppose the quest of moral value, virtue, and beatitude to a search for the useful, presupposing a concept of finality that transcends the order of utility, a concept that is directly moral and not technical like our own. But there remains for us a difficulty in interpretation: St. Thomas and the Fathers did not know the modern concept of finality with its technical aspect and experienced no need to explain the difference. It is indispensable therefore that the interpreter should engage in serious reflection and understanding, and her efforts will be well repaid.

The difference between finality of the technical type and moral finality consists principally in this: the first abstracts from the nature of realities taken as means and ends, considering only their useful qualities, in such a way that everything can become a means to an end and can also be seen as an end for a series of means. In contrast, moral finality is determined by the very nature of realities; some things are ends by nature and can never, as such, be legitimately considered as means, while others are by nature means and can never be seen as ends properly understood.

This is the case with human persons; we should love them for themselves, with an intention that rests in them as in an end, and we should transcend considerations of our own interest or utility to the point of accepting sacrifices for their sake. We cannot love our neighbor as ourselves in accordance with the second commandment unless we love this person as an end, not a means, thus rising above the order of utility and purely technological finality. Note that here we touch the heart of Gospel morality.

In the same way, personal goods and qualities such as virtues, truth, goodness, friendship, etc. cannot be acquired unless we seek them for their own sake, as ends, and are willing for their sake to renounce self-interest, immediate gratification, and even a hidden utilitarian attitude toward them. The Aristotelian analysis of the kinds of friendship, taken up by St. Thomas in his study of charity, is very clear on this point. True friendship ranks higher than interested and enjoyable friendship and pertains to those who know how to love virtue and practice it for its own sake, rather than for pleasure or utility, and this holds true especially for charity. This is precisely the virtue that enables us to love others effectively for their own sake. As Saint-Exupéry said, one cannot purchase friends in the market. The same holds true for every authentic virtue.[19]

19. We can also distinguish between moral and technical finality by considering the difference between morality and art or technology, and more precisely according to the choice that directs the action. Technical action is directly concerned with some external matter that it transforms. The technician's choice establishes the relationship of means to end strictly at this level. It has nothing to do with personal dispositions, one's own or those of others. A good engineer could be a dishonest person, just as an excellent person might have no talent for engineering. Moral action, on the contrary, has to do principally with interior matter, with persons themselves and the moral qualities it produces in them. Moral choice, which, according to St. Thomas, has for its object *ea quae sunt ad finem,* presupposes therefore a certain reflection of subjects acting on themselves, or at least an interior perception of their dispositions as persons, and consists in their ordering themselves with the help of action and all its elements, interior and exterior acts,

However, these natural ends—human persons and their moral qualities or virtues—are not ultimate ends. It is precisely on this point that Christian morality is most clearly, sometimes forcefully distinguished from pagan morality. According to Christianity, human persons are not their own ends, even did they possess the most spiritual activity and the highest virtue, in which the philosophers placed beatitude. Through this spiritual nature itself, which makes them ends, human persons are ordered to the God whose image they are as to their ultimate end. They are in no sense means, but rather beings capable of knowing God in himself and loving him for himself to the point of self-forgetfulness, with the help of grace, and then of tending toward him consciously and willingly as to their own ultimate end.

Here we are dealing with a finality very different from the technical type. It applies particularly to persons and takes their spiritual nature into account. It comprises two degrees in the order of ends itself: the ultimate end, alone absolute and universal, and the ends that we may call secondary, at the level of the human person, and that must be clearly distinguished from means. St. Thomas used a broad formula for this, not foreseeing its abuse: the expression *ea quae sunt ad finem*. This could be extended to viewing secondary ends as means, persons as instruments; but it has been too easily translated as "means" in the sense of something one uses to reach an end. This has inevitably led to confusion.

It is well for us to note also the link between moral finality and the acts of love and desire placed at the source of morality, while the sentiment of obligation in no way implies finality and tends to marginalize it in morality, together with desire and love.

The Specificity of the Moral Order in Relation to the Useful

In connection with our problem, let us consider two essential differences between the moral finality we have just described briefly and the technical type of morality. Moral finality permits us to situate the moral order directly at

to the end that is chiefly sought, ultimately, as persons, that is, to the end they love and seek above all. At this level the relation of means to end (if one wishes to retain these terms) which defines the choice is obviously of a nature other than technical, and so far surpasses the consideration of material utility, regarding the external act, that to lower it to that point would produce a serious degeneration, a sort of demoralization, a fall below the moral level. In any case, moral choice can in no way be separated from the consideration of the dispositions of the moral person, that is, the virtues and vices, for this is its primary, specific matter.

the level of persons, and to demonstrate that we do not enter the moral order until the very moment when we detach ourselves from the useful, and transcend it in order to discover realities that deserve to be loved for themselves and so to be called final. On the other hand, finality of the technical type that is used by proportionalism especially when it situates it at the ontic or pre-moral level, leads to centering the system in the order of the useful. This seriously compromises the very concept of values and of the moral order.

We return here to an old problem: the distinction between the useful and the *honestum* or righteous and the fact that the righteous cannot be reduced to the useful. I shall take as an example one of the earliest systematizations of Christian morality, the *De officiis* of St. Ambrose, which merits profound study. The principal purpose of the bishop of Milan was to show, with the help of scriptural examples, that the Christian should absolutely prefer the righteous to the useful, even more than the philosopher, because the Christian has placed his end in future realities and ought to be ready, for the sake of the righteousness taught by the Gospel, to endure joyfully renunciations and sufferings that surpass human wisdom. Ambrose then reinforces this with the paradox that only the righteous is truly useful, which brings the useful back to the righteous and transforms the notion of it. For a Christian who aspires to the vision of God far more than for a philosopher, only the righteous is useful (but in a sense diametrically opposed to utilitarianism). Righteousness means justice, benevolence, kindness, mercy, preferring another's advantage to one's own, and finally, friendship. In affirming the priority of righteousness over utility, an affirmation all the more cogent for the Christian, St. Ambrose is the clear-sighted and sure interpreter of the great Christian moral tradition. Now it is precisely this primacy that is endangered in a system where finality is placed in the vanguard without a prior distinction between technical and moral finality.

We should also mention that our definition of moral finality brings up the famous Augustinian distinction between three kinds of reality: *ea quibus utitur; ea quibus fruitur; ea quae utuntur et ea quae utuntur et fruuntur,* which serves as a basis for Western theological thought up to the end of the Middle Ages.

The Objectivity of Moral Finality

The second difference between finality of the technical type and moral finality touches directly on the problem of objectivity and intrinsic morality. The former finality leads us to consider all reality as a means for attaining an end, which end will itself then become a means to a further end, in an indefinite succession regulated by the utility of the subject. Moral finality, on the contrary, takes the nature of what it attains so fully into account, particularly through love, that it refuses to reduce this reality to utility of any kind whatsoever when its own nature is opposed to it, as in the case of the person. This finality is based on the grasping, through knowledge and love, of the intimate nature of the external reality, apart from the subject. Hence this finality possesses a dimension of objectivity that is essential to it, and that is very different from the instrumental and material objectivity that we may speak of in the case of technical finality. It is an objectivity that culminates in a relation to the person of another who has become the object of knowledge and love and as such is an end of the will. It presupposes a penetration into the "selfhood," the interiority of the personal reality, thus founding a morality that we may call intrinsic in a far deeper sense than is understood by casuistry.

It is not surprising, on the other hand, that in favoring finality without making these distinctions, proportionalism compromises the objectivity of the moral judgment and the intrinsic character of morality that traditional morality had tried to safeguard, giving it as well a quasi-physical content, impoverished to say the least.

If we would restore its essential role to finality in morality, it is indispensable that we discern clearly the particular nature of moral finality which alone permits a true objectivity befitting persons. Thanks to this, we can firmly establish that finality has a primordial need for objectivity and consequently we can account for one of the specific traits of Christian thought found in the Fathers as they encountered the philosophers and in St. Thomas: the objectivity of their response to the question of beatitude and of the "end of goods."[20] For them the question of beatitude is primarily objective and is determined by the goods that one desires and loves. Their response is above all objective, be-

20. Cf. Etienne Gilson, *L'Esprit de la philosophie médiévale* (Paris, 1944), 336ff.; K. Ragnar Holte, *Béatitude et Sagesse, saint Augustin et le problème de la fin de l'homme dans la philosophie ancienne* (Worcester, Mass.: Augustinian Studies, Assumption College, 1962).

cause beatitude resides not strictly in virtue or in the full development of the human person, as the philosophers thought, but in an external reality higher than the human person, in God who calls us to know him in himself and to love him for himself, which cannot be accomplished without self-renunciation. But for the last three centuries moralists of obligation have cast the question of beatitude out of the moral domain, and they seem unable to imagine its having an objective dimension and response. We are thus very far from the Fathers, and doubtless from the Gospel, and face a veritable divorce between moral thought and the sense of beatitude, and still more of love.

In rediscovering the objective character of moral finality, we can root the objectivity that befits the external act in the will itself, with its acts of desire and love, giving it true moral substance. This objectivity establishes a proper coordination between these two parts of the moral action. By the same token we will be providing a solid foundation for moral laws within the acting subject.

Finality in the order of utility, on the contrary, leads us almost unfailingly into the dilemma that separates the subjective from the objective, in a morality of intention opposed to a morality of external and material objectivity.

The Ontic or Pre-moral Order

We need another clarification. It concerns the basic category of proportionalism: the establishment of an ontic order preceding the moral order, in which the judgment takes place as it weighs the balance between goods, the pre-moral effects or consequences. The moral order proper then consists in the engagement of the will regarding the result of this technical type of judgment.

For Knauer, the category of the pre-moral or ontic is based on a direct experience of the good which he calls metaphysical, but which does not seem to be clearly distinct from a physical, biological, or psychological experience according to the areas of reality in which this appropriation of goods takes place. It seems that here the proportionalist authors are establishing a slightly confused combination: a category of modern Scholasticism that departs, for the study of the moral act, from the quasi-physical order to rise to the moral order through a relation to reason and law, and the ontic categories in philosophy and then biology, psychology, and sociology, distinguished by the human sciences. The pre-moral category would regroup them all while distinguishing them from the moral category, which comes into being only through the engagement of the will and the intentional direction to these goods and evils.

In my opinion this is an unduly narrow view of goods and evils, corresponding to a too-subjective concept of the moral dimension.

There is no doubt that science can break up the human reality into various areas according to its particular object. But the distinctive quality of morality that would direct the concrete action consists precisely in a judgment about the totality of the reality in which the action will take place, implying the synthesis of all the levels and sectors distinguished by scientific analysis, and this beginning at the center, which is the consideration of the person. Let us take the example of health. From the moral point of view, health is not simply a biological good, which would become moral because of my will to restore health to another. It is already moral in itself because of the fact that it is the health of a human person, with demands upon me very different from the health of an animal. Likewise, to take a person's life is not a pre-moral and neutral act for the moralist, even though the expression does not yet convey a moral qualification. In effect, in reality, a person's life, because it belongs to the very nature of that person, is already in itself a moral object that as such elicits in me moral sentiments and behavior.

Morality is therefore not a dimension hidden in some way within the intention of my will; it already lies in realities external to me as soon as these are human or personal. The moralist who limits her consideration to the analytical division of reality into sections by the sciences or even by philosophy commits a serious error of perspective, for the proper nature of her science is to grasp the human reality as a whole, including the total concrete reality within which the action is performed. Above all, she may not, in his consideration of the goods in view, abstract from the person they affect and consider them as if they were simply pre-moral. It is precisely this moral nature of goods, created by their relation to the person, that will give rise at the heart of finality to the distinctions we have spoken of between means, secondary ends, and the ultimate end.

Once more we face the problem of objectivity. Is morality all on the side of the will of the acting or does it include the correspondence between the subject and the objective reality which, taken in its totality, is already a moral good by reason of its relation to a person, to another, or to God?

The Separation between Formal and Material Norms

The division established by proportionalists between transcendental or categorically formal norms and concrete or material norms also requires a clarification because of the fact that the virtues are ranked alongside formal norms that still remain abstract, distanced from the concrete. We have already noted the grave inconvenience occasioned by this viewpoint: it takes away from the virtues, understood here as the theologal virtues, all real hold over moral judgment at the level of the action; it indicates a morality still centered upon obligations, that does not really know how to accord to the virtues a principal function in moral action.

But additionally, in thus treating the virtues as abstract principles, proportionalists, like the casuists of former times, show that they possess only an effectively abstract concept of virtue, far different from the reality of virtue revealed by the experience to which the ancients testified. For the latter, virtue meant attraction, dynamism, novelty, and joy. Without doubt the expressions "to be just, temperate, charitable" are general and abstract, but the reality, the personal quality they designate, is so far from abstract that it can only spring from what is concrete in the action and maintain itself by returning to it. In effect, it is by the repetition of personal and progressive acts of quality that virtue is formed in us and that we become just, courageous, prudent, self-controlled, charitable. Then, thanks to this increasing experience and love, we acquire the capacity to judge and perform concrete acts conformable to virtue. In this sense there is nothing more concrete, realistic, and experiential than true virtue, for it accustoms us to grasp the real with accuracy and penetration far better than any norm or law and to transform it with patience, and in the end even with ease and joy. Virtue is so inseparable from concrete action that it lessens and is lost when we cease to practice it.

This explains why St. Thomas stopped with the study of particular virtues in the *secunda pars* without going on to the examination of particular cases. For him, the moralist's work consisted in the teaching of virtue, because he knew that the virtuous person, formed by practice and experience, was by the same token best able to enter into the concrete realm of action and resolve cases, in fact that person was the only one who could do this fully. Here is an essential difference between St. Thomas and the casuists, for whom virtue was actually nothing more than an impoverished abstraction, a category into which obligations and precepts fit.

The separation between virtues and concrete norms established by the proportionalists results in rendering virtues inoperative in action as well as in morality. The moralist can work out a system of morality and do his work of determining norms and cases without any real need for the virtues, even charity. In this scenario, we remain fixed in the categories and limitations proper to moral systems of obligation.

Proportionalism according to Louis Janssens

We have studied proportionalism particularly as portrayed in Knauer's article, which presents the system in a fairly clear way. However, I should add a few words about Janssens' articles,[21] where we find the same approach, but amplified by interesting references to St. Thomas, particularly to his analysis of the moral act, and by applications to current problems connected with the *ordo caritatis* [order of charity]. These articles are well thought out, vigorous, and open to current events. They make a serious effort to construct a morality adapted to the mentality of our times.

For a disciple of St. Thomas who attempts to penetrate his original thought beyond the writings of commentators, the first article on ontic and moral good starts out very well. It shows how St. Thomas studies morality by carefully distinguishing the interior act, whose object is the end, from the external act with its matter, in order to give priority, in the formation of the moral judgment, to the intention and the end; and this without making any use of the distinction between the *finis operis* and the *finis operantis* which had become classic according to him in this connection. Thus St. Thomas considers moral action from the point of view of the acting subject and not of the external object.

The analysis, perfectly correct thus far, begins to shift when Janssens treats the external act as a means in view of the subject's end and hence denies it a proper moral quality. Yet it suffices to read question 20 of the *prima secundae* on the morality of the external act, to see that in St. Thomas's view this part of the action possesses its own moral quality, determined by the relation of its object and circumstances to reason. This is explicitly stated in almost every article. I quote simply the first one: *"Bonitas autem vel malitia quam habet actus exterior secundum se, propter debitam materiam et debita circumstantias, non*

---

21. See Janssens, "Ontic Evil and Moral Evil" and "Norms and Priorities."

derivatur a voluntate, sed magis a ratione. Unde, si consideretur bonitas exterioris actus secundum quod est in ordinatione et apprehensione rationis, prior est quam bonitas actus voluntatis." One could not be clearer. Janssens indeed saw it, without a doubt; and he wonders if St. Thomas is contradicting himself.[22] Evidently such texts contradict the proportionalist system which establishes the judgment of morality by the relation of means to end, and they are all grist for the mill of traditional morality and its objectivism. This is why Janssens will try to interpret question 20 by directing it at once to finality, by way of the relation of matter to form between the external and interior acts, recalled in the response to the third objection of article 1, which Janssens attempts to reduce to the relation of means to end. But this is to approach the question through a secondary response, in order to make it say almost the contrary of what is explicitly affirmed throughout the body of the articles.

We can only gather from this that St. Thomas is not a proportionalist, nor is he a casuist, a Kantian, or a Cartesian, for he recognizes the moral specificity of both the interior act, whose end is the proper object, and of the external act, whose object is the matter with its circumstances, and he coordinates them intimately and vitally as matter and form, as body and soul, if you will. In establishing the essential role of finality, St. Thomas passes beyond the interpretation of his casuist commentators. In recognizing the proper contribution of the external act, he contradicts the proportionalists. In uniting these two parts of the action substantially so that they communicate their moral quality to each other, he transcends Cartesian dualism and the Kantian separation of the formal and material that the division between moral and pre-moral rejoins.

Thus we discover in St. Thomas the same unity in the composition of the morality of acts as exists in the human composite, so characteristic of his thought. There is no contradiction here, but a remarkable balance, taking into account as adequately as possible the richness of human action with its two essential dimensions of interiority and outward expression. Nevertheless, to grasp the connection between the interior and exterior act, we must have a deeper concept of finality than that of the proportionalists, a technical type of relation between means and end.

The second part of Janssens' article holds a surprise for the attentive reader. Following St. Thomas, he had introduced the interior act as the heart of

22. Janssens, "Ontic Evil," in Curran and McCormick, 50.

morality. But now, without further reference to St. Thomas, he brings in as a basis for the study of morality the distinction of later moralists between *malum physicum* and *malum morale*, which becomes, in modern language, the distinction between *ontic* and *moral evil*, and gives place to the division between the ontic or pre-moral order and the moral order. As we have seen, this division is so important for proportionalism that, with the entire judgment involving the object, the circumstances and end will develop at this level. Proportionalists will doubtless say that this judgment is still pre-moral. Nevertheless, this is what will determine when an act is good and when its good effects outweigh its evil ones in proportion to the end, such that the will need only assume this in order to render the act morally good. Here we basically move to what St. Thomas called the external act, in a way that is at least as extrinsic as casuistry.

So what has happened? How did we move from an interiority that rejected the moral specificity of the external act to an exteriority that plainly calls itself pre-moral but intends nonetheless to determine the entire moral judgment?

Quite simply, we never really abandoned the exteriority or rational extrinsicism that predominates in proportionalism, as it already did in the casuist system, whatever be the new terms used. Doubtless the interior act evoked at the beginning by Janssens places us on the side of the acting subject, too much neglected by casuist morality, but the entire judgment and the problematic will be returned to the level of the external act, considered as pre-moral or ontological.

I believe the crux of the debate lies, once again, in the concept of finality brought into play by proportionalism. It is a finality of the technical type, consisting in the rational and rigorous ordering of means to end and abstracting from all that cannot be reduced to this relationship, particularly the profound nature of the realities to which this finalizing scheme is being applied. Now that which it is least possible to reduce to this sort of finality is precisely the human person, possessing qualities constituting the moral order, for we can never attain these except by considering them as ends, and by acts that engage personal interiority as such, in an encounter with God and neighbor.

Again, when Janssens invites us to return to St. Thomas at the level of the interior act where finality predominates, it is certainly a clever move, like a maneuver to trip up the traditional moralists from the rear by showing them that their principal authority is against them when they make the object the only essential criterion of the moral judgment. It is also a useful argument to safeguard the cornerstone of the proportionalist system, the ordering of means to end. But in reality Janssens never has us penetrate interiority, where St. Thomas places the source of morality; he almost seems in a hurry to get away from it. In fact, hardly has he established the primacy of finality with the support of St. Thomas, when he turns from the interior act to the pre-moral order, that is, to external acts; and it is there that he will apply the relation of means to end and make of it the determining criterion of the moral judgment. Actually, the technical type of finality used here is not suitable for considering interior acts of love, desire, faith, etc.; it only works well in the realm of external matter that is easy to handle, like physical objects.

Thus proportionalism will develop as a sort of technique for forming a pre-moral judgment, where all the elements of an action, especially the proximate and remote effects, will be taken into account according to the relation of means to end and the calculation of proportion. The moralist will thus become a kind of engineer of pre-moral acts who prepares and determines the matter of moral decisions.

Thus an inevitable consequence of the utilization of finality of the technical type is to situate the moralist's work principally at the level of external acts. Expositions of the theologal and other virtues, of personal values, and Gospel morality, such as Janssens makes in his second article, will remain additions or will always constitute a separate order that will be called the moral or transcendental order, or again, spirituality—it matters little which. The connection will never be anything but accidental.

The success of proportionalism among contemporary moralists stems precisely from the application to morality of this finality which aligns it with modern technology, with its prodigious methods and achievements, and also with the human problems it sparks today, which sometimes drive the scholars themselves to appeal to the moralists. It is quite significant that proportionalists draw their examples by preference from the problems of modern life that simultaneously engage both technology and humanity: production, pollution, etc. These moralists are perfectly right to deal with problems that preoccupy the people of our times and to handle them in a broader and better-informed manner than did moralists of former days. But the fundamental question remains: can we, in treating moral and properly human problems, use the same methods as modern technology, that is, set up as our chief criterion of moral material a finality of a technical type which, moreover, operates and orders the elements of action at a level qualified as pre-moral, exactly like technology or art in the sense of the ancients?

The danger of such an application of technical finality in morality is first of all that it will lead to the neglect of certain qualities that cannot be reduced to the strict relation of means to end and that, for example, render an act evil in itself regardless of the end of the subject, as traditional teaching firmly maintains.

This is to introduce into morality a basic relativism for, in regard to technology, the relation of means to end is in continual evolution, the future always being open to new techniques, as they say. Likewise, in proportionalist morality one can never determine in advance that an act will always be evil, for one can always imagine that it might be ordered to an end and to effects so important that they would render it good, as a necessary means, despite the evil effects that subsist. Proportionalism presents no solid theoretical barrier to the legitimization of an action commonly recognized as evil in itself, any more than does technology. It cannot defend itself against this technical relativism, so insidious today, except by way of concessions (such as recognizing that torture would practically always be evil, for example) or by allowing the intervention of considerations that come out of the system of finality, like the Kantian principle that a person can never be used as a means (after all, why not, since everything is both end and means?). Someone will doubtless say that persons belong to another order, properly moral; but we can retort to the proportionalists that they have practically separated the moral and pre-moral orders, which amounts to submitting them to the calculation of effects in proportion to the end.

The Separation between Morality and the Gospel

I shall close with a fundamental question touched upon by Knauer in the last sentence of his article: "Someone may object that my essay is limited to the rules of natural ethics without any regard for the supernatural order and for the transformation this order is supposed to bring to morality. To which I reply: the Incarnation in no way changed the content of the human nature of Christ, but on the contrary assumed it in its integrity; likewise and in consequence, the supernatural order, far from changing the content of ethics, assumes it to its own dimension and consecrates its value."[23]

23. Knauer, "La détermination du bien," 376. [Editor's note: The "Hermeneutic Function"

From the viewpoint of Christian morality, the question raises the whole problem of the coordination between the natural and supernatural order. It is particularly acute. Think of de Lubac's book *Surnaturel* or of discussions on Christian philosophy.[24] The objection indicated inevitably comes to mind as one reads proportionalist writing. As already noted on several occasions, all discussion on moral problems unfolds on a purely natural plane, without any felt need to question revelation unless to get from it a confirmation or an illustration. Knauer's response is a bit facile for a problem of this importance, but it is logical and very significant. Not only does it confirm the fact of the treatment of ethics on a purely natural plane, but legitimizes it in principle. If revelation changes nothing in nature (but how could it not change a person's view of life and way of acting?), if it rather confirms it, we may, even must, remain on a purely natural plane as we treat the content of ethics, thus assuring the complete autonomy of human nature and of ethics.

Henceforth the field of Christian morality is divided into two levels, the one natural and the other supernatural; they remain parallel but have no profound interrelation. In this situation, the moralist's best efforts will obviously be made on the natural and rational plane. In his work, Gospel teaching will be a surplus benefit, as spirituality was added on to morality in former times for those who were interested in it.

Proportionalism fits well into the tradition of Suarez and his self-sufficient nature, and also of the rational humanism of the Scholasticism of recent centuries. It is not too difficult for it to agree on this point with the rationalism of the Enlightenment.

In his second article, Janssens tries to inject the Gospel into the proportionalist system, if I may use the expression, so as to set out duties to one's neighbor according to the order of charity and also with the partial intention of avoiding the criticism we mentioned. But in my opinion the connection with Scripture is far from being reestablished in a satisfactory way. The Gospel teaching is brought in by way of the interpretation of a philosophical notion: the "impartial" and universal love that becomes the rational principle of a totality of obligations, in the Kantian manner. This too-abstract and rationalistic love cannot envisage the personal character, the sensibility, and the

---

version of Knauer's article does not retain this concluding sentence, nor make reference to either the Incarnation or a supernatural order.]

24. Henri de Lubac, *Surnaturel: Etudes Historique* (Paris: Aubier, 1946).

power of the Gospel *agape* that St. Paul places at the source of Christian morality as a gift and an attraction prior to all obligations. As far as essentials are concerned, we remain on the natural and rational plane. On the plane of interpersonal relations also, for there is no question of the source of *agape*, which is in God. Proportionalism seems in fact to want to maintain itself on the human plane even in its reading and use of Scripture.

The problem is a serious one for Christian theology. This concept of morality explains in great part the breach that has been created between moralists on the one hand and on the other, exegetes, patrologists, dogmaticians, etc; and still more profoundly between morality and Scripture and the Gospel. It is easy to verify this: while the teaching of the Fathers and the great Scholastics was continually and methodically nourished by Scripture, which they constantly quoted, we have here a morality that would set itself up, in fact and by reason of its method, without recourse to Scripture for the substance of its labor. Let us note that the Christian intentions of proportionalist moralists are not being directly challenged here; the question has to do with the objective work they are accomplishing in morality and the system that has been elaborated. The problem is rendered more acute, furthermore, by the rationalist and positivist temptation that has penetrated the Church in recent years.

I believe it is impossible to reestablish authentic and profound bonds between Christian morality and Scripture, the Gospel, and revelation, without a reconsideration of the relationship between the natural and supernatural and between reason and faith at the heart of moral theology, traditional as well as proportionalist.

Gratia non tollit, sed perficit naturam

The question can be expressed simply by relating it to the interpretation of St. Thomas's oft-quoted and famous principle: *Gratia non tollit, non destruit naturam, sed perficit eam* [grace does not destroy nature, but perfects it]. The current interpretation which lies just beneath the surface of Knauer's sentence quoted above concludes that it is proper to study and to establish human nature in its integrity first of all, since grace, far from destroying this work, will confirm and perfect it. So we must begin with nature and with the human in morality as elsewhere, and consider grace later on. This method seems obvious, at least for Catholic theology after Trent. It returns the treatise on grace and the main part of the treatise on faith to dogmatics, and all that is specifically evangelical and Christian to spirituality.

However, there is another interpretation that reverses the terms and seems to me more in keeping with the first intention of the *Summa theologiae*. We can put it this way: "Do not be afraid to surrender to grace, faith, and revelation, for far from harming your nature and reason they will confirm, develop, and perfect them." Here faith and Scripture are placed first, as the principal sources of theology. For the moralist this means that it is fitting to give the New Law, expressed in the Sermon on the Mount and in Sts. Paul and John, priority over the Decalogue and even natural law, and to restore to faith its practical dimension as the first source of Christian action, in keeping with the Letter to the Romans, etc. Such a concept of Christian morality corresponds well to the theological method of the Fathers as well as to the perspectives and main intention of St. Thomas in the *Summa*. Addressing Christians and pagans alike, St. Thomas wished to preach the Gospel, presenting Christian doctrine to all in the form of theology and showing how this teaching corresponds with human reason and the aspirations of the human heart and nature. It is an adequate, full, and universal correspondence that expresses effectively the saying "Grace does not destroy nature, but perfects it." It is precisely evangelical perfection that characterizes the new justice in St. Matthew, in relation to the Decalogue, and the relations of the New Testament with the Old according to the teaching of the Fathers.

The Question of Beatitude and the Relation of Morality to the Gospel

This fundamental problem of theological method, which conditions the relation of morality to Scripture, goes hand in hand with the very concept of morality. If the essential question in morality is that of obligation, particularly at the ontic or pre-moral level, we reach our conclusion quickly: there are not many texts in Scripture that answer the question thus posed, and probably Scripture is not too interested in morality. Does this not show that the question has been put too narrowly, and does not correspond to morality as Scripture sees it? On the other hand, if we ask our moral question as the Fathers did—In what does true human beatitude consist, in view of the suffering, poverty, violence, etc. that make up the human condition? What is true and noble love? What are true justice and authentic wisdom in a world so often unjust and foolish?—then the relationship of morality with the Gospel is easily reestablished. It suffices to ask these questions to see the answers pour forth from Scripture, as was experienced by the Fathers and theologians who based their moral teaching on the Gospel.

We may wonder whether the proportionalist moralists, like the casuists of former times, have not elaborated their concept of morality in a way that prevents them from maintaining a real and vibrant contact with Scripture. These are the limitations of a human nature closed in upon itself, too rationalized and conceptualized, and then subjected to the destructive criticism of scientific reason and the rebellion of freedom: the narrowness of a morality of obligation that discards the great questions about beatitude and suffering, noble love and wisdom, which, however, are of interest to everyone.

Thus proportionalism, which is a crisis of casuist morality, many of whose perspectives of thought it inherits, strikes us as insufficient, not only from the viewpoint of the moral objectivity defended by the manuals, but also from that of finality, which it makes its strongest point. Remaining fixed on the question of obligation, it is unable to handle competently the principal "final" questions, which have been practically banished from morality for four centuries and to which the Gospel brings the best and sometimes the only answers in a very direct manner. It runs the risk of enclosing itself within a very restricted finality, and the constrained limits of the intentions of the subject and of singular acts, inevitably open to the danger of subjectivism and relativism, which threaten the personal conscience. We can only hope it does not lend itself to the manipulation of morality through its submission to a technical finality that develops with ease in the domain of the sciences, economics, and politics. And there, it could escape only with great difficulty from the rationalism and naturalism that despite all setbacks remain the great temptation of moderns.

As for St. Thomas, the proportionalist authors interpret him according to their own system and make use of him by drawing from the *Summa theologiae* choice morsels that suit their taste, if I may express myself so mundanely. They pay no more attention to traditional moralists than to St. Thomas's structure of morality, which is profoundly different from theirs and which is nonetheless clearly inscribed in the plan of the *Summa*. On the one hand we have a morality of law and norms of conscience, focusing on obligation; on the other, a morality of beatitude, virtues and gifts, law, particularly evangelical, and grace, focusing on the attraction of truth and goodness. We cannot interpret St. Thomas correctly without being aware of such differences, which have consequences, in all the treatises that compose morality, for the study of all problems, however concrete they may be, and notably for the relations between morality and the Gospel.

SECTION IV　Passions and Virtues

13 ❧ Reappropriating Aquinas's Account of the Passions   (1990)

Divergences concerning the Place of the Emotions in Morality

St. Thomas accords a remarkable place to the study of the emotions in the moral part of the *Summa theologiae*. This treatise counts the largest number of questions: 27, containing 132 articles. It is more expansive than his treatises on human beatitude *(beatitudo)* and on human agency combined, or on the virtues and on the gifts, or on law and on grace. This quantitative comparison does not necessarily mean that the treatise on emotions is the most important in the eyes of Aquinas, but it does indicate that he pays particular attention to it. In his carefully elaborated outline, the emotions form part of what he calls the universal consideration of moral agency, and what was later called fundamental moral theology.

His previous works demonstrate the growing attention that St. Thomas paid to human emotions. In the *Commentary on the Sentences* (III 15), he took the opportunity presented by Peter Lombard's treatment of the human deficiencies assumed by Christ, notably the sorrow and the pain of the Passion, in order to study the nature of human emotions; in particular, Thomas focused on the emotions that the Gospels attribute to Jesus. Furthermore, it is very significant that he devoted a question to *delectatio,* to pleasure and joy, as a constitutive part of beatitude, at the end of his *Commentary on the Sentences* (IV 49). Aquinas returns to the subject in the *De veritate.* He devotes one question with ten articles to the emotions, after the study on free will and on sensuality, and before that on grace; here he maintains the traditional order with the Pas-

Originally published as "Les passions et la morale," in *RSPT* (1990): 379–91. Translated and edited by Craig Steven Titus for publication in *The Pinckaers Reader*.

sion of Christ. In his *Summa,* St. Thomas finally gives free reign to his own genius and undoubtedly to his desire to write on the subject: his treatise on the emotions developed without constraint, ripening as a cluster of fruit. To my knowledge, there does not exist, either among the Fathers of the Church or in the Middle Ages, a treatise on the human emotions comparable in length and quality. It is a unique classic that is generally neglected.

In order to avoid misunderstandings, I would like to note that for St. Thomas the term "passion" does not carry the pejorative connotation that it acquired in the modern era, signifying a violent sentiment that overpowers reason. It simply concerns sensate movements. We could speak of the sentiments or the emotions, either good or bad.

The importance that Thomas attaches to the emotions seems that much more significant in contrast to the role that modern Catholic morality attributed to them. Let us take, for example, D. M. Prümmer's valuable manual, written "according to the principles of St. Thomas Aquinas."[1] This manual deals with emotions in its treatise on human acts entitled *De hostibus voluntarii* (the "enemies," the obstacles to the voluntary character of human acts). It treats emotions alongside violence, fear, and pathological bodily states. As a disciple of Aquinas, Prümmer does provide, in four pages, an outline of the emotions; nonetheless, this piece remains evidence of the negative conception of the emotions that imposed itself as traditional in moral theology: the emotions are obstacles to the freedom and moral quality of acts. How can we explain such a difference of viewpoint within the Thomist school? How can we understand, on the other hand, St. Thomas's creative interest, as we might say, in the emotions?

Two Conceptions of Morality

There is a fundamental reason for these differences in the treatment of the emotions: it concerns two conceptions, two systematizations of morality, one based upon beatitude, the other based upon obligation. St. Thomas is a spokesman for ancient thought, which conceived of morality as a response to the question of beatitude. Indeed the first experience of beatitude that is offered to human beings is that of pleasure, to which are linked the other senti-

1. *"secundum principia S. Thomae Aquinatis."* D. M. Prümmer, *Manuale Theologiae Moralis,* 11th ed. (Freiburg im Breisgau, 1953).

ments that form the different emotions. The manuals, on the contrary, center morality on the question of obligations.

The moral adjudication of emotions is determinant in the major schools of philosophy in antiquity. The Epicureans place their beatitude at the level of the emotions, in a calculated search for pleasure and the absence of pain. The Stoics consider, on the contrary, emotions as disorders and propose the ideal of *apatheia,* that is, of the soul as indifferent to emotions. The Platonists favor the overcoming of the sensible pleasures in order to attain the joy caused by contemplation of Ideas. Aristotle's thought is more nuanced. It puts at the center of its perspective human action, with the virtue that renders it perfect. Beatitude consists in the highest human activity that achieves the best kind of pleasure. Pleasures and other passions are morally adjudicated from the actions that accompany them. The emotions are thus good if they contribute to a good action, and bad in the opposite case.

However, even if there are discrepancies between the schools of antiquity, the study of the emotions always occupies a place of primary importance in moral matters, even among the Stoics. The Fathers of the Church, while of course rejecting Epicurean laxity, found insight, according to their own inclination, in the positions of other schools. Indeed they conceive of Christianity as a response to the question of beatitude as well, but a response coming from God through the mouth of Christ. While they vigorously lead a spiritual combat against the flesh, in the manner of St. Paul, they adopt in general a line of balanced conduct concerning the emotions that resembles the Aristotelian position. The example of Christ, who experienced sadness, joy, pain, and anger, keeps them from Stoic rigorism. St. Thomas follows this same line while constructing the *Summa theologiae.* The emotions are a necessary component to human agency: they depend on the acts and on their interior principles, the virtues, in view of attaining beatitude. His analysis is precise, detailed, and well articulated, a masterpiece in the manner of the buildings of his time.

By contrast, beginning in the following century, morality concentrates progressively on two poles: liberty and law, competing with each other through the intermediary of obligation. The consideration of beatitude became very marginal in morality and the treatise on beatitude disappeared from the manuals. As a logical consequence, emotions were given a minor role in the study on human acts. The emotions are considered henceforth as a threat to the sovereignty of liberty and reason, since they originate from obscure regions of human sensate knowledge. We are in the age of rationalism and voluntarism. Sensate knowledge and emotions no longer have the right to a place in a morality that only concerns itself with establishing and defending restrictive laws. Nevertheless, they will assert themselves in hidden ways, and even find their way into the exercise of human freedom.

If we wish to understand the import and the richness of Aquinas's treatise on the emotions, we must place ourselves in the profoundly human perspective of the moralities of beatitude that he systematized. Emotions are one of the direct and necessary components of the response to the question of beatitude. We cannot construct a morality that is truly human without taking them into consideration.

The Relation of the Emotions to the Spirit according to St. Thomas

Let us press on in Aquinas's treatise on the emotions. It is enough to read the table of contents to notice immediately that the author, who defines the emotions as movements of the sensible appetite, does not restrict himself to the level of sensation. Already the problem of the moral quality of the emotions situates them in relation to reason and will, and attributes to them a dimension that they do not have among the animals. St. Thomas considers them as human emotions, integrated in the human composite. But the way in which we surpass pure sensation seems still more manifest in the study of love, when he distinguishes between love, delight, charity, and friendship; he considers love the most common term, encompassing the others (*ST* I-II 25.3). It is clear that, at this moment, he is already referring to the virtue of charity. This is confirmed when he distinguishes between concupiscible love and friendship-love (*ST* I-II 25.4). Indeed it is clear that this latter does not belong to the order of sensation; it serves to define the virtue of charity as a friendship with God. Further on (*ST* I-II 27), he presents the causes of love, good, beauty, knowledge, and resemblance, before applying them at the sensate level. Finally the effects of love (*ST* I-II 28): union, mutual indwelling, ecstasy, zeal, and wounding directly evoke the language and experiences of Christian mysticism; the numerous citations from *The Divine Names (De divinis nominibus)* of Dionysius the Areopagite are there in order to confirm it (*ST* I-II 28). The study of pleasure or *delectatio* has the same dimensions. St. Thomas distinguishes between pleasure and joy. He specifies that the latter is a pleasure that proceeds from reason, and is therefore of a spiritual nature. This leads him to investigate the existence of a *delectatio* in the intellectual appetite and to compare the corporal pleasures with spiritual ones. We could multiply the examples.

Thus, in his study of the emotions, St. Thomas does not isolate sensation from the spirit. Rather, he continually moves from the level of sensation to the higher realm of moral and spiritual life. His perspective is that of the theologian whose dominant aim, as he says concerning circumstances (*ST* I-II 7.2), is to demonstrate how human acts, with their components, are ordered to beatitude. Such is his perspective: St. Thomas conceives the emotions as a constitutive element of human agency ordered to beatitude in God by the means of the virtues and the gifts, as internal or personal principles of action. His treatment of the emotions points to the virtues and the gifts. Indeed, the treatise on the emotions is the direct preparation for that on the virtues: the study of love prepares for that of charity; it is the same for desire or "concupiscence" in regard to hope. Concerning the study of *delectatio*, he immediately relates it to the questions on beatitude, as the parallel text of the fourth book of the *Sentences* demonstrates (IV 49), where he dedicates question 3 (with its five articles and its fifteen *quaestiunculae*) to it in his first redaction of the treatise on beatitude.

In the *Summa theologiae*, Aquinas does not treat the emotions as a physiologist nor as a psychologist nor as a pure philosopher, but as a theologian. Indeed, he meets the psychologist's perspective at the level of sensation, but his aim extends beyond it toward human relationships with God, who constitutes true beatitude for human beings. Aquinas's particular interest in the emotions comes from their contribution to moral action and to human progress in one's journey toward God; it relates to the fact that sensation provides humans with a primary image and a basic vocabulary in order to express spiritual realities.

Similar Language

Effectively, the relation that Aquinas establishes between the emotions and spiritual realities, notably the virtues, rests on the solid foundations found in cognitive processes and in his very conception of humanity. As Aquinas often recalls, our knowledge proceeds from sense perception. Our first subjective reactions are of the same order; they are precisely the emotions: pleasure and pain, attraction and fear, love, anger, and so forth. Since language follows knowledge, we spontaneously employ the images and vocabulary of the emotions in order to describe analogically the movements of the spirit in us on the affective and cognitive levels. The whole art of the ethicist consists in distinguishing similarities and differences, while delicately assuring the transition from the senses to the spiritual realm. If we think of the subtle play of evangelical language, we can affirm that the emotions are a parable of the movements through which the spirit accesses the world and God.

A Unified Conception of the Human Being and Human Action

We must go further and say that the place given to the emotions in the *Summa* rests on a unified conception of the human being and human action. The human composite is not formed of two substances that are artificially united but often continue to oppose one another. For St. Thomas there is a substantial union and natural harmony between the body and the soul, between sensation and spirit, in spite of the frictions that we can experience. We can find the same harmony in the interplay of the human faculties: reason, will, sensation, and sense perception; they tend to function together in coordination, for example, in free choice (which consists of a judgment and an act of the will, which include the sensate desire that corresponds to them). In this view, sensation is perfected by serving the spirit, with the aid of the virtues that educate it. Thanks to the natural union between body and soul, and to the fundamental harmony that it creates between our faculties, humans can spontaneously move from the emotions to the spiritual, and, on the contrary, the spiritual can rebound through sensation, for good and for bad. There is a marked difference from the Franciscan theology that distinguished several souls in the human composite, and separated more clearly the intellectual and the sensate faculties. Then nominalism disrupted this harmony by concentrating freedom only in the will, and morality in the law, as the principle of rational obligation; it left no other choice than strict obedience or rebellion.

In passing we should recall that the way in which Aquinas coordinates sense experience and the life of the spirit aptly corresponds, in spite of the differences, to scriptural language. Scripture typically specifies things in our concrete sensory experience, although its interior extension attains the heights of the spirit. Thus, poverty evokes humility of heart and riches suggest self-sufficiency and pride. At the same time, according to Christian tradition, the Holy Spirit himself accomplishes his work with a commitment to the body that involves even the physical suffering of the Passion (the meditation on which is historically at the origin of the treatise on the passions). Consequently, the most humble suffering, such as sickness or fear, is able to acquire an authentic spiritual value, significantly beyond the physiological level. In this perspective, Thomas establishes a continuous reciprocal interaction between spirit and our sense experience that is linked to the body. This interaction involves the very nature of human beings, which, accordingly, can then acquire a supernatural dimension thanks to charity and its penetration into the fibers of sensation, with the aid of the other virtues, especially courage and temperance, as well as patience, which St. Paul always cites in his lists alongside charity.

In our opinion, this explains the efflorescence of the *Summa theologiae*'s treatise on the emotions. Its constituent studies are in close contact with the whole of this great work—in particular, with the studies on beatitude, on the virtues, and on the gifts. Other conceptions of humanity and morality do not attribute to the emotions as positive a role—neither Platonism nor Stoicism, and later, neither nominalism nor Descartes, whom we shall revisit shortly.

Aquinas's treatise on the emotions is both philosophical and theological. For Aquinas, these two dimensions interpenetrate. The treatise definitely attains a theological goal through its integration in a theological work (a summary of theology), through its intent (the ordination to beatitude in God and the preparation for the study on the virtues, especially the theological ones), and through its sources (principally from the Christian mystic tradition).

Comparison with Descartes

It is interesting to compare Aquinas's study on the emotions with Descartes' treatise *Passions of the Soul.*[2] We should not, however, be intimidated by the latter's devastating declaration: "[T]he teaching of the ancients about the passions are so meager and for the most part so implausible that I cannot hope to approach the truth except by departing from the paths they followed."[3] How can we explain such disdain except from the novel point of view on the emotions that gave Descartes the impression "to need to write here as

2. René Descartes, *The Passions of the Soul* (*Les Passions de l'âme,* orig. 1649), trans. S. Voss (Indianapolis: Hackett, 1989).
3. *The Passions of the Soul,* in *The Philosophical Writings of Descartes,* trans. Robert Stoothoff (Cambridge: Cambridge University Press, 1985), vol. 1 (pt. 1, art. 1) 328.

though I were treating a topic which no one before me had ever described."[4]

The base on which Descartes constructs his study of the emotions is strictly philosophical; it builds on a conception of man that he indicates from the start. The principle is the following: in order to study emotions we have to begin with the difference that exists between the soul and the body, by attributing to the body all that we experience in us that can be attributed to non-human bodies, and to the soul that which cannot conceivably belong to the body, such as ideas. This separation between thought and phenomena that depend on the body leads us to conceive of the emotions as if they were movements of a "machine that moves itself," of a robot like a watch whose "movement is produced only by its spring and wheels."[5] This physiological explanation of the emotions focuses on the interaction of bodily organs, the heart, the brain, the muscles, the nerves, the production and circulation of animal spirits. However, in contrast to physical robots, emotions are the sentiments of the soul, or "the emotions that we particularly attribute to [the soul]," but they have their principal cause in the corporeal side; they "are caused, sustained, and strengthened" by the movement of the animal spirits provoked by the small gland in the brain "in which the soul particularly exercises its functions" and which is its principal center. By this gland the body acts on the soul and produces in it the emotions, and the soul can also act on the body. The emotions have as a principal effect "that they incite and dispose the soul to will the things for which they prepare the body."[6] As Malebranche writes: "the emotions are the movements of the soul that accompany those of the spirits and the blood, and that produce in the body, by the construction of the machine, all the necessary dispositions in order to maintain the cause that gives them birth."[7] Thus understood, the emotions have above all as a goal to assure the well-being of the body. The emotions pose for Descartes a delicate and interesting question arising from the fact that they engage the soul and the body in interaction.[8] He resolves it through his anthropology, which views man as a composite of two substances: the soul, which thinks and is in no way

4. Descartes, *The Passions*, trans. S. Voss, First Part, Art. 1.

5. Ibid., Art. 5.

6. Ibid., Art. 40.

7. Nicolas Malebranche, *Treatise on Ethics* (orig. 1680), trans. Craig Walton (Boston: Dordrecht, 1993), bk. I, ch. XIII, IV.

8. *The Passions of the Soul* is a response to a critical remark of the Princess Elizabeth, the daughter of the Palatine Elector Frederick V. She wrote to Descartes: "The senses show me that

extensive; and the body, which is extensive and does not think in any way, as Malebranche puts it.[9]

Descartes thus introduces a new relationship between the spirit that concentrates on clear ideas and the body subsequently conceived of as a machine. He inaugurates a new attitude toward the spirit vis-à-vis the body, which one could call the view of a mechanic or engineer. Even if the emotions affect the soul, they will be viewed subsequently through this lens, because of the corporal processes that they involve and that constitute a sort of mechanics. Descartes focuses his attention primarily on the physiology of the emotions.

The vision of the emotions is henceforth radically different from that of the ancients, St. Thomas included. That is the source of Descartes' scorn: he does not find any good in the authors that precede him simply because he can no longer understand them nor share their views. Even the relationship of the spirit to emotion has changed. The ancients saw the emotions as a human phenomenon engaging the spirit and the body. They observed the interior, as someone who experiences them and who is interested above all in their moral dimension in view of beatitude. Descartes introduces a radical separation between thought and the emotions by the attitude he adopts: he construes them from a distance that separates thought, with its clear ideas, from corporal phenomena; he observes emotions as from the exterior and they appear to him henceforth as a simple piece of machinery, no matter how complex the cogs. It is only a mechanism that touches the soul. One must beware of them if one wants to avoid illusions and favor progress of rational knowledge, as well as the mastery of free will.

The import of Descartes' innovation is to have laid the philosophical foundation of modern experimental psychology. We cannot fail to recognize it. Nor should we hide the losses incurred by it. In short, Descartes contributed in a decisive way to dehumanizing the emotions. For him, the emotions no longer involve the whole human being, spirit and body together; thus they lose their moral and spiritual repercussions. The Cartesian method can give us a ration-

IMP.

---

the soul moves the body, but they do not teach me in any way, not more than the understanding and the imagination, the way in which the soul makes the body; and for this reason, I think that there are properties of the soul that are not known to us. These unknown properties might be able to undo that which your metaphysical meditations persuaded me by such good reasons of the extension of the soul" (letter of 1 July 1643).

9. Malebranche, *Treatise on Ethics,* bk. I, ch. X, XIII.

al knowledge of the emotions, a rational knowledge that came to be called scientific; but this is based on a materialized experience, rendered exterior as if concerning physical bodies. Thereby, Descartes turns his back on the intelligence of the emotions that interior experience procures; here these emotions predominantly connect with the spirit that is in us, with the person that we are. He personalizes the emotions. In his perspective, the natural passage of sensibility to the spiritual world no longer exists. There remains only an accidental link, an "occasional" parallel, as Malebranche says. The language of emotions can no longer be applied to spiritual movements except in an artificial manner, full of confusion.

We should not discard Aquinas's treatise on the emotions after Descartes. Thomas can, on the contrary, help us to rediscover the internal aspect of the emotions, which renders them properly human and integrates them into the moral life, with the movements of the spirit and of grace. This in no way demands that we reject the achievements of modern psychology but permits us to perceive its limits and to fill in its gaps. If we want to integrate again the emotions as important and significant human factors, this is of capital importance for the morality and theology that are grounded on spiritual interiority.

Let us note another consequence of the Cartesian perspective on the emotions. By separating the spirit from bodily and emotional mechanics, Descartes severed the will from the emotional spontaneity that is exercised in desire, love, pleasure, and so on. He thus favors a voluntarist conception of morality based on the liberty of indifference and on pure voluntarist resolve. Thus, spiritual spontaneity and sensibility will disappear from the horizon; there remain only two extremes: voluntarist rigorism and the irrational manifestation of sentiments and emotions.

Between St. Thomas and Descartes: Nicolas Coeffeteau

Between St. Thomas and Descartes, there is probably only one author, forgotten today, who served as an intermediary: the Dominican Nicolas Coeffeteau (1568–1623). Jean de La Bruyère wrote of him in 1688: "A sober, serious, scrupulous style that penetrates deeply. We still read Amyot and Coeffeteau; which of their contemporaries are still read?"[10] Coeffeteau wrote several theological works that lay out the doctrine of St. Thomas, notably "Table of the

---

10. Jean de La Bruyère, *Les caractères; ou, Les mœurs de ce siècle,* ch. 1.

human emotions, of their causes and of their effects," which he published in 1620 and which went through sixteen editions before 1664, with an English translation in 1621.[11] Recall that Descartes' *The Passions of the Soul* dates to 1649.

It would be interesting to compare Coeffeteau with Aquinas and with Descartes. In the seventeenth century, there were several indications of change of perspective concerning the emotions among the readers and disciples of St. Thomas; we shall focus on one. Coeffeteau starts by defining emotion as "a movement of the sensitive appetite, caused by the perception, or the imagination of good or evil, which is followed by a change that happens to the body, against the laws of nature."[12] This last part of the definition surprises us. St. Thomas did not include it in his definition, since his goal as a moralist is rather to assure the conformity of the emotions to human nature. Coeffeteau explains later on: the emotions produce a change that acts on the body against the laws of nature, since the emotions "push the heart beyond the limits of movement that nature prescribed for it and agitates it unusually."[13] Therefore we call the emotions of the soul "the maladies by which it is tormented and troubled, like pity, fear, embarrassment, desire, anger, and the others." The emotions are the sensible movements that involve a corporal change. That is why Coeffeteau carefully discusses the bodily organs affected by the emotions. For him, the emotions that certain thinkers attribute to different organs (like the liver for love, and the spleen for anger) have their center instead in the heart, which is the source of life and of all vital operations; from the heart proceed the vital spirits that travel throughout the body and rouse its members. We note at the same time the qualification of the emotions as "illnesses," which recalls the Stoic position.

It is noteworthy that Coeffeteau later challenges this stance of the emotions as illnesses,[14] but it is nonetheless clear that Coeffeteau adopted a point of view that differed from that of St. Thomas. Coeffeteau focused on the sensations linked to the changes that the emotions cause in the body. The moral and, above all, spiritual import of the emotions is no longer in the foreground.

---

11. Born in 1574, at Château-du-Loir (Maine, France), Coeffeteau was Regent and Priory of the Convent Saint-Jacques of Paris. He died there on 21 April 1623. We cite his "Tableau of the Passions" from the 1632 edition.

12. Coeffeteau, 2.   13. Coeffeteau, 16.

14. Coeffeteau, 67.

Thus he judges that "if someone gives the name of the Emotions to the movements of understanding or of the will, it is in an improper sense and through allusion to sense emotions, with which they have some relationship." This signifies that employing the names of emotions for spiritual movements is artificial, while for St. Thomas it proceeds from a natural analogy. Undoubtedly Coeffeteau affirms that the soul is the form of the body, following Aquinas; but to explain the emotions, he prefers to consider the soul as the cause that moves the body.[15] This idea clearly recalls the Platonic conception of the relationships between the soul and the body that St. Thomas extensively critiques in order to establish his own position against the Franciscan school.[16] There we see again how the study of the emotions depends on the anthropology that one adopts and utilizes.

I have specified several divergences between Coeffeteau and his master, St. Thomas. Nonetheless, we can congratulate him for having perceived the treatise on the emotions' importance and for having deemed it worthy of presentation to the cultivated public of his era.[17]

Pleasure, Joy, and Beatitude

I would like to end this overview of Aquinas's treatise on emotion by showing the considerable influence that it can have on the conception of morality, in particular regarding the place attributed to the consideration of beatitude in the construction and the presentation of morality. More precisely, I shall say a few words on the impact of the study of *delectatio* on the question of eudaemonism (beatitude). This issue highlights the opposition of moral systems such as that of Immanuel Kant not only to that of Aquinas, but also to those of the Church Fathers and ancient philosophy.

Our thesis is the following: the Kantian critique of eudaemonism rests on the image of happiness (beatitude) formed by sensate experience and pleasure. By contrast, St. Thomas's morality, when it establishes beatitude as the

15. Coeffeteau, 11.

16. *ST* I 76.

17. This task, however, presented him with unexpected difficulties. In 1607, Coeffeteau had announced a translation of the theological texts of St. Thomas. The Sorbonne reacted by asking him to retract this initiative for fear "that St. Thomas's doctrine would lose its value, if one were to submit it to the judgment of women or ill-disposed people."

ultimate end of morality, takes as the principal basis of its representation of beatitude the spiritual experience of joy, according to St. Augustine's famous definition: beatitude is "joy of the truth." We have therefore on each side two "eudaemonisms" of different natures: the first, which Kant rejects, directs the search for pleasure as the supreme principle of action, and thus corrupts morality, rendering it utilitarian and egoistic. Therefore one is not able to save morality, except by expelling this interested desire of beatitude; yet this leads to a sort of divorce between the morality of pure duty and the search for beatitude. The other form of eudaemonism, if we would still like to keep the term, is built on a moral and spiritual experience. It involves an active surpassing of the search for pleasure and for tangible utility by the generous opening to God and to others, an opening achieved by friendship-love and more particularly by the virtue of charity, of which joy is the direct fruit.

At the heart of the discussion on eudaemonism we find the study of *delectatio*. St. Thomas places this study in his treatises on the passions, although he links the study to his analysis of beatitude (as he did already in his *Commentary on the Sentences*—Book IV) and revisits it in the treatise on charity (*ST* II-II 28).

St. Thomas's analysis is nuanced. When he compares *delectatio*[18] to joy,[19] he makes the following distinction: *delectatio* can be employed on the tangible level as well as on the rational or the spiritual level, while joy only relates to reason and spirit. Joy cannot be attributed to animals but only to humans, and—we can add—to angels and to God. In the two following articles,[20] Aquinas compares the tangible pleasures (that are linked to the body) to spiritual joys in order to demonstrate how the latter outstrip the former by their nature, quality, and power. He concedes nonetheless that our attachment to tangible pleasures can give them more control over us.

Here we can clearly see how St. Thomas, while maintaining the connection with the experience of tangible pleasure, carefully prepares the way leading to spiritual experience. We develop this spiritual experience through the practice of the virtues of which joy is the effect, and principally through the act of charity in which is condensed the grace of the Holy Spirit that defines the

---

18. When *delectatio* is translated as "pleasure," the English has a narrower connotation, which is more linked to the tangible.

19. *ST* I-II 31.3.

20. *ST* I-II 31.4–5.

New Law.[21] Such work cannot evidently be done without overcoming the control of sense pleasure and without the purification of heart in order to cleanse it of the roots of egoism; we can hardly accomplish this without the intervention of an Other through the grace of love. This is the purification that the evangelical Beatitudes notably describe, according to Aquinas's interpretation, which directs them toward the Beatitude of the pure of heart and puts them at the center of the source of his treatise on beatitude.

In the *secunda secundae,* Aquinas dedicates a question to the joy that charity causes, while describing its nature and purity.[22] Spiritual joy is twofold: it flows primarily from the consideration of divine goodness taken as such according to benevolent love—and this is the best source of joy; secondly, it comes from our participation in divine goodness and as such it is linked to the virtue of hope. The latter allows us to tend toward God's presence and is measured by its level of charity (*ST* II-II 8.1 corpus and ad 3).

Such is the experience of spiritual joy, from which St. Thomas drew his conception of beatitude and which becomes the cornerstone of his morality. It is a participation in God's beatitude and joy, which has been revealed in Christ and communicated through the Holy Spirit. Obviously Kant does not offer any comparable study of pleasure, and even less so of spiritual joy. The kind of eudaemonism that he fights comes from the beginnings of British utilitarianism, which is oriented toward an increasing wellness, toward beatitude intended as enjoying the greatest number of goods by the greatest number of people. Its determination to build its philosophy solely on sensate experience in the order of knowledge manifests itself in its treatment of the emotions as well, which brings it to a conception of beatitude based solely on sensate pleasure. As far as spiritual experience, Kant seems to have turned away from it since the beginning of his career, when he criticizes Emanuel Swedenborg's flights of fancy in *Dreams of a Spirit-Seer, Illustrated by Dreams of Metaphysics.*

Anyway, the very structure of the Kantian moral system—which was inherited from nominalism probably through Luther—prevented him from giving a positive role to emotions, in particular to pleasure and beatitude. This is caused by the radical separation between freedom, which is jealous of its absolute independence, and the inclinations, which are rejected at the sensate

---

21. *ST* I-II 106.1, 108.1.
22. *ST* II-II 8.

level. Therefore, the emotions could be considered only as a threat against the empire of freedom, a "gangrene" of moral life, as he says. As a consequence, Kant failed to recognize the spiritual inclinations and the spiritual experience of which they are a source. However, what distinguishes joy from pleasure is notably that pleasure comes from an exterior source, which is found in sensate goods, whereas joy comes from the interior of man, by his most personal and spiritual agency. But this interiority is opened toward God and neighbor through love beyond the grasp of mere sensation.

I shall conclude with a quotation from Henri Bergson, from one of the most clear-sighted critiques of Kant. Bergson intuited the difference between pleasure and joy and he expresses it according to this own philosophical experience:

Nature warns us by a clear sign that our destination is attained. That sign is joy. I mean joy, not pleasure. Pleasure is only a contrivance devised by nature to obtain for the creature the preservation of its life; it does not indicate the direction in which life is thrusting. But joy always announces that life has succeeded, gained ground, conquered. All great joy has a triumphant note. Now, if we take this indication into account and follow this new line of facts, we find that wherever there is joy, there is creation; the richer the creation, the deeper the joy.[23]

I imagine that St. Thomas experienced a similar kind of joy after finishing his treatise on emotions.

23. Henri Bergson, *Mind-Energy: Lectures and Essays,* trans. H. Wildon Carr (New York: Henry Holt and Company, 1920), 29.

14 ∾ The Role of Virtue in Moral Theology
(1996)

Introduction: The Debate about Virtue

Virtue is back. Especially in the United States, a widespread discussion about its role in moral theology has been initiated, a discussion modeled on Aristotle's *Ethics,* particularly as Aristotle's thought was developed in the Middle Ages by Thomas Aquinas.

Accompanying this rediscovery of virtue is a criticism of modern ethical theories. These theories, having broken with Aristotelian tradition, have led to a burgeoning of contradictory systems: a morality of obligation on the Kantian model; utilitarian morality; and a radical critique of morality by Nietzsche. Because of such divergences any discussion between moralists, especially where the foundations and principles of morality are involved, has up to the present seemed doomed to failure.[1]

Originally published as "Redécouvrir la vertu," *Sapientia* 51 (1996): 151–63; "Rediscovering Virtue," *The Thomist* (1996): *361–78*. Translated by Sr. Mary Thomas Noble, O.P. Edited for publication in *The Pinckaers Reader* by John Berkman.

1. The author who has contributed most to this discussion of virtue is undoubtedly Alasdair MacIntyre in *After Virtue: A Study in Moral Theory* (Notre Dame, Ind.: University of Notre Dame Press, 1981; 2nd ed. 1984); *Whose Justice? Which Rationality?* (Notre Dame, Ind.: University of Notre Dame Press, 1988); and *Three Versions of Moral Inquiry: Encyclopedia, Genealogy, and Tradition* (Notre Dame, Ind.: University of Notre Dame Press, 1990). See also the article by Martha Nussbaum, "Virtue Revived," *Times Literary Supplement* (July 3, 1992): 9–11; and a recent book by André Comte-Sponville, *Petit traité des grands vertus* (Paris: Presses Universitaires de France, 1995). This work is very interesting because it proposes to a wide readership a moral system drawn from Aristotle that is at the same time based entirely on modern philosophy. The author unintentionally confirms the thesis of the incompatibility of modern ethical systems of obligation and the Aristotelian construct of the virtues held by MacIntyre. With the

In view of this ethical pluralism, certain philosophers have undertaken to set up ethical norms through reflection on justice, using the methods of discussion and decision prevalent in our democratic societies. The initiative has been designated "procedural ethics."[2]

In this rather chaotic situation, other writers have thought a return to Aristotelian ethics opportune—a move that would enable us to reconnect with the long tradition of virtue-based morality represented therein, while bringing it up to date. In fact, the introduction of the concept of virtue offers many opportunities for the shaping of a morality that takes the human person into account. Virtue is a dynamic human quality acquired through education and personal effort. It forms character and assures continuity in action. Furthermore, it is set within the framework of community and a strong tradition, to whose development it contributes. Teaching on virtue would seem to be a good corrective for excessive individualism. This is what the so-called "communitarian" trend has emphasized.[3]

The debate on virtue has also surfaced within traditional Catholic teaching. Since the first half of this century, under the inspiration of St. Thomas, several authors of moral theology textbooks have undertaken to reorganize special moral theology on the basis of the virtues rather than the Ten Commandments, as had been done since the seventeenth century.[4] Admittedly, the change remained superficial, since the virtues served only to classify obligations and prohibitions in a new way. The focus was still obligation, not virtue.

moderns he rejects a natural foundation for morality, within man, and thus robs the virtues he treats of their deep roots. Virtue is not spontaneous; it remains voluntaristic.

2. To mention a few titles: Karl-Otto Apel, *Towards a Transformation of Philosophy* (London: RKP, 1979); Apel, *Ethique de la discussion* (Paris: Cerf, 1994); Jurgen Harbermas, *The Theory of Communicative Action*, 2 vols. (Boston: Beacon Press, 1985); Jean-Marc Ferry, *Philosophie de la communication* (Paris: Cerf, 1994); John Rawls, *A Theory of Justice* (Cambridge, Mass.: Harvard University Press, 1971).

3. See, for example, John H. Yoder, *The Politics of Jesus* (Grand Rapids, Mich.: Eerdmans, 1972); Stanley M. Hauerwas, *The Peaceable Kingdom: A Primer in Christian Ethics* (Notre Dame, Ind.: University of Notre Dame Press, 1983); W. Reese-Schäfer, *Was ist Kommunitarismus?* (Frankfurt, 1994); Charles Taylor, *Sources of the Self: The Making of the Modern Identity* (Cambridge, Mass.: Harvard University Press, 1989); Charles Taylor, *The Malaise of Modernity* (Cambridge, Mass.: Harvard University Press, 1991); Charles Taylor, *Multiculturalism and "the Politics of Recognition"* (Princeton, N.J.: Princeton University Press, 1992); Michael Walzer, "Les deux universalismes," *Esprit* 187 (December 1992): 114-33.

4. Two examples: D. M. Prümmer, O.P., *Manuale theologiae Moralis ad mentem divi Thomae* (Barcelona, 1946); J.-B. Vittrant, S.J., *Théologie morale* (Paris, 1948).

Nonetheless, these authors drew attention to the inadequacy of a moral teaching limited to the commandments, and indicated the direction to be followed for a renewal of the presentation of moral theology.

In the opposite direction, reacting to Paul VI's encyclical *Humanae vitae,* certain Catholic moralists worked out a new concept of morality and criteria of judgment based principally on the weighing of the good and evil consequences of human actions, seen as means in view of the end sought. This has been called "consequentialism" and "proportionalism." It amounts to a modern translation of casuistry combined with reflections based on Kantian categories. This construct, tending to utilitarianism, harmonizes well with the technological mindset of our age.

Taking as its point of departure a pre-moral judgment formed by relating an action to its circumstances and external consequences, this system is unable to assign a determining role to virtue, which is an interior principle of human action. If virtue is referred to at all, it is associated with a habitual, general good intention. "Consequentialism" avoids the consideration of virtue even more decisively than did traditional casuistry.

The *Catechism of the Catholic Church,* too, has encountered the problem of virtue. In organizing the subject matter of morality it had to choose between using the commandments or the virtues as a base. While it opted for the commandments, in order to lend firm support to the teaching of the Decalogue, it has been at pains to elucidate them by their relationship to the virtues. Nor has it hesitated to reintroduce into moral theology the too-long-neglected teaching on the New Law and the gifts of the Holy Spirit that perfect the virtues.[5]

The problem of the role of virtue has far-reaching ramifications in philosophy as well as in theology. In order to resolve this problem, it is not enough to assign a place to virtue in a moral system based on concepts of obligation, duty, or utility. The nature of virtue calls for a specific systematization in which the other elements, particularly obligations, commandments, and means, play a subordinate role. We are no longer dealing with a morality of individual actions that are either allowed or forbidden by law. Virtue builds up a moral system around those qualities inherent in man that enable him to perform with freedom good actions involving continuity and development.

5. See S. Pinckaers, O.P., "Catechisme de l'Eglise catholique," *Sources* 19 (1993): 49–59. [Editor's note: See also "The Return of the New Law to Moral Theology," essay #19 in *The Pinckaers Reader.*]

Obviously, I cannot treat the question of the place of virtue in moral theology exhaustively here. I should simply like to offer some reflections that may help us to rediscover the true nature of virtue, and more particularly, its rightful role in the making of practical judgments and in the study of moral cases.

Toward a Morality of Dynamic Interiority

It is very important to situate virtue accurately in its relationship to moral action. Our actions are actually richer and more complex than the ordinary treatment of cases of conscience would have us believe. According to Aristotle's analysis, in order for an action to be voluntary and hence moral, two conditions are required: it must proceed from within the acting subject; and the agent must be aware of the component elements of his or her act. Spontaneity and awareness are, therefore, the two essential notes of a moral action.

Awareness of our actions, like consciousness, operates at two levels. The first level draws our initial attention. This is the "external action" with its purpose, circumstances, and the result sought: for example, a job to be done, a role to exercise, a debt to pay, or a duty to perform. The second level goes deeper. It stems from our capacity to reflect upon ourselves, our personal dispositions, desires, intentions, and feelings. This is the level of "interior action," where the roots and causes of our actions lie. Now the question becomes: Am I acting out of self-interest or out of a concern for justice? Out of vanity and egoism, or out of devotion? From a sense of duty, or out of love? Here we are at the moral level of voluntary and rational commitment, at the level of the "heart" in the biblical sense of the word. This is where the virtues have their place (vices also), as stable and personal dispositions to do good (or evil). These dispositions are dynamic and shape human persons together with their actions, according to Aristotle's definition: "Virtue renders its possessor good, and also his actions."[6]

There are two elements, therefore, in every moral act: inward and outward action. Note well, we are not speaking of two separate acts, for the first stands to the second as soul to body. We can therefore speak of the two dimensions of a human act: its inwardness and its outwardness. The interior act is paramount because it emanates directly from the will, from the person. It takes

---

6. Aristotle, *Nicomachean Ethics*, II, 6 (1106 a 15); see Aquinas, *ST* I-II 20.3, obj. 2.

place at the source of human morality. Virtues are likewise interior principles of action as contrasted with law, which, by its origin, is an external principle.

Casuist morality has focused on the external action considered as individual, for example, a case of conscience, relating it to law, the source of moral obligation. In this way morality is closely linked to law and justice. Casuist morality abstracts from interiority or reduces interiority simply to a good or evil intention. Being concerned about rationality, it will also avoid the intervention of affectivity in the forming of a moral judgment. Although careful to consider concrete circumstances, the moralist will study human action in an impersonal, abstract way, as "one case" falling under the general law. The expression "consequentialist" is significant in this regard: judgment of actions should first be made at the pre-moral level, by an adjustment of circumstances and means to the end, in a technological type of relationship. Morality will only intervene at a later stage, with the intention.

Such a break with the interior dimension of human action logically leads to relegating the virtues to a position outside the moral realm, thus constricting them. Virtue becomes a kind of habit of obeying the law.

The restoration of a virtue-oriented morality calls therefore for a fundamental change. The central focus of morality needs to be returned to the level of the interior act and seen from the viewpoint of the person who is acting, with all his intellectual and affective dispositions—beginning with the "discerning mind" that Scripture attributes to Solomon.[7] This was the point of the ancient Socratic maxim "Know thyself!" which was deepened by St. Augustine in the brief prayer at the beginning of his work on free will: "That I may know myself, that I may know Thee!" This interiority is the realm of the virtues, theologal as well as human. From this center, they enlighten and direct moral action.

I should like to make it clear that in placing morality once more at the level of interiority we are not taking up a morality of intention, after the manner of Kant and others. If virtue remains merely a good intention it risks being no more than an illusion. It only becomes real and effective when it produces good actions, as a tree produces fruit. Virtue is altogether ordered to actions and to their excellence, as well as to the object that specifies them. One of the tasks of virtue is precisely to effect coordination between the interior and ex-

7. 1 Kgs 3:12.

ternal act, between our disposition to act and its realization in actions done and done well.

The Treatment of Cases of Conscience

If virtue is oriented to action, it cannot remain a general principle. It must enter the concrete area of action. The first change it effects is a deepening of the approach to the study of cases of conscience. The difference between virtue-based morality and that of the casuists stands out clearly when we compare their contrasting procedures with St. Paul's method of solving moral questions in First Corinthians. Let us take the case of food offered to idols. The Apostle first states that such food cannot contaminate, since idols have no real existence. Christians, therefore, may eat it. This reasoning establishes a general norm of what is allowed and forbidden. St. Paul is of the opinion, however, that this material, external judgment does not go far enough. As a more basic criterion he introduces the consideration of charity toward the weak, taking into account their persons and their dispositions. The concern to avoid scandal and to practice fraternal charity modifies the practical judgment and calls for abstinence from the idol offerings. Thus reflection rises to the decisive level of personal interiority, which opens out to others and to the common good. The quality of the Christian's actions and his or her perfection will depend more on charity than on abstract knowledge.

St. Paul solves other cases in the same way. He first examines the external data involved and then introduces as his principal criterion the personal bonds that faith and charity establish with Christ and the Holy Spirit.

Thus the Apostle provides us with models for analyzing and solving cases of conscience. The virtues, human and Christian, predominate, in conformity with the moral catechesis exposed in his letters.[8] Here we have a clear, authoritative invitation to renew casuistry by way of a virtue-oriented morality.

Such a change of method in the study of conscience cases will also have its pastoral effects. In order to handle a problem of conscience properly, it is not enough to examine it in itself as if it were a general case. It needs to be seen within the life context of the person concerned, and we should reflect with him or her on the underlying intentions directing and inspiring his or her actions. Very often the clarification of a case brings to light some personal prob-

8. *CCC*, n. 1971 [which identifies RM 12–15, 1Cor 12–13, Col 3–4, Eph 4–5.]

lem involving relationships with God and others. Deeper exploration shows the important bearing of the virtues, especially faith and charity, on our actions. The moral question undergoes a transformation. It is no longer limited to what is legally permissible and forbidden, but is inserted into the dynamism of a life, into the heart of personal relationships, against a background of an advancing progress toward goodness and beatitude. The commitment and dispositions of the person make up the essential data where cases of conscience are being considered in the concrete.[9]

Two Concepts of Justice

A moral system based on the virtues includes a significant change in the concept of justice. In many current theories that limit ethics to interpersonal relationships, the idea of justice plays a determining role. Justice, which governs societal relationships by means of laws, seems capable of providing ethics with rational foundations not to be found elsewhere. In a pluralistic society like ours justice thus seems to be the final court of appeal in laying down moral norms and in establishing criteria for evaluating human actions. Justice and morality tend to merge.

The beginnings of this kind of merger could already be seen in handbooks of moral theology of recent centuries. Morality, being based on obedience to legal obligations, was conceived of and often exercised in a juridical manner. Canon law and morality used almost the same methods. The section on justice in the textbooks was particularly well developed. This casuistry, however, recognized natural law, the expression of the divine will, as the first foundation of morality, and affirmed its superiority over all human law. In spite of its similarity to law, morality remained distinct from justice and maintained its primacy.

Modern theories have abandoned natural law and rights because of the opposition that has been directed at them, and no longer take into account a person's relationship with God. Deprived of these supports, ethics clings to justice and law as the only foundations generally acceptable in the name of reason. Thus morality may hope to exercise once again a role in modern societies where, moreover, the need for ethical criteria is becoming more and more

9. For the study of actual cases, see S. Pinckaers, O.P., "Le cas du Dr. Augoyard," in *Ce qu'on ne peut jamais faire* (Fribourg, 1986); and S. Pinckaers, "Le jugement moral sur les problèmes de la vie naissante," in *L'Evangile et la Morale* (Fribourg, 1992).

widely felt. But in doing this, ethics becomes subservient to theories of justice and society.

I should like to clarify once more precisely what is meant by justice. In our liberal societies justice results from a rational organization that aims at establishing equality between the rights of individuals, that is, the right of each person to satisfy his or her needs. We are dealing here with a basically self-centered concept of man. We could call it "rational egoism" and "solipsism."[10] Justice becomes the art of organizing society, viewed as "a collection of egoisms," by dint of laws that will avoid violent confrontation, favor collaboration, and contribute to the well-being of the majority. To assure their rational and scientific character, these theories will, moreover, abstract from what pertains to affectivity and personal factors which do not lend themselves to generalization.

If we now consider the virtue of justice in the setting of a virtue-oriented morality, as described by Aristotle, St. Augustine, or St. Thomas, for example, it will be easy to note some profound differences. According to the traditional definition, the virtue of justice consists in "a permanent and constant will to give to everyone his due."[11] Going back to Cicero's *De officiis,* St. Ambrose adds some fine-tuning: "Justice renders to each one what is his and claims not another's property; it disregards its own profit in order to preserve the common equity."[12]

Such a definition makes it clear that the virtue of justice is quite different from the balance of "egoisms" discussed above. It could almost be called its opposite, since its focus is not self but the other. Its proper activity is not receiving, but rather giving to others what is due them. In order to do this, it will even transcend the consideration of one's own profit out of love for the common good. Justice is a virtue of the will, which it renders constant and firm, in conformity with reason, which discerns the law to be respected and carried out. It is a quality that perfects man in his most personal aspect, his free will and his relationship with others.

Such an idea of justice presupposes a different concept of the human person. Beyond needs to be satisfied, it implies the existence within us of a capac-

10. J.-M. Ferry, *Philosophie de la communication* (Paris, 1994), 2:63.
11. Aquinas, *ST* II-II 58. 1.
12. St. Ambrose, *De Offic.,* I, c. 24; quoted in Aquinas, *ST* II-II 58.11 *sed contra.*

ity to open ourselves to others, to recognize their rights and honor them. Justice is more than respect and the desire not to infringe on others' rights. It is the beginning of a certain kind of love, an esteem for another that inclines us to give the other his or her due.

Seen in this light, the virtue of justice is rooted in the natural inclination to live in society with others, which proceeds from an innate sense of the other, as expressed in the golden rule and the commandment to love others as oneself. Justice will be expressed in laws seen less as constraints than as means of education, effecting coordination and harmony between members of society in view of the common good. It will find its perfection in friendship, which goes beyond the measure of legal obligation and is exercised through liberality or generosity. Virtue forms a love of justice in us and through this it opens the way to charity.

Two Remarks

I should like to make two important distinctions. Seen as a balance of "egoisms," justice presupposes that man is morally undifferentiated. The recognition of "egoisms" is a precondition for the distinction between good and evil that will precisely determine the formation of laws. Let us note, however, that it is difficult to see how a balance of "egoisms," whatever the skill and imagination of the legislator, could logically produce anything more than a multiple and reinforced "egoism," and how such an amalgamation of "egoisms" could produce a moral system that would improve man's condition.

The virtue of justice, on the contrary, bases the distinction between good and evil within us, in our natural sense of what is true and good, in our will and desire intent on what is just or unjust. The question of moral excellence is of prime importance here. It affects both ourselves and our actions. The virtue of justice is both a challenge and a demand, urging us on and judging us.

My second point is that modern theories of justice, inspired by rationalism, separate reason from affectivity. Norms are established with the aid of purely rational procedures on the basis of material data which form the matter of law. A human person is viewed as a thinking being, for whom the command of duty or law is sufficient motivation. This concept is too cerebral. It is impossible to deny that affective factors such as patriotism, family attachments, class solidarity, fidelity to tradition, or a passion for freedom can play powerful roles in politics and society, and that they must be taken into account in the areas of law and morality.

Casuist morality manifests the same tendency. Its rational and juridical character causes it to banish affectivity from moral judgment. In the textbooks, passions are viewed simply as obstacles to the voluntary and free character of actions and threats to their moral excellence. This school of morality requires an obedience of the will alone; it is distrustful of sensibility and affection. Moral judgment ought therefore to be purely rational and should beware of the intervention of any emotion.

In a virtue-oriented morality, the situation is quite different. Doubtless the virtue of justice has a material objective—the law—and this distinguishes it from the affectivity-related virtues, courage and temperance. As a quality of the will, however, justice has its seat in affectivity; it is a disposition of the personal will, an efficacious love of what conforms to the law. In particular it will generate love for the common good.

Furthermore, in order to be practiced concretely, justice requires other moral virtues. We cannot perform a work of justice without possessing sufficient control over our feelings and passions, and without having enough courage to overcome obstacles such as fear and resistance. Better still, in moderating affectivity, these virtues render it capable of contributing to moral action. Thanks to them justice will not operate in a stiff, dry way but rather with upright and firm sensitivity in regard to others. Virtue engages the heart as well as the reason.

The virtues connected with affectivity also collaborate in the prudential discernment that directs justice, at both legislative and personal levels. They prevent the passions—avarice, ambition, fear, and anger—from blinding the vision and disturbing the judgment. They contribute to a clear view of things and a perceptive discernment.

A morality based on the virtues includes therefore a connectedness between reason, will, and sensitivity. It tends to effect the dynamic unification of our faculties in the exercise of justice, among other virtues. This work is achieved thanks to moral education and to our gradual progress through actual experience.

Virtue and Concrete Moral Judgment

Let us return to the objection made against a morality based on the virtues, namely, that it remains on a general plane without indicating concrete norms or precise determinations for judging cases of conscience. For example, to be just, chaste, charitable, or temperate are universal precepts. They do not define which actions are just or unjust, chaste or impure, charitable or not. Thus a moral system based on the virtues remains on a general and abstract level. It cannot resolve the chief ethical problem, which is to move from the universal to the particular, from the general to the concrete in moral judgment.

I hold exactly the opposite position. Only a morality based on the virtues can truly assure a connection between the universality of principles and the particularity of human action.

In order to understand this, we need to rediscover the meaning of virtue. Virtue cannot be reduced to a simple idea or proposition, however precise. It is a specific reality and is only revealed in the experience of action and life.

Virtue Is Formed by Repetition of Interior Actions and through Experience

What then is the experience in which virtue manifests itself or exercises its ability to relate the universal to the particular?

Let us consider virtue at its origin. It is commonly taught that virtue is acquired through the repetition of actions. This is true, but has to be understood correctly. Repetition of the same material actions engenders, certainly, a habit—a kind of psychological mechanism that inclines us to repeat the same actions, smoking or drinking for example. But this is not virtue. Virtue is much more than a habit.[13] It is formed by the repetition of interior actions that insure excellence and progress in performance. For example, we exercise ourselves in overcoming our laziness or timidity, in controlling our impulses, or in practicing justice, generosity, or patience. Virtue is formed in us by the repetition of personal actions, by a series of successful efforts that enable us to keep improving. Virtue is properly called a *habitus,* to use the classical term which has unfortunately been lost in our modern languages. Whatever the outmodedness of the word, it is through such active experiences that we learn what virtue really is.

---

13. See S. Pinckaers, O.P., *Le Renouveau de la Morale* (Tournai: Casterman, 1964), especially "La vertu est tout autre chose qu'une habitude," 144–61.

Prudential Discernment and Knowledge Attained
through Connaturality

In the formation of virtue, prudence plays a major role through the discernment and decision that are its functions.[14] Thanks to the repeated experience of acting appropriately and well in a given area such as justice or temperance, we learn to relate the universal to the particular as we discern what is most fitting and profitable in the various circumstances that arise. This is how an artisan learns his trade, training himself by applying the rules, or how an artist perfects herself in her art and makes progress, profiting even by her mistakes. In this work where we encounter reality, both interior and external, we develop a kind of knowledge that is proper to virtue, a knowledge attained through connaturality: a rapid, sure, penetrating, and intuitive ability to judge. We see things at a glance, as skilled and experienced workers do. This kind of knowledge is accompanied by inspiration, which favors invention and creativity.

Thus it is by the repeated experience of good actions that we acquire the art of applying rules and laws in the moral order. Experience is all the more necessary here since prudence is distinguished from the other intellectual virtues in that it not only gives us the ability to act, but also causes us to act effectively. This is its essential activity: the decision to act, which leads to action and gives experience. All the virtues are engendered in this ambiance and develop under the aegis of prudence.

I shall illustrate this teaching with a few texts from St. Thomas. He did not hesitate to adopt Aristotle's affirmation that "the virtuous man himself sets the measure and standard for human acts."[15] He explains this by the connaturality and inclination to the good that the moral virtues develop in us, prudence for example, in combination with the other moral virtues, particularly chastity, according to the classic example. This would be most especially the case with charity, which conforms us to divine realities and renders us capable of judging them in the light of the gift of wisdom.[16] Here are two passages dealing with this subject:

14. We also need to rediscover prudence. It is not simply the virtue of being cautious. True prudence is enterprising. It is exercised in active discernment and practical decision. It joins practical judgment to the determination that leads to action (the "precept" or "command" of St. Thomas). Only he is prudent who acts effectively, at the right time and in the best way.

15. *ST* I 1.6 ad 3.   16. *ST* II-II 45.2.

Since having a formed judgment characterizes the wise person, so there are two kinds of wisdom according to the two ways of passing judgment. This may be arrived at from a natural bent that way, as when a person who possesses the habit of a virtue rightly commits himself to what should be done in consonance with it, because he is already in sympathy with it; hence Aristotle remarks that the virtuous man himself sets the measure and standard for human acts (*Ethics,* Bk. X). Alternatively, the judgment may be arrived at through a cognitive process, as when a person soundly instructed in moral science can appreciate the activity of virtues he does not himself possess.[17]

As by the habits of natural understanding and science, a man is rightly disposed with regard to general truths, so, in order that he be rightly disposed with regard to the particular principles of action, namely, their ends, he needs to be perfected by certain habits, whereby it becomes, as it were, connatural to him to judge rightly about an end. The virtuous man judges rightly of the end of virtue, because, as Aristotle says in *Ethics* III, "as a man is, so does the end seem to him."[18]

Let us simply note that these maxims of Aristotle, "The virtuous man himself sets the measure and standard for human acts" and "As a man is, so does the end seem to him," would lead to pure subjectivism if we applied them to a morality of obligation, in which morality is imposed from without, by law, upon an indifferent will. The maxims presuppose the interior rule of virtue, itself rooted in a person's natural inclination to the true and good. In a moral system based on the virtues, law will intervene in relation to this interior morality, acting as a tutor.

The Need for Right Experience

Thanks to the experience acquired at the level of intelligence and action, knowledge of morality, itself universal like the laws or norms it studies, can reach its full development through the virtue of prudence, which is personal, and can be transformed into an active, experiential knowledge. Through virtue a kind of reciprocity is established between science and prudence, thought and action, reflection and experience.

In a morality based on the virtues, the ethicist cannot remain at a distance from her object, nor can she maintain a kind of neutral attitude toward good and evil. Her personal commitment to the good and the true is needed, lest

17. *ST* I 1.6 ad 3.
18. *ST* I-II 58.5.

she be lacking in the experience indispensable for the perception of profound ethical realities. This is why Aristotle insisted on the need for experience before one could study morality, and therefore thought it ill-suited to the young. We could also maintain that an experience of the life of faith is indispensable for a proper treatment of moral theology. Faith constitutes a richer source of knowledge than any book. Actually, it is at the heart of such experience that practical wisdom is formed in us. The experience of faith is like a source of light that clarifies and directs the virtues in the concrete, ordering them to their end.

The Gap between Science and Experience in Moral Systems Based on Actions and Norms

In a moral system based on actions and norms, the situation is not the same. The universal, which is operative on the side of law, is in a permanent state of tension with the singularity of actions that operate in freedom. In the framework of this concept of morality, the problem of moving from the universal to the particular can only persist and in fact remain insoluble, since the tension between law and freedom is irreducible. Experience cannot play its unifying role here. Actually it is viewed as a kind of subjective data that cannot be universalized as the norms require. It is also viewed as indifferent in itself, like the acts it leads to, and can acquire moral significance only through the intervention of law. We are not dealing here with an experience of right action in accord with virtue, but with the experience of an action that is blurred as to its moral quality, or is pre-moral, so to speak.

In such a system, knowledge and experience can remain completely separated. The knowledge one acquires through study is one thing; moral experience, a personal matter, is something else again. It is not necessary to be an honest man in order to be a competent ethicist, any more than one needs to have faith and live by it in order to study moral theology. It even seems that the rational exigencies of knowledge demand that the ethicist distinguish clearly between her study and her personal belief or devotion. She may even consider this separation a necessary form of asceticism that will guarantee the objectivity and universality of her research. This way of seeing things has certainly played an important role in recent debates over the existence of a Christian morality. One cannot understand the latter without a certain experience of faith joined to moral reflection.

Another effect of this separation will be the impoverishment of morality. Obliged to disregard experience, this science is deprived of knowledge attained through connaturality. It becomes dry and abstract in thought and language, even when it discourses on the importance of the concrete and of experience in morality.

Conclusion: The Need for Varied Terminology in Virtue-Based Morality

We shall conclude these reflections by touching on a difficulty encountered in a morality based on the virtues: the problem of terminology. A virtue-oriented morality requires a richer and more varied vocabulary than does one based on acts and norms, precisely because of its link with experience.

In order to reach a scientific level, every moral system tends to create for itself a universal language which cannot help including a certain amount of technical and abstract terminology. We can take St. Thomas's work as an example. It offers us a model of theological language that has reached a high degree of perfection, now become classical. But if it is true that experience is essential to virtue, we cannot really understand the moral teaching of St. Thomas without relating it to experience. In the light provided by personal experience this teaching, which at first appears abstract and impersonal, comes to life and reveals its power, precision, and capacity for disposing and directing concrete action.

If it is to be fruitful, the reading of St. Thomas's works on moral theology therefore calls for contact with experience. Yet even then, in my opinion, it cannot be totally fruitful unless complemented by the reading of authors who use a language more directly associated with experience, such as the great spiritual writers. Among Thomas's own sources, I would mention St. Augustine, St. Gregory the Great, Dionysius the Areopagite, Cassian, and St. John Chrysostom, without overlooking their common and higher source, the Word of God in the sapiential books of the Old Testament and in the moral catechesis of the New Testament, particularly the Lord's Sermon on the Mount. Obviously we should add to this list modern authors who help make the Gospel teaching clear to our age.

A virtue-based morality calls for various types of terminology. Narration and examples are also necessary, as well as a broad, well-ordered synthesis. St.

Augustine, for example, is more expressive and personal but less precise than St. Thomas, who excels in definitions and analyses but is less rich in images and examples. So it seems to me that no single author can utilize all genres with equal expertise. Does this not show that we can only attain to an understanding of moral and spiritual reality through collaboration and communion?

It will even be true to say that a virtue-based morality, however precise and perfect, will always remain incomplete. Its real function surely is to open our minds and hearts to the mystery of the human person and God, so that our actions may participate in the "unsearchable riches of Christ" in his mystery (Eph 3:8). No philosophy, no theology can fill such a role. Only the Holy Spirit possesses the power of the Word who reveals the truth to us interiorly and gives the grace that transforms our hearts and actions.

15 ❧ Capreolus's Defense of Aquinas

A Medieval Debate about the Virtues
and Gifts   (1997)

In his writing on the virtues, John Capreolus (1380–1444) speaks directly to our time, from a distance of more than five hundred years. Capreolus undertook to defend St. Thomas's moral theology, which is based on the doctrine of the virtues and gifts, against a trend which he called "new" and which, beginning with the consideration of particular acts, called into question and strongly reduced the role of the virtues. Today we observe a renewal and strengthening of virtue-based morality. For example, we find modest but real evidence of such morality in the *Catechism of the Catholic Church* and in the encyclical *Veritatis splendor,* although it coexists with the morality of casuistry and of commandments that has prevailed since the end of the Middle Ages, that is, the time of John Capreolus. The continuity of the moral problematic of Capreolus down to our own times is real. This is not surprising, for the movement of ideas at the level of thought-categories is as slow as the shifting of geological substrata, which can take centuries. Capreolus can help our reflection and can throw light on the moral problems we face today, revealing the deep foundations on which they rest.

Capreolus can also teach us how to think in a straightforward manner and reason in a firm and disciplined way. He belongs to the Scholastic tradition formed in the universities during the thirteenth century. In him we still find

Originally published as "La defense par Capreolus de la doctrine de S. Thomas sur les vertus," in *Jean Capreolus et son temps* (Paris: Cerf, 1997). Also published in Jean Capreolus, *On the Virtues,* translated with an introduction and notes by Kevin White and Romanus Cessario, O.P. (Washington, D.C.: The Catholic University of America Press, 2001). Edited for publication in *The Pinckaers Reader* by John Berkman.

this tradition in its vigor, before it was discredited by a proliferation of argumentation and logical excesses. Today's students would certainly profit from reading him and would learn how to listen attentively to opposing opinions, assess arguments accurately, and make nuanced and precise responses. Capreolus is a master at these intellectual maneuvers. He knows how to dialogue, and at the same time to sustain firmly the truth he is defending. In this work of theological combat he is never overcome by the ardors of the joust. Careful as he is to expound objections and responses thoroughly, he never becomes prolix. His thinking remains concise and sticks to the essentials.

Hence Capreolus knows how to reason. He does so with strength and precision. Yet he is not a "creative" theologian. He is a commentator on St. Thomas, or rather a defender, as the title of his work indicates: *Arguments in Defense of the Theology of Saint Thomas Aquinas.* He is not commenting on Aquinas as a teacher would for students in a class. His object is to defend the doctrine of St. Thomas against the attacks of adversaries: Duns Scotus, Peter Aureolus, Durandus of Saint-Pourçain, and others, whose names he does not always mention. In order to answer them, he has St. Thomas speak for himself, in texts so well chosen that one would think St. Thomas had prepared them in advance in order to reply to objections formulated after his time.

Capreolus's *Defense* follows the *Book of Sentences* of Peter Lombard, which was still the basic text for teaching in the universities of Capreolus's day. He regularly divides his exposition into three parts, called articles. The first article gives the "conclusions," that is to say the principal points of St. Thomas's teaching on the subject under discussion, which a later period will refer to as "theses." The second article proposes the objections of adversaries to these various "conclusions," with their more or less numerous arguments. The third article contains responses, point by point, to these objections and arguments. The responses are composed largely of texts of St. Thomas taken from his *Summa theologiae,* his *Disputed Questions,* and the *Commentary on the Sentences.* Thus Capreolus ensures the defense of Aquinas by having him speak for himself in the manner that best fits the objections of his adversaries. Capreolus adds very little of his own devising, and intervenes only when he feels the need to connect quotations or to harmonize texts that seem contradictory. Thus he effaces himself in the presence of St. Thomas, but his work shows a penetrating understanding of theology, sure and faithful. He is a good representative of the Thomist school at war.

The Teaching on the Virtues

Peter Lombard treats the subject of virtue in Distinctions 23–36 of Book III of his *Book of Sentences*. Thomas Aquinas first elaborates a treatise on the virtues in his *Commentary on the Sentences*. This shows that from his earliest writings, St. Thomas's moral theology was a morality based on virtues and not commandments, as some have maintained.[1] Capreolus follows the plan of St. Thomas, while limiting his exposition and discussion to the chief controversial theses.

Let me comment briefly on the significance of the following questions addressed by Capreolus:

1. Whether "habitual virtues"[2] are necessary to man (Distinction 23);

2. Whether virtuous *habitus* are acquired by human acts, and whether they exist in the sensible appetite, concupiscible and irascible, as their subject (Distinction 33);

3. Whether the gifts of the Holy Spirit are *habitus* distinct from the virtues (Distinctions 34–35);

4. Whether the cardinal virtues are interconnected in such a way that he who possesses one possesses all (Distinction 36).[3]

The following discussion is accordingly limited to four topics: the necessity of virtuous *habitus,* either acquired by repeated actions or infused; their location in the sensible appetite; the distinction between the virtues and the gifts; and the interconnection between the virtues.

The Necessity of Virtuous *Habitus*

At first glance we would seem to be dealing with hoary scholastic discussions. However, if we know a bit about the problematics involved, we see on closer inspection that Capreolus is witness to a vastly important episode in the history of Western moral theology: the cleavage, initiated at the beginning of the fourteenth century and widening thereafter, between a morality based on virtue, which was that of the Fathers and which received from St. Thomas its

---

1. See Giuseppe Abbà, *Lex et virtus* (Rome: Las, 1983).

2. *Virtutes habituales* is an expression not found in the writings of St. Thomas.

3. N.B.: Capreolus includes the remaining distinctions of Book III (i.e., distinctions 37–40, which concern the Ten Commandments) under this question.

classic form, and a morality based on individual acts, which was to take over in the modern era, particularly in the form of casuistry. On one hand, a morality concerned with interior qualities and awareness of the perdurance and continuity of actions in an overall personal development; on the other hand, a morality concerned with individual actions in their particularity. The latter stems from a freedom that is always variable and is confronted with a law which limits it from without by obligations and prohibitions.

The whole debate centers on the question of *habitus*. What are *habitus*, if not precisely those acquired capacities, those dispositions to action which ensure the quality and continuity of our actions and enable us to act better and better? *Habitus* are like forces that link actions together, forming and coordinating them from within so as to improve them.

The rejection of the doctrine of *habitus* was tragic, for it led to the loss of the word itself, so much so that we no longer use it in our modern languages to express the human experience signified by *habitus*. What shall we call the skill acquired by an artisan or an artist, which makes them masters of their art? The ordinary term "habit" is inadequate and misleading, because it designates a psychic mechanism that tends to diminish the human engagement that such work demands. It cannot signify an advance in perfection or in the power to create a work. Can we explain the masterly composition or performance of a musician by saying that he has a habit of playing the piano or the violin? But this is precisely what a *habitus* is, the capacity of acting to perfection, of creating a new and excellent work.

Virtuous *habitus* are thus defined as powers of acquiring and exercising our human "works" in accord with truth and goodness, producing excellence in action and progress in living. The problem is a vast one therefore: to maintain the necessity of *habitus* means to establish morality on the foundation of good *habitus* and to organize it around the theological and cardinal virtues, perfected by the gifts. The *habitus* thus gains priority over action as the interior principle of the latter's production and quality, and as the prolongation of the natural inclination to the good. The teaching on *habitus* is a necessary element in a morality which tends to ensure excellence of action ordered to an ultimate end, in which human perfection and beatitude are completed.

To refuse the necessity of *habitus* and to reduce them to simple habits, more or less useful in performing acts, leads to another conception and organization of morality resting on the primacy accorded to individual actions.

These are seen as the emanations of a freedom endowed with the power to choose at each instant between contraries, regardless of all inclination or pre-determination, natural or acquired. This is called freedom of indifference. On the other hand, a morality based on *habitus* and virtues presupposes a freedom which is naturally ordered to quality and excellence—freedom for the good.

Let us note in passing that with this problem we approach the basic question dealt with in the encyclical *Veritatis splendor* in its critique of freedom considered as an absolute, and its stance in favor of freedom for the good and for truth.[4] It is necessary to mention these matters so as to show what is at stake in Capreolus's debate. How does he proceed? He recalls what is essential in St. Thomas's teaching.[5] A *habitus* is necessary when three conditions are present:

1. when something which requires a disposition is ordered to something other than itself in a relationship of potency to act, as happens with our faculties;

2. when it may be determined in more than one way;

3. when several elements concur in an action and may be combined in several ways, good or evil.

These conditions are fulfilled especially in our spiritual faculties, intellect and will, whose sphere of action is the broadest, opening out onto the universality of the true and the good. Grafted on the potentiality of these faculties, the *habitus* is necessary to them as a stable disposition, a determination in view of the perfection of their action.

Capreolus limits himself strictly to St. Thomas's texts, which he selects judiciously. He does not prolong the consideration by showing the larger systematization involved.

The Objections of Durandus of Saint-Pourçain

Let us now look at the arguments advanced by the adversaries of the teaching on *habitus*. We shall try to discern the differences in viewpoint which reveal another way of considering action.

4. [Editor's note: See, e.g., *VS*, no. 31–34, 72.]
5. He refers to *ST* I-II 49 and 55; *In Sent.* III.23.1.1.

The chief adversary in this matter is Durandus of Saint-Pourçain. A Dominican, and a dissident in the area of theology, he was called in his day Doctor *modernus* and Doctor *resolutissimus,* because of his cleverness in resolving theological problems. Durandus belonged to the second generation following St. Thomas. Born between 1275 and 1280, he was a contemporary of the English Franciscan William of Ockham and was with him at Avignon in the papal court of John XXII. He was to be a member of the commission which would censure fifty-one propositions taken from the works of Ockham, whom he knew well. His commentary on the *Sentences* ran into several editions, the last of which was dated between 1317 and 1327.

We shall accept Durandus's teaching as Capreolus presents it to us. We will not go into all the details of the debate, but will simply try to bring out some characteristic features of this rather subtle and technical confrontation.

Durandus attacks the doctrine of the necessity of *habitus* on three points: the determination to good and evil by *habitus;* the facility of action provided by *habitus;* and the greater intensity of action caused by *habitus.*

Regarding the first point, which is the most important, Durandus introduces a preliminary distinction between the act in its natural being *(quantum ad esse naturae)* and the act in its moral being *(quantum ad esse morale).* He begins with the universal concept that we can perform an action, independently of all determination as to its kind, this or that, and its moral quality, good or evil, and therefore in this sense the act is an indifferent one. If I understand it rightly, he is considering the act as an expenditure of energy. This universal concept does not really differ from an individual action, which is, in itself, determined, since the distinction is made only at the conceptual level. The real determination of the individual act is inherent to it and does not come to it by means of any other agent.

From the point of view of the *esse naturae* we have to say, on the one hand, that the *habitus,* when it exists in a faculty, determines it to some qualification which excludes the contrary qualification; but that, on the other hand, if we consider the determination of the faculty to its action as caused by the *habitus,* we have to say that the good or evil *habitus* does not determine the natural being of the act, for the latter is a general effect calling for a cause common to all acts, whether they precede or follow the *habitus.*

We also have to say that no *habitus* determines or inclines any faculty whatsoever to produce an act in its individuality according to its natural being, for this is a case of an effect common to all actions, whatever they may be.

As to its moral character, the act receives it not from the sole singularity of its real existence, but from its conformity or lack of conformity to right reason alone. From this point of view, as to the determination to good or evil, we have to say that the *habitus* does not cause such conformity or nonconformity by itself, but accidentally, through the mediation of the foundation, the natural being, of the act. In effect, acts which precede the *habitus* and form it are already determined to good or evil, which determination cannot therefore be produced by the *habitus*.

Let us pause for a moment. Durandus clearly places in the foreground of his study, no longer the *habitus* in its dynamism, but the act taken in its singularity, able, as such, to precede or follow the *habitus,* and included under the general concept "undifferentiated act" that we can determine for ourselves. The point is no longer to show the role of the *habitus* in the formation of acts, but to discover whether there is still a need for it in the determination of individual acts.

The preliminary distinction between the *esse naturae* and the *esse moris* is characteristic. It can doubtless be related to the distinction between the natural goodness of acts, caused by God, and moral goodness, a distinction that was common enough among Lombard's commentators to account for human sin in the tradition of the Augustinian problematic of evil. We find it in St. Albert and St. Bonaventure. But St. Thomas shifted the perspective and gave priority to the *esse moris* in the voluntary act, following upon its ordering to the end.[6] In Durandus the distinction becomes conceptual and is more clear-cut.

This consideration of the act as starting with its physical being, which then becomes moral by its relation to reason and law, is encountered once more in casuistry and, in our own day, in a more pronounced manner, in consequentialism, which bases the evaluation of acts on their consequences at the pre-moral, physical, or ontic level, as distinguished from the moral level, which is constituted by the intervention of the will following the rational judgment.

When the question is put this way, from the point of view of acts each sep-

6. For further discussion, see S. Pinckaers, "Le role de la fin dans l'action morale," in *Le Renouveau de la Morale,* 2nd ed. (Paris: Tequi, 1979), 114–24.

arate in their singularity, *habitus* can only play a secondary and limited role, for *habitus* implies a continuity between acts owing to an interior finality we can call "long-range," because it links acts in an ordered whole in view of a distant or ultimate end, God as the end of life, in contrast to a "short-term" finality that subsists in individual acts in relation to the immediate intention of the subject, such as, for example, the act of stealing by someone who wishes to buy drugs. *Habitus,* virtues, finality, everything that assures continuity between acts, are relegated to the background in this view of the human act; only traces of them remain, the minimum.

This kind of analysis is diametrically opposed to that of St. Thomas, who gives priority to the moral dimension of the human act, determined in the first place by its end, the direct object of the will, and the principle of its dynamism through the succession of acts.[7]

Capreolus's Answer

How does Capreolus answer Durandus? If we compare his questions to an article of St. Thomas, we perceive that for him the objections/responses are primary, while the "body" of the article is practically limited to selected texts from St. Thomas, and does not provide the original overview of the totality of all the data—that masterly determination which gives to the responses of Aquinas their forcefulness. We are dealing rather with a "defense," which has the drawback of accepting to some degree the position of the problems posed by the adversary, such as, here, the distinction between the *esse naturae* and the *esse moris,* which St. Thomas would surely have critiqued.

Nonetheless Capreolus's responses are pertinent. He observes rightly that, at the level of their nature as of their morality, acts are not determined formally by themselves but by their principle, the acting subject, and by their term distinct from the subject, such as the object, circumstances, and end, particularly at the level of the interior act. Also, according to him, the *habitus* determines the faculty to produce its act or to receive it in *esse naturae* as well as in *esse moris.*

Even so, we perceive a weakness in Capreolus's argument. Though he

---

7. For further discussion, see S. Pinckaers, *The Sources of Christian Ethics,* trans. Sr. Mary Thomas Noble, O.P. (Washington, D.C.: The Catholic University of America Press, 1995), part one.

firmly establishes the necessity of *habitus* to determine faculties to their acts, he does not seem to see that *habitus* are rooted in the natural inclinations to goodness and truth which are components of our spiritual faculties and which assure their development. He writes in conclusion:

... a habitless power [*potentia non habituata,* a term not found in St. Thomas and which seems to indicate a tendency to habitude] is not more inclined to an act that is morally good than to one that is morally evil; nor is it inclined to acting pleasurably or easily or readily; rather it remains in an indistinct potentiality to this and that object, and similarly to a good and an evil act, and similarly again to a certain way of operating and its opposite—or rather, it is of itself indisposed to one of the two, but through habit is inclined towards one object and away from its opposite (and the same is true of the act and the manner of operating). This is clear in the case of the habit of temperance, which inclines the concupiscible power to certain objects and to certain acts and modes of operating. (D.23, a.3).

It seems therefore that for Capreolus the entire determination of acts comes from *habitus,* which increases their necessity in a morality based on virtues, but takes away their natural root. On this point one might wonder whether Capreolus is influenced by the theory of freedom of indifference that holds for the radical indetermination of the will in its action, notably in regard to natural inclinations, onto which, in St. Thomas's account, the *habitus* are grafted.

Other Objections: Durandus and Peter Aureolus

The other arguments are similar to those we have just considered. Durandus again attacks *habitus* from the angle of the facility attributed to them. According to him, this facility comes not from the *habitus* but from the acting subject. It can perfectly well happen, therefore, that an act preceding a *habitus* should be exactly like an act following it and have the same intensity. It should be added that for him, if the *habitus* by itself rendered the act easier, it would diminish its merit and would thus be more harmful than helpful to the act. Here we see the idea that virtue is connected with difficulty and valued in accordance with it, like merit.

With the help of St. Thomas's texts Capreolus responds that the act which precedes a *habitus* is never quite like one which follows it and is elicited by it; the latter is normally more perfect. As to the question of ease, Capreolus shows that merit depends more on the perfection of the act, assured by the *habitus,* than on the difficulty entailed, which could result from the weakness of the subject. He sums up his reply thus: the *habitus* does not render the act either easy or difficult in itself, but lets us perform it either easily and promptly, or with difficulty.

Finally, Durandus tries to show that the *habitus* does not contribute to the intensity of the act. For example, the act of knowing is no more intense after than before the acquisition of an intellectual *habitus;* the *habitus* only renders the subject's adherence to the known truth firmer.

Furthermore, if the *habitus* were a force capable of increasing the intensity of the act, it should eventually be able to produce the act alone, which is not the case, since the faculty's contribution is always required.

Capreolus rules out the separation made by Durandus between the contribution of the faculty and that of the *habitus* to the intensity of the act, as if it were a case of two separable forces. Faculty and *habitus* are coordinated as that which acts *(quod agit)* and that by means of which it acts *(quo agit).* He opportunely recalls the difference between a purely intellectual *habitus,* which Durandus cites in his example, and moral *habitus;* these last not only confer the power to act easily *(facultas bene operandi),* but also determine effective action *(ad usum).* This is the special case of prudence, which is not limited to judging what ought to be done but determines that it shall be done through *praeceptum* or command. Finally, contrary to Durandus's assertion, the faculty endowed with a *habitus* can act more intensely than before, that is, in the order of knowledge, for the intellectual *habitus* throws a greater intensity of light, coming from the *habitus* of first principles, on the acting intellect.

We should note that in his objections Durandus tends to remove *habitus* from the realm of knowledge in order to introduce them into the appetitive order. Here they would no longer be able to contribute directly to the formation of a moral judgment, to the development of moral knowledge or of prudence, or to the formation of conscience. We are heading for moral voluntarism.

Let us set aside this lengthy discussion with Durandus and listen briefly to the objections of the Franciscan Peter Aureolus, traditionally called Doctor *facundus,* and of the others whose names are not cited. Peter was born at Gourdon in le Quercy in 1280 and died at Avignon in 1322. He was thus a contemporary of Durandus and Ockham.

Peter's objections as set forth by Capreolus tend to reduce the importance of *habitus* by affirming that virtue is not an absolute form but an accidental being, a pure relation of fittingness or non-fittingness, which can eventually change as a person's state changes. Thus what is a virtue in one man can be a vice in another; for example, taciturnity is a virtue in the young, but in the old a vice.

To illustrate the subtlety of the argumentation, I quote from among ten responses of Capreolus to Peter Aureolus and unnamed adversaries, in a veritable battle of logic over the definition of a snub nose, the conclusion of which is that *simitas* ("snubness") occurs principally and directly in the concavity, but as a terminus and obliquely in the nose (ad 8) (!).

Capreolus's answer can be summed up as follows: in the thought of St. Thomas, virtue is not a pure relation, but it includes a certain relationship in a secondary and oblique order, notably to the subject, the nature, and the operation which is its end.

We get the impression that here Capreolus accepts too easily the problematic of his adversaries and concedes too much. As they see it, virtue must have a nature of its own in order to be considered. Neither do they see its dynamic nature to be necessary for the realization of a finality which carries man toward divine beatitude. And, like virtue, morality itself becomes a simple relation of congruence, the fitness of acts with regard to reason and law. The powerful system worked out by St. Thomas falls to the ground in the view of his adversaries, because in their account the cement linking the virtues has disintegrated.

The Moral Virtues in the Sense Appetites

A second thesis defended by Capreolus has to do with the positing of virtues in the sense appetites. St. Thomas, contrary to the Franciscan doctors, situated certain moral virtues, such as temperance and courage, in the concupiscible and irascible appetites, and not only in the will.

The question is still of interest today. It is a matter of determining the part sensibility plays in the moral life. Does the latter unfold entirely at the level of will and reason, as was held by Descartes and Kant as well as by the casuists—in which case the movements of the sense appetites will be regarded with suspicion and reduced to a psychic mechanism—or can sensibility indeed be actively associated with the moral life, that is, at the theological level, as St. Thomas thought? St. Thomas actually took the trouble to compose a vast treatise on the passions as a preparation for the study of the virtues: a study of desire, for example, in view of hope, and a study of love in view of charity. Once more we note that we are dealing with two different moral systems and even two anthropologies, the one separating the component parts of man, the other tending to harmonize them.

To be brief, let me simply mention the opposing positions. Duns Scotus is foremost here. For him, the virtues are located in our higher faculties, particularly in the will, which, being indeterminate in regard to contraries, needs an inclination to determine it to act rightly. This is virtue. Scotus invokes the opinion of Aristotle for this proposition, then St. Augustine, who defines the moral virtues as forms of charity, which is a virtue of the will. Peter of Aureolus, for his part, adopts a compromise and situates the virtues equally in the sensible and rational appetites.

The position of St. Thomas is very different. The will, which tends naturally toward the good, needs virtue only in view of a good that surpasses man, whether as an individual (the virtue of justice) or in his nature (the virtue of charity). According to Capreolus, Aristotle never denied the existence of virtue in the sensible appetite, and the affirmation of St. Augustine that every virtue is a form of love does not oblige us to situate the virtues exclusively in the will.

The discussion moves on to the acquisition of virtues by means of the repetition of acts, which Durandus criticizes, maintaining that this repetition is not an active but a passive principle of the formation of acts, like a disposition to receive similar acts, as soft wax is disposed to receive different forms.

Then comes the attack on St. Thomas's teaching on the infused moral virtues, led by Durandus: the theological virtues and the grace given by baptism suffice for salvation; the infused moral virtues are in no way necessary or useful. The consideration of the effects of baptism at the moral level, the comparison between the state of a sinner before and after conversion, or of a pagan trained in virtue, do not indicate the influence of the infused virtues, which would be evidenced by more perfect conduct.

Behind St. Thomas's teaching on the infused moral virtues there is at stake the practical influence of the grace of the Holy Spirit upon the action of the Christian, which raises him to a higher level according to spiritual experience. This teaching goes hand in hand with that on the gifts and the Gospel Beatitudes.

Capreolus takes up a final point regarding the permanence of the moral virtues after this life: they do not perdure in regard to their material object, which is in the sensible order, but they do in regard to their formal object, the *ordo rationis,* the submission of acts and passions to reason.

The Distinction between the Virtues and the Gifts of the Holy Spirit

The discussion of the virtues extends to the gifts of the Holy Spirit: Are they distinct from the virtues, and are they necessary, as St. Thomas holds?

Aquinas's teaching on the virtues and gifts finds its place in the spiritual tradition represented by St. Gregory the Great, which thirteenth-century theologians tried to develop. Elaborated in an original reflection on Isaiah 11, which furnishes the list of the gifts in the Augustinian tradition, this doctrine seems to be truly the fruit of St. Thomas's personal experience. The gifts are properly speaking inspirations: "We are obviously given to understand that these seven which are enumerated [in the text of Isaiah] are in us by divine inspiration."[8] Moral theology based on the virtues should thus culminate in the doctrine of the gifts of the Holy Spirit, so as to take Christian experience into account and to clarify the mode of collaboration between the virtues and the movements of the Spirit. Virtue represents the active aspect of the spiritual life, while the gifts, seen as dispositions to receive spiritual impulses with docility, represent the passive aspect. In the *Summa theologiae,* St. Thomas is careful to relate each principal virtue with the corresponding gift. St. Thomas's moral theology is therefore profoundly spiritual.

We note that this richness of moral teaching was soon to be lost after Capreolus. Following the line of nominalism, post-Tridentine moralists were to separate morality, focused on obligations, from asceticism and mysticism. They would place the virtues, joined with personal effort, under asceticism, and the gifts of the Holy Spirit would fall under a mysticism reserved for those enjoying extraordinary graces.

But we have not yet arrived at this point. The principal adversary here is Duns Scotus, who takes issue with the distinction of the gifts in the name of the adequacy of the virtues. His argument is to become classic. We come

8. *ST* I-II 68.1.

across it, for example, in Dom Lottin, that excellent historian of the thirteenth century, when he expresses his personal opinion.

In the thought of Duns Scotus, there is no need to consider the gifts, any more than the beatitudes or the fruits of the Holy Spirit, as *habitus* distinct from the virtues. It is reasonable to retain only the necessary *habitus,* taught by the Church. These are, for us wayfarers, the theological virtues relating to God, and prudence and the other moral virtues relating to creatures. These suffice, if brought to perfection. It is not necessary to add other *habitus.*

Scotus also rejects the distinction between the human mode of action of the virtues and the supra-human mode of the gifts. According to Scotus, the virtues—especially charity—dispose humans to act with the greatest perfection as well as with the least.

Here we see a separation from the spiritual sap of moral theology, or at least a different orientation. According to St. Thomas, the sap rises through the virtues as in a tree in springtime. The more branches, the more clearly the power of life is manifested. Hence the spreading of the tree of virtues, to which are added the gifts, beatitudes, and fruits of the Spirit. For Scotus everything leads to charity, since virtue is centered in the will. In his eyes, the necessity of joining *habitus* to the virtues has yet to be proved. At this point we are no longer dealing with a moral theology organized around virtue. The Franciscan tradition is already oriented toward a morality based on commandments, which is what the morality of nominalism will be.

Capreolus replies by using the argumentation of St. Thomas to set up the distinction between virtues and gifts, and by responding in detail to the objections formulated by Duns Scotus. He likewise answers the objections of Durandus of Saint-Pourçain against the permanence of the gifts in patria: the gifts will not perdure in regard to their material objects, it is true, but they will in regard to their formal object, which is conformity to the rule of the Holy Spirit.

The Interconnection of the Virtues

The discussion with Duns Scotus subsequently takes up St. Thomas's teaching on the interconnection of the virtues through the work of prudence and charity. The establishment of the precise way in which the virtues form an organism of action is the centerpiece of virtue-based morality. In his exposition of moral theology, in which analysis dominates, St. Thomas studied the multiplicity of virtues in detail; it is essential for him to show how they yet constitute a dynamic unity, an organism comparable to the human body with its various members acting together. This unity is assured by prudence at the level of the moral virtues and by charity for the totality of the virtues. The sense of unity in the life of virtue is predominant in St. Augustine, for example, for whom the four principal virtues became forms of charity. It was equally the case with the Stoics, who presented virtue as basically one.

The discussion will bear essentially on prudence. For St. Thomas, prudence cannot exist without the moral virtues, nor the moral virtues without prudence. This means that in the concrete all the virtues coexist and act together. This argument presupposes a close, natural collaboration between our spiritual faculties, intellect and will, to form moral action, especially in choosing, which is the proper act of freedom. The entire Thomistic analysis of freedom and choice rests on this connection between the sense of truth and the aspiration to the good.[9]

In Scotus's objections we can see that this link between the spiritual faculties and the virtues is in the process of being dissolved. Duns Scotus wants to show that prudence can perfectly well exist without the moral virtues: a right prudential judgment could perfectly well be accompanied by a voluntary, bad choice. It is also possible to acquire perfection in the realm of one virtue, while remaining imperfect in regard to others, he holds.

Capreolus rightly replies that a capital point in this matter is to understand that prudence is not limited to judging and counseling well, but finds its completion in the "command" or imperium which forms the choice; we could call this the decision to act joined to the impetus to act. We should note that, in the analysis of the prudential act, the command is not external to but interior to the acting subject, and proceeds from his "willing reason." In order to form this command to act, and to act in this particular way, prudence has need of the appetite's rectitude, which is produced by temperance, courage, and justice.

Capreolus also observes that the *habitus* of prudence is not acquired by a single act, but requires much experience and also hindsight, which contribute to its connection with the moral virtues. A morality of individual acts could not account for all that prudence presupposes. He might have added that, in a

9. See Pinckaers, *Sources of Christian Ethics,* part three.

morality based on virtues, prudence presupposes not only a succession of acts which form a *habitus* but also deep-seated intentions and a long-range view, which order action to its ultimate end and procure for prudence higher criteria of judgment. This is the way that prudence is linked to charity.

Conclusion

I have tried to disentangle the principal threads of Capreolus's problematic of virtue while indicating their historical connections, as they go back to St. Thomas and forward to ourselves. This introduction has not gone into all the details of Capreolus's treatment of virtue, nor does it presume to have untangled all the threads. Many points still remain to be clarified, and I trust that the contemporary reader will find the present volume a great help in this task.

The interesting thing about Capreolus's work is that it represents a stage in the vast debate on Christian morality which has gone on for several centuries in Scholastic theology. It can be summed up in the confrontation of two principal orientations. On the one hand, there is a morality based on the organic structure of the virtues and gifts, with the teaching on *habitus* as its capstone. St. Thomas provided the most systematic model for this morality, and so handed on the heritage of the Fathers and of ancient philosophy. On the other hand, very soon after the Angelic Doctor died, the system of virtues was attacked: by a reduction to charity and the moral virtues; by a separation among these virtues; and by a change of perspective which favored the consideration of the individual act to the detriment of those elements which assure continuity in acting, namely, the *habitus* and finality. These developments opened up the road to the casuistry that was to flourish from the seventeenth century on.

Capreolus was not an innovator but a defender. In the fifteenth century—when nominalism was largely taking over in Western universities, and imposed, in the name of the divine law and reason, a morality regulated by obligations—Capreolus was a courageous and skillful defender of a stronghold: the teaching of St. Thomas on the virtues and gifts. It is somewhat surprising that he does not quote contemporary authors, and that all his adversaries come from the preceding century. Doubtless time passed more slowly in the Middle Ages, especially for speculative minds not much concerned about the historical dimension of doctrines.

What is important to remember is that Capreolus took up his defense when the earliest controversies regarding St. Thomas were formulating their major objections. He replied point by point, always solid and faithful to the Master. He could not know the later development of the teaching of moral theology in the Church, which helps us to see his value more clearly.

I shall close by mentioning an impression I have had throughout my study of Capreolus. On rereading the texts of St. Thomas which he quotes, I felt as if I were present at the flow of a powerful intellectual and spiritual torrent, all the more vigorous for having been well channeled by Capreolus. In the end, then, I had the impression of a creative energy unleashed. We should be grateful to Capreolus for having vigorously defended the doctrine of the virtues and gifts at a time when it was "out of season," and for having contributed from afar to the current renewal of virtue-based morality.

16 ∾ Conscience and Christian Tradition

(1990)

Christian teaching on moral conscience is extremely firm regarding prescriptions and moral rules; at the same time, it is flexible when dealing with the conscience's field of action, the theological organization of the moral domain. In order to treat adequately the Christian concept of moral conscience, we need to scan the history of moral theology, not simply for erudition's sake, but rather to make contact with the living sources of Christian moral teaching that continually influence the Church through the working of the Holy Spirit.

I propose, therefore, a study of what we might call the history of the Christian moral conscience, in three main stages: the New Testament; the theology of St. Thomas, heir of patristic thought; and finally the modern manuals of moral theology which have formed priests and faithful through preaching and catechesis since the Council of Trent, that Council which is so often reflected in current discussions of ethics.

I shall choose some characteristic features to describe the Christian conscience during these three periods, which may help us to discern how to rejuvenate it today through renewed contact with the sources of inspiration that make up the richness of our moral inheritance.

Previously published as "La conception chrétienne de la conscience morale," in *NV* (1990): 81–99. Translated by Sr. Mary Thomas Noble, O.P. Edited for publication in *The Pinckaers Reader* by Craig Steven Titus.

Moral Conscience according to St. Paul

A Model in the Treatment of Cases of Conscience

First of all we shall consult St. Paul. Rather than make a study of the use of the word "conscience," which you can find elsewhere,[1] I propose that we first observe St. Paul in action in the treatment of "cases of conscience" submitted to him in his first letter to the Corinthians: the cases of incest, of an appeal to pagan law courts, of fornication, of the problem of eating food offered to idols, and so on. In all these passages, we can observe a procedure that remains constant throughout the variety of thoughts put forward. Paul makes use of a twofold argument, which proceeds in two stages.

Let us take the case of fornication, which is the clearest. First the Apostle proposes arguments and criteria based on common sense and right reason, things a philosopher might suggest, which everyone can understand:

All things are lawful for me, but not all things are helpful. . . . The body is not meant for immorality. . . . Do you not know that he who joins himself to a prostitute becomes one body with her? Shun immorality. Every other sin that a man commits is outside the body; but the immoral man sins against his own body.[2]

Then immediately, in the same train of thought, Paul introduces a new dimension from the order of faith, based on our belonging to Christ through the action of the Holy Spirit:

Do you not know that your bodies are members of Christ? Shall I therefore take the members of Christ and make them members of a prostitute? . . . Do you not know that your body is a temple of the Holy Spirit within you, which you have from God? You are not your own; you were bought with a price. So glorify God in your body.[3]

This is the model St. Paul offers us for the handling of cases of conscience and for moral reflection. Reason and faith interact reciprocally in a progressive argument that throws light on the case at a new depth stemming from a relationship with Christ. The rule of conduct thus established is given a richness of content which philosophy alone could not have provided. It is indeed in the

---

1. Cf. Philippe Delhaye, *The Christian Conscience,* trans. C. U. Quinn (New York: Desclee Company, 1968).

2. 1 Cor 6:12, 14, 18.

3. 1 Cor 6:15, 19–20.

light of the wisdom of the Holy Spirit, of whom Paul has just spoken at the beginning of this letter, that he treats cases of conscience. At the same time, while firmly denouncing its inadequacies, he makes use of whatever is useful in human wisdom. In Paul's view, rational and spiritual wisdom can thus be joined to form together a single ray of light.

The Moral Teaching of Romans

The study of cases of conscience calls for moral teaching that will furnish general rules of conduct and precise directions. Let us look for moral teachings in St. Paul which will serve, for example, to form what we call an examination of conscience, or for statements that can be used for molding or directing consciences.

The texts abound. We can find them in almost all the Apostle's letters. This is hardly surprising. After the announcement of the Gospel of Jesus Christ, which awakens faith and leads to baptism—exegetes call this kerygma—Christians need to be taught how to live as disciples of Christ. This is moral catechesis.

I shall take as an example the Letter to the Romans, which is clearly divided into these two parts: first the preaching of faith in Jesus, which wins us justification and the wisdom of God; then the moral teaching which flows from this and which renders the grace of Christ active in the disciples' daily lives, under the movement of the Holy Spirit. We find this in chapters 12–15.

St. Thomas understood this very well, as we can see when he introduces this passage, at the beginning of chapter 12 in his commentary: "Here [Paul] teaches the way to use grace (received through faith and the Spirit), and this is the moral instruction." (Ad. Rom., Cap. XII) In these four chapters we have a typical exposition of apostolic moral catechesis, intended to form the conscience of Christians in the light of faith. As he has written, Paul wishes to provide his readers with "the armor of light," that they may "put on the Lord Jesus Christ" (Rom 13:12–14). This is his idea of catechesis.[4]

---

4. Here I should like to pause for a moment to answer an objection that could lead us astray. In some Bibles, the title "Parenesis" has been inserted before chapter 12 of Romans. This is done to indicate that this second part of the letter is a moral or spiritual exhortation—that is the meaning of the term parenesis—rather than moral teaching properly so called. The latter is the domain of imperatives, obligations, or duties. But such a division between morality on the one hand and parenesis or spirituality on the other was unknown to St. Paul and to the Fathers. I

Consciousness of Sin and Grace

In order to be faithful to St. Paul, I should add that the division of Romans into dogmatic and moral sections, which has become the classic procedure, is not at all adequate and can be deceiving. For if we seek the content of St. Paul's moral conscience, we discover that the basis of his moral teaching is to be found in his exposition in the first part of the letter. The bottom line, so to speak, of St. Paul's moral conscience consists in his clear perception of his sin, which has been manifested to him by the blinding light of the grace of Jesus on the road to Damascus. Paul sees the root of this sin as human pride, which feeds even on the justice achieved by observing the Law, as happened with the Jews, whose zealous follower he was. The same pride vitiated the search for wisdom, in which the Greeks excelled, causing the corruption of their pretended virtue.

But this is only the negative aspect, the shadow side of Paul's experience. The center of his consciousness is filled with God's light, shining through the revelation of Christ's love, the love that forgives him and transforms his heart. This is effected by faith and the reception of the Spirit of Jesus, which will henceforth animate both his life and his preaching. This is why for Paul the Christian life will be a life *with* Christ, a life *in* Christ through love, and also a life *according to the Spirit,* who is the source of the virtues and gifts, beginning with charity. At the heart of Paul's moral conscience is the experience of liberation from sin through the grace of Christ. And in spite of the necessary struggle against what he calls the flesh and against evil spirits, the moral teaching of St. Paul retains as its predominant note in the midst of all his trials the invitation to joy and the promise of God's peace. This is why Paul's teaching is truly a hymn to joy in the name of Christ our liberator. It proceeds wholly from the Apostle's consciousness of the living presence of Christ Jesus within him as the source of the justice and wisdom of God, that is, of the entire moral life.

An understanding of this is indispensable as an introduction to my exposition of chapters 12 to 15. A precise moral teaching is given here, which can well be used as an examination of conscience.

---

even go so far as to think he would reject it, because for him morality is life in the Spirit, basically a spiritual thing. Let us therefore avoid trying to project our own ideas and divisions on the writings of St. Paul. Let us allow him to teach us what Gospel morality is. Let us allow our consciences to be formed by him without imposing our categories.

A "Liturgical" Morality

The background of this moral teaching is very beautiful: the Christian life, which consists in a "spiritual" worship—according to the wisdom of the Spirit—in which we offer *our body,* our person and our life, "as a living sacrifice, holy and acceptable to God." This transforms our idea of life and shows us "what is the will of God, what is good and acceptable and perfect."

Moral life thus becomes the prolongation and activation in our daily life of the Eucharistic liturgy where we communicate in *the Body of Christ* to which we have been united by baptism. There is a close bond, therefore, for Paul, a vital contact between liturgical prayer and the moral life. Before all theory and doctrine, the moral life is first nourished by the Body of Christ, his presence in the Eucharist. Today we can once more affirm this relationship between the liturgy and morality, since in the Mass readings, preserved through the ages, the texts of St. Paul are still offered for our meditation, texts far more helpful than any books on morality. But do we, whether theologians or the faithful, pay close enough attention to them?

In any case, for St. Paul moral conscience has a liturgical dimension. This is why prayer cannot be relegated to the margin of the moral life, to the realm of spirituality or anywhere else. Its place is at the center of the moral conscience, even as the liturgy is celebrated in the midst of the Church. Through prayer the Holy Spirit nourishes us with the grace of Christ and makes us aware of his presence. The recommendation to pray will be repeated unceasingly in the moral teaching of Paul.

An Ecclesial Conscience

Let us read on. The Apostle continues his teaching by relating the offering of our body and our life to God with our insertion in *the Body of Christ which is the Church,* of which we become the members: "So we, though many, are one body in Christ, and individually members one of another" (12:5). This ecclesial body is a living spiritual reality whose soul is charity. Charity gives each member an awareness of the fraternal bonds uniting him to the others in Christ. It inspires humble and generous devotedness in the exercise of the gifts the members have received and the functions entrusted to them: prophecy, teaching, exhortation, and the various ministries. The Church, considered in its deep self-awareness, is therefore far more than a juridical society. It forms a spiritual organism whose soul is charity, present and active in the conscience and heart of each member.

Charity and the "Body" of the Virtues

St. Paul's repeated use of the word "body" indicates that we are not dealing with a purely spiritual reality. In the Church, the Christian commits his body and soul in concrete and material actions that involve his heart and hands.

Thus charity, which forms the Church and which Paul calls "the bond of perfection," will group around itself all the virtues that enter into our concrete actions in the Church, as Paul lists them. They are like multiple facets of charity, its qualities and servants.

Paul often delights to describe charity in this way, pointing out a succession of precise and practical characteristics. His texts are made up of short phrases with frequent use of alliteration (they really ought to be read in Greek), and are easily memorized. Take for example the one which follows the passage we have just been looking at: "Let love be genuine . . . hold fast to what is good; love one another with brotherly affection . . . rejoice in hope, be patient in tribulation, be constant in prayer . . . practice hospitality" (Rom 12:9–13). We see from this that Paul's moral teaching is about the virtues, which form, so to speak, the body of charity, itself rooted in faith in Christ.

Dynamism and Breadth of Conscience

The moral teaching that forms Paul's conscience is full of animation. After having insisted that in daily life we should be considerate of others, he leaps upward to the culminating point of the Sermon on the Mount, and opens up to us infinite horizons, which might be called, in philosophical language, concrete expressions of the universal. "Bless those who persecute you, and do not curse them. Rejoice with those who rejoice, weep with those who weep. Live in harmony with one another. . . . Repay no one evil for evil, but take thought for what is noble in the sight of all. If possible, insofar as it depends upon you, live peaceably with all. . . . Do not be overcome by evil, but overcome evil with good" (Rom 12:14–21).

The dynamism of Paul's conscience unfolds under the movement of charity. Charity should inspire all the members of the Body of Christ with a warm, effectual good will toward all, most evident in times of persecution. The latter had become a common and crucial experience for the first generation of Christians: persecution by both Jews and Romans.

Paul's moral conscience is broad. On the one hand he knows how to make allowances for the humble and weak, sharing their needs, joys, and sorrows. On the other, he reaches out to everyone, transcending all divisions and even that gravest of obstacles, the hatred which engenders persecution. Through charity, Paul's conscience is both gentle in humility and all-embracing as the world itself.

Paul's moral conscience is not individualistic, as ours often is. He does indeed enjoy a profoundly personal, unique relationship with Christ, who called him, loved him, and gave himself up for him. But this very love causes him to forget all self-interest and to work day and night for the Gospel without counting the cost, bearing the burden of his concern for all the Churches, seeking the salvation of both Jews and Greeks, to whom he feels responsible because of his mission as Apostle to the Gentiles. "Woe to me," he says, "if I do not preach the Gospel!" (1 Cor 9:16).

Let us sum up the results of our reading. Paul's conscience differs from that of the philosophers; it is deepened by the perception of the sins of men, particularly "the worldly-wise." It is illumined by the revelation of Christ's loving grace. Hence its source is faith; it becomes prayer, liturgy. Paul's conscience is not static, limited by rational imperatives determining what is allowed and what forbidden. It is animated by charity's thrust toward what pleases God, toward the perfect. At the center of Paul's conscience dwells the person of Christ. This is why his moral teaching is both spiritual and realistic, and at the same time ecclesial: it is life with Christ, in Christ. It stretches forward to the knowledge of the mystery of Christ.

The Christian Conscience and the City

There is one more passage we need to mention, and this will lead us to a very concrete problem still on our agenda: the attitude of Christians toward civil authority. The civic or social dimension of Paul's conscience flows from its ecclesial dimension. It was a delicate question, for it concerned Roman authority, which the Jews supported with difficulty and which could disturb Christians since they were not a recognized religious group.

In his answer to this problem we note once again the method he applied to cases of conscience. In order to establish the rule of conduct that he prescribes, submission to the authorities in charge, Paul uses an argument based on good sense and reason, as a philosopher might do. Authority receives its power from God; it is established for the punishment of those who do evil and the reward of those who do good. Justice requires that we render to the authorities, as to everyone, what is due them, particularly taxes. We also find an expression, which interests me highly: we must obey the authorities not only to avoid their wrath, but also for the sake of our conscience *(dia ten suneidesin)*.

In reality, the context of this passage invites us to understand it as an application of what has just been said about charity. It is formative, and urges Church members to place themselves at the service of all, which implies being open to the teaching and exhortations of those who have received this mission.

Civil society also forms a kind of body willed by God, for according to the philosophers themselves, it comes about because of a natural inclination of human beings. In civic life, therefore, the service and devotion proper to charity translate into an attitude of frank submission and constructive service vis-à-vis authority, which is entrusted with the common good. This obedience receives a new dimension, for it no longer proceeds from fear but from good will toward all, rooted in charity. It is directed not only to men but to God, who has revealed himself to us in the service and obedience of Christ. This is an obedience "based on conscience," a conscience animated by the Holy Spirit. Paul establishes, in this way, the basic foundation of the Christian attitude toward civil authority, which ought to be maintained even when it is a case of "overcoming evil with good," and "blessing those who persecute us."

This well-disposed submission to those in power in no way prevents Christians from resisting authority when it would have them deny their faith. In this case, according to the same teaching of the Apostle, if civil authority opposes the God from whom it receives its power, we must "obey God rather than men." This is "conscientious" resistance for the sake of Christ. But there is no allowance for lack of submission in matters concerning the legitimate welfare of the commonwealth. An ever more active effort for the good of all, including the persecutors, is called for, so that in the midst of trial witness may be given to the superior strength of benevolence inspired by the love of Christ. Paul does not go into the problem of persecution here, however. He is teaching us about conduct toward authority in general, as it is inspired by the charity of Christ. This will serve as a criterion in difficult cases, which may arise. In fact, the attitude Paul recommends is universal, transcending Jewish nationalism in favor of Greeks, Romans, and barbarians. By this very fact it relativizes the political order, which henceforth will be transcended by the inauguration of a different kind of community, the Church of Christ, which is open to all nations and races.

Moral Conscience in St. Thomas

After having reread these passages from St. Paul, which were constantly commented upon and explained to the Christian people by the Fathers of the Church, it is now time for us to consult a classic representative of Christian theology, St. Thomas Aquinas. By reason of his office, as Master of theology, but also because of his vocation to the apostolic life, he is an interpreter and disciple of St. Paul. His commentaries on the letters of the Apostle were a direct preparation for the composition of the *Summa theologiae.* We should note too that he always interprets Scripture with the help of the Fathers, especially St. Augustine and St. John Chrysostom. He thus gives us the example of reading with the Church, in the mainstream of living tradition. In the *Summa* we rediscover the joining of the two dimensions we spoke of in Paul's treatment of cases of conscience, and they are developed theologically. (This is reproduced also in the Fathers.) A reflection in the rational order, at the level of the philosophers, is combined with a reflection in the light of faith, permeated by the teaching of Christ and the work of the Holy Spirit.

Practical Reason and Conscience

Let us open the *Summa theologiae* and see what St. Thomas has to say about the moral conscience. We are surprised to find that he speaks of it very little. He treats it directly in only two places: firstly, when he is studying the intellectual faculties in *prima pars,* question 79, at the very end in article 13, where he affirms that conscience is not a faculty, but a certain act of knowledge; secondly, in his study of the morality of human acts, where he touches upon the question of the erroneous conscience.[5] Does this mean that St. Thomas did not perceive the importance of conscience? This would be very odd.

5. *ST* II-II 19.5 and 19.6.

Doubtless the facts I have just indicated pose a difficult problem for modern ethicists, who have introduced a special treatise on conscience in fundamental moral theology, while claiming that they are followers of St. Thomas.

Aquinas himself provides the solution when he writes: The question, Is one obliged to follow an erroneous conscience? brings us to the question of whether the will is evil when it is at variance with erring reason. St. Thomas's terminology is different, therefore. He prefers to speak of practical reason rather than of conscience. So we shall find his thought on what we call the moral conscience in his teaching on practical reason. This terminology will be used in moral theology among Scholastic theologians and continued into modern philosophy, as for example in Kant, who will write a critique of practical reason rather than a critique of conscience.

St. Thomas attributes the discernment of the moral quality of human acts to practical reason perfected by the virtue of prudence. Therefore for him the treatise on prudence occupies the central position later to be given to the treatise on conscience. St. Thomas's moral teaching is a morality of the virtues, organized around charity and prudence, rather than a morality of commandments and obligations imposed upon conscience.

The Source of Practical Reason

For the moment I propose that we consider practical reason, the seat of the moral sense, from above and from below. From above first, because practical reason receives its light and strength from a lofty source. This source is formed by the joining of our two fundamental spiritual inclinations: the yearning for truth and the attraction to the good, which are at the origin of the moral sense in the heart of all persons and enable us to discern the difference between good and evil. They are, as it were, the spiritual instinct for the true and the good within us. St. Thomas calls this the *instinctus rationis*.[6]

The first expression of this moral sense resides in the *habitus* of the first principles of the practical reason, to which, following the Greek tradition, the rather odd name of *synderesis* is given. It is the original moral light in the depths of the human mind and heart.

This terminology may seem cold and abstract when applied to such profound, personal realities. This is the fate and the limitation of all technical lan-

6. *ST* I-II 68.

guage, in theology as in the other sciences. Let me translate it for you, by means of an image.

The Prologue of the *secunda pars* refers us to Genesis,[7] where we read that God made human beings in his image. St. Thomas interprets this by seeing this image in our freedom, where the light of the intellect and the movement of the will are concentrated and render us master of our actions, which resembles the mastery of God over his works. The image of God in human beings is precisely this light of truth and attraction to the good, like a warming ray within us rendering us capable of imitating God in knowing and loving him freely and personally. Thus things become personalized, and we can say, moving from the sense of sight to that of hearing, that this light and this attraction to the good are like the voice of God in the depths of the human heart, and that they form what we commonly call "the voice of conscience."

The image of God in us, at the base of our freedom, will become still more personal through the intervention of Christ, who came to restore this resemblance, effaced by sin, by conforming us to himself, the perfect Image of God, and causing us to enter into intimacy with the Father.

The action of the Holy Spirit in particular will be engrafted precisely upon this moral source in our depths, the *synderesis,* by infusing within our spirit new principles of action through the theological virtues, which will effect our conformation to Christ by making us children of the Father through grace. St. Thomas's moral teaching will thus be built upon faith, hope, and charity, to which are joined the gifts of the Holy Spirit which have been too much neglected by ethicists.

Prudence, the Virtue of the Practical Reason

Let us return to the practical reason and consider it now from below. We shall see how it works in view of action, which is another way of saying, how the moral conscience is formed and educated.

The practical reason, like all human faculties, is developed and perfected by virtue, particularly the virtue of prudence, which, in St. Thomas's system, occupies almost the same position that the modern manuals give to the treatise on conscience.

Here we need to pause for a moment before the terms virtue and pru-

7. Gn 1:17.

dence, to rediscover their original meaning, which has become very impoverished in our language.[8] Briefly, let me say that virtue signifies the quality of a person insofar as she is human and the master of her own actions. It designates our ability to act with excellence and perfection in all areas, business, the arts, science, and most especially at the moral level where we act as persons with willing, free commitment. Virtue implies an aim and thrust toward perfection, which cause us to transcend spontaneously the lowest demarcation between the allowable and the forbidden and to become engaged in an ongoing effort to grow and develop.

Prudence, for its part, is the virtue proper to practical reason. It is a far cry from the habit of taking precautions to avoid inconvenience. To be truly prudent, we need to have gained mastery over our emotions, and to possess the courage to take action effectively in confronting obstacles and trials, as well as the patience to wait for the opportune moment. The proper action of prudence is a clear, active discernment of the conditions for action and of oneself, a discernment gained by personal experience and by the kind of reflection that knows how to profit by the opinions and experience of others as well. Thus prudence collaborates with other virtues, which lend it their support but which would go astray without it. It is like the directing eye, or, to use the expression of the ancients, the charioteer of the virtues. Above all, prudence is at the service of that love of truth and good of which we were just speaking, which provides it with its light and active movement. Thus prudence is, together with the virtues that it directs, the flowering of our moral sense. It contains within it what the ancients called the *semina virtutum*, the seeds of the virtues and of all moral excellence.

From this we can understand what Christian prudence is. It is a kind of practical wisdom receiving a new, profound light from faith and a higher strength from charity, which unites it to God and deepens its understanding of the neighbor. Furthermore, it is disposed through the gifts of counsel, understanding, and wisdom to correspond to the movements of the Holy Spirit. Thus enlightened and penetrated, prudence becomes capable of fulfilling its role as director of action according to the designs of God. Its intervention is

---

8. Incidentally, it is good to note that in the United States people have progressed in rediscovering the importance of virtue, a philosophical ethic, notably in the Aristotelian tradition. Obviously, I am alluding to the works of Alasdair MacIntyre. In Europe, we have not come so far.

indispensable, because by means of prudence the theological virtues, like the others, can be embodied in concrete action. Without it, even charity could not discern and follow the right path with precision.

Such is prudence: the intelligent handmaid of the human virtues. Without its help no virtue, no gift, could bear its fruit, which is excellence. To what shall we compare it? It is like the eye to the painter, the ear to the musician. It is neither the root of the plant nor the sap nor simply a branch. Is it not rather that mysterious sense of increase that makes the tree grow and stretch forth its branches to the sun? The life of a human person is concentrated in the glance of prudence, the searchlight. Through it the whole person becomes a conscience in action, even the unconscious being drawn in to take its share in the concrete action and show forth its own particular reflection.

The Question of Beatitude

We cannot leave St. Thomas without saying a word about the primary and principal question which prudence must address. This will open up to us at a glance the wide horizon where all ultimate moral questions are written large.

The primary question the prudent man needs to address is not that of law, norms, obligations, duties, or the boundary line between the permissible and the forbidden. At the very start of prudential research is a question which lies deep in the heart of every man, that of the good and of beatitude. These two are one. This question determines the ultimate end, the goal, which orients and draws one's whole life and all one's actions to itself. This question is answered, far better than any philosophy can do, by the Gospel Beatitudes, which offer us, through the lips of the Lord himself, the conquest of the Kingdom of Heaven as the principal goal and the highest criterion of our actions. At the same time, the Beatitudes trace before our astonished gaze a path that begins with poverty and humility, is pursued through the testing of hunger for justice, the practice of mercy, purity of heart, and the peace of the children of God, to finish with the overwhelming joy of those who suffer persecution for the love of Christ. The treatise on beatitude, which opens the discussion of morality in the *Summa*, is but the theological expression of this first part of the Sermon on the Mount. It communicates to the moral teaching of St. Thomas and to its central virtue, prudence, the sap that rises from the roots of the Gospel as preached by St. Matthew, St. Paul, and their successors.

Clearly, the horizon of prudence or the Christian conscience is as broad as the Gospel of the Kingdom of Heaven, which the apostles were commissioned to preach to the whole world. This means, among other things, that while being entirely personal, Christian prudence cannot be constrained within the limits of an individual life or a beatitude focused on self. It is called to open outward and to collaborate with God's plans for the Church, to become an ecclesial prudence or conscience, whose work will consist in building up the Body of Christ in great affairs as well as small, according to each one's vocation, under the movement of charity. I should add that this kindly prudence— it is right to describe it so—should include within its scope everyone inspired by a desire for the good and true, everyone to whom the promises of the Gospel appeal in the name of Christ. Prudence is at the same time fully human and wholly Christian.

"Political" Prudence

One last point before we leave St. Thomas. He devotes part of his study of prudence to its political dimension.[9] In the tradition of Aristotle he shows how this virtue is at the service of justice and should extend as justice does to the consideration of the common good in the setting of city, family, and even the military. In these areas of the social order prudence will even play a primary role, for it is concerned with lawmaking. Law is, for St. Thomas, an *ordinatio rationis,* a work of practical reason having both positive and constraining force as needed. Prudence will also direct the obedience of subjects to the law, appealing to their reason as well as to their good will. In this way, prudence should be a light shining out over the whole social body to create bonds of understanding and solidarity among all its members.

Finally, we recall that the Holy Spirit can intervene at this level to enlighten and sustain us through the gift of counsel and the gift of piety which is connected with justice as a loving movement toward God who is our Father, but also to every man called by God to his Kingdom. Thus in the heart of the Christian there develops an awareness of God as Father, an awareness of the Church, and an awareness of humanity which becomes active and concrete through the work of prudence.

9. *ST* II-II 50.

Conscience in Post-Tridentine Moral Teaching

Let us take one last leap in history and look at the domain and role of conscience in modern Catholic moral teaching. The textbooks that have proliferated since the Council of Trent are classic examples of this. These manuals are all the more important because their principal object was the formation of priests in seminaries, particularly in view of the administration of the sacrament of Penance. Because of this, they provided material for preaching and influenced the moral sections of catechisms, as well as the examinations of conscience found in our devotional books.

Let us open a manual and look at the table of contents. The first section is called general or fundamental morality. It consists of four treatises, on human acts, conscience, laws, and sins. This is the foundation on which special morality is constructed, usually being divided according to the commandments of God and of the Church, together with the study of cases of conscience. A simple look at the plan followed shows us that the treatise on conscience has been given a place among the foundations of moral teaching, even a central position. It has replaced practical reason and prudence. From now on it presides over moral discernment between law and human acts. Morality has become a matter of conscience. We see precisely what function has devolved upon it within the combination of the four fundamental treatises. Let us note in passing that the treatises on beatitude, the virtues, the Gospel Law, and grace, characteristic of St. Thomas's moral teaching, have disappeared from this table of contents.

Conscience, Intermediary between Law and Freedom

In this system, which is rigorous enough in its logic, conscience plays the role of intermediary between law and human acts, or more precisely between law and the freedom that is at the origin of human acts. Conscience makes the law known to the free will and presides over its application, which includes a certain role of interpretation, for the law is general and has to be applied to particular, concrete actions with many attenuating circumstances. Also, in this application, whenever any doubt or incertitude is present, conscience may be either broad or rigorous.

The work of conscience will be determined above all by the relationship between freedom and law. Here we are dealing with freedom of indifference,

freedom of indifference

conceived as <u>the will's power to choose between contraries</u>, between the yes and the no, at each instant—at least in theory. The origin of morality resides in the law, the expression of the free and sovereign will of God the Creator, which is imposed upon man under the form and with the force of obligation. Human acts, indifferent in themselves, become moral through their connection with legal obligations. They will be good if they conform to the law; evil, and sins, if not. <u>Such is the domain of conscience: obligations imposed by the law, refined by the commandments.</u> This realm is dominated by tension. Freedom and law are opposed to each other, like two landowners, disputing over the territory of human acts. Again, it is generally held among moralists that such and such an act falls under the law, and another under freedom. For example, according to the law of Sunday rest, Sunday will be said to fall under the law, while week-days, "workdays," fall under freedom. The law limits freedom by its com-mandments; it takes away the power to perform various actions: to steal, to commit adultery, etc. The <u>principal task of conscience, as of moralists,</u> will therefore be <u>to mark off the limits between the domain of the law and the do-main of freedom.</u> It is a question of what is allowed, what forbidden; what is obligatory, what remains free. How far does obligation go? Where does sin be-gin?

<u>At the heart</u> of this moral system <u>is the idea and feeling of obligation</u> or duty, something no one would dream of questioning. <u>Obligation</u> becomes cen-tral to such a point that it <u>circumscribes the domain of morality.</u> All actions that fall under a moral obligation, <u>whether they are commanded or forbidden,</u> belong to morality properly so called. Other actions, particularly those which tend toward higher perfection, are considered free, simply matters of counsel, and they are relegated to an annexed science such as asceticism or mysticism, later to be called spirituality or, in the language of the exegetes, parenesis or moral exhortation. <u>We are no longer looking at a morality of the virtues,</u> where the tendency toward a certain perfection is of the essence. Rather, <u>the determi-nation of the legal minimum now predominates.</u>

Conscience, Interpreter of Law

Situated between law and freedom, conscience occupies a difficult posi-tion and carries out a delicate function. It is the representative of the moral law in the human subject. As the messenger of the law it makes obligations known and imposes them. It plays the role of a judge who commands or forbids, who condemns and punishes, but who cannot modify the law. In this role, conscience appears as the interpreter of an external law, acting always with a certain constraint because of the fact that it limits the subject's freedom. This sense of being external is reinforced by the manner in which moralists treat cases of conscience. In resolving doubtful cases, they always adduce what they call "external reasons," that is, authority and the number of moralists who hold such and such an opinion, and who form a kind of jurisprudence in the moral field.

I should add, however, that with deeper experience of the moral life, conscience can manifest itself as the interpreter of a law that is expressed within a man's interior, like the voice of the divine legislator speaking through the intimate voice of conscience. Conscience then becomes a witness to God within a man. This is how Cardinal Newman, for example, understood it. But in this case, conscience has the tendency to extend its field of action beyond legal obligations and to embrace the entire spiritual life. This is how Newman was converted and chose a consecrated form of life, in order to obey his conscience. Here we transcend the horizon of the manuals and discover what the term "conscience" has been able to recoup of all that is best in the moral lives of many Christians. It no longer designates the awareness of a law that obliges and constrains, but rather the knowledge of a law that appeals to the heart and touches it.

But let us return to our manuals of moral theology. Conscience should apply the law to the subject without attenuating it, with precision, without compromise. It should be objective and imperative. It may appear rigorous, even severe. Moralists who fulfill a like role in regard to freedom will be the masters and counselors of conscience.

The Subjective Conscience

On the other hand conscience is a faculty of the subject. In the last analysis it is up to the conscience to penetrate, in some way, the free will and the concrete action, with all their objective and subjective conditions. We could even say that conscience is part of the subject in his most intimate and personal depths. In the conscience lie the subject's sentiments, aspirations, and all his reactions to the law, including those in his "unconscious."

This explains why many moralists favor freedom and personal conscience, which is shown by their perfectly legitimate concern not to overburden consciences with a multiplicity of precepts and obligations applied too rigorously. Again, they show a marked preference for freedom in doubtful cases. But the balance has not always been respected. The debate over conscience was loud and heated during the quarrel over probabilism, which occupied moralists for several centuries. The concern to adapt morality to Christians living in the world has led some moralists to favor freedom to the point of laxity. This is the reproach Pascal made to Jesuit moralists. At the opposite end of the spectrum, Jansenists sustained the moral law to the point of rigorism. So the moral conscience has been tossed from one extreme to the other, according to whether freedom or law has been preferred.

New Dimensions of Conscience

If we glance back now and compare all this with St. Paul and St. Thomas, we observe that in one sense conscience has expanded, and in another, it has shrunken. It has expanded so far as to occupy a primary position in fundamental moral theology. Morality has become a matter of conscience, and its principal subject matter consists in cases of conscience. On the other hand, however, by concentrating on obligations, the field of conscience studied by moralists has become much narrower. It no longer includes spirituality, which is the noblest part of the Christian experience. Conscience no longer seems to be concerned with the great human questions of beatitude and suffering, of love and the virtues, even the theological virtues, for it no longer considers anything but the obligations involved. The contact between this type of morality and Scripture is thus greatly reduced, for moralists are interested in nothing beyond the Decalogue and imperative texts of the same nature. They care no longer for the Sermon on the Mount or parenetic and sapiential texts. In moral textbooks and in catechisms destined to form the conscience of the faithful, Scripture is no longer quoted, not even the Gospel.

Conscience and the Magisterium

Finally, let us note the very individualistic character of this concept of morality and conscience. The moral act is solely the work of the subject's free and voluntary decision; morality becomes a private affair, relevant only to the personal conscience. For St. Paul, conscience was profoundly ecclesial, because of its insertion in "the Body of Christ" through faith and love. For St. Thomas, it was ordered to the common good by the virtue of prudence. In the morality of recent centuries man sees himself as a free individual in confrontation with the law, which limits his freedom exteriorly. His relationship to Church and society will take the form of a relationship to authorities that make laws: the Magisterium in the Church, the state in civil society. This will mean a certain rapport between powers. Questions about the legitimacy of authority and the limits of its powers will predominate. Once again we think of the comparison of the two landowners, disputing like rivals over the field of human acts. Personal conscience and the Magisterium are seen as external wills which confront each other in competition rather than collaboration. In this setting, conscience will vacillate between a too servile obedience and the excessive claims of freedom. The question of the Magisterium will rise to prime importance among moral and dogmatic discussions, as if it were the source of moral obligation and doctrine. Henceforth in the study of moral problems and other similar questions people will be far more concerned about formal problems in the exercise of authority than with basic questions. Yet in discussions about abortion and so forth, should not the quality of actions in view of man's nature and relationships be the first consideration? Should not his relationship to another life that is born of him be the primary concern, even before the positions taken by the Magisterium, which are at the service of reason enlightened by Revelation?

The Vacillations of Conscience

In the course of these changes the very concept of conscience has been subtly modified. Since the Council and the human sciences' invasion of ethics, we have passed from a rigorous conscience, seen as the interior voice of the divine legislator, to a morality which favors freedom and in the end settles for the subjective conscience as the judge of good and evil. We are not too far from the concept of conscience which Newman attributed to the English people of his time: "The right of every Englishman to act according to his own will; the right to believe what he pleases and to ask no one's advice," without too much concern for what the priest or the pastor may say.[10] Clearly, variations in our view of conscience can be very important.

However this may be, a sure sign of conscience's authenticity is that it is

10. John Henry Newman, *A Letter Addressed to His Grace the Duke of Norfolk* (New York: Catholic Publication Society, 1875), chap. 5.

exacting in our regard, as are truth, goodness, and reality, which resist our desires like rugged ground beneath our feet. Conscience sets us upon an astonishing road. It calls for effort that lifts us high after humbling us in submission to the moral law. It is an illustration of the Gospel principle: he who humbles himself shall be exalted. The key to this paradox is in the hands of love, which finds its joy and fulfillment in the humility of service, after the example of Christ.

I can sum up my whole study in three words. We have looked at three types of Christian conscience, which I shall describe as follows: a Christ-centered, ecclesial conscience with St. Paul; a virtuous, community-centered conscience with St. Thomas; and a conscience that is at once legal and subjective, found in the manuals of moral theology. This is the moral patrimony bequeathed to us; it has formed our Catholic culture. In current debates on moral questions we are basically conditioned by the third type, the legal conscience, whether we are defending it in the name of morality or attacking and criticizing it in the name of the free subject.

We have certainly changed our terminology, to adapt it to the modern world. We prefer to speak of ethics rather than morality. Laws have been replaced by norms. Asceticism has become spirituality, and then parenesis. Obligations have turned into imperatives. But beneath the changes in terminology the problems and mental categories are still there. We may fairly suspect that the moral crisis we know today is a resurgence of the old quarrel over probabilism, which we thought long dead and buried. The moral systems elaborated in our times—consequentialism and proportionalism in their various forms—are more closely related to the systems in the manuals than we may realize. They can be traced back to these directly sometimes, through their interpretation of the theory of double effect, or through their method of comparing the consequences of actions or the opinions of moralists.

However this may be, I hope I have rendered you some small service by bringing out in stronger relief the riches of our Catholic moral tradition, and suggesting that in our day the Christian conscience is able to recapture the broad, comprehensive horizons of St. Paul, the Fathers, and the theology of St. Thomas. In our current crisis, which we have inherited from recent centuries, it seems to me indispensable to control the moral categories which have boxed us in excessively, so as to rediscover in all their light and vigor the primary sources of Revelation, those choice instruments forged by the Holy Spirit and used to communicate an understanding of the designs of God and the mystery of Christ to successive Christian generations, first to the Church, then to each believer, be he a theologian or not. Now we face the decisive question: Do we have the courage to believe that these ancient, familiar texts contain a word of God for us capable of renewing our consciences and hearts far more effectively than can the wisdom of philosophers and the science of the learned? Do we know how to receive this word with openness and love?

17 ∾ Conscience and the Virtue of Prudence
(1996)

As stated in Cardinal Ratzinger's article "Conscience and Truth," the central problem encountered in moral theology at the present time is the relation between conscience and truth.[1] Is our personal conscience the ultimate judge of the truth of our acts? Is it their very source? Or, is our conscience the witness within us of a superior truth perceived as a voice, a lawgiving light? In a word, is it a consciousness of truth? This question coincides with the pivotal point of the encyclical *Veritatis splendor*. Our freedom is not absolute; it is a freedom for truth; it grows and fulfills itself while serving the truth of which moral law is the expression. The love of truth, at the core of freedom and conscience, is certainly the most profound, the most decisive point of the present moral debate.

Our Heritage: Moral Doctrine on the Commandments and on Virtue

To present clearly the problem of the relation among freedom, conscience, and truth, and to see its implications, it is useful to study the moral heritage we have received. Catholic teaching on morals comprises two traditions, which have produced two systems of thought. The modern tradition, of which the manuals are the classic expression, introduced the treatise on conscience in place of the treatise on virtue in fundamental moral theology. Special moral

Originally published in John Haas, ed., *Crisis of Conscience* (New York, 1996), 79–92. Translated by Sr. Mary Thomas Noble, O.P. Edited for publication in *The Pinckaers Reader* by Craig Steven Titus.

1. Joseph Cardinal Ratzinger, "Conscience and Truth," in *Catholic Conscience Foundation and Formation*, ed. Russell E. Smith (Braintree, Mass.: The Pope John Center, 1991), 7–27.

theology was divided following questions based on the Ten Commandments, considered as the expression of natural law for which conscience is the witness and the interpreter.

This tradition covers the study of acts, of cases of conscience, and the obligations determined by law or norms, as we say today. It is likened to the moral imperatives in the tradition of Kant. The theological virtues are doubtless mentioned in the manuals but serve in fact only as categories under which obligations and sins are listed. The study of virtue was left to ascetical theology in keeping with the search for perfection, which goes beyond the limit of right and wrong proper to morality.

The other tradition, a much older one, which claims its beginnings with the Church Fathers and found in St. Thomas its finest systematic expression, builds Christian morality on the theological and moral virtues, perfected by the gifts of the Holy Spirit. The practical virtue par excellence, which leads the moral judgment to its conclusion, is prudence rather than conscience (as thought in the other tradition).

We find in St. Thomas, however, a conjunction between, on the one hand, the virtue of prudence, analyzed through the resources of the Aristotelian tradition, with the contribution of the monastic tradition of discernment, and on the other, the doctrine of conscience from St. Paul and the Church Fathers, especially St. Jerome. Two levels can be distinguished: synderesis, defined as the *habitus* of the first principles of practical reason; and conscience itself, understood by Aquinas as the act of applying these principles in concrete actions. Having said that, prudence plays incontestably the main role here on the practical level; conscience works for prudence.

It is important to consider the placing of conscience in the organization of moral doctrine in the one view or the other, because its role and even its conception depend on its relation to the other elements of the system.

The Freedom of Indifference and Conscience

But let us return to our problem: the relation among freedom, conscience, and truth. The manual tradition was explicitly linked to the freedom of indifference, as the choice between opposites, for or against. This resulted in a certain opposition, an exteriority, between freedom and law. Freedom and law can be compared to two landlords who are contesting the field of human behavior. The moralists say, *"Possidet lex, possidet libertas,"* conscience is seen as the intermediary between law and freedom like a judge in court. It applies law to human acts. Conscience speaks in the name of the law, but it resides in the subject to whom it dictates the law. And so, that is why it can easily fluctuate between a zeal for the law, capable of turning into rigorism, and excessive concern for the subject, which can lead to laxity. The whole argument on probabilism lies in this fluctuation. We see today the pendulum of conscience, which once held firmly to the side of the moral law, forcefully swinging to the side of freedom as the criterion of moral values, so much so that some moralists are beginning to consider that which favors freedom as itself the criterion of moral law.

In this tradition freedom of indifference has given rise to a moral voluntarism that, beginning with freedom as the source of choice, communicates to the law itself understood as the pure will of the divine legislator. It does not allow for complete awareness of the role of truth in moral actions. On one side we have a will that dictates and makes the law, and on the other a will that obeys. Between the two, it is the function of conscience to make known the commands and imperatives but not to explain them or to give any reasons, because the sole reason is the will of the legislator. Therefore, obedience to the law imposed by conscience through the force of obligation becomes the main virtue in this conception of morality, because it exercises a general role. It gives moral form to all acts, even to all virtues. Current claims in favor of freedom and personal conscience are the exact opposite of this conception. They indicate the passage of the will of the legislator to the will of the subject as the principal dynamic within the individual conscience.

The Freedom for Excellence

The encyclical *Veritatis splendor* wished to reestablish firmly the bonds among freedom, conscience, and truth, and to show that truth frees us and favors the growth of true freedom and that consequently the law, with conscience as a manifestation of moral truth, helps form freedom and exercises over it a pedagogical role.

Using these terms, the encyclical follows the tradition of a conception of freedom analyzed by St. Thomas. He received it from the Greek philosophers and the Church Fathers. It can be called a freedom of quality or excellence. It can be defined as a power to carry out acts of quality that are perfect in their order. This freedom is rooted in the natural inclinations proper to our spiritual nature created in the image of God. These are the inclinations to truth, goodness, beatitude, and life in society, associated with the inclinations toward the preservation of human beings and to the gift of life.[2] We are dealing with a freedom of attraction and not one of indifference. It proceeds from the aspiration to truth and goodness; it is fundamentally a freedom for what is true and good. As such, it is a participation in Divine freedom.

These inclinations are the basis for the natural law, which presides over the development of human freedom; one could say the development of personality. They provide the first principles for moral judgment in the application of positive acts that are the work of reason. These are also the principles that synderesis makes known to us and that direct the judgment of conscience.

Let us note that in this conception of freedom, intellect and will stand together at the source of what we call free will, and that reason and affectivity go to form the choosing of what is its proper activity. There is no longer any question of voluntarism. Reason, which grasps truth precisely as the real good, plays an essential part in choice. Practical judgment is inseparable from choice. Intelligence has, equally, a part in the elaboration of the law, which is the work of wisdom, as well as in obedience, which requires the discernment of prudence.

Freedom for Charity

Freedom, as a power to accomplish acts of quality that are true and good, is given to us as a seed. Under the movement of natural inclinations it tends to develop progressively, as a spiritual growth.

At the origin of this growth is a spontaneous attraction for truth, goodness, beatitude, and an inclination toward life in human community. It also comes from a concern for the well-being of others, which in real terms signifies a certain natural love of God and neighbor prior to all instruction. St. Basil could say at the outset of his Rule (Qu.2) that the love of God, like our affection for our parents, is unteachable, *adidaktos*. It is so spontaneous that no schooling is necessary to learn it; it precedes all teaching. Love of God cannot be taught.

2. Cf. *VS*, no. 51, and reference to *ST* I-II 94.2.

No one taught us to enjoy the light of day, or to cling to life above all, or to love those who brought us into the world. In the same manner, or even in a stronger way, exterior instruction does not teach us to love God. The very nature of the human being contains a seed that possesses the principle of this ability to love. It is at the school of the commandments of God that this seed should be gathered, cultivated diligently, nourished with care, and brought to fulfillment through Divine grace.

We have a natural basis for receiving charity. It precedes any exterior intervention in the form of an obligation or a prohibition. On this basis we can build a morality of charity in which it is both the principle and the form: as principle, it inspires free acts; as form, it is the force that guides the other virtues toward their ultimate end.

The encyclical introduces an important change in the interpretation of the Decalogue. The Ten Commandments are not reduced to a code of obligations imposed by God. Rather, they are presented as a gift of his wisdom and mercy, demanding a response of love.[3] Since charity is grafted onto the natural love of which we have just spoken, it remains the principle of the moral life, even before that of moral obligation. In other terms, the encyclical changes the cornerstone of moral life. Morality must be built on the greatness of love rather than on a legalistic obedience, as was the case in the manuals of moral theology. It was left to spiritual theology to talk about the virtue's growth and perfection.

Freedom, as a capacity to act on our own according to truth and goodness, is given as a seed. It is ourself, our being, our spiritual nature. How can we develop it?

The Necessity of Law for the Growth of Freedom

First of all, we need law to guide us in our consideration, especially in the first phase of our moral growth. Law has a unique place for us. It is both exterior and interior, superior and immanent. Moral law comes to us from above and may even be surrounded by thunder and lightning, as on Mount Sinai. However, it corresponds precisely to the dictates of our natural inclinations to truth, goodness, and our intimate sense of God and others. It is exactly what we perceive in our conscience when the voice of God sounds, when divine

3. *VS*, no. 11.

light shines in the depth of our soul. We can say that this law, even though it is proclaimed exteriorly, even though it is chiseled on stone tablets, is nonetheless inscribed in the heart of man. As written in *Gaudium et spes:*

Deep within his conscience man discovers a law which he himself has not laid upon himself but which he must obey. Its voice, ever calling him to long to do what is good and to avoid evil, tells him inwardly at the right moment: do this, shun that. For man has in his heart a law inscribed by God.[4]

The Religious Dimension of Law and Conscience

Let us remark also with the encyclical, concerning the moral questions asked by the rich young man, that law, like conscience which bears it witness, has a spiritual and ecclesial dimension. Whether it be from the top of Mount Sinai or from the depths of the heart of man, moral law comes from God, from his wisdom and his holiness. It is addressed to those whom it touches in its sense of what is true and good in order to make them part of the People of God. Conscience, therefore, is part of the movement of man's aspiration toward God in company with "those who seek justice." They receive the cultural and religious legacy contained in scripture and stored in human wisdom.

A passage from Newman can be cited here on the Christian conception of conscience. A part of it is given in the *Catechism of the Catholic Church:*

This at least, is how I read the doctrine of Protestants as well as Catholics. The rule and measure of duty is not utility, not the beatitude of the greatest number, nor State convenience, nor fitness, order and the *pulchrum.* Conscience is not a long-sighted selfishness, nor a desire to be consistent with oneself; but it is a messenger from Him, who both in nature and in grace, speaks to us behind a veil and teaches and rules by his representatives. Conscience is the aboriginal Vicar of Christ, a prophet in its information, a monarch in its peremptoriness, a priest in its blessings and anathemas, and, even though the eternal priesthood throughout the Church could cease to be, in it the sacerdotal principle would remain and would have a sway.[5]

---

4. *Gaudium et spes,* no. 16.
5. John Henry Newman, *A Letter Addressed to His Grace the Duke of Norfolk* (New York: Catholic Publication Society, 1875), chap. 5.

The Necessity of Virtue

However, law and conscience are not sufficient in order to develop fully in us the power to act according to the truth and the good that for us is the freedom of quality. It is the particular work of the virtues to direct the natural inclinations.

We must give to the word *virtue* its original meaning. It has been impoverished and deformed through a particular usage by the school of obligation-based morality. Virtue became the habit of submitting to the law and, from that point, it turned into boring conformism. But there is nothing more surprising and fresh than real virtue. It is comparable to the talent of the artist or the excellence of the craftsman. It possesses a lucidity and an energy that contribute to the perfection of our most personal ability to act. Proceeding from within us, it makes us independent with respect to the outside world. Virtue develops our natural inclinations toward truth and goodness. It gives us the power to accomplish excellent works for ourselves and for many others and thereby participate in the creative and providential power of God according to our capacity and with his help.

Thus, a virtue-based morality covering all the active qualities that man acquires through intellectual, moral, and spiritual faculties has roots in his natural inclination to goodness and truth, the source of his freedom.

For a long time, virtue-based morality was predominant in the Church. It was developed gradually from Holy Scripture in conjunction with human and Christian experience.[6] It was not formed by human effort (as in the virtue-based philosophies) but accepted as a gift from God; it is both infused and acquired, passive and active. It was St. Thomas who would give the morality of the virtues their most authoritative systematization, which became the classic one. To give a complete account of the teachings of revelation and Christian experience, and inspired by the writings of St. Augustine, he combined the virtues with the gifts of the Holy Spirit as well as the Beatitudes and the fruits

---

6. In Greek and Latin philosophy, starting from the question of beatitude, which covers all natural inclinations, morality was ordered around the four cardinal virtues: prudence, justice, fortitude, and temperance, already present in the Book of Wisdom. Taken up by the Church Fathers, the doctrine of the virtues became part of a new system governed by the theological virtues of faith, hope, and charity as taught by St. Paul. Accordingly, the significance and reality of virtue was profoundly transformed by this Christian integration.

of the Holy Spirit, which St. Paul enumerated in Galatians 5:22. *The Cate-chism of the Catholic Church* restated this doctrine in the section on virtue, which follows the teaching on conscience and precedes the treatment of sin.[7] St. Thomas divided the study of morality into the theological and cardinal virtues, adding for each one the study of the corresponding gift of the Holy Spirit and relevant Beatitude. After that, sins against the virtues are examined as well as the commandment pertaining to each case.

Prudence as the Link between the Virtues

When expounded and studied in all its detail, the morality of virtues appears rich and complex. It must be noted, however, that all the virtues, regardless of their number and diversity, form a whole, which is similar to our body with its members and organs. They all act together when we carry out a concrete act. It is here that we meet prudence, and it is here that we can perceive its role and its relation to conscience.

In his analytical exposition on the virtues, St. Thomas made clear that they were connected and thus worked together. He showed how this connection was guaranteed by charity and prudence.[8] Charity unites the virtues by ordering them to God, our ultimate end and our complete beatitude. Charity enables us to love him with all our heart, all our strength, and all our virtues. Prudence, on the other hand, the virtue of practical reason, takes up the other end of the chain. It governs each concrete action and fulfills its function of judgment for all the other virtues, including the theological ones. Prudence discerns *hic et nunc*, according to the circumstances, what is best in order to practice each virtue in its particular place. St. Anthony taught this to his followers when he asked them which virtue could save the monk from the devil's snares and help him rise to the summits of perfection. St. Anthony said that without discernment all the other virtues go astray, to the left or to the right, by excessive fervor or by laxity.[9]

Here again, we must give back its original and powerful significance to an old word that has been worn out and distorted. *Prudence* is not a safe or tutior-

7. *CCC,* part 3, ch. 1, art. 7, nos. 1803–45.

8. *ST* I-II 65.

9. John Cassian, *Conferences,* trans. Colm Luibeid (New York: Paulist Press, 1985), chap. 2, second conference: "On Discernment."

ist ("protectionist") virtue stemming from fear of breaking the law. It is the virtue of discernment, of decision, of action. Prudence does not consist only in careful deliberation or wise advice. Its proper action is what St. Thomas calls the precept that follows choice, that is, the decision which produces the action.[10] It is by this positive and active choice that prudence directs the acts of the other virtues to their end. This, then, is the concept of prudence that we can compare with conscience.

Synderesis, Conscience, and Prudence

Before comparing conscience and prudence, let us look upstream at their source. It is all the more useful since St. Thomas's analytical study can tend to hide their natural union due to differences he distinguished in his definitions.

Let us begin with conscience. It originates in the natural and primitive light of synderesis, which St. Thomas defines as the *habitus* of the first principles of practical reason. There is a sense of good and evil bound to the very nature of the human spirit. Conscience is found at the conjunction of the two faculties, reason and will, according to the measure of their inclination to truth and goodness.

Since it belongs "to the very nature of the soul," this light is permanent and unchanging. Its function is to condemn evil and tend toward the good. It provides the primary basis for our moral judgments and cannot err. It enlightens all mankind and is indestructible, regardless of the sins and errors that veil and darken it in our heart.[11] Synderesis is therefore the original source of all judgments of conscience. They are the reflection of this original light in the distinctiveness of our actions and all they involve.

Let us stop and make two brief remarks. First, note the importance of the doctrine of synderesis in the recent debate. It offers a solid base for the recognition of the universal and permanent character of moral laws coming from within us in the form of a light that illuminates our intellect. The strength of moral law derived from this light does not come to man from a merely exterior will; it has its roots in man's intellect and is at the origin of his freedom.

Second, it is regrettable that the word "synderesis" is so foreign to our

10. *ST* II-II 47.8.
11. *De Verit.* 16.3.

modern languages. This is due in part to the weakness of our vocabulary, bound as it is to the experience of the sense and lacking words to designate the deeper and higher realities; it is too often reduced to using abstract and technical terms. Cardinal Ratzinger has suggested the substitution of the word "synderesis" with the word "anamnesis," and has given good reason to support his suggestion. It can be debated. It is very difficult, however, to replace such a classical term. To better understand the meaning of synderesis, an image given by St. Thomas can be helpful. St. Jerome, in his commentary on Ezekiel's vision of the four animals, spoke of synderesis as the "spark of conscience" that was not quelled even in the heart of Cain after his crime. He compared it to the eagle that corrects from above when reason and sensitivity err. The other animals are symbolized in his vision by the man, the lion, and the bull. St. Thomas went to the trouble of explaining St. Jerome's comparison and made the distinction between the spark, the purest part of fire, which shoots out above the flame, and the fire itself, which is mixed with alien matter that alters its purity. The spark is synderesis, the pure light of truth; the fire is conscience, which can err accidentally by attaching itself to a particular object that is inferior to reason.[12] Synderesis is, strictly speaking, the spark of conscience, the origin of the light that illuminates it.

Let us look at prudence. The Thomistic doctrine of prudence directly follows the Aristotelian tradition in its analysis of the faculties and the virtues. Prudence is the specific moral virtue particular to practical reason, but it is not so in an isolated manner. Prudence uses all the data provided by moral science. It is worth clarifying that this science, insofar as it is a virtue, is anterior to prudence and that it directs prudence just as acquired knowledge guides the judgment. Moreover, like knowledge, prudence draws its wisdom from the *habitus* of the first principles of practical reason (synderesis), which it applies in concrete behavior. Conscience and prudence, therefore, share the same source of light and join in the same work, the elaboration of moral judgment. What is it, then, from that moment which distinguishes them, particularly in an author like St. Thomas, who associates both of them even though he studies them separately?

12. *De Verit.* 17.2 ad 3.

Comparison between Conscience and Prudence: How They Differ and How They Converge

St. Thomas, to our knowledge, did not explicitly compare prudence and conscience, but he did analyze them so specifically that it is easy to establish their differences.

First, the passage pertinent to our question is the answer given to an objection in the *De veritate*,[13] where Thomas compares the judgment of conscience and the choice of the free will. The latter contains practical judgment, which is part of reason and therefore part of prudence in choice. There is, however, the following difference: the judgment of conscience remains at the level of knowledge, whereas the judgment of the choosing as well as the judgment of prudence includes the involvement of the "appetite," that is, of the affective will. Prudence, in fact, as we have seen, is not content to deliberate, to counsel, or to judge in the abstract. Its distinctive action is the command, that is, the decision to act, which necessarily includes the participation of the will. Such is the practical judgment where prudence finds its fulfillment. And that is why it is not only an intellectual virtue but also a moral one; prudence can ensure the connection between the other moral virtues. Conscience, on the other hand, although it judges the moral quality of our behavior, is not a virtue; it is the application of synderesis in the appraisal of acts we have carried out or will carry out.

This difference should not prevent us from seeing the close collaboration of prudence and conscience. They are two beacons that join and penetrate one another to produce good actions.

Another difference: St. Thomas was the heir to a tradition whereby conscience was bound to the idea of obligation with regard to the law. A demonstration of this is the way St. Thomas asks the question about erroneous conscience in the *Summa*. He asks whether erroneous conscience creates an obligation and if the will that disagrees with mistaken reason is evil, with the aim of bringing the problem of conscience back to that of reason, which he had very carefully studied, following Aristotle. In spite of the similarity, the perspective is rather different. Legal obligations bear directly on exterior acts and determine "that without which no virtue is possible" or the minimum re-

13. *De Verit.* 17.1 ad 4.

quired of everyone. Virtue is a principle interior to our actions and tends spontaneously toward the quality of perfection of action. Conscience sees action within the limits of what is obligatory, but prudence sees action in view of its perfection.

The difference between the two is reduced to a nuance in St. Thomas, who places law at the service of virtue, but it became decisive when nominalism concentrated moral theology strictly on what was legally compulsory. Soon after that, the moralists introduced into fundamental moral theology a treatise on conscience that replaced the treatise on virtues and the treatise on prudence. Conscience became the authority of moral judgment in the subject faced with freedom. Moralists had at this point great difficulty in defining the role of prudence.

A third difference: the judgment of conscience is concerned with past actions. It carries with it either an accusation and so causes remorse, or an approval and thus excuses. On future actions it either incites or forbids on the strength of obligation.[14] But prudence, after having deliberated on the action to be carried out and perhaps calling to mind past experience, is directly concerned with the present moment of the action, because it is through the decision that it brings the action into being in a particular way. It is perhaps why St. Thomas directly associates solicitude or vigilance with prudence, similar to the active attention to the present.[15]

Whatever may be said of these differences, it is clear that St. Thomas saw conscience and prudence as two converging lights coming from the same source. Both are prompted by our aspiration to the truth and both share the object of the discernment between good and evil. They are located on two different levels. Prudence goes beyond mere knowledge in order to enter into our actions and direct them toward truth. Both will come up against the problem of error, which can always affect human judgment in contingent realities like the circumstances of an action.

Prudence and the Formation of Conscience

By associating prudence and conscience in the establishment of moral truth, consideration of the former sheds important light on what we call the

14. *De Verit.* 17.1.
15. *ST* I-II 47.9.

formation of conscience. The doctrine on virtue provides us with a classification that is not included by the moralists of conscience. We can show this in two ways.

First, the doctrine on virtue implies the idea of growth, distinguishable in different stages of education, based on the model of the growth of charity described by St. Thomas. He distinguishes among beginners, the proficient, and the perfect.[16] Two main elements contribute to this growth: the help of teachers and the acquiring of personal experience.

Prudence, like all virtues, needs outside assistance in the form of teachers, authorities, or other intermediaries, especially in the first phase of its growth. These people inculcate by word and example, the rudiments of prudence, the principles of good behavior that transmit the heritage of wisdom and culture of a religious or secular kind. Prudence develops thanks to the assimilation of what we acquire from our cultural milieu or from revelation, as in the case of the Ten Commandments. The progressive formation of the virtue of prudence benefits conscience and gives it a solid base and greater clarity as to the differences between good and evil or what is compulsory or forbidden.

The second element that contributes to growth is especially obvious in the second phase (proficient), when personal experience is acquired which calls for our own initiative and a prolonged commitment in keeping with the virtues. It is here that knowledge develops connaturally through repeated contact with the very substance of the action, whether perceptible or spiritual, whether concerning things or persons. It is the fruit of the just and lawful experience of the work of human hands and of the Spirit. This type of knowledge is different from that acquired by reason or observation. It would be preferable to call it wisdom. Connatural knowledge is particularly important in moral theology because it is synthetic and intuitive, and because of that, it is suited to forming judgments of action that require the facts to be grasped in their entirety and discernment as to the order to be given to them. It is, at the same time, a picture of the whole and a view that unites and finalizes.

Connatural knowledge aims directly at progress by the quality and excellence of our action. Nonetheless, it enlightens conscience in the discernment of what is or is not in conformity with the moral law and its obligations: it helps in guaranteeing a fruitful application of synderesis, a real participation in

16. *ST* I-II 24.9.

its light, a true echo of the voice of God. Furthermore, conscience can be attributed with a directional role that goes beyond legal obligations and can help in the choice of a career, in a conversion, or in a vocation, as seems to be the case with Cardinal Newman. Conscience is then an inner light guiding along the way of truth. The more common use of the term, however, in moral theology links conscience with the obligations set by law.

The conjunction between prudence and conscience appears to be the best way to explain the formation of conscience, which is required in order that it be faithful to truth; this is because of the development of prudence, which is the specific virtue of the truth in action. We can see, therefore, that conscience and prudence are the organs of truth within us. They become deficient, distorted, or corrupt as soon as their connection with the truth is weakened or broken.

SECTION V   Law and Grace

18 ∾ Aquinas on Nature and the Supernatural
(1992)

To begin with an observation: the original title of this essay, "Nature and Supernature," is not exact as far as St. Thomas is concerned. He never used the noun "supernature,"[1] but only the adjective "supernatural." This means that the concept of "supernatural" is, for him, something relative to an existing nature, but it constitutes neither a subsistent reality nor a kind of order floating somewhere up above nature. The terminology "nature/supernature" has its origin in modern discussions and is based on the hypothesis of a state of pure nature, embodying the concept of a nature that is self-sufficient and independent, at least conceptually, of any appeal to a lofty and gratuitous end, the vision of God.

Next, let me note the difficulty encountered in our reading of Aquinas. We cannot study his concept of nature as if we were living in the thirteenth century, because this fundamental notion has undergone a profound evolution in modern times. We ourselves are marked, impregnated by the problematics and interpretations elaborated by later theology, notably in regard to the relationship between human nature and the supernatural. In order to go back to Thomas, we need to take into account what has transpired since his day, particularly the critique of Ockham, then the concept of nature in its relationship to grace among theologians of the Renaissance, and finally the concept of nature in the philosophy of the Enlightenment and in modern sciences.

Originally published as "Nature-surnature chez Saint Thomas d'Aquin," in *Ethique et natures* (Geneva, 1992), 19–28. Translated by Sr. Mary Thomas Noble, O.P., with the assistance of Craig Steven Titus. Edited for publication in *The Pinckaers Reader* by Craig Steven Titus.

1. Cf. Roberto Busa, *Index Thomisticus*.

The question of nature is a complex problem, unceasingly raised anew. We must be content to deal with a few ideas that are particularly important for our discussions.

The Meaning of "Nature"

Since "supernatural" stands in relation to "nature," we first need to clarify the meaning of the latter. Aquinas has explained the different meanings of the word "nature," notably in the *tertia pars,* question 2, article 1, where he treats of the Incarnation of the Word: was the union of the Word with flesh wrought in a nature or a person?[2] This context shows us clearly the perspective and the sources. We are in the theological context of a reflection on the mystery of the Incarnation; the sources are Aristotle, the teaching of the Greek Fathers in dealing with Christological and Trinitarian problems, citations from Cyril and Athanasius and, as the foundation of faith, the Council of Chalcedon.

St. Thomas, taking his inspiration from Aristotle,[3] who was also used as a source by the Greek Fathers, distinguishes four meanings of the word "nature":

1. In the first sense, the term comes from "nativity," nature signifying the generation of living things, more specifically the act of generation.

2. Thus "nature" has come to signify the source of generation.

3. And because the source of generation in any living thing is something within it, "nature" came to signify the inner principle of movement, either form or matter.

4. Furthermore, since the end of generation is the essence of the species (as humanity is common to father and son), "nature" will also signify the essence of a being as expressed by its definition, its *quod quid est* or "whatness."

I should like to make two comments here.

It is certainly necessary to distinguish these different meanings clearly, but we must avoid separating them, because they belong together, and together bear on a concrete experience, that of birth, which should be understood not

---

2. *ST* III 2.1. This is also the case concerning the definition of "person" in connection with the Trinity, in *ST* I 29.1 ad 4.

3. *Metaphysics,* IV (1014b16ff.); cf. St. Thomas, *Commentary on Metaphysics,* V.5 (n. 809ff).

only as a biological act but as a primitive fact, the coming into existence of a being taken in its concrete totality, the human person with its form, that is, a soul or spirit, and its matter, a body. In the case of the birth of Christ, divinity itself will be involved; the problem is to know how. The term "nature" thus seems to designate an all-encompassing and dynamic reality.

We note especially the dimension of interiority as essential to the concept of nature. What characterizes "natural" action is that it proceeds from inner principles or sources. Thus nature is different from technology: it acts from within. Because of this, nature is linked with the person in view of all the external causalities that may affect him. At the core of the person it forms an essential component of human interiority.

This interiority is not only biological or psychological; it is dynamic. The concept of nature invites our reflection, beginning with our experience of the way we produce acts and works, as though by a kind of generation, and going on to their intimate sources: our free will and our spiritual nature. We are thus led to seek the causes of human morality.

Nature and Freedom: Two Concepts of Their Relationship

The basic question is the relationship between nature and freedom. Historically, it depends upon two interpretations of the definition of free will proposed by Peter Lombard in his *Sentences of the Fathers,* the foundation of theological teaching up until the Renaissance: "Free will is the faculty of reason and will, through which good is chosen with grace assisting, or evil with grace desisting."[4] Here in brief are the two interpretations: according to Aquinas, free will *proceeds from* reason and will; according to Ockham, free will *precedes* reason and will, like a first faculty.

The Spiritual Nature at the Source of Freedom according to St. Thomas

For Thomas, free will proceeds from reason and will. It is a consequent faculty formed by the conjunction of the intellect and the will.

---

4. "Liberum arbitrium est facultas rationis et voluntatis *qua bonum eligitur gratia assistente, vel malum eadem desistente*" (*In Sent.* II, 24.3).

This means that the first source of free action resides in the two natural inclinations that move our spiritual faculties: the sense of truth and the attraction to the good, which are expressed in the first principles of the theoretical and practical intellect; more precisely, in the desire for beatitude and perfection which raised, for Aquinas as for all the ancients, the first moral question: what is true beatitude?

In this concept, nature—but let us understand this as spiritual nature—is the very source of free and moral action.

We can also say that the human person is moral "from birth," possessing within, by nature, the primitive criteria of morality and the seeds of the moral life, the *semina virtutum*. This holds true not only in the temporal sense of the day of birth, but also in a structural sense: at the origin of life of the mind and heart, there is within us a certain higher nature that inclines us to truth and goodness.

Obviously, it is here in these faculties which render a person *capax Dei,* capable of knowing and loving God, that the image of God, of which Genesis speaks, resides.

Thus we shall see the possibility taking shape of a harmony between, on the one hand, the *spiritual nature* of the person, whose primitive inclinations function in *freedom* (for a person is free because of, not in spite of, these inclinations) and, on the other hand, *the call of grace* to a supernatural life.

The Fundamental Harmony between Nature and Grace. Natural Desire and Sin

For St. Thomas and for the Fathers, before the tragedy of sin took place and underneath the struggle and damage caused by it, human nature is still God's greatest work, according to Genesis. This, by its universal opening to the infinity of truth, goodness, and being, renders a person at once free and capable of receiving the gratuitous gift of God which surpasses the active possibilities of creatures, whether human beings or angels, and which, for this reason, is rightly called supernatural.

The passive capacity to receive the vision of God, and the grace leading to it, will be expressed in the famous theme of the natural desire to see God, which still startles Catholic theologians, even Thomists, and which nonetheless constitutes an original and central argument in Thomas's demonstration of the possibility of the human person's seeing God, contrary to the opinions of Jewish and Arabian philosophers. This argument had already appeared in the *Summa contra Gentiles* and becomes the dominant principle of the treatise on beatitude in the *Summa theologiae,* particularly in questions 2 and 3. These demonstrate that human beatitude, from the point of view of its object, cannot consist in obtaining any created good, but in God alone. From the point of view of its subject this beatitude can only be obtained in the act of the vision of God. We see this basic reflection, therefore, focusing on the desire for the good and for beatitude, which gathers within itself all the natural inclinations and traces, in its development, the trajectory of ordering to the final end. This will prevail in the moral theology of St. Thomas, explained in the *secunda pars* in connection with the study of God, the Trinity, and its work, and with the study of Christ and Redemption in the *tertia pars.*

In this concept, there is a basic harmony between human nature, which is at the source of our human freedom and personality—whence proceeds our action—and the gratuitous gift of supernatural life. This unique harmony includes a certain paradox, because our ideas and words are incapable of expressing such a reality: the human person is both capable and incapable of God. We are capable of receiving the vision of God, and absolutely incapable of attaining it by ourselves. The gift depends first on the free divine initiative, but it also engages our human freedom by way of acceptance. Our free will aspires to it naturally as it aspires to beatitude, but we can also miss the mark and refuse it, particularly because of the exigencies of the divine call.

At this point the tragedy of sin makes its entrance. It is useful to say a word about it, because Thomas's teaching might seem too serene, in its insistence on harmony, to take into account the drama of the Redemption and the mystery of the Cross, as contrasted with Luther, for example, and the Augustinian tradition.

In Aquinas's teaching, the tragedy of sin is not diminished; it is put in context. It is even explained in greater depth. Sin does not consist only in being at variance with an external law that expresses the will of God. It sets up a contradiction in the depths of the human person between a free choice, made explicitly or implicitly in view of a given beatitude, and the natural human aspiration to truth and goodness expressed by the natural law in the depths of our conscience. Sin stirs up the tension of polarity within the human person: our spiritual nature with its decision is pitted against our free commitment to the contrary.

Sin is obviously a refusal of God's call; but it wounds the human person as well, because God's offer is made to a nature, a heart "capable of God." We are able to welcome grace and desire it obscurely as our end, even before we know it.[5]

We gain light on the drama of sin in the Genesis accounts of the temptation: "You will be like gods." The demands of grace are great: that a human being should recognize and love God as the source of his being, the one true God; that he should detach himself from his very being that he has received and place his center in God, not in himself; all of which will be effected through faith and love.

The temptation is also strong: that captivated by his own spiritual power, a human being should establish his center in himself and set himself up "as god." But in doing this, he cuts himself off from the source of truth and goodness and falls into illusion and vanity.

In brief, it is a question of faith: will a person put his faith in God and love God above all else? Will he make God his beatitude and his end, acknowledging God as the supreme Judge of good and evil?

Or will the person put his faith in himself, loving himself even to the point of despising God and others, seeking his beatitude in himself alone and setting himself up as the judge of good and evil?

Freedom, the First Faculty, Separate from Nature and Grace, according to Ockham

Let us now turn to Ockham. With him, we witness a complete reversal of anthropology and moral theology, beginning with his interpretation of the definition of free will which we mentioned above: free will *precedes* reason and will because it regulates their actions of thinking and willing. St. Bonaventure had already mentioned the opinion that free will is first, since the Father, in the Trinity, precedes the Word and the Spirit. This faculty is defined as the power to choose between contraries, to decide as one pleases between a yes and a no, beginning from the will alone. One can speak of a kind of creative power of choice in regard to one's decision.

Now this power of choice will operate first of all in regard to the natural inclinations, and more precisely, to the inclination to beatitude that draws them

5. Cf. *ST* I 62.8 ad 3.

all together. Ockham will maintain that I can choose indifferently to follow or not follow the inclination to beatitude, to be or not to be happy.

In doing this, Ockham breaks the link connecting freedom and nature; he thrusts the latter to a position outside of freedom and places it in opposition to it. A radical difference is inaugurated in the relationship between freedom and nature. The latter, henceforth to be subject to freedom and the spirit, is relegated to a lower level, to the physical, biological, or sensitive plane.

The isolation of freedom in relation to nature, as to everything outside of itself, has a direct consequence: morality will no longer be something belonging to the human person "from birth." Free actions are of themselves indifferent; they become moral only through the intervention of a law that expresses the will of an external freedom, notably the will of God. He, all-powerful and sovereign, can impose his will with the force of obligation.

Self-Sufficient Nature and the Addition of the Supernatural

This concept will also modify the relationship of nature to the supernatural. We are considering human nature as possessing freedom at its core. Isolated from divine freedom, human freedom now addresses its relationship with the supernatural. In the tradition of nominalism, one will tend to see nature as self-sufficient, autonomous, possessing its own end and laws. This will be the concept of Renaissance theologians, to be concretized in the hypothesis of a state of pure nature existing at the beginning of history.

Faced with this kind of nature, the supernatural can only be added on as a supplement, and we can no longer show where it is rooted or grafted into the human person. It will come to be represented as something of a parallel order; in this way we can turn it into a noun and speak of a "supernature." The relationship between nature and the supernatural becomes competitive and dialectical, as if between antagonistic freedoms. The situation is aggravated by the fact that within the context of freedom of indifference the idea of sin assumes a preponderant importance. Where there is freedom for excellence, the backbone of action is formed by the desire for truth and goodness; sin is a weakness and resembles illness. With freedom of indifference, on the other hand, the ability to sin is essential. It enters into its very definition as the power to choose between what the law decrees and its contrary, between sinning and not sinning. We can even say that this kind of freedom is especially prone to affirm itself through sin, seen as a claim to independence of law and all authority.

Moral systems based on freedom of indifference will always give pride of place to the consideration and study of sins and the law.

"Grace Does Not Destroy Nature, But Perfects It"

It remains for us to say a word about the relationship between nature and grace as expressed in the adage: grace does not destroy nature, but perfects it. When we look for quotations from St. Thomas on this subject, we are surprised at their scarcity. He has no article explaining the formula, and he uses it only twice in the *Summa*. [6] Nevertheless, this saying is a perfect formulation of the concept of the relationship between nature and grace, which Thomas applies in his theology. The first citation is of great importance. It determines the relationship between philosophy and theology: it legitimizes our appeal to philosophers and explains our use of their arguments in theology; at the same time, it situates them within the framework of the service natural reason can render to faith, in connection with the relationship of the will's natural inclination to goodness as the basis of the virtue of charity: thus the philosophers provide preambles to the articles on faith.[7]

If we consider the formula simply, it has two parts: 1) the denial of opposition between grace and human nature; 2) the manner in which they are ordered by a relationship of perfecting, which harmonizes with the concept of freedom for excellence, inspired by the natural inclination to truth and goodness. The relationship here is of a special kind, however, because of the infinite distance between the divine nature bestowing grace and human nature, simply *capax Dei, capax gratiae*.

Since time does not permit a further clarification of these relationships, it will be enough to offer a correction of a frequent interpretation of our saying. It is often taken as a guarantee to reason and the natural virtues: we can rest assured that their work, carried on according to their own rules and methods, even independently of faith, will be taken up by grace and will receive from it

---

6. "*Fides praesupponit cognitionem naturalem, sicut gratia naturam et ut perfectio perfectibile.*" "Faith presupposes natural knowledge, even as grace presupposes nature, and perfection supposes something that can be perfected." *ST* I 2.2 ad 1 (Translation of the Fathers of the English Dominican Province); *ST* I 1.8 ad 2.

7. *ST* I 2.2 ad 1.

an additional perfection. Some also say that the work of reason should precede that of grace as a necessary preparation. This interpretation presupposes and favors a principle of separation between the work of nature and grace, in keeping with the hypothesis of self-sufficient nature. Since reason's work is never finished, grace might have to wait a long time, in this scenario.

This is certainly not St. Thomas's idea. For him, as a theologian, the gift of grace has primacy in theology, since it is a participation in the very source of the divine light and love, whence theology ensues.

I believe, therefore, that Thomas's saying should be interpreted from the vantage point of grace, under a twofold aspect:

1. First of all, for us, it means: do not be afraid to hand yourself over to grace, to open your mind to its light through faith; for faith, far from destroying reason's work, will develop it and give it a new dimension.

2. Then, for believers, it means: do not be afraid of philosophers and scholars, do not be afraid to make use of their research and their arguments, for in the measure in which they contain truth, they can perfectly serve the work of grace. It is up to you to sort out the teachings proposed to you and weigh their precise value, with the help of the Holy Spirit. This is how the Fathers of the Church made use of the philosophers of their times, in full Christian freedom.

Nature, beyond Ideas and "Phenomena," at the Heart of the Moral Experience

I shall close with a remark that was made to me when I was preparing this paper. I had observed that the question of nature persists and is always turning up in the course of the many concepts, theories, treatments, and critiques it has occasioned over time in the various schools of philosophy and science. It seems that nature designates a basic reality that offers philosophies and sciences a sort of prime matter, beyond their reach yet lurking in the heart of all their undertakings. We see it, for example, rising up today to confront science and technology and to raise problems for ecology and bioethics.

To use Kantian categories, which have to be handled with caution, we shall willingly say that nature belongs to the world of the "nomena," beyond the "phenomena" that the sciences reach, and that there nature joins freedom itself. We do not know whether Kant would have admitted this, but everything leads us to think it was his position.

To return to the debate between Aquinas and Ockham, we shall say that the banishing of nature from the realm of freedom ought to be rethought, and also the separation of the world of the spirit and that of nature, which is ranked with the body and matter by Descartes. Nature is not beneath freedom and the spirit. It is on the same level with them, and even at their source, assuming that in this case we are dealing with a spiritual nature. It is at the origin of the ideas that reason forms and the choices that freedom works in view of the true and the good.

This is of the greatest importance, particularly for moral theology.

First of all, nature enters fully into the moral domain. It is no longer a sort of biological barrier limiting freedom, but becomes once more a source of inspiration whence flow moral rules, from within conscience and reason. Nature designates the image of God as the direct work of the creator in the human spirit, at the heart of its freedom.

It is, then, in the moral experience itself, rather than in scientific experiences in the modern sense, that this nature is most clearly revealed, thanks to the method proper to morality. The latter proceeds not so much by external observation as do the sciences, but rather by reflection about personal action leading us back to its source, to the free will where our commitment to faith and love is engendered.

This is why St. Thomas was able to base his moral theology on a twofold interior foundation:

—first on the natural law, inscribed in the conscience of every person and formulated by the Decalogue in the setting of the Old Covenant,

—then on the Evangelical Law, written by the Holy Spirit in the human heart by means of faith and defined as the very grace of the Holy Spirit operating through charity. Its specific text is the Sermon on the Mount; its instruments are the sacraments and their liturgy.

The moral law thus has its source in the profound interiority of the human being, where the Holy Spirit encounters human nature to heal, vivify, and sanctify it, and to create progressively a dynamic harmony which will find expression chiefly in the fruits of the Spirit according to St. Paul: joy, peace, patience, kindness, goodness, self-control.[8]

8. Cf. Gal 5:22–23.

19 ✌ The Return of the New Law to Moral Theology (1999)

Our object here is briefly to retrace the history of the reintegration of the New Law in Catholic moral teaching, from the deliberations of the Second Vatican Council up to two major recent documents, namely *The Catechism of the Catholic Church* and the encyclical *Veritatis splendor*.

A Foreword: Post-Tridentine Morality

In order more fully to appreciate the history of Catholic moral theology since the Council, and in order to observe the starkly contrasting originality and innovative character of recent Roman publications, it is imperative to take into account preconciliar Catholic moral theory such as was dispensed in the manuals of moral theology in the aftermath of the Council of Trent. The presentation of moral theory that one finds there constituted the common cultural currency of the Church. Molded in the classical manualist tradition, it oversaw the formation of priests in seminaries and the instruction of the Christian people through catechesis and preaching. This approach to morality, characterized by its pastoral orientation to the sacrament of Penance and the resolution of *casus conscientiae* (cases of conscience), even found its way into the Dominican tradition through the addition of a *cursus minor,* or course in practical morality. This was evidenced in a particular way at Fribourg, in the shape of Dominic Prümmer's three-volume manual of moral theology. In order to

Originally published as "Le retour de la Loi nouvelle en morale," in *Praedicando et docendo: Mélanges offerts au Père Liam Walsh* (Fribourg: Editions Universitaires, 1998), 281–93. Original English publication in *The Irish Theological Quarterly* 64 (1999): 3–15. Translated by Hugh Connolly. Edited for publication in *The Pinckaers Reader* by Craig Steven Titus.

avoid any misconception, we should at the outset make it clear that the critique of the manuals of moral theology which we are about to undertake is in no way a rejection of their teaching, but seeks instead to correct their limitations, especially those concerning their relationship to the Gospel.

The following is in large part the plan followed by the manuals in their presentation of moral theology. It is not difficult to discern in them the understanding of Catholic morality that was in vogue in recent centuries. Moral theology is divided into two sections: namely fundamental and special moral theology.

Four tracts constitute fundamental moral theology:

—*Law* is essentially Natural Law, as identified with the Decalogue. Emanating from the will of God, law appears as the source of obligation and thus forms the basis of morality over against human freedom, which it restricts. As St. Alphonsus says, "All is freedom for man except that which the law prohibits."

—*Conscience* interprets, applies, and makes known the moral law; thus it plays the role of interior judge.

—*Human acts* are considered as material for the *casus conscientiae,* a fact which, in turn, results in this type of morality becoming known as *casuistry.*

—*Sins* constitute the raw material of the sacrament of Penance; they are a major preoccupation of post-Tridentine morality, and are thus studied in detail according to their species and their gravity.

The absence of tracts on the Beatitudes and the virtues (except for a brief reference to the theologal virtues in some authors) is worthy of note.

Special moral theology is divided according to the Ten Commandments, to which in turn are added the commandments of the Church, certain prescriptions of canon law, and rules concerning the reception of the sacraments. Thus conceived, moral theory is presented as the domain of strict ethical obligation, which is to be imposed on everyone, and the Decalogue takes the form of a code of commands and prohibitions dictated by God. Morality thus takes on a juridical tone. Accordingly, a correspondent of French television at Rome was able to explain that the moral portion of the *Catechism* constituted the civil code of the Church, which was, in turn, complemented and completed by the penal code!

To moral theory thus presented are added, as if by way of auxiliary disciplines, asceticism and mysticism, which today we prefer to call spirituality or spiritual theology. Asceticism and mysticism deal with the ways of perfection, which go beyond common obligation and are presented as counsels to be followed freely rather than precepts. They are therefore the concern of an elite, usually taken to be those in religious life. Asceticism studies the search for perfection by way of the virtues with the help of ordinary grace, while mysticism presupposes special graces (easily confused with extraordinary phenomena), which are attributed to the gifts of the Holy Spirit.

These are essentially the divisions and categories that have now become classic in moral theology, and have been generally adopted. We should also add that, in tying morality to the will of God as supreme Legislator, this moral theory is above all rational, and therefore makes little recourse to Scripture.

We would be wrong to believe that the manuals were somehow destined henceforth to gather dust on library bookshelves. They were originally composed by theologians of the Society of Jesus who were *au fait* with the ideas of their times. They clung to these ideas with a relentless logic across the span of three centuries. Indeed, the morality of duty as taught in the manuals remains very much alive in the memory of many Christians today. It belongs to the same stable as the theory of the categorical imperative as elucidated by Kant. It is not far from social prohibition theory still used by psychologists and sociologists. In exegesis one also comes across similar categories in the distinction which is often made between ethics, as expressing obligations in the form of imperatives; and parenesis, which puts forward simple exhortations in the shape of spiritual counsels, as is to be seen for instance in the Sermon on the Mount, and those passages classified as parenetical in the apostolic letters. Perhaps we are closer to the thought patterns of the manuals than we sometimes think.

Finally, insofar as our subject is concerned, we should note that in the manuals of moral theology the Law of the Gospel and the Sermon on the Mount never receive more than a cursory mention, often reduced to a footnote. Indeed, the teaching of the Sermon on the Mount, which speaks to the values of the human heart, is ultimately incapable of assimilation by a moral theory centered on legal obligations and external acts, such as murder, adultery, and the like.

The Schema *[De re morali]* and Its Demise at the Council

We can now move on to examine the history of the theme of New Law in moral theology beginning with the Second Vatican Council. It is unquestionably surprising that the Council documents have so little to say—at least in explicit fashion—about moral theology. In fact, the only brief mention is to be found in the decree *Optatam totius:*

Special care should be given to the perfecting of moral theology. Its scientific presentation should draw more fully on the teaching of Holy Scripture and should throw light upon the exalted vocation of the faithful in Christ and their obligation to bring forth fruit in charity for the life of the world.[1]

In fact, the moral question did occupy an important place in preparations for the Council.[2] It was one of the preoccupations of John XXIII. A special commission was charged with compiling a document on morality. It worked according to directives provided by the Holy Office and had to take account of responses to enquiries made among bishops and theological faculties. These consultations provided evidence of a theological malaise in the area of morality and a great desire for renewal. After many discussions and amendments, their labors gave rise to an initial draft entitled *Constitutio de re morali,* dated 1961. Franz Hürth, S.J., was the principal redactor, assisted by Louis-Bertrand Gillon, O.P., and Ermenegildo Lio, O.F.M.

A simple glance at the document reveals that it is situated firmly in the long line of classical manuals of moral theology with their four fundamental tracts: law, conscience, human acts, and sins. A first chapter deals with the foundation of the moral order. It affirms the existence of an objective and absolute moral order. The basis of this moral order is God, who is the author, guardian, judge, and agent of retribution, and more precisely, the divine will, which is the source of moral obligation. (Recent criticisms have borne out the voluntaristic nature of this document.) The will of God is manifested in Natural Law, which is known by reason and in divine positive law, first of all in the Decalogue, which expresses Natural Law, and then in the Law of the Gospel. However, the document is at pains to point out that the latter is not in opposi-

1. *OT,* n. 16.
2. The following information on the schema is taken largely from the doctoral thesis of Pierre D'Ornellas, who has reviewed this section.

tion to Natural Law; rather, the Law of the Gospel contains and perfects Natural Law (n. 4). A listing of the various different errors follows, notably subjectivism and ethical relativism, to which a chapter is devoted.

For the authors of the document it is clear that the moral order that issues from the will of God rests entirely on the Natural Law. The Law of the Gospel serves only to confirm this law and its obligatory character through the authority of the Son of God. If the document grants more space to the New Law than did the manuals, this undoubtedly is due to the demands for renewal, as expressed in the foregoing enquiry. However, this concession does not alter one whit the underlying classical conception of moral theory; on the contrary, it seeks to reinforce it all the more.

Cardinal Döpfner's Critique

It is precisely to the role of the Law of the Gospel in moral theory that the two critiques that interest us here are addressed. The first observations come from Julius Cardinal Döpfner, made during the third session of the Central Commission in February 1962. In a rather long and detailed intervention, the Archbishop of Munich called for a more biblical presentation of morality. He proposed that the articulation of the "moral order"—a term that he noted is more philosophical than biblical—should be more scriptural and should take as its starting point the "salvific action of God in Christ, through whom his sanctificatory will is revealed to us and written on our hearts."

The Cardinal goes on to criticize the manner in which the Natural Law and the New Law are dealt with. The impression is created that unlike the Natural Law, which is known internally by reason, the New Law comes to man and is imposed on him by God from without and that it is "above all a clarification and amplification of Natural Law." The Cardinal suggests that the definition of St. Thomas should be taken up again: "That which is foremost in the Law of the New Testament and in which all its virtue resides, is the grace of the Holy Spirit given by faith in Christ; the New Law is therefore, above all, the grace of the Holy Spirit, which is given to Christ's faithful ones."[3]

The Cardinal laments the fact that nothing is to be said on how the positive legislation given by God in the two Testaments is known. Corresponding to the natural light of reason, he argues, there must also be "the light of faith by

3. *ST* I-II 106.1.

which the law of grace is made known to man." He proposes to use the expression "law of grace" for the New Law. Therefore he distinguishes clearly between Natural Law and New Law. The latter can be considered neither as a mere elucidation of the former nor as its simple fulfillment with the help of grace.

In this intervention we clearly see the beginnings of a line of renewal in the sense of a better biblical grounding for moral theology, and more particularly a revaluation of the New Law in fundamental moral theology, thus avoiding the tendency to reduce it to the treatment of Natural Law.

Le Guillou's Critique

The second intervention criticizing the *De re morali* schema came from Marie-Joseph Le Guillou, O.P. This was a later development, and dates from April 3, 1963, the beginning of the Council. The Dominican's assessment is quite severe:

The reading of *De ordine morali christiano* [he says] is more than disappointing. Dominated by an intellectual climate of conceptualist rationalism and written in a deficient style, which is not that of the great theological tradition, [the document] represents a lack of appreciation of true Christian values. . . . The more essential exhortations of the Gospel and of contemporary thought are radically disregarded.

The criticism gets even more pointed: "The Schema is characterized by an almost total absence of the mystery of Christ and of the New Law given in the Spirit and constituted by love." What is this central mystery?

In one great vision of the mystery of Christ everything could be presented—*the Natural Law, the Christian law of the Old Testament, the interior law* (the New Law) as three aspects of participation in the Law of Christ, in His Mystery, which finds its full realization in glory. Only a presentation of this kind would render Christian moral theology more attractive.

What links therefore should be established between the Natural Law and the New Law? It cannot simply be a question of setting the New Law in opposition to the Commandments because "the Son of Man came to fulfill the precepts of the Decalogue." However we do need a Christocentric morality, based on the New Law "which in turn demands the fulfillment of the Commandments and not vice versa." The schema, on the contrary, "seems entirely built on the internal coherence—one is tempted to say autonomy—of the Natural Law, *as if that were to be the starting point.*"

The fundamental ambiguity of the whole Schema rests on the notion of Divine Law used as a univocal concept. All the statements presuppose, more or less deliberately, a homogenous hierarchical link between Natural Law and supernatural Law, without sufficiently distinguishing the unevenness that exists between these two levels of participation in Divine Law, corresponding to the Natural Law and the supernatural Law.

This primacy of Natural Law is also aggravated by "an extrinsicist and voluntarist conceptualism." The fact that *"the existence of the moral order rests, essentially, on the will of God"* is constantly emphasized. "Exteriority seems to be to the forefront and law is never presented *as a principle of justification.*"

For his part, Le Guillou insists on the internal coherence of the New Law. One might ask: how does he square this with Natural Law? According to him, Divine Law can be understood as

the free intervention of God, calling humanity to share His own life, His beatitude, and to be a constituent part of this supernatural order. By giving man this *super*natural end, he is at the same time given another law, that of a calling which nature does not contain nor does it demand, and which for man will be "Divine" in a manner other than that of Natural Law; a manner that is not only essential, in the sense of participation in the Eternal Law, but also "historic" in the sense of instituted positively by God.

"This supernatural end," he goes on, "does not contradict nature, but, on the contrary, presupposes it, confirms it, and makes it its own."

Le Guillou, therefore, sets himself against the position of *De re morali:* he strives to prove the internal coherence of the supernatural order, whilst the schema, on the other hand, seeks to preserve that of the natural order. He looks forward to a morality founded on Holy Scripture. His ethical reflections on law are inspired by the work of St. Thomas, especially his questions on the New Law. From a morality based on the Commandments, which is to be accomplished with the help of grace, there is a progression toward a morality of grace or of the New Law, which enables and allows the fulfillment of the Commandments. Christian morality as proposed by Le Guillou is ordered by the New Law, an internal law coherent in itself, which awakens a specific calling in man. This morality is Christological and theological. At its core is the grace of the Holy Spirit.

The Failure of the *De Re Morali* Schema

The two aforementioned reports pointed to an important current of thought among the bishops and the theologians of the Council, which was conscious of the need for renewing the way Catholic morality was presented, particularly its biblical dimension, by having recourse to the teaching of St. Thomas on the New Law. We have every reason to believe that the future John Paul II was attentive to this current, but he didn't participate directly in the discussions on the *De re morali* schema.

The criticisms of Cardinal Döpfner and Le Guillou did not obtain the desired effect. Their proposals in favor of the New Law were not heard. Despite later revisions, among which were the interventions of Jean Cardinal Daniélou, the *De re morali* schema was not judged sufficiently ready to be presented to the assembly of Council Fathers. The preoccupation with the relationship between the Church and the modern world had become dominant, which led to the document being sidelined. Apparently the time was not yet ripe; minds had not yet been prepared for the carrying through of the desired renewal of moral theology. This explains the relative silence of Vatican II on moral theology.

An Attempt at Dialogue between Moralists

Unquestionably, Paul VI's encyclical *Humanae vitae* of 1968 played a decisive part in the crisis in moral theology. This encyclical provoked a shock wave, which, in one particular case—the condemnation of artificial means of contraception—led to the calling into question both of the traditional teaching that moral law was based on the Natural Law, and of the manner in which this law was applied. Detaching itself from post-Tridentine morality, a new moral theory gradually developed and resulted in the emergence of proportionalism, which eventually came under scrutiny in the encyclical *Veritatis splendor*. What is perhaps less well known, because of the confidentiality involved, was the remarkable attempt made by Rome, at the instigation of the future Cardinal, Jerome Hamer, to set up a dialogue between those who were referred to as the "innovative moralists" and the "classical moralists," as well as to improve contact with the Magisterium. This took place at a symposium, which was held in March 1981. It brought together moralists and exegetes, patristic scholars and historians, and had as its subject the universal and immutable character of the moral law. It is of interest to our discussion, because its treatment of the New Law provided the framework within which the work of the symposium was to be undertaken. The first part dealt with Holy Scripture and it comprised two contributions, one from A. L. Descamps[4] and the other from Jacques Dupont,[5] dealing with the Sermon on the Mount. The final session took up all the preceding interventions, in order to bring them into the perspective of the Law of the Gospel. It took the form of an exposition by Philippe Delhaye[6] and a further one by myself, "The Universality and Permanence of Moral Laws in the Law of the Gospel."[7] This attempt at rapprochement failed, notably because of difficulties of communication between specialists from different disciplines, and because of the technicality of the language and subject matter with which the moralists were working. The reports were published separately by P. W. Kerber for the German- and English-speaking group, under the title *Sittliche Normen*,[8] and for French-speakers and other participants by myself and C. J. Pinto de Oliveira in the publication *Universalité et permanence des Lois morales*,[9] which followed the plan of the symposium ordered around the New Law.

The Doctrine of the New Law Perfected by St. Thomas Aquinas

Before coming to consider the *Catechism* and the encyclical, it is worth taking a look back at the teaching on the New Law, or the Law of the Gospel, as put forward by Thomas, who devotes three lengthy questions to this in the *prima secundae* (106–8). The definition of this Law is set down in the first article of question 106, and is completed at the beginning of question 108. The very posing of the problem is already significant: is the Law of the Gospel an interior law? Contrary to common opinion, which saw the Law of the Gospel

---

4. "Le Discours sur la montagne: Esquisse de théologie biblique," in Pinckaers and Pinto de Oliveira, eds., *Universalité et permanence des Lois morales* (Fribourg: Editions Universitaires, 1986), 43–72.

5. "Le langage symbolique des directives éthiques de Jésus dans le sermon sur la montagne." Ibid., 74–89.

6. "Le Sermon sur la montagne. Suggestions théologiques et pédagogiques," Ibid., 408–41.

7. "L'universalité et la permanence des lois morales dans la Loi évangélique," Ibid., 442–54.

8. P. W. Kerber, *Sittliche Normen* (Düsseldorf, 1982).

9. Pinckaers and Pinto de Oliveira, *Universalité et permanence des Lois morales*.

as an external law by virtue of the simple fact that the Gospel is a written work (obj. 1), Thomas held that the New Law is a law internal to the human person, although it has its origins externally, in God.

To demonstrate this, Thomas draws on some of the richest texts of Scripture. Firstly, he invokes a passage from Jeremiah, which is a prophecy about the New Testament: "Behold the days are coming when I will make a New Covenant with the House of Israel, I will put my Law into their minds and I will write it on their hearts." This proclamation is confirmed by St. Paul, in Aquinas's view, because, it is taken up again, explicitly, in the Letter to the Hebrews (8:6–13) and applied to the New Covenant established by Christ.

Aquinas also meditates on the Letter to the Romans, where the apostle speaks of a "Law of Faith," since the Justice of God comes to us through faith in Jesus Christ (Rm 3:27), and of a "Law of the Spirit which gives us life in Christ Jesus" (Rm 8:2). In addition Thomas, reading the Word of God with the Fathers, draws inspiration from Augustine's treatise *De Spiritu et Littera,* which is a long meditation on the texts which we have just cited. Here he finds a good definition for the New Law: it is "the presence of the Holy Spirit in the souls of the faithful."

Having established these scriptural and patristic bases, Thomas now sets out to construct a nuanced answer: the New Law is an internal law by virtue of its main element, the grace of the Holy Spirit; it is, nevertheless, external by virtue of certain secondary elements, which are like instruments of this grace. The principal element of the Law of the Gospel is the very same grace of the Holy Spirit, received through faith in Christ and animated by charity.[10] It is, therefore, through faith in Christ and love and along with these, by means of hope and the other virtues, that the Holy Spirit writes the New Law on the hearts and in the lives of the faithful. All the energy of this law comes from the Holy Spirit. Thus the active principle of justification and of sanctification, of forgiveness and of perfection, is within us.

However, because Christ became Flesh, "full of Grace and Truth" as the Prologue to St. John tells us, "it was appropriate that certain realities from the order of the senses should bring to us the grace which flows from the Incarnate Word, and that this interior grace should in turn give rise to those works which submit the flesh to the spirit."[11] These would be considered the sec-

10. *ST* I-II 108.1.   11. *ST* I-II 108.1.

ondary elements of the New Law. Their importance, however, should not be understated. The words of the Gospel, focused on the moral teaching of the Sermon on the Mount would become the specific text of the New Law, as the Decalogue text had been for the Old Law. This is the summit of Scripture, which provides theology with its raw material. Moreover, there are also the sacraments which the Holy Spirit makes use of in order to communicate to us His grace, and these in turn form the basis of the Christian liturgy.

The grace of the Holy Spirit, received through faith in Christ, animated by charity, using the Scriptures and the sacraments, such are the defining elements of the New Law, which were to be taken up again in a more complete fashion in the documents which we are now to consider. Before that, we should at this point add two further historical observations:

The Thomist definition of the New Law is the theological expression of a powerful spiritual current from the thirteenth century, illustrated both by the figures of St. Dominic and St. Francis, and by the Orders which they founded. One might see it as a fitting expression of the particular kind of evangelism that was prevalent in that era. On the one hand, it avoids an excessive spiritualization both of the Gospel, to the detriment of its true meaning, and of ecclesial institutions. On the other hand, it equally avoids a materialization of Scripture, which would obstruct the spiritual sense and the dynamism of the interior life.

The teaching of St. Thomas on the New Law, which renders such an accurate account of the evangelical dimension of morality by placing it in the foreground of the action of the Holy Spirit and the theologal virtues, was by all accounts unsuccessful. From the fourteenth century onward, the understanding of morality evolved under the influence of nominalism, in the direction of a concentration on obligation and the Natural Law. Aquinas's commentators were scarcely interested in these matters. Cajetan (1469–1526), the most widely read of these thinkers, after having dealt at length with the Decalogue and the Natural Law in his commentary on the *Summa,* contents himself, insofar as the New Law is concerned, with advising his readers to learn by heart the exposition of Thomas, because, he says, "no one has spoken so well about these matters as he." This is more or less all that he has to say on the subject. Two centuries later a very popular commentator, Billuart (1685–1757), observes that one did not discuss the New Law in the schools of his time, and continues without further comment. Nonetheless, one does find an interesting commentary on the questions on the New Law in the writings of a Dominican of that era, Vicenzo Patuzzi (1700–69), who was an adversary of St. Alphonsus on the question of probabilism.

All the same, it took until the middle of our own century for a rediscovery of the teaching on the New Law to take shape among theologians and exegetes.[12] It was precisely from this renewal that the *Catechism* and *Veritatis splendor* were later to benefit.

The New Law in the *Catechism of the Catholic Church*

The Catechism of the Catholic Church has the great merit of presenting a veritable synthesis of the corpus of Christian teaching set down in a simple and succinct manner. Its language is accessible without being too technical. Its treatises are peppered with numerous citations, which have been well chosen from Scripture, the Fathers, and spiritual writers; these help to place the reader in contact with the Word of God, and enable one to discover the riches of the Christian inheritance and the experience of the saints.

A simple reading of the table of contents of the *Catechism* shows that in its moral section the post-Tridentine tradition has clearly not been abandoned: the four treatises which make up fundamental moral theology are still to be found there. They have however been revised and several important articles have been added. The first chapter deals with the dignity of man, created in the image of God, and it begins by reintroducing to moral theology the treatise on beatitude, a tract that had been expelled for some four centuries. The study of human acts is improved by a return to the thought of St. Thomas and by a more positive presentation of the passions or movements of the senses. Next to conscience, one sees the reappearance of a treatise on the human and theologal virtues, followed by the gifts and the fruits of the Holy Spirit. A further chapter is devoted to the social dimension of human action. The third chapter deals with the Law and brings the treatise on grace and justification back into

12. Let us cite some publications: J.-M. Aubert, "Loi et Evangile," *Dictionnaire de Spiritualité* 9 (1976): 966–84; Philippe Delhaye, "La Loi nouvelle dans l'enseignement de Saint Thomas," *Esprit et Vie* 84 (1974): 33–41, 49–54; S. Lyonnet, *Liberté chrétienne et loi nouvelle* (Paris, 1953); S. Pinckaers and L. Rumpf, *Loi et Evangile* (Geneva, 1981); P. R. Regamey, "La Loi nouvelle," *Vie spirituelle* 138 (1984): 28–45; G. Salet, "La loi dans nos cœurs," *NRT* 79 (1957): 449–62, 561–78; J. Tonneau, *La Loi nouvelle (Somme de La Revue des Jeunes)* (Paris, 1981).

the heart of moral theory. (After all, how could one describe Christian action without having some recourse to the notion of grace?) Finally, it also adds an article on the ecclesial dimension of morality. Fundamental moral theology is thus profoundly renewed and in great measure enriched.

The section devoted to the moral law in particular interests us here. It is divided into three parts: the Natural Law, the Old Law, and the New Law, the latter presented as "the perfection here below of the Divine Law, both natural and revealed" (*CCC* n. 1965). The New Law is the work of Christ, which he brought to light in the Sermon on the Mount, and a gift of the Holy Spirit, who turns it into the interior law of faith and of love. The *Catechism* takes up again the definition of Thomas, and explains how this Law fulfills the Old Law, following the categories of the Sermon: by the promise of the Beatitudes, by the interiorization of the Commandments in the heart, by the practice of religious duties "in secret where the Lord alone sees us," and by the Golden Rule. The New Law is presented as a law of love, of grace, and of freedom. It is realized, notably, in the evangelical counsels, which are aimed at promoting the advancement of love and manifesting its fullness. The Law of the Gospel is, therefore, reestablished in its rightful place in fundamental moral theology, as the summit of the Christian moral life toward which all paths and precepts lead.

In order to measure the importance of this change and its consequences one might also look at the articles that deal at greater length with Christian holiness (*CCC* n. 2013-14). They abolish the boundary which once separated post-Tridentine morality from asceticism and mysticism, as outlined in this observation from *Lumen gentium* (n. 40): "The call to the fullness of the Christian life and to the perfection of love is addressed to all those who believe in Christ, whatever their class or status may be." Similarly, the New Law is aimed at all Christians in whom the grace of the Holy Spirit works through faith and love.

As for special moral theology, this poses a deeper problem: should the traditional divisions, as determined by the Ten Commandments, be maintained, or should they be replaced by an exposition of the virtues and the gifts of the Spirit, as set down by Thomas in the *Summa* in his treatise on the New Law? I feel that the solution that was adopted, conserving the divisions according to the Commandments, was the best one for a *Catechism* ultimately destined for the Universal Church, and which therefore had to take into account different traditions. Above all, the *Catechism* could not give the impression that the Church was abandoning the Decalogue, which for so long has constituted the cornerstone of Christian moral teaching; it was necessary, moreover, to revitalize the understanding of the Commandments, which had become too static and negative. The *Catechism* thus attempted to infuse a new dynamism into its account of the Commandments by putting them once more in contact with their corresponding virtues. The outcome was perhaps not exactly perfect, but it was a step in the right direction.

The Encyclical *Veritatis Splendor* and the New Law

The encyclical does not have the same sort of overarching focus as the *Catechism.* By a circumstance one might consider providential, it was issued after the *Catechism,* thus affording it a keener focus. It sets out to answer two stated aims:

1. Polemical: To make the necessary corrections concerning certain theological opinions in morality which were at variance with the doctrine of the Church, and which had become widespread in seminaries and faculties of theology. The encyclical wishes thus to reestablish a more solid moral teaching which is faithful to the greater tradition.

2. Corrective: To improve the teaching of moral theology by reestablishing a thorough and sustained contact between Catholic moral theory and the Gospel (chap. I).

The encyclical does not set out to give a complete exposition of the doctrine of the New Law, but it does draw on some of its elements according to its needs and within its own perspectives. By and large we can say that the work of the encyclical consisted in reestablishing the two pillars of Christian morality: in the first place the Decalogue, which was threatened in its solidity by new theories; and secondly the Sermon on the Mount, the key text of Evangelical Law, for too long neglected by post-Tridentine tradition.

The encyclical suggests, from the outset, a reinterpretation of the Decalogue, which should be subtle, but nonetheless radical, beginning with the love of God and neighbor. It holds that the Commandments seek a *response of love* from us rather than strict legal obedience (*VS* n. 10). This reintroduces into moral theology, right from the start of Christian life, that dynamism of love which carries us toward perfection. Next it deals with the Sermon on the Mount (*VS* n. 15–16), which, with reference to St. Augustine's Commentary on the same, it describes as the "Magna Carta," the great charter of biblical morality. It shows how Jesus brings to fulfillment the Commandments of God by interiorizing their demands and making them more radical in accordance with the Sermon's teaching: "You have heard it said . . . but, I say to you . . ." Deepening our interpretation of the episode concerning the rich young man who was dissatisfied with mere observation of the Commandments, the encyclical explains that Jesus perceived in him "a yearning after that fullness which goes beyond a legalistic interpretation of the Commandments," by inviting him to enter into the way of perfection, which is taught in the Beatitudes. The latter are not separated from the Commandments, nor are they opposed to them; but they constitute invitations to follow Christ and to live in communion with Him. In effect, the Beatitudes "are a sort of *self-portrait of Christ*." Thus the encyclical repositions the Sermon, and with it the New Law at the heart of Christian morality; it furthermore reestablishes the close link with the Decalogue, which the Sermon brings to perfection.

In chapter II, at number 45, after having dealt with the Natural Law—the writing of the Eternal Law in the heart of man—the encyclical again explicitly takes up the idea of the New Law set forth by Thomas, as gift of God. It is an internal law, written not with ink, but with the Spirit of the living God. It quotes from St. Thomas's *Commentary on the Epistle to the Romans* (8:2), where Aquinas sketches the definition of the New Law, which he will clarify in his *Summa*. This law is "either the Holy Spirit, or else the very effect of the same Holy Spirit."

So we can see then that both the *Catechism* and the encyclical invite us to give a central place in Christian morality to the New Law and to the Sermon on the Mount. In addition to the Sermon we should also mention those passages from the epistles which set forth the apostolic moral catechesis, such as Romans 12–15. The *Catechism* (*CCC* n. 1971) is stronger on this point than the encyclical (*VS* n. 26).

Conclusion

Having arrived at the end of our historical survey, we can take a look back at the past thirty years and admire the work of the Spirit. The Spirit has traced a straight and unerring path through an era which encompasses the failure of the *De re morali* schema, the criticisms of it made in the name of the New Law, the failure of the symposium in 1981 and its attempt at dialogue, and even the failure in some respects of St. Thomas himself. At last, after seven centuries of negligence, the Law of the Gospel now finds its true place at the heart of Christian morality, thanks to the *Catechism* and the encyclical.

All the same we should not be tempted to believe that everything has now been resolved. Few commentators in fact have been attentive to the renewal of Christian morality and to all of its implications. A pointer to ongoing difficulties may be seen in the fact that the thematic index in the French edition of the *Catechism* (which has been copied by the Italian edition) made no mention of the Sermon on the Mount, even though several articles are devoted to it (*CCC* n. 1967–70). The German edition took care to compose a new index, but the term "Bergpredigt" is not to be found, nor indeed is the equivalent term in the Dutch edition, which follows the German and English, even though the biblical index does manage to include 139 quotations from chapters 5–7 of St. Matthew. So the key feature of the New Law, the Sermon on the Mount, does not yet seem to be part and parcel of our current reflection on morality. Our mental categories are still lagging behind. We can only pray to the Holy Spirit that we might be granted the grace of rediscovering this Gospel pearl more precious than all the textbooks of moral theology, this seed of the Word of the Lord, which alone is capable of giving moral theology new strength and life.

20 ∾ Morality and the Movement of the Holy Spirit

Aquinas's Doctrine of *Instinctus*   (1991)

Distrust of Instinct

We would like to tackle the role of spiritual instinct in Christian ethics, especially as it appears in St. Thomas's ethics. Instead of associating morality and instinct, we are accustomed to opposing them and to distrusting instinct. Is it not the role of ethics to teach us to fight against our instincts? Is not its goal to restrain them through precepts and interdictions, through the virtues of moderation, chastity, and courage? To place instinct at the heart of Christian ethics seems to introduce a subversive principle into it.

The issue becomes more complicated when one realizes that modern moralists have a deep distrust—which we could qualify as instinctive—for the very term "instinct." For example, St. Thomas's translators feel uneasy with his frequent use of the word, especially when it refers to the action of the Holy Spirit. They often look for alternative words, such as "impulse," in order to avoid the misunderstandings that they fear.[1]

Even some recent commentators, like E. Schillebeeckx, who are very experienced and even audacious, in their own ways express a certain distrust. In

---

Originally published as "L'instinct et l'Esprit au coeur de l'éthique chrétienne," in *Novitas et Veritas vitae* (Fribourg, 1991), 213–24. Translated and edited for publication in *The Pinckaers Reader* by Craig Steven Titus.

1. In the last century Father Drioux, in his translation of the *Summa theologiae* (Paris, 1852), translated *instinctus* as *impulsion*. The more recent translations are more literal. The same difficulty appears in German. The *Thomasausgabe,* referring to the gifts, translates *instinctus* as *Antrieb* rather than *Instinkt.* In English, "impulse" is preferred.

his long and interesting review of the book by Max Seckler *Instinkt und Glaubenwille nach Thomas von Aquin,* Schillebeeckx writes: "since it concerns in the first place a historical analysis, the term *instinctus* doesn't frighten us. [Nonetheless] a modern reflection on faith will rightly avoid it. 'Instinct and religion' evokes today a totally different level of thought and, moreover, the word *instinctus (motio)* doesn't suit us particularly well in a more personalist perspective. But it does concern Thomas's conception of faith, such as it should appear today in a contemporary conception."[2]

Instinct and Freedom

In choosing this topic, we were urged on by a certain intellectual instinct, which suggested to us that St. Thomas's doctrine on instinct was richer and maybe more relevant today than we had thought. Furthermore, we should not be hindered by lexical difficulties, which might be a sign of a deeper problem that we must address.

We have been encouraged to pursue this perspective by an idea expressed by J. H. Walgrave in the conclusion of his interesting article, "*Instinctus Spiritus Sancti:* An Attempt to Interpret St. Thomas."[3] In his final synthesis, the author makes the following observation:

The instinct (of the Holy Spirit) comes from outside but works from inside: it is *exterior* by its origin, but *interior* by its way of working within us. The more perfect its work, the more interiorized it becomes; and our will and the Holy Spirit work together as if they were forming a unique principle. The growth of the motion received by our spirit does not diminish the very motion of freedom. Indeed, under the New Law, the instinct of the Holy Spirit becomes in us our own instinct. The instinct of the Holy Spirit builds up the very movement of the free will. This highlights, in the context of the analogy that regulates the use of the word "instinct," the radical opposition between the highest and the lowest position on the scale of analogates. To be moved by natural instinct is a sign of a lack of freedom; to be moved by an instinct led by the Holy Spirit is the sign of a growing freedom, which belongs to God's children.[4]

2. E. Schillebeeckx's book review of Max Seckler's *Instinkt und Glaubenwille nach Thomas von Aquin,* in *RSPT* (1964): 393.

3. J. H. Walgrave, "*Instinctus Spiritus Sancti.* Een proeve tot Thomas-interpretatie," *Ephemerides Theologiae Lovanienses* 5 (1969): 417–31.

4. Ibid., 430.

Walgrave gives us direction for our research: what is the nature of this instinct of the Holy Spirit which, rather than hindering our freedom, favors it and allows it to grow? The type of instinct that we are dealing with here is a spiritual instinct, which is very different from animal instinct. The essence of the question is found in the relation between such an instinct and the conception of human freedom. Let us ask only a little question of Fr. Walgrave: he speaks of a "radical opposition" between the lowest and the highest form in the use of the word "instinct." Wouldn't such an opposition risk breaking the analogy? Does it correspond perfectly to St. Thomas's thought? It is useful to highlight in our perspective the peculiarity of spiritual instinct in its conjunction with human freedom.

The Use of the Word "Instinct" in St. Thomas

Before tackling our question directly, it is useful to take a look at Aquinas's texts. Let us start with some statistical observations. Fr. Busa's *Index thomisticus* lists 298 occurrences of the word *instinctus*. If we counted them properly, 51 of them involve the expression *instinctus Spiritus Sancti,* and about 30 more speak of a divine instinct, referring to prophecy among other things. More than 50 instances entail man in his moral life, the motion of the will in the discernment of good and evil, and the relationship with law. About 15 refer to the demon's instinct, which is the cause of sin through temptation. There are more than 50 that imply animal instinct. This simple categorization shows us that references to the spiritual and moral life constitute the bulk of Aquinas's usage of *instinctus.* Apparently St. Thomas, in his vocabulary and his conceptualization, was not as tied to animal instinct as we are.

Let us enter into our subject now. An evolution has been observed in St. Thomas's use of the word *instinctus.* Expressions such as "divine instinct" and "instinct of the Holy Spirit" multiply in his mature works, particularly in the *Summa theologiae.* There this term plays a much more important role than in his rebuttal of semipelagianism in the *Commentary on the Sentences.* Aquinas builds upon his deep reflection on grace and the formation of faith thanks to a more careful reading of St. Paul and St. Augustine; moreover he employs the help of one of Aristotle's texts, which speaks of those who are moved by a divine instinct which outstrips reason.[5]

5. "The Philosopher says in the chapter *On Good Fortune* (*Ethic. Eudem.,* vii, 8; 1248a, n.

The Gifts As "Instincts of the Holy Spirit"

As a matter of fact, we find the highest concentration of the word "instinct" and its more typical use in question 68 of the *prima secundae*, which St. Thomas dedicates to the gifts of the Holy Spirit. That is where Aquinas defines the gifts of the Holy Spirit as *instinctus divinus* and where he exhibits a preference for the expressions *"moveri quodam superiori instinctu Spiritus Sancti"* (a. 2 ad 2), and *"sequi instinctum Spiritus Sancti."*[6]

Someone might claim that this question is an exceptional case. In fact, subsequent theology has rather minimized the importance of the Thomistic theory on the gifts of the Holy Spirit, under the influence of the separation between morality and mystical theology. Certain thinkers have restricted the gifts to mysticism and have questioned their necessity. Did not Dom Lottin, an excellent historian of St. Thomas, after rethinking this issue, claim that the theologal virtues were sufficient for Christian life in the order of grace, that the doctrine of the gifts was superfluous, and that Thomas had supported it only because he was dependent on his time, without fully believing in it?[7]

The Doctrine of the Gifts as the Apex of St. Thomas's Morality

On the contrary, from our perspective, it seems that in his study of the gifts of the Holy Spirit, St. Thomas reaches the apex of his theological reflection and of his effort to account for the best of Christian experience, in the light of Scripture and tradition.

Here are two reasons why we came to this conclusion.

Because of the Originality of the Doctrine

The first article of question 68 communicates one of Thomas's discoveries. In the long theological argument on the distinction between the gifts and

---

4ff.) that for those who are moved by Divine instinct, there is no need to take counsel according to human reason, but only to follow their inner promptings, since they are moved by a principle higher than human reason." *ST* I-II 68.1.

It is interesting to note what Marcel Proust says about instinct in the literary domain (cf. "Le temps retrouvé," in *A la recherché du temps perdu*, Bibliotéque de la Pléiade [Paris: Gallimard, 1983], 893; cf. 879).

6. *ST* I-II 68.2 corpus et ad 3; 68.3 corpus; 68.4 corpus.

7. Odon Lottin, *Morale fondamentale* (Tournai, 1954), vol. 1, 427–34.

the virtues—an argument which questions the very nature and existence of the gifts—St. Thomas states first the different opinions that have arisen since St. Augustine and then refers to an important illumination that he had while he was meditating on the text of Isaiah 11, where the enumeration of gifts are found.[8] He noticed that Isaiah does not use the word gifts, but rather *spiritus*, *spiritus sapientiae et intellectus*, etc. This was a revelation for Thomas: what we call gifts are inspirations of the Holy Spirit. He explains: like any inspiration, the gifts define a motion coming from above, from outside, namely from God who takes the initiative, whereas virtue, in the literal meaning of the word, enables us to act from ourselves. More precisely, the gift is a disposition to receive the action of the Holy Spirit, which penetrates to the very heart of our spirit, our freedom, and our virtues, in order to give us a superior impulse in the form of inspiration. In that way we can achieve this unique conjunction between God's action and ours, of which Fr. Walgrave writes: "The more perfect the work of the Holy Spirit (namely the inspiration), the more it is interiorized and the more our will and the Holy Spirit work together (with our virtues), as if they formed a common principle."

This is the peculiar effect of inspiration or of the gifts: to achieve the unity of action between the superior principle, which is God's Spirit, and the interior principles which are the virtues, at the level of our free and reasonable will, at the source of our actions.

Now, the word "instinct" is perfect, according to St. Thomas, to describe such an action moved by inspiration: it refers to an interior impulse, whose origin is nevertheless exterior, or rather superior, such as the action of the Creator in animals. In order to be applied to the action of the Holy Spirit, however, the word instinct has to undergo a major transformation: it is a spiritual instinct, a Spirit that inclines us in a very personal way toward the truth and the divine goods that are revealed to us. In his commentaries on the Romans and Galatians, St. Thomas quotes the example of the vocation that can be caused by an exterior calling, as in Peter's, Andrew's, or Saul's case, or by an interior calling, "which is nothing other than a certain instinct of the soul *(quidam mentis instinctus)* by which God moves the human heart to give its assent to faith or to virtue." One approach does not exclude the other, however, because

8. "*Et requiescet super eum Spiritus Domini: spiritus sapientiae et intellectus, spiritus consilii et fortitudinis, spiritus scientiae et pietatis; et replebit eum spiritus timoris Domini.*" *ST* I-II 68.1.

[the exterior calling usually gives rise to the corresponding spiritual "instinct."]

This leads us to a methodological remark. In order to understand the nature of the spiritual instinct of which St. Thomas writes, should we not invert our usual method, which starts from the representation of the animal instinct? Otherwise we risk never overcoming it; we might continue to imagine the instinct of the human being as always blind and determined. Would it not be better to reflect directly on the spiritual experience, so as to discern in it the action of the Holy Spirit? [The inspiration (both an impulse and an illumination) that deserves to be called "instinct" acts immediately, surely, with a superior origin and goal, as in the case of a vocation or a conversion. We know that this method is the opposite of that of St. Thomas, who likes to describe the most spiritual movements with examples from the material world, as in his study on the unfolding of contemplation.[9] Why could we not start from the other side of the scale of analogy, since we have more difficulty than he does in seeing God's work in the physical or animal world and we risk remaining entangled in it? In that way, we would see more clearly how this doctrine on the gifts of the Holy Spirit is the expression of Christian experience, and even of the personal experience of St. Thomas. Indeed, we think that an original idea, such as his definition of the gifts, can only come, like a spark, at the heart of a direct experience, in the passionate contact with the reality that we examine.[10]

Because of Its Extension to Morality as a Whole in Relationship with the Virtues

Let us tackle the second reason supporting the importance of the doctrine on the gifts of the Holy Spirit in St. Thomas; it shows us the relevance of the spiritual instinct of which he speaks when referring to the gifts. We recognize this reason when we simply look at the structure of the *Summa* and observe the importance given to the gifts of the Holy Spirit. The gifts are related directly to the Evangelical Law that St. Thomas defines—in a very original

---

9. *ST* II-II 180.6.

10. St. Thomas has a different representation of nature from ours. For him, nature is still in harmony with the world of the spirit. He considers it permeated with divine action; therefore he uses its movements as examples to talk about those of the spirit. Modern thought is characterized by rupture, by the opposition between spirit and nature, which is reduced to measurable phenomena. In such thinking, the analogy between nature and spirit does not work. However, if we start from spiritual experience, we shall discover in creatures with which we have connatural relationships the deep impulses that connect them to God.

way—as the grace of the Holy Spirit, which is received through faith in Christ and which is active through charity. He transformed a law that appeared as exterior—as the text of the Gospels in the common view—into an interior law. More precisely, this law was *indita,* inscribed by the Holy Spirit in the heart of the faithful, which highlights once more that unique relationship between an exterior principle, God's Spirit, and our personal interiority where faith and charity are formed. At this point, we need to suggest an important clarification: the type of exteriority concerning the Holy Spirit and the New Law, as in the case of the spiritual instinct, is not the one which makes us different from material objects; it is rather the exteriority or otherness which forms our relationship with God (or with our neighbor) when we believe in Him and love Him, the exteriority which distinguishes people and then reunites them in friendship and love. Therefore, we can discern the nature of the spiritual instinct involved in the Law that the Holy Spirit inscribes in us, and in the relationship between the gifts and the experience of faith and love.

The range of the action of the gifts in St. Thomas's morality appears clearly through the table of contents of the *Summa theologiae.* Aquinas associates one gift of the Holy Spirit with each virtue. In so doing, he clearly shows that in his view the gifts have a general effect in morality and in the life of Christians. Thus, the gifts are not restricted to the elite; neither do they belong to a particular science like mystical theology, as it was later believed. St. Thomas clearly states that the gifts are necessary for salvation and that their function is to help us to act in a perfect way, namely to help us grow toward perfection through the virtues, starting with faith, hope, and charity.

The coordination between gifts and virtues—understood as vital and dynamic principles—is important for our study. It shows that this spiritual instinct formed in us by the gifts does not act in a sporadic way, through sudden inspirations, but in a constant way, supporting the enduring patience required by the practice and progress of virtues. We could compare it to the plant's instinct, which directs it toward the sun, which makes the sap rise in spring and lets it flow until the fruit ripens. Even the blossoming of flowers, which appears to occur quite suddenly, has been in preparation for a long time. Likewise the spiritual instinct, formed in us in our initial yes to a vocation, continues its inspiring work in the secret of the soul, all throughout our life, if we are faithful to it. This spiritual instinct guides our choices, suggests initiatives, guards us from dangers, and helps us to surmount errors. The same

IMP.

observation is true for any Christian life that is animated by faith and charity.

More deeply, would not the spiritual instinct indicate the implementation of God's plans in our life, their penetration into our heart of which St. Paul speaks? They go beyond our ideas and our projects. But don't they nevertheless become ours through faith, which reveals them; through hope, which allows us to desire them; through charity, which attracts us to the point of making us able to leave everything to fulfill them?

The relationship between the virtues and the gifts teaches us as well that the instinct of the Holy Spirit, which acts through the gifts, is not blind even if it goes beyond human reason. The list of the gifts clearly shows that they bring us a light: such are the gifts of understanding and of knowledge, which perfect faith and provide it with the *intellectus fidei* that is a solid and firm perception of revealed realities and goes beyond words and appearances; the gift of counsel, which is particularly useful for moral theologians, and develops prudential judgment through connaturality; and finally the gift of wisdom that St. Thomas must have appreciated very particularly, since his major work is one of the major models of sapiential construction. We even guess that Aquinas must have harbored this work in his mind long before writing it, that he felt attracted to it by a certain spiritual instinct, maybe even since his childhood; but he certainly experienced in writing his masterpieces that the help of the Holy Spirit did not spare him the need for reason, for effort in his work, and for patience in research, reflection, and discussion.

Thus, through the gifts associated with the virtues, Christian life can really become a life according to the Spirit, as St. Paul expounds it in the Epistle to the Romans, on which Thomas wanted to commentate a second time in order to prepare himself to write the *Summa theologiae.*

Why Moral Theologians Have Neglected the Doctrine on the Gifts and Why They Are Reluctant to Use the Word Instinct

We still have to say a few words about an important problem: how can we explain why St. Thomas's doctrine on the gifts of the Holy Spirit and on the New Law has elicited so little response, including in his commentators and in the modern moral theologians who wrote *ad mentem sancti Thomae?* More precisely: why does the word *instinctus*—the very word that Thomas chose to describe the gifts in their spontaneous qualities—raise even today such distrust that one tends to avoid it?

The reason is very deep. It refers to the conception of freedom—and thus the conception of man—and afterwards the conception of morality that has been formed since the sixteenth century. We have, on the one hand, the freedom of indifference, implemented by nominalism, and on the other hand, the freedom of quality or perfection, which belonged to St. Thomas. For him, freedom comes from intelligence and will, the latter of which is the faculty to desire and to love. Freedom grafts itself onto a spiritual nature, which is moved by what we can call an instinct for truth and love, notably expressed in the spontaneous desire for beatitude. These converging aspirations form what Thomas called at times the *instinctus rationis,* particularly in question 68, which is dedicated to the gifts of the Holy Spirit.[11] This "instinct" expresses itself in the inclinations toward truth and good, which preside over natural law and tie together the five inclinations of which they are formed, according to the *Summa* (I-II 94.2).

Fifty years later, however, William of Ockham directly attacked St. Thomas by defining freedom as an indifferent choice between opposites. He saw it as a sort of absolute beginning, independent of any movement of reason and any natural inclination. He supported this thesis by claiming that we are perfectly free to follow or to refuse the inclination to beatitude, to being, and to life, and that freedom appeared even more clearly through resistance and denial. He thus broke the connection between freedom and nature, as well as the connection with all the things proceeding from nature that could be called inclinations, attractions, or instincts. As a consequence, people would marginalize nature and all that comes from it in an area considered inferior to freedom, to reason, and to spirit. From then on, the natural inclinations could only be blind, irrational, and threatening for freedom; similarly the instincts were con-

---

11. Fr. Walgrave seems to have been frightened by this expression. He writes in a footnote of his interesting article on the instinct of the Holy Spirit: "The expression *'instinctus rationis'* is rather surprising. In the previous article, Thomas focused on the fact that 'inspiration' and 'instinct' refer to a movement coming from an exterior source, as opposed to the movement of reason. It is possible that St. Thomas used this word by mistake, under the influence of the opposition that he would stress later with the *'instinctus Spiritus Sancti.'* However, we also have to take into account Thomas's freedom in his word choice on the basis of the play of analogy. Since reason is fundamentally different from will and the powers of execution, it is exterior in a certain sense and acts as if it came from an exterior source. This way of speaking is certainly misleading, but it is not forbidden by Thomas's language rules. In another context, he speaks for example of the desires that are caused *'ex instinctu cogitationum nostrarum' (In Ephesios,* 2, lect.1, *in fine)"* (Walgrave, *"Instinctus Spiritus Sancti,"* 428, footnote 36).

sidered inferior and confined to human animality. This conception favored the formation of the moralities of obligation founded on the imperatives issued by the arbitrariness of divine will. As a logical result, the compulsory commandments would predominate over the virtues, including charity; as for the gifts of the Holy Spirit, moral theologians would no longer talk about them. This ethical voluntarism, united with the logical rationalism that goes with it, would result in the separation between an increasingly conceptualized theology and the spiritual experience, as well as the relegation of mystical theology and spirituality to the margins of morality. We can add that the emotions were relegated to the chapter on the obstacles to voluntariness,[12] in spite of St. Thomas's long, original, and very positive study, which, through the analysis of love, desire, and joy, prepared for his description of spiritual progress and of union with God.

Rediscovering the Spiritual Instinct

In this debate that involves so many issues, the question of instinct appears to raise a fundamental problem: are we able to rediscover in human beings— beyond rationalistic reason and voluntaristic freedom, with their categories upon which we are still dependent—the existence of a spiritual instinct which leads us toward truth and good with the spontaneity of a natural impetus? Thus are we able to prepare ourselves to receive again the impulses of the Holy Spirit that we dare call, according to St. Thomas's definition of the gifts, the "instinct of God"? Indeed the Spirit makes us groan toward God like newborn children who call God "Abba! Father!" Moreover, the Spirit urges us to worship God, as is fitting according to the gift of piety, which completes the virtue of justice.[13]

If the word instinct still frightens us, we could rephrase the same question by focusing on the source of morality. Is morality a barrier, which restrains our freedom from the outside, like a constraint coming from God or society to prevent us from harming our neighbor? Or does the source of morality dwell in us like a birthright, established at the very origin of our freedom by God, who modeled us in his image to make us seek Him? This source belongs to us,

12. In his Thomist manual, even when it was updated, Fr. Prümmer still accepted that emotions had only negative potential.

13. *ST* II-II 121.1.

since it flows from our inner self and it allows us to be and to act in truth and goodness; at the same time, this source does not belong to us, because it flows as a continuous gift from God, who grants us the greatest gift, the Holy Spirit, according to the teaching of the Lord to the Samaritan: "the water that I shall give him will become in him a spring of water welling up to eternal life";[14] or: "as the scripture has said, 'Out of his heart shall flow rivers of living water.' Now this he said about the Spirit, which those who believed in him were to receive."[15]

We will stop here, because there is no better way to end this presentation than this invitation of St. John, who was the contemplative evangelist and, it seems, the one that St. Thomas preferred.

14. Jn 4:14.
15. Jn 7:38–39.

Bibliography of Servais-Théodore Pinckaers, O.P.

Compiled by John Berkman and Craig Steven Titus

BOOKS

1. *Le renouveau de la morale.* Tournai: Castermcan, 1964. (RM)

   (Italian translation, Turin: Boral, 1968.)
   (Spanish translation, Estella: Verbo Divino, 1971.)

   "Le renouveau de la théologie morale." *Vie intellectuelle* 27 (October 1956): 1–21.

   "Qu'est-ce que le bonheur?" *Vie spirituelle* 488 (November 1962): 507–24.

   "Recherche de la signification véritable du terme 'spéculatif.'" *NRT* 81 (July–August 1959): 673–95. (significant revisions)

   "Le rôle de la fin dans l'action morale selon saint Thomas." *RSPT* 45 (1961): 393–412.

   "La vertu est tout autre chose qu'une habitude." *NRT* 82 (April 1960): 387–403. (some revisions)

   ("Virtue Is Not a Habit," trans. Bernard Gilligan. *Cross Currents* (Winter 1962), 65–81.)

   "L'espérence de L'Ancien Testament est-elle la même que la nôtre?" *NRT* 77 (1955): 785–99. (revised)

   "La nature vertueuse de l'espérance, de Pierre Lombard à saint Thomas." *RTh* 58 (1958): 405–42; 623–44.

   "Peut-on ésperer pour les autres." *Mélanges de Science Religieuse* (1959). (revised)

   "Der Sinn für die Freundschaftsliebe als Urtatsache der thomistischen Ethik." *Sein und Ethos*, ed. Paulus M. Englehardt. Mainz: Matthias-Grünewald-Verlag, 1963.

2. *La faim de l'Evangile.* Paris: Téqui, 1977. (FE)

   "La vie intérieure." *Kerit* 1 (1975): 5–14.

   "Aime et fais ce que tu veux!" *Kerit* 6 (1976): 7–19.

   "Vous a-t-on déjà parlé du courage?" *Kerit* 5 (1975): 28–42.

   "Etre chaste aujourd'hui?" *Kerit* 2 (1975): 28–36.

   "Pour une théologie du repos." *Kerit* 3 (1975): 18–29.

"C'est aujourd'hui Dimanche." *Kerit* 4 (1975): 19–27.
"Du nouveau sur la Vierge Marie?" *Sources* 3 (1977): 12–17.

3. *La quête du bonheur.* Paris: Téqui, 1979. (PH)

(*The Pursuit of Happiness—God's Way: Living the Beatitudes.* New York: Alba House, 1998.)

"Le Sermon sur la montagne." *Kerit* 11 (1976): 8–21.
"Les beatitudes." *Kerit* 12 (1977): 23–34.
"Bienheureux les pauvres en esprit." *Kerit* 13 (1977): 5–16.
"Heureux les doux." *Kerit* 14 (1977): 18–30.
"Heureux les affligés." *Kerit* 15 (1977): 19–32.
"Heureux ceux qui ont faim et soif de la justice." *Kerit* 16 (1977): 3–17.
"Bienheureux les miséricordieux." *Kerit* 17 (1977): 31–42.
"Heureux les coeurs purs." *Kerit* 18 (1978): 22–35.
"Heureux les pacifiques." *Kerit* 19 (1978): 22–36.
"Heureux les persecutes." *Kerit* 20 (1978): 27–42.
"Les commentaires de saint Augustin et de saint Thomas sur les béatitudes." *Kerit* 21 (1978): 31–41.

4. *La Morale: somma di doveri? legge d'amore?* trans. P. Cozzupoli. Roma: Edizioni "La Guglia," 1982.

5. *Les sources de la morale chrétienne.* Fribourg: Editions Universitaires, 1985. (SCE)

(*The Sources of Christian Ethics.* Washington, D.C.: The Catholic University of America Press, 1995.)

"Existe-t-il une morale chrétienne?" *Sources* 1 (1975): 11–23, 49–59.
"La morale de saint Thomas est-elle chrétienne?" *NV* 51 (1976): 93–107.
"La théologie morale à la période de la grande scolastique." *NV* 52 (1977): 118–31. (an expansion)
"La théologie morale au déclin du moyen âge: le nominalisme." *NV* 52 (1977): 210–21.
("Ockham and the Decline of Moral Theology." *Theology Digest* 26 (1978): 239–41. [summary of longer essay above])
"La théologie morale à l'époque moderne." *NV* 52 (1977): 269–87.
"Morale catholique et éthique protestante." *NV* 53 (1978): 81–95.

6. *La justice évangélique.* Paris: Téqui, 1986. (JE)

"Comment faire du bon pain avec l'Ecriture." *Kerit* 52 (1983): 20–29.
"Le sel de la terre." *Kerit* 24 (1979): 28–42.
"La lumière du monde." *Kerit* 25 (1979): 37–43; 26 (1979): 23–31.
"La justice nouvelle." *Kerit* 27 (1979): 34–43; 28 (1979): 27–36.
"Les préceptes de la justice nouvelle." *Kerit* 29 (1979): 12–21.
"La colère et l'amour fraternel." *Kerit* 33 (1980): 29–37; 34 (1980): 23–29.
"La convoitise." *Kerit* 35 (1980): 36–41; 36 (1981): 13–18.

"L'amour de la vérité." *Kerit* 37 (1981): 14–20; 38 (1981): 22–25.

"La générosité évangélique." *Kerit* 39 (1981): 41–46; 40 (1981): 34–40.

"L'amour plus grand." *Kerit* 41 (1981): 26–31; 42 (1982): 46–50; 43 (1982): 39–47.

"L'Evangile et la liberté." *Kerit* 30 (1980): 25–34; 31 (1980): 27–32; 32 (1980): 20–26.

"De l'obligation à l'admiration." *Kerit* 59 (1984): 25–32.

"L'Evangile et la prière." *Kerit* 48 (1983): 22–35.

"Prier sans jamais se lasser." *Kerit* 57 (1984): 36–41.

"Prière du soir." *Kerit* 49 (1983): 34–37.

7. *Ce qu'on ne peut jamais faire.* Fribourg: Editions Universitaires, 1986. (PJF)

"Le cas du Dr Augoyard." *Sources* 9 (1983): 193–200.

"Le problème de l'Intrinsece Malum. Esquisse historique." *Freiburger Zeitschrift für Philosophie und Theologie* 29 (1982): 373–88. Reprinted in Pinckaers and Pinto de Oliveira, eds. *Universalité et permanence des Lois morales.* Fribourg: Editiones Universitaires, 1986, 277–90. (This article is a resume, "giving the essentials" of a much longer study published in PJF.)
("A Historical Perspective on Intrinsically Evil Acts [1986]." Essay 11 in *The Pinckaers Reader.*)

"La question des actes intrinsèquement mauvais et le proportionalisme." *RTh* 80 (1982): 181–212.
("Revisionist Understandings of Actions in the Wake of Vatican II [1982]." Essay 12 in *The Pinckaers Reader.*)

"La question des actes intrinsèquement mauvais." *RTh* 84 (1984): 618–24.

"A propos du volontarisme dans le jugement moral." *RTh* 85 (1985): 508–11.

"Università delle lege morale e libertà." *La scuola cattolica* 115 (1987): 591–609.

8. *La prière chrétienne.* Fribourg: Editions Universitaires, 1989.

9. *La grâce de Marie.* Paris: Mediaspaul, 1989. (GM)

"L'Ave Maria." *Kerit* 74 (1987): 5–10.

"L'Annonciation à Marie." *Kerit* 75 (1987): 3–8.

"La salutation angélique selon saint Thomas d'Aquin." *Kerit* 76 (1987): 15–23.

"La grâce de Marie." *Kerit* 77 (1987): 23–32.

"L'excellence de Marie." *Kerit* 78 (1988): 9–16.

"Le fruit de Marie." *Kerit* 79 (1988): 3–11.

"Sainte Marie, Mère de Dieu." *Kerit* 80 (1988): 4–10.

"L'intercession de Marie." *Kerit* 81 (1988): 3–7.

"Ce que Dieu en pense." *Kerit* 46 (1982): 3–4.

10. *L'Evangile et la morale.* Fribourg: Editions Universitaires, 1989. (EM)

(Italian translation, *La Parola e la coscienza.* Torino: Società editrice internazionale, 1991.)

(Spanish translation, *El Evangelio y la Moral.* Barcelona: Eiunsa, 1992.)

First Part (at L'Evangile et la morale)

1. "Morale et Evangile." *Sources* 14 (1989): 249–60.
2. "Esquisse d'une morale chrétienne. Ses bases: la Loi évangélique et la loi naturelle." *NV* 55 (1980): 102–25.

   Italian translation, "La legge evangelica e la legge naturale nella morale cristiana." *Renovatio* 13 (1978): 356–81.
3. "La Loi évangélique, vie selon l'Esprit, et le Sermon sur la montagne." *NV* 60 (1985): 217–28.
4. "L'agir chrétien et ses dimensions selon le Sermon sur la montagne." *Sources* 12 (1986): 97–106.
6. "Lecture positive et lecture 'réelle' de la Bible." *Sources* 3 (1977): 108–18.
7. "La morale chrétienne et ses sources: Ecriture, Tradition et Magistère." *Anthropotes* (1987): 25–42.

Second Part

1. "La béatitude dans l'éthique de saint Thomas." *Studi tomistici* 25 (1984): 80–94.
2. "Amour de Dieu, amour unique." *Sources* 5 (1979): 105–17.
3. "Faut-il encore des moines après Vatican II?" *Sources* 2 (1976): 1–13.
4. "Ce que le Moyen-Age pensait du mariage." *Vie Spirituelle Supplément* (May 1967): 413–40.
5. "La chasteté: de la servitude à la liberté." *Sources* 11 (1985): 97–106. [in collaboration]
6. "Les conseils évangéliques et la morale chrétienne." *Sources* 12 (1986): 249–54; 13 (1987): 9–12.
7. "Convertir la violence." *Sources* 10 (1984): 1–11.

Third Part

1. "Etre d'Eglise." *Sources* 2 (1976): 177–87. [in collaboration]
2. "L'Esprit dans la Loi nouvelle. Esprit et institution." *NV* 62 (1987): 242–62.
3. "Le mystère de l'obéissance et de l'autorité dans l'Eglise." *Sources* 3 (1977): 245–56. [in collaboration]
4. "Comment être chrétien aujourd'hui? Une étude du livre *Etre chrétien* de Hans Küng." *NV* 54 (1979): 134–56.
5. "Suivre sa conscience." *Sources* 9 (1983): 97–102.
6. "Le cas de la conscience erronée." *Sources* 11 (1985): 55–62.
7. "Le jugement moral sur les problèmes de la vie naissante." *NV* 63 (1988): 254–71.
7a. "Sommes-nous moraux de naissance? Les relations entre la morale et l'économie." *La gestion, carrefour de l'économie et de l'éthique.* Fribourg, 1990.
11. *La morale catholique.* Paris: Cerf, 1991.

(Morality: The Catholic View, with a preface by Alasdair MacIntyre. South Bend, Ind.: St. Augustine's Press, 2001.)
12. *La Vie selon l'Esprit. Essai de Théologie spirituelle selon saint Paul et saint Thomas d'Aquin.* Luxembourg: Saint-Paul, 1996.
    Italian translation, *La Vita spirituale del cristiano.* Milan: Jaca Book, 1995.
13. *Un grand chant d'amour. La Passion selon saint Matthieu.* Saint-Maur: Socomed Madiation, 1997.
14. *La Spiritualité du martyre.* Versailles: Editions St. Paul, 2000.
15. *A l'école de l'admiration.* Versailles: Editions St. Paul, 2001.
16. *La béatitude* (Thomas d'Aquin. *Somme Théologique* Ia–IIae, qq. 1–5. Traduction française, notes et appendices). Editions le Revue des jeunes. Paris: Cerf, 2001.

DISSERTATIONS

Le "Surnaturel" du P. De Lubac. S.T.L. Thesis. La Sarte, 1952.
La Vertu d'espérance de Pierre Lombard à St. Thomas d'Aquin. S.T.D. Thesis. Angelicum, 1958.

EDITED BOOKS

1. With six others. *La souffrance, valeur chrétienne.* Tournai-Paris: Casterman, 1957.
2. With L. Rumpf. *Loi et Evangile.* Genève: Labor et Fides, 1981.
   "La Loi de l'Evangile ou Loi nouvelle selon saint Thomas d'Aquin."
   "Conclusion: Panorama de nos recherches et regard en avant."
3. With C.-J. Pinto de Oliveira. *Universalité et permanence des Lois morales.* Fribourg: Editiones Universitaires, 1986.
   "Avant-Propos."
   "Le problème de l'Intrinsece Malum. Esquisse historique." *Freiburger Zeitschrift für Philosophie und Theologie* 29 (1982): 373–88.
4. With C.-J. Pinto de Oliveira. *Sainte Thérèse d'Avila: Contemplation et renouveau de l'Eglise.* Fribourg: Editiones Universitaires, 1986.
   "L'oraison thérésienne dans la prière chrétienne." *Kerit* 44 (1982): 17–28.

ESSAYS IN COLLECTIONS

"Zonde." *Theologisch Woordenboek.* Maaseik, 1958.
"La découverte de l'existence de Dieu par saint Augustin." *L'existence de Dieu.* Paris: Casterman, 1961.
"Der Sinn für die Freundschaftsliebe als Urtatsache der thomistischen Ethik." *Sein und Ethos.* Mainz, 1963. (see RM)
"Eudaimonismus und sittliche Verbindlichkeit in der Ethik des heiligen Thomas." *Stellungname zum Beitrag Hans Reiners.* Mainz, 1963.

"Le langage scolastique, langage rationnel." *Le Langage,* vol.1. Neuchâtel, 1966.

"Autonomie et hétéronomie selon saint Thomas d'Aquin." *Dimensions éthiques de la liberté.* Fribourg: Editions Universitaires, 1978.

("Aquinas and Agency: Beyond Autonomy and Heteronomy? [1978]" Essay 10 in *The Pinckaers Reader.)*

"La Loi de l'Evangile ou Loi nouvelle selon saint Thomas d'Aquin." *Loi et Evangile.* Geneva: Labor et Fides, 1981. (See LE)

"Le Commentaire du Sermon sur la montagne par S. Augustin et la morale de S. Thomas." *Mémoires Gillon.* Rome, 1982. (See SCE)

"La Loi évangélique, vie selon l'Esprit, et le Sermon sur la montagne." *Le Christ, notre vie.* Notre-Dame de Vie, 1984. (See EM)

"La béatitude dans l'éthique de saint Thomas." L. J. Elders and K. Hedwig, eds. *Studi tomistici* n. 25. Vatican: Libreria Ed. Vaticana, 1984. (See EM)

"Les Actes humains (I) notes et (II), traduction, introduction et notes." *Thomas d'Aquin, Somme théologique.* Paris, 1984.

"La foi au Christ rèdempteur comme première source de la morale chrètienne." *Jèsus-Christ, Rèdempteur de l'homme.* Venasque: Carmel, 1986.

"La prière de sainte Thérèse dans la prière de l'Eglise." S.-Th. Pinckaers and C.-J. Pinto de Oliveira, eds. *Sainte Thérèse d'Avila. Contemplation et renouveau de l'Eglise.* Fribourg: Editions Universitaires, 1986.

"La dignité de l'homme selon Saint Thomas d'Aquin." *De dignitate hominis.* Fribourg: Editions Universitaires, 1987.

("Aquinas on the Dignity of the Human Person [1987]." Essay 9 in *The Pinckaers Reader.)*

"Liberté et préceptes dans la morale de S. Thomas." *Studi tomistici* n. 30. Vatican: Libreria Ed. Vaticana, 1987.

"L'Eglise dans la Loi nouvelle, Esprit et Institution." *Le Christ et l'Eglise.* Venasque: Centre Notre-Dame de Vie, 1987. (See EM)

"Le thème de l'image de Dieu en l'homme et l'anthropologie." *Humain à l'image de Dieu.* Geneva, 1989.

("Ethics and the Image of God [1989]." Essay 8 in *The Pinckaers Reader.)*

"Réflexions sur les relations entre la philosophie et la théologie." *Actualité de la philosophie.* Paris, 1989.

"Sommes-nous moraux de naissance? Les relations entre la morale et l'économie." *La gestion, carrefour de l'économie et de l'éthique.* Fribourg, 1990. (See EM)

"L'instinct et l'Esprit au coeur de l'éthique chrétienne." *Novitas et Veritas vitae.* Fribourg, 1991.

("Morality and the Movement of the Holy Spirit: Aquinas' Doctrine of *Instinctus* [1991]." Essay 20 in *The Pinckaers Reader.*)

"Nature-surnature chez Saint Thomas d'Aquin." *Ethique et natures.* Geneva, 1992.

("Aquinas on Nature and the Supernatural [1992]." Essay 18 in *The Pinckaers Reader.*)

"La voie spirituelle du bonheur." *Ordo sapientiae et amoris.* 1993.

("Aquinas' Pursuit of Beatitude: From the *Commentary on the Sentences* to the *Summa Theologiae* [1993]." Essay 6 in *The Pinckaers Reader.)*

"La ley natural." J. L. Bruguès, ed. *Ensename tus caminos para que siga en tu verdad. Comentarios y "Veritatis splendor."* Valencia, 1993.

"La Ley nueva y el papel del Espiritu Santo." J. L. Bruguès, ed. *Ensename tus caminos para que siga en tu verdad. Comentarios y "Veritatis splendor."* Valencia, 1993.

"Consecuencialismo y proporcionalismo." J. L. Bruguès, ed. *Ensename tus caminos para que siga en tu verdad. Comentarios y "Veritatis splendor."* Valencia, 1993.

"La Ley nueva, en la cima de la moral cristiana." G. del Pozo Abejon, ed. *Comentarios a la "Veritatis splendor."* Madrid: BAC, 1994.

"L'enseignement de la théologie morale et saint Thomas." *Saint Thomas au XXe siècle. Actes du colloque du centenaire de la Revue thomiste.* Paris: Saint-Paul, 1993.

"Lo que esta en juego. El capitulo II de la 'Veritatis splendor.'" J. A. Martinez Camino, ed. *Libertad de Verdad. Sobre la "Veritatis splendor."* Madrid: San Pablo, 1995.

"Bioetica e coscienza." G. Russo, ed. *Bioetica fondamentale e generale.* Torino, 1995.

"La Loi nouvelle, sommet de la morale chrétienne, selon l'encyclique 'Veritatis splendor.'" *Gesu Cristo, Legge vivente e personale della Santa Chiesa. Atti del IX Colloquio Internazionale di Teologia di Lugano.* Lugano, 1996.

("The New Law in 'Veritatis splendor.'" *Josephinum Journal of Theology* 3 [1996].)

"Coscienza, verità e prudenza." G. Borgonovo, ed. *La Coscienza.* Vaticano, 1996.

"Conscience and the Virtue of Prudence." John Haas, ed. *Crisis of Conscience.* New York, 1996.

("Conscience and the Virtue of Prudence [1996]." Essay 17 in *The Pinckaers Reader.*)

"La defense par Capreolus de la doctrine de S. Thomas sur les vertus." *Jean Capreolus et son temps.* Paris: Cerf, 1997.

("Capreolus' Defense of Aquinas: A Medieval Debate about the Virtues and Gifts [1997]." Essay 15 in *The Pinckaers Reader.*)

Pour une lecture de "Veritatis splendor." Paris: Cahiers de l'Ecole Cathédrale, Mame, 1995.

("An Encyclical for the Future: Veritatis splendor." J. A. DiNoia and Romanus Cessario, eds. *Veritatis Splendor and the Renewal of Moral Theology.* Chicago: Scepter, 1999.)

"The Sources of the Ethics of St. Thomas Aquinas." Stephen Pope, ed. *The Ethics of St. Thomas Aquinas.* Washington, D.C.: Georgetown University Press, 2002.

"The Sources of the Ethics of St. Thomas Aquinas [2002]." Essay 1 in *The Pinckaers Reader.*

JOURNAL ARTICLES

"La structure de l'acte humain suivant S. Thomas." *RTh* 55 (1955): 393–412.

"Les origines de la définition de l'espérance dans les Sentences de Pierre Lombard." *RTAM* 22 (1955): 306–12.

"Une morale sans péché." *Evangéliser* 10 (1955): 147–59.

"L'espérance de l'Ancien Testament est-elle la même que la nôtre?" *NRT* 77 (1955): 785–99. (See RM)

"Le renouveau de la théologie morale." *Vie intellectuelle* 27 (October 1956): 1–21. (See RM)

"Espérance personnelle et espérance communautaire." *Evangéliser* 13 (1958): 182–99.

"La nature vertueuse de l'espérance, de Pierre Lombard à saint Thomas." *RTh* 58 (1958): 405–42; 623–44. (See RM)

"L'espérance chrétienne." *L'Echo de N.-D. de la Sarte* 71 (1958): 16–18.

"Recherche de la signification véritable du terme 'spéculatif.'" *NRT* 81 (July–August 1959): 673–95. (See RM)

"Peut-on espérer pour les autres." *Mélanges de Science Religieuse* (1959). (See RM)

"La vertu est tout autre chose qu'une habitude." *NRT* 82 (April 1960): 387–403. (See RM)

"Le rôle de la fin dans l'action morale selon saint Thomas." *RSPT* 45 (1961): 393–412. (See RM)

"Qu'est-ce que le bonheur?" *Vie Spirituelle* 488 (November 1962): 507–24. (See RM)

"L'examen de conscience est-il un exercice démodé?" *Vie Spirituelle* (May 1963): 537–53.

"Qu'est-ce-que la liberté?" *Evangéliser* 18 (1964): 332–50.

"Ce que le Moyen-Age pensait du mariage." *Vie Spirituelle Supplément* (May 1967): 413–40. (See EM)

"La pauvreté religieuse est-elle une vraie pauvreté?" *Vie consacrée* 42 (1970): 55–64.

"La question des actes intrinsèquement mauvais." *RTh* 80 (1982): *181–212*. (See PJF) **("Revisionist Understandings of Actions in the Wake of Vatican II [1982]." Essay 12 in *The Pinckaers Reader*.)**

"Le Sermon sur la montagne et la morale." *Communio* 7 (1982): *85–92*.

"Le problème de l'Intrinsece Malum. Esquisse historique." *Ce qu'on ne peut jamais faire*. (See PJF) **("A Historical Perspective on Intrinsically Evil Acts [1982]." Essay 11 in *The Pinckaers Reader*.)**

"La question des actes intrinsèquement mauvais." *RTh* 84 (1984): 618–24. (See PJF)

"A propos du volontarisme dans le jugement moral." *RTh* 85 (1985): 508–11. (See PJF)

"La morale chrétienne et ses sources: Ecriture, Tradition et Magistère." *Anthropotes* (1987): 25–42. (See EM)

"Università delle lege morale e libertà." *La scuola cattolica* 115 (1987): 591–609. (See PJF)

"La foi en Jésus-Christ." *Voix de Saint-Paul* (June 1988): 5–7.

"Actualité de la morale." *L'Echo illustré* 47 (November 26, 1988): 18–19.

"Les sources de la morale chrétienne (Discussion avec René Simon)." *Supplément* 169 (June 1989): 193–202.

"Les Sources de la théologie morale." *Seminarium* 39 (July 1989): *376–88*.

"Les passions et la morale." *RSPT* (1990): 379–91. **("Reappropriating Aquinas' Account of the Passions [1990]." Essay 13 in *The Pinckaers Reader*.)**

"La méthode théologique et la morale contemporaine." *Seminarium* 29:2 (1991): 313–27.

"La vive flamme d'amour chez S.Jean de la Croix et S.Thomas d'Aquin." *Carmel* 63:4 (1991): 3–21.

"La conscience et l'erreur." *Communio* 18 (July 1993): 23–35.

"L'Enseignement de la théologie morale à Fribourg." *RTh* 93 (1993): 430–42.

("Dominican Moral Theology in the 20th Century [1993]." Essay 5 in *The Pinckaers Reader.*)

"L'usage de l'Ecriture dans la théologie morale." *NV* 2 (1995): 23–36.

("Scripture and the Renewal of Moral Theology [1995]." Essay 3 in *The Pinckaers Reader.*)

"Veritatis splendor: The New Law and the Role of the Holy Spirit." *Ethics and Medics* 20/1 (January 1995): 3–4.

"Veritatis splendor: Human Freedom and the Natural Law." *Ethics and Medics* 20/2 (February 1995): 3–4.

"Veritatis splendor: Consequentialism, Proportionalism and Christian Morality." *Ethics and Medics* 20/3 (March 1995): 3–4.

"Redécouvrir la vertu." *Sapientia* 51 (1996): 151–63.

("The Role of Virtue in Moral Theology [1996]." Essay 14 in *The Pinckaers Reader.*)

"Les anges, garants de l'expérience spirituelle selon saint Thomas." *Rivista teologica di Lugano* 1 (1996): 179–91.

"Linee per un rinnovamento evangelico della morale." *Annales theologici* 10 (1996): 3–68.

"La Parole de Dieu et la morale." *Le Supplément de la vie spirituelle* 200 (March 1997): 21–38.

"Thérèse de l'Enfant Jésus, Docteur de l'Église." *RTh* 97 (July 1997): 512–24.

("Thérèse of the Child Jesus, Doctor of the Church." *Josephinum Journal of Theology* 5 [Winter–Spring 1998]: 26–40.)

"Morale humaine et morale chrétienne." *Cahiers Saint-Dominique* 250 (December 1997): 15–24.

"Entretien avec le Père Servais Pinckaers." *Montmarte* (June–July 1998): 21–24.

"The Desire for Happiness as a Way to God." *Maynooth University Record*, 1998.

("Beatitude and the Beatitudes in Aquinas's *Summa Theologiae* [1998]." Essay 7 in *The Pinckaers Reader.*)

"The Return of the New Law to Moral Theology." *The Irish Theological Quarterly* 64 (1999): 3–15.

("The Return of the New Law to Moral Theology [1999]." Essay 19 in *The Pinckaers Reader.*)

"The Place of Philosophy in Moral Theology." *L'Osservatore Romano* (June 16, 1999): 14–15.

("The Place of Philosophy in Moral Theology [1999]." Essay 4 in *The Pinckaers Reader.*)

"La morale et l'Eglise: Corps du Christ." *RTh* 100 (2000): 239–58.

("The Body of Christ: The Eucharistic and Ecclesial Context of Aquinas's Ethics [2000]." Essay 2 in *The Pinckaers Reader.*)

In *Nova et Vetera*

"La morale de saint Thomas est-elle chrétienne?" 51 (1976): 93–107. (See SCE)

"Le désir naturel de voir Dieu." 51 (1976): 255–73.

"Réflexions pour une histoire de la théologie morale." 52 (1977): 50–61. (See SCE)

"La théologie morale à la période de la grande scolastique." 52 (1977): 118–31. (See SCE)

"La théologie morale au déclin du moyen âge: le nominalisme." 52 (1977): 210–21. (See SCE)

("Ockham and the Decline of Moral Theology." *Theology Digest* 26 (1978): 239–41. [résumé])

"La théologie morale à l'époque moderne." 52 (1977) 269–87. (See SCE)

"Morale catholique et éthique protestante." 53 (1978): 81–95. (See SCE)

"La violence, le sacré et le christianisme." 54 (1979): 292–305.

"Esquisse d'une morale chrétienne. Ses bases: la Loi évangélique et la loi naturelle." 55 (1980): 102–25. (See EM)

Italian translation, "La legge evangelica e la legge naturale nella morale cristiana." *Renovatio* 13 (1978): 356–81.

"La Loi évangélique, vie selon l'Esprit, et le Sermon sur la montagne." 60 (1985): 217–28. (See EM)

"L'Esprit dans la Loi nouvelle. Esprit et institution." 62 (1987): 242–62. (See EM)

"Le jugement moral sur les problèmes de la vie naissante." 63 (1988): 254–71. (See EM)

"Autonomie du devoir et du bonheur. La question de l'eudémonisme." 64 (1989): 98–114.

"Amour et devoir. Une réponse à la question de l'eudémonisme." 64 (1989): 179–97.

"Qu'est-ce que la spiritualité?" 65 (1990): 7–19.

"Le bonheur d'après Aristote." 65 (1990): 180–202.

"Le bonheur d'après Aristote. II. Une lecture chrétienne de l'éthique d'Aristote." 65 (1990): 268–286.

"La conception chrétienne de la conscience morale." 65 (1990): 81–99.

("Conscience and Christian Tradition [1990]." Essay 16 in *The Pinckaers Reader*.)

"La contemplation au temps de la science." 69 (1994): 129–41.

"L'usage de l'Ecriture en théologie morale." 70 (April–June 1995): 23–36.

"L'Evangile de la vie face à une culture de mort." 70 (July 1995): 5–17.

"La Bible et l'élaboration d'une morale chrétienne." 70 (October 1995): 16–27.

"Alasdair MacIntyre et la morale des vertus." 71 (April 1996): 77–86.

"Un Symposium de moral inconnu." 76 (2001): 19–34.

In *Sources*

"Nous misons sur la foi." 1 (1975): 3–9.

"Existe-t-il une morale chrétienne?" 1 (1975): 11–23; 1 (1975): 49–59. (See SCE)

"Faut-il encore des moines après Vatican II?" 2 (1976): 1–13. (See EM)

Italian translation, "Ancore monaci dopo il Vaticano II?" *Vita Consecrata* 13 (1977): 443–53.

"Que faut-il en penser? 'Le chrétien doit apprendre à vivre sa foi dans l'insécurité.'" 2 (1976): 102–4.

"L'Esprit Saint et l'amitié." 2 (1976): 105–10. [translation and presentation of a text of St. Thomas]

"Le mystère de l'Assomption." 2 (1976): 160–61.

"Etre d'Eglise (en collaboration)." 2 (1976): 177–87. (See EM)

"Du nouveau sur la Vierge Marie?" 3 (1977): 12–17. (See FE)

"La foi et les apparitions." 3 (1977): 83–84.

"Lecture positive et lecture 'réelle' de la Bible." 3 (1977): 108–18. (See EM)

"Le feu et les divisions." 3 (1977): 175–76.

"Le mystère de l'obéissance et de l'autorité dans l'Eglise" (in collaboration). 3 (1977): 245–56. (See EM)

"Que faut-il en penser? 'L'homme est un être-pour-les-autres.'" 3 (1977): 274–77.

"Dix années de formation sacerdotale aux Pays-Bas. Histoire d'un échec." 4 (1978): 22–26. [translation]

"La 'Lettre aux martyrs' de Tertullien." 4 (1978): 167–73.

"La jalousie et la bonté dans la parabole des ouvriers de la vigne (25e dimanche)." 4 (1978): 220–21.

"Simples réflexions sur notre condition d'adultes." 4 (1978): 269–71.

"Le service de la prédication et de la vie." 5 (1979): 28–29.

"Amour de Dieu, amour unique." 5 (1979): 105–17. (See EM)

"Ce que je crois." 5 (1979): 175–78.

"L'Immaculée Conception." 5 (1979): 271–73.

"Le 'Cantique des Cantiques': invitation à le lire." 5 (1979): 55–56.

"L'humanisme chrétien de Jean-Paul II. Les lignes de force de l'encyclique 'Redemptor Hominis.'" 6 (1980): 67–75.

"Fête de la Sainte-Trinité, mystère 'révélé aux tout-petits.'" 6 (1980): 128–29.

"L'annonce à Joseph." 6 (1980): 264–65.

"L'encyclique 'Dives in misericordia.'" 7 (1981): 49–58.

"Notre-Dame du Rosaire." 7 (1981): 220–23.

"La Loi et la morale." 7 (1981): 272–75.

"L'encyclique sur le travail et l'homme." 8 (1982): 11–19.

"Prions avec la Prière du Fils. Saint Cyprien: de l'Oraison dominicale." 8 (1982): 124.

"Les bénédictins vus par Newman." 8 (1982): 228–30.

"L'Epiphanie et les Mages." 8 (1982): 264–66.

"Suivre sa conscience." 9 (1983): 97–102. (See EM)

"Réflexions sur la prière du dimanche." 9 (1983): 158–62.

"Comment user habilement de l'argent (25e dimanche)." 9 (1983): 168–70.

"Le cas du Dr Augoyard." 9 (1983): 193–200. (See PJF)

"Convertir la violence." 10 (1984): 1–11. (See EM)

"Morale dynamique (7e dimanche)." 10 (1984): 35–37.

"Le mystère de saint Joseph." 10 (1984): 72–73.

"Souffrance des hommes, souffrance du Christ." 10 (1984): 193–97.

"Le cas de la conscience erronée." 11 (1985): 55–62. (See EM)

"La chasteté: de la servitude à la liberté" (in collaboration). 11 (1985): 97–106. (See EM)

"Un sermon inédit de saint Thomas d'Aquin (translation)." 12 (1986): 9–22.

"L'agir chrétien et ses dimensions selon le Sermon sur la montagne." 12 (1986): 97–106. (See EM)

"Les conseils évangéliques et la morale chrétienne." 12 (1986): 249–54; 13 (1987): 9–12. (See EM)

"L'encyclique 'Redemptoris Mater' ou le Pèlerinage de la Vierge Marie." 13 (1987): 202–6.

"Les neuf degrés de l'amour fraternel." 14 (1989): 193–98.

"Morale et Evangile." 14 (1989): 249–60. (See EM)

"L'examen de conscience au miroir de l'Evangile." 16 (1990): 54–59.

"Réflexions sur le temps qui passé." 16 (1990): 241–48.

"Notre Père. Pardonne-nous nos offenses." 17 (1991): 26–35.

"Le catéchisme au temps des apôtres." 17 (1991): 177–84.

"Le catéchisme de l'Eglise catholique." 19 (1993): 49–58.

"L'encyclique 'Veritatis splendor.'" 20 (1994): 49–64.

"Plaidoyer pour la vigilance." 22 (1996): 208–17.

In *Kerit*

"La vie intérieure." 1 (1975): 5–14. (See FE)

"Etre chaste aujourd'hui?" 2 (1975): 28–36. (See FE)

"Pour une théologie du repos." 3 (1975): 18–29. (See FE)

"C'est aujourd'hui dimanche." 4 (1975): 19–27. (See FE)

"Vous a-t-on déjà parlé du courage?" 5 (1975): 28–42. (See FE)

"Aime et fais ce que tu veux!" 6 (1976): 7–19. (See FE)

"L'humilité, cette princesse méconnue." 8 (1976): 29–38.

"L'Evangile et la joie." 9 (1976): 10–19; 10 (1976): 3–12.

"Le Sermon sur la montagne." 11 (1976): 8–21. (See PH)

"Les beatitudes." 12 (1977): 23–34. (See PH)

"Bienheureux les pauvres en esprit." 13 (1977): 5–16. (See PH)

"Heureux les doux." 14 (1977): 18–30. (See PH)

"Heureux les affligés." 15 (1977): 19–32. (See PH)

"Heureux ceux qui ont faim et soif de la justice." 16 (1977): 3–17. (See PH)

"Bienheureux les miséricordieux." 17 (1977): 31–42. (See PH)

"Heureux les cœurs purs." 18 (1978): 22–35. (See PH)

"Heureux les pacifiques." 19 (1978): 22–36. (See PH)

"Heureux les persécutés." 20 (1978): 27–42. (See PH)

"Les commentaires de saint Augustin et de saint Thomas sur les béatitudes." 21 (1978): 31–41. (See PH)

"L'Evangile et l'argent." 22 (1978): 27–33; 23 (1978): 35–43.

"Le sel de la terre." 24 (1979): 28–42. (See JE)

"La lumière du monde." 25 (1979): 37–43; 26 (1979): 23–31. (See JE)

"La justice nouvelle." 27 (1979): 34–43; 28 (1979): 27–36. (See JE)

"Les préceptes de la justice nouvelle." 29 (1979): 12–21. (See JE)

"L'Evangile et la liberté." 30 (1980): 25–34; 31 (1980): 27–32; 32 (1980): 20–26. (See JE)

"La colère et l'amour fraternel." 33 (1980): 29–37; 34 (1980): 23–29. (See JE)

"La convoitise." 35 (1980): 36–41; 36 (1981): 13–18. (See JE)

"L'amour de la vérité." 37 (1981): 14–20; 38 (1981): 22–25. (See JE)

"La générosité évangélique." 39 (1981): 41–46; 40 (1981): 34–40. (See JE)

"L'amour plus grand." 41 (1981): 26–31; 42 (1982): 46–50; 43 (1982): 39–47. (See JE)

"L'oraison thérésienne dans la prière chrétienne." 44 (1982): 17–28. (See STA)

"Ce que Dieu en pense." 46 (1982): 3–4. (See GM)

"L'Evangile et la prière." 48 (1983): 22–35. (See JE)

"Prière du soir." 49 (1983): 34–37. (See JE)

"Faut-il honorer le Saint Sacrement?" 50 (1983): 27–33.

"Pour prier le 'Notre Père.'" 51 (1983): 33–37.

"Comment faire du bon pain avec l'Ecriture." 52 (1983): 20–29. (See JE)

"L'Ecriture et la confession." 53 (1983): 30–38.

"Le Sermon sur la montagne commenté par saint Augustin." 54 (1984): 42–51.

"L'itinéraire de la vie chrétienne." 55 (1984): 44–49; 56 (1984): 24–30.

"Prier sans jamais se lasser." 57 (1984): 36–41. (See JE)

"De l'obligation à l'admiration." 59 (1984): 25–32. (See JE)

"La prière du Seigneur. Explication du 'Notre Père.'" 60 (1985): 35–40; 61 (1985): 11–19; 62 (1985): 7–12; 63 (1985): 41–50; 64 (1985): 13–21; 65 (1985): 33–42; 66 (1986): 42–49; 67 (1986): 41–50; 71 (1986): 14–25; 72 (1987): 29–36.

"Le mystère de saint Joseph." 73 (1987): 3–6.

"L'Ave Maria." 74 (1987): 5–10. (See GM)

"L'Annonciation à Marie." 75 (1987): 3–8. (See GM)

"La salutation angélique selon saint Thomas d'Aquin." 76 (1987): 15–23. (See GM)

"La grâce de Marie." 77 (1987): 23–32. (See GM)

"L'excellence de Marie." 78 (1988): 9–16. (See GM)

"Le fruit de Marie." 79 (1988): 3–11. (See GM)

"Sainte Marie, Mère de Dieu." 80 (1988): 4–10. (See GM)

"L'intercession de Marie." 81 (1988): 3–7. (See GM)

"La foi pour accueillir l'Emmanuel." 83 (1988): 38–41.

"La foi de notre baptême." 84 (1989): 14–18.

"La foi dans sa dimension personnelle." 85 (1989): 29–36.

"La foi, et le problème de la souffrance." 86 (1989): 34–38.

"La prière du dimanche." 87 (1989): 21–27.

"Les neuf degrés de l'amour fraternel." 90 (1990): 40–47.

"Je fais pénitence." 91 (1990): 42–43.

"La pêche miraculeuse et la vocation des apôtres." 92 (1990): 25–29.

"Le pharisien et le publicain." 93 (1990): 41–44.

"1,6,12 heures de travail pour le même salaire." 94 (1990): 40–45.

"On l'appellera le Prince de la Paix." 95 (1990): 44–49.

"Une vive flamme." 96 (1991): 32–39.

"L'espérance chrétienne." 97 (1991): 40–43.

"La parabole du festin nuptial." 99 (1991): 36–40.

"La blessure d'amour chez S.Jean de la Croix et S.Thomas." 100 (1991): 6–10.

"La Passion selon saint Matthieu." 102 (1992): 42–48.

"Marie de Béthanie et Judas Iscariote." 103 (1992): 19–26.

"L'Eucharistie et la trahison." 104 (1992): 38–48.

"Le scandale de Pierre et la prière de Jésus." 105 (1992): 37–47.

"Judas arrête Jésus." 106 (1992): 44–48.

"Le témoignage de Jésus et le contre-témoignage de Pierre." 107 (1992): 30–36; 108 (1993): 25–29.

"Le témoignage de Judas." 109 (1993): 31–37.

"Le procès devant Pilate." 110 (1993): 37–47.

"Le Catéchisme de l'Eglise catholique." 111 (1993): 34–45.

"Le bon Pasteur." 113 (1993): 20–25.

"Le couronnement d'épines ou le Roi outrage." 114 (1994): 31–36.

"Le portement de la croix et la crucifixion de Jésus." 115 (1994): 38–47.

"Jésus crucifié par les railleries." 116 (1994): 31–36.

"La mort de Jésus." 117 (1994): 37–46.

"Veritatis splendor." 118 (1994): 36–43; 119 (1994): 35–39; 121 (1995): 31–38.

"La descente du Christ aux enfers." 122 (1995): 38–46.

"Les femmes qui regardaient de loin." 123 (1995): 13–19.

"L'Evangile de vie face à une culture de mort." 124 (1995): 41–50; 125 (1995): 24–32.

"L'audace de Joseph d'Arimathie." 126 (1996): 43–49.

"La vaine garde du tombeau." 127 (1996): 20–22.

"Le grand chemin d'amour." 128 (1996): 31–41.

"La Loi nouvelle et le rôle du Saint-Esprit." 129 (1996): 42–46.

"'Veritatis splendor': conséquentialisme et proportionnalisme." 130 (1996): 44–47.

"La loi naturelle." 131 (1996): 38–41.

"La parabole des talents." 133 (1997): 40–43.

BOOK REVIEWS

Le précepte de la prudence chez saint Thomas d'Aquin, by Th. Deman. *RTAM* 20 (1953): 40–59; *Bulletin thomiste* 9 (1954–56): 345–62.

S. Maxime le Confesseur et la psychologie de l'acte humain, by R. A. Gauthier. *ibidem.*

"Le Dr Hesnard et la morale sans péché." *Revue Générale Belge* (15 September 1956): 147–59.

"Une morale pour notre temps. A propos d'un livre recent." *NRT* 88 (1966): 503–6.

"La vie après la mort (recension d'un livre de R. Moody)." *Sources* 4 (1978): 86–88.

Grammaire de l'assentiment, by J. H. Newman. *Sources* 4 (1978): 226–27.

Eglise missionnaire ou Eglise démissionnaire? by A. Piettre. *Sources* 5 (1979): 33–35.

"Comment être chrétien aujourd'hui? Une étude du livre *Etre chrétien* de Hans Küng." *NV* 54 (1979): 134–56. (See EM)

"Engagement de Dieu et fidélité du chrétien." *NV* 55 (1980): 230–35.

"Catholicisme." *La vie spirituelle* 136 (1982): 115–18.

Problèmes de morale fondamentale. Un éclairage biblique, by Pierre Grelot. *NV* 58 (1983): 76–79.

Norbert et l'origine des Prémontrés, by F. Petit. *Sources* 8 (1982): 174–75.

Nous, convertis d'Union soviétique, by T. Goritchéva. *Sources* 11 (1985): 84–86.

Camille C. ou l'emprise de Dieu, by H. Caffarel. *Sources* 11 (1985): 132–34.

Au commencement Dieu créa le ciel et la terre, by J. Ratzinger. *Sources* 12 (1986): 275.

Die Begründung des Sittlichen. Zur Frage des Eudaemonismus bei Thomas von Aquin, by B. Bujo. *RTh* 86 (1986): 133–37.

After Virtue, by Alasdair MacIntyre. *RTh* 86 (1986): 137–41.

L'expérience spirituelle selon Guillaume de Saint-Thierry, by J. A. Baudelet. *Sources* 13 (1987): 38–40.

Bonum hominis. Die anthropologischen und theologischen Grundlagen der Tugendethik des Thomas von Aquin, by E. Schockenhoff. *RTh* 89 (1989): 118–25.

"De persoonlijke dimensie van het geloof." *Emmaüs* 20 (1989): 101–7.

"Les sources de la morale chrétienne." *Le Supplément de la vie spirituelle* (June 1989): 193–202.

"Christ, moral absolutes and the good: recent moral theology." *The Thomist* 55 (1991): 117–40.

Dictionnaire de morale catholique, by J.-L. Bruguès. *RTh* 91 (1991): 685–87.

S. Thomas d'Aquin et le mal, by L. Sentis. *Choisir* (May 1994).

Dictionnaire de Spiritualité, fasc. CIV–CV. Freiburger Zeitschrift für Philosophie und Theologie 41 (1994): 285–86.

"Alasdair MacIntyre et la morale des vertus." *NV* 71 (1996): 77–86.

Petit traité des grandes vertus, by André Comte-Sponville. *Sources* 23 (March 1997): 68–72.

Index of Holy Scripture

Old Testament

Genesis, 4, 9, 12, 140, 195,
    362, 364; image of God,
    133–135, 331
    1:26, 133

Exodus, 4, 136

Deuteronomy, 4, 192

Joshua, 4, 11

Judges, 4, 9

Ruth, 4

1 Samuel, 4, 25

2 Samuel, 4, 9

1 Kings, 224

2 Kings, 4, 17

1 Chronicles, 2, 4

2 Chronicles, 4, 13

Tobit, 4, 8

Judith, 3, 4

Esther, 4

1 Maccabees, 4, 6

2 Maccabees, 4, 10

Job, 4, 11, 72

Psalms, 4, 11, 103, 246
    4, 11

Psalm 102, 121

Proverbs, 4, 166
    14:28, 35

Isaiah, 11

Song of Solomon, 4, 7
    1:3, 36

Wisdom of Solomon, 4, 103

Sirach, 4, 172

Isaiah, 4, 132, 316, 389
    11, 126, 316, 389

Jeremiah, 4, 56, 378

Lamentations, 3, 4

Baruch, 2, 4

Ezekiel, 4, 38

Daniel, 4

Hosea, 4, 21

Amos, 4, 8

Jonah, 4, 5

Micah, 4

Nahum, 3, 4

Habakkuk, 1, 4

Zechariah, 4, 7

Malachi, 4, 14

New Testament

Matthew, 66, 82, 86, 94,
103–4, 106, 112, 123, 126,
146, 269, 333, 384; Ser-
mon on the Mount, xii,
10, 16, 27, 30, 32, 42, 47,
63, 69, 83, 85, 104, 117,
126, 188, 197, 207, 269,
302, 326, 333, 338, 368,
371, 377, 379; and law,
52–54; and moral cate-
chesis, 56–57; and New
Law, 178–79, 206,
381–84
  1:21, 29
  19:9, 49
  23:8, 110

Mark, 14

John, 4, 126, 146; prologue,
378
  3:2, 102, 118
  4:14, 395
  6:54, 40
  7:35–39, 395

Acts, 56, 4
  15:9, 106
  27:9, 22, 55

Romans, 4, 9, 41, 68, 177,
269, 313, 323, 378, 383,
392; moral paraclesis of
chs. 12–15, 31–34; mod-
el of apostolic catech-
esis, 56–58
  1:20, 110
  3:8, 238
  3: 27, 378
  8:2, 378, 383
  12:1, 31–32, 55, 326
  14:19, 32

1 Corinthians, 12, 30, 54, 83,
88, 108, 293; source of
moral catechesis, 57–58
  2:15, 183
  3:7, 180
  6:11, 59
  6:12, 14, 18, 322
  6:15, 19, 322
  6:18, 58
  6:19, 58
  9:16, 327
  12 and 13, 30
  13, 12, 33, 58, 88
  13:4, 33, 58

2 Corinthians, 4
  12, 113

Galatians, 4, 80, 129, 349,
389
  5:18, 180
  5:22, 129, 349

Ephesians, 4, 31, 37, 41, 58,
81; source of apostolic
catechesis, 33–34
  1:22, 31
  3:8, 303
  4, 41
  4:1, 34
  4:4, 33
  4:15, 31
  4:16, 33
  4 and 5, 30
  5:32, 95

Philippians, 4
  1:21, 26
  4:8, 68, 87, 111
  4:8–9, 111

Colossians, 4, 29, 33, 38, 133;
source of apostolic cat-
echesis, 31–34
  1:18, 33
  2:19, 31
  3:10 133
  3:11, 34
  3:15, 33: 38
  3 and 4, 30

1 Thessalonians, 4, 15

2 Thessalonians, 4

1 Timothy, 81, 4

Titus, 4, 12

Philemon, 2, 4

Hebrews, 4, 111
  12:2, 109

James, 4, 63

1 Peter, 4, 21

2 Peter, 4, 15

1 John, 4, 67
  3:2, 102, 118

2 John, 1, 4

Jude, 1, 4

Revelation, 4, 23

Index of Patristic, Ancient, and Medieval Sources

Patristic Sources

St. Ambrose, *De officiis*, 189, 257; *Book I, ch. 24*, 295

St. Augustine, *Confessiones: Book I, ch. 1.1*, 123; *Book IX, ch. 10.23–26*, 121; *Book X*, 107, 111; *Book X, ch. 27*, 136–37

St. Augustine, *De doctrina Christiana*, 12, 191; *Book I, ch. xxii, 20*, 17–18; *Book I, ch. xxxv, 39*, 52

St. Augustine, *In Ioannis evangelium tractatus: Tract. 26, n. 13*, 40; *Tract. 82, n. 3*, 51; *Tract. 7, n. 7*, 195

St. Augustine, *De mendacio*, 198–99

St. Augustine, *De moribus ecclesiae catholicae*, 12, 17; *1.2*, 5

St. Augustine, *De spiritu et littera*, 9–10, 378

St. Augustine, *De Trinitate*, 133–34, 136, 145; *Book XIII, ch.3*, 118

St. John Damascene, *De fide orthodoxa: Book II, 12*, 132

St. Leo the Great, *Seventh Christmas Homily*, 143

St. Leo the Great, *Sermons*, 131–32

Ancient and Medieval Sources

Aristotle, *Eudemian Ethics*, 387

Aristotle, *Metaphysics*, 360

Aristotle, *Nicomachaean Ethics*, 8, 117, 121, 288, 299, 301; *Books I and V*, 17; *Book II, 6, 291*; *Books VIII and IV*, 12; *Book X*, 300

Boethius, *Consolation of Philosophy*, 116

Cicero, Marcus Tullius, *De finibus bonorum et malorum*, 190–91

De officiis, 295; *Book I, ch. IV*, 69

Dionysius the Areopagite, *De Divinis nominibus*, 276

Peter Lombard, *Sententiae in IV libris distinctae*, 4–5, 7, 16, 305; *Book I, dist. 23*, 145; *Book II, dist. 24, ch. 3*, 137, 212, 361; *Book II, dist. 40*, 198–99; *Book III, dist. 13*, 38; *Book III, dist. 23–36*, 306

Index of Proper Names

Abelard, Peter, 6, 194–99, 205, 214; on the primary of intention, 194–97

Adam, 14, 131, 132, 162, 195

Aelred of Rievaulx, St., 13

Albert the Great, St., 5, 7, 84, 205, 206, 310

Alexander of Hales, 8

Alexander the Aphrodite, 98

Alexander the Great, 139

Ambrose, St., 4, 84, 115, 295; on righteous vs. useful, 188–89, 257

Amyot, Jacques, 282

Andrew, St., 389

Andronicus of Rhodes, 13

Anselm of Canterbury, St., 84

Anthony, St., 349

Apel, Karl–Otto, 289

Aquinas, St. Thomas. *See* index of Aquinas texts.

Aristotle, 20, 174; as source for Aquinas, 3–5, 8, 11–17, 21, 81, 112–14, 117, 123, 126, 183, 199, 201, 352; on nature, 360; on divine instinct, 387; as source for Scotus, 315; Aquinas's transformation of, 67; Aquinas's commentaries on, 116; on end/beatitude, 8, 23, 65–66, 80, 105–7, 115, 121, 123, 171, 190, 207; on action, 201, 275, 291, 299–301; on conscience, 352; on courage, 44; on freedom, 143; on friendship, 8, 12; on genius, 139; on human nature, 8, 145; on memory, 136–37; on virtue, 8, 61, 275, 288, 291, 299–301; justice, 168, 295–297; prudence, 334; and appetite, 315

Athanasius, St., 360

Aubert, Jean Marie, 24

Augustine, St.: action, 195–99; as contrast to Aquinas, 30, 44, 303, 389; as source for

Aquinas, 3–4; beatitude, 10, 17–18, 49, 65, 80, 86, 107, 117–26, 171, 188, 284–85; charity/love, 12, 315, 318; eucharist, 40; gifts and beatitudes, 94, 124–26, 316, 348, 388–89; humility, 14; image of God/person, 133–36, 145, 156, 203; intrinsically evil acts, 210, 232, 244; moral finality, 206–7, 257; New Law, 9–10, 177, 378; Sermon on the Mount, 10, 104–6, 383; spiritual experience, 111, 302; Theological method, 5; virtue, 68, 292, 315, 318; evil, 207, 310; love, 191, 193; love vs. commandments, 51–52; lying, 193, 196, 198–99; sin, 195, 363

Averroes, 8, 98

Avicenna, 8

Azor, Juan, 117

Basil, St., 345

Baudelet, Yves–Anselme, 132

Benedict, St., 4, 14, 87

Bergson, Henri, 52, 287

Bernard, St., 4, 197–98

Billuart, Charles, xxi, 73, 227–30, 249, 379

Bloch, Oscar, 150

Boethius, 4; on action, 199, 201; on beatitude, 8, 16–17, 65, 115–16, 121; on 'person', 147–50, 153

Bonaventure, St., 8, 94, 137, 364; on person, 147, 151; on action, 205–6, 310

Borne, Etienne, 142

Busa, Roberto, 4, 28, 146, 359, 387

Cain, 351

Cajetan, 226, 379

Capreolus, John, 304–20

Cassian, John, St., 87, 302, 349

Cessario, Romanus, xviii, 304
Charlier, Louis, xiii, 74–75
Chenu, Marie–Dominique, xiii, xv, 74–75
Chrysostom, John, St., 14, 19, 302, 329
Cicero, 4, 14, 67, 138, 188; On action, 199, 201;
    On virtue, 8, 13, 61; Justice, 13, 88, 295; On
    natural inclinations, 69; On wisdom,
    190–91
Coeffeteau, Nicolas, 282–84
Comte-Sponville, André, 288
Connery, John, 245
Curran, Charles, 245, 247, 248
Cyril of Alexandria, St., 360

Damascene, John, St., 4, 188, 207; on image of
    God, 132, 133, 135, 137
D'Ambrosio, Marcellino, xiii
Danie?lou, Jean Cardinal, xiii, 376
de Groot, Johannes, 77
de Lagarde, George, 141
de la Bruyère, Jean, 282
de Langen-Wendels, J., 76–77
de Lille, Alain, 151
de Lubac, Henri, xiv, 267, 401
Delhaye, Philippe, 322, 377, 380
Delville, Fr., 76
Deman, Thomas, xiii, 73, 75, 77–78, 79–80,
    82, 84
Descamps, A. L., 377
Descartes, René, 20, 279, 280, 281, 282, 283,
    314, 368
Dionysius the Areopagite, 9, 115, 276, 302
Döpfner, Julius Cardinal, 373–76
Draguet, René, 74, 75
Driessen, Theodore, 76
Drioux, C.J., 385
Dupont, Jacques, 377
Durandus of Saint-Pourçain, 305, 308–13, 315,
    317

Ermenegildo, Lio, 372

Ferris, Daniel, xxii
Ferry, Jean-Marc, 289
Fuchs, Joseph, 244, 246

Garrigou-Lagrange, Reginald, xiv
Garvens, Anita, 211

Gauthier of Bruges, Blessed, 81
Gauthier, René Antoine, 73, 410
Gerson, Jean, 219
Gillon, Louis-Bertrand, 372
Gilson, Etienne, 189–90, 258
Gregory of Nyssa. See Nemesius of Emesa
Gregory the Great, St., 4, 9, 14, 68, 115, 133;
    on experience & reason, 87, 99, 113, 302,
    316; on beatitude & contemplation, 99, 113
Grossi, Filippo, 225–26
Guelluy, R., 74

Haas, John, 342
Hamer, Jerome, xiii, xiv, xvii, 75, 376
Harbermas, Jurgen, 289
Hauerwas, Stanley, 289
Hegel, George W. F., 168
Hendrickx, Marie, 108
Henry of Ghent, 81
Hilary of Poitiers, 4
Holte, Knut R., 189, 258
Hürth, Franz, 372

Ignatius of Loyola, 136
Isidore of Seville, 4, 13, 14

Janssens, Louis, 243, 244, 246, 262–66, 267;
    on evil effects, 240–41, 249, 266
Jerome, St., 4, 108, 343, 351
John of the Cross, St., 78, 86–87, 107, 136
John Paul II, xxi, 47, 376
John XXIII, Pope, 211, 372
Judas Iscariot, 195

Kerber, P. W., 377
Kerr, Fergus, xiv
Knauer, Peter, 240–46, 248, 259, 262, 266–68

Labourdette, Michel, 87
Le Guillou, Marie-Joseph, 374–76
Leclercq, Jacques, xiii, 76, 131, 236
Leo the Great, St., 131–32, 143
Leonard, Augustine, xiii, 75, 76
Liguori, St. Alphonsus, 77, 380
Lio, Ermenegildo, 372
Lombard, Peter, xiv, 4, 73, 306, 397, 401; as
    theological authority, 5, 7, 305; influence
    on Aquinas, 24; action, 199, 205, 310; beati-

tude, 26, 93, 94, 96, 117, 207; emotion, 273; free will, 137, 361; freedom, 212; grace of Christ, 38; human person, 145; sin, 310; on action, 198–99; on intention, 198–99; on philosophy, 108

Lottin, Odon, 81–82, 200, 317, 388

Luther, Martin, 56, 286, 363

Lyonnet, S., 380

Macintyre, Alasdair, 85, 288, 332, 412

Macrobius, 4, 13, 67

Maimonides, 8

Malebranche, Nicolas 280–82

Maritain, Jacques, 78, 86

Marx, Karl, 168

Mary of Bethany, 99

McCormick, Richard, 244, 245, 248

Meier, Anton Meinrad, 220

Mersch, Emile, 33

Murtagh, J., 231

Nemesius of Emesa, 4, 8, 133, 201

Newman, John Henry, 337, 339, 347, 355

Nietzsche, Friedrich, 288

Nussbaum, Martha, 288

Ockham, William of, 81, 141, 170, 180, 211–15, 219, 220, 233, 309, 313, 359, 361, 368, 393, 406; freewill precedes reason, 212–13, 364–65; Freedom and nature, 365

Olivier, B., 75–76

Origen, 14

Pascal, Blaise, 338

Patuzzi, G. Vincenzo, 380

Paul, St., xii, xviii; as source for Aquinas, 4, 11, 13, 44–45, 86, 89, 103, 329, 333, 343; Beatitudes, 126, 129; body of Christ, 34–36; Church, 35–36, 38; contemplation, 113; grace, 387; image of God, 133; New Law, 177; philosophical wisdom, 108–11; teaching, 20; virtue, 183, 279; body (of Christ), 31–34, 58, 71; casuistry (cases of conscience), 57–59, 71, 293, 322–29; catechesis, 30–34, 44, 54–59; civil authority, 327–29; conscience, 338, 340 (see also casuistry); freedom, 184; fruits of the spirit, see spiritual gifts; gifts, see spiritual gifts; good

from evil, 238; grace, 59, 323–24, 327; ignored by moralists, 26–27; law, 177, 378 (see also new law); love/charity, 268, 326–27, 348 (see also virtue); moral life, 47; new law, 10, 269, 378; paraclesis (moral teaching), 30–34, 54–59; paranesis; passions, 275; spiritual gifts/charisms, 32–33, 83, 324, 349, 368, 392; virtues, 14, 32–33, 58–59, 61, 68, 87–88, 324, 326, 348; wisdom, 191, 323, 327; worship/liturgy, 325

Peter Aureolus, 305, 312, 313–15

Peter, St., 106, 389

Philip the Chancellor, 7

Pinto de Oliveira, Carlos-Josaphat, 25, 377

Plato, Platonism, 4, 61, 168

Plotinus, 136

Princess Elizabeth, 280

Proust, Marcel, 388

Prümmer, Dominic, xiii, 76, 274, 289, 369, 394

Ptolemy, 4

Ramirez, Santiago, xiii, 77–78

Ratzinger, Joseph, 342, 351, 412

Rawls, John, 289

Regamey, Pie-Raymond, 380

Richard of St. Victor, 7

Rousseau, Jean-Jacques, 193

Salet, Gaston, 380

Schillebeeckx, Edward, 385–86

Schlier, Heinrich, 55

Schüller, Bruno, 244, 246

Scotus, John Duns, 219, 305, 315–18

Seckler, Max, 386

Seneca, 8

Smith, Timothy L., 64

Solignac, Amédée, 136, 137

Spicq, Ceslas, 76

Struyker Boudier, C. E. M., 77

Suarez, Francisco, xxi, 75, 218–23, 225, 227, 267

Swedenborg, Emanuel, 286

Taylor, Charles, 289

Teresa of Avila, 121

Thomas, St. See Aquinas

Torrell, Jean-Pierre, xx, 104, 108, 116

Van Den Berge, Roger, 194
Vereeke, L., 211
Vincent de Paul, St., 128

Waldstein, Michael, 25
Walgrave, Jan Hendrik, 386–87, 389, 393
Walzer, Michael, 289

Wartburg, Walter von, 150
Weisheipl, James A., 108
White, Kevin, 304
William of St. Thierry, 132
William of Tocco, 122

Yoder, John Howard, 289

Index of Works of St. Thomas Aquinas

Commentary on Galatians, 389
Commentary on Ephesians, 37–38, 393
Commentary on Colossians, 38
Commentary on Hebrews, 156
*Commentary on Aristotle' Nicomachean
    Ethics,* 116
Commentary on Aristotle's Metaphysics, 360
*Compendium theologiae: Book I, cap. 201,*155;
    Book I, cap. 214, 38; *Book II,* 116
Contra errores Graecorum, 151

De Rationibus Fidei, 155
De unione Verbi incarnates, 151

In Epistulam ad Romanos, 34–35, 37, 68, 323,
    378, 383, 389, 392; *Cap. XII, lect. 1, no.
    953,* 31; *Cap. XII, lect. 1, no. 955,* 30

*Lectura super evangelium secundum
    Matthaeum,* 15, 49, 66, 103, 123, 146;
    lect. V, n. 404, 85, 112–13; *lect. V, n. 434,*
    106; *lect. V, n. 435,* 106; *lect. V, n. 443,*
    105; *Ch. 1, lect. 8.3,* 155

Quaestiones disputatae de veritate: Q. 16.3, 11,
    350; *Q. 17.1,* 353; *Q. 17.1 ad 4,* 352; *Q.
    17.2 ad 3,* 351; *Q. 29.4–5,* 38; *Q. 29.4–7,*
    39, 273–274; *Q. 16.3,* 350
Questiones quodlibetales, 183

Scriptum super libros sententiarum, 16, 116,
    387
    Book I: 10.1.5, 146–47; *16.2,* 156; *23.1.1,*
        146–47, 151; *26.1.1,* 146–47; *40.1,* 205,
        207; *44.1,* 152; *44.1.4,* 153

Book II: 1.2.1, 210; *12.4,* 210; *2.1,* 153; *23.1,*
    308
Book III: dist. 34, 16, 93ff., 124
Book IV, 208; 16.3.1 [2 and 3], 210; *dist. 49,*
    38; *49.3,* 277; *k IV,* 208; 285, 305–6
Sermon 12, The Feast for All Saints, 116
Summa contra Gentiles, 101, 116, 146, 363;
    Book III, 95–100; *Book III, ch. 1–63,* 16;
    Book III, 129, 200, 214; *Book IV,* 54, 155;
    Book IV, ch. 21–22, 180
Summa Theologiae
    ST I: 1.10, 23; *1.6 ad 3,* 299–300; *1.8 ad 2,*
        170, 366; *2.2 ad 1,* 366; *29.1 ad 4,* 360;
        29.1, 148, 360; *29.2,* 149; *29.3 ad 1,*
        145; *29.3 ad 2,* 151; *29.3,* 145, 149–51;
        62.8 ad 3, 364; *76,* 284; *79.6,* 137;
        79.8, 11, 19; *103,* 120; *117.1 ad 1,* 11;
        117.1, 11, 20
    ST I-II: prologue, 101; *1.3,* 119; *1.7,* 120; *1.8,*
        120; *2 and 3,* 101; *2,* 12, 13, 17, 66,
        101–2, 119, 207–8, 276, 291, 354; *2.2
        ad 1 and ad 5,* 207; *2.8,* 102; *3,* 83, 101,
        118–19, 122, 285; *3.3,* 122; *3.4,* 83, 122;
        3.5, 122; *3.6,* 122; *3.7,* 122; *3.8,* 102,
        118, 122; *4,* 14, 102, 119, 121, 123, 308,
        353; *4.4,* 123; *4.6,* 123; *4.7,* 123; *4.8,*
        123; *5,* 12, 102, 118–19, 123, 300; *5.7,*
        12; *5.8,* 118; *6, prologue,* 117; *6.1,* 148,
        149, 207; *7.2,* 201, 277; *7.3 ad 3,* 202;
        7.3, 201, 202; *17,* 73; *18.6,* 204; *19 and
        20,* 206; *20.3, obj. 2,* 291; *23.1,* 12–13;
        23.3, 13; *23.4,* 13; *23.8,* 13; *24.9,* 354;
        25.3, 276; *25.4,* 276; *27,* 17, 276; *27.1,
        sed contra,* 17; *28,* 276; *31.3,* 285; *47.9,*
        14, 353; *49 and 55,* 308; *58.5,* 300;

ST I-II: prologue, (continued)
62.1, 117; 65, 349; 68, 100, 316, 330,
388–89; 68.1, 316, 388–89; 68.2 corpus et ad 3, 388; 68.2, 100, 388; 68.4
ad corpus, 388; 69, 10, 15–16, 66,
124–28; 69.1, 127; 69.2, 125,127; 69.3,
15, 126–28; 70, 10, 129; 70.4, 10; 72.5,
117; 79.6 ad 4, 219; 85, 159; 90.2, 117;
94.2, 96, 345; 94.3, 224; 106.1, 9, 22,
43, 126, 286; 107.1, 117, 181; 108.1,
286, 378; 108.2 ad 1, 172; 108.2, 10,
172; 108.3, 104; 108.4, 12; 161.1, 14;
161.5, obj. 1, 14; 161.5, obj. 4, 14;
ST II-II: 2.3, 110; 2.7, 28; 8, 41, 286; 8.1 corpus, 286; 8.1 ad 3, 286; 19.5 and 19.6,
329; 23.1, 12; 23.2, sed contra, 12; 23.3,
sed contra, 12; 24.9, 113; 28, 285; 39.1,
41; 45.2, 299; 47.8, 350; 50, 334; 58.1,
295; 58.11, 295; 63, 159; 64.2 ad 3,
160; 88.4 ad 3, 41; 104, 88; 121.1, 394;
124, 14; 136.3, 67; 141.6 ad 1, 210; 161,
88; 163, 43; 175.1 ad 1, 157; 180.6, 113,
390; 182.1, 113; 183.2, 28, 41; 188.6, 113
ST III: prologue, 120; 1.2, 155; 2.1, 360; 2.2
ad 2, 154–55; 2.2, obj. 2, 154; 4.1, 154;
7, 40, 42, 83, 128; 7.7, 83, 128; 8, 38,
40; 49.1, 43; 48.4, 43; 48.1, 39; 60.3,
sed contra, 40; 73.3 ad 1, 40; 80.4, 40;
82.9 ad 2, 40; 83.5, 40
Super evangelium secundum Ioannis, 146
Super I ad Corinthianos, 31; Ch. I, lect. III,
108–9; Ch. I, lect. III, n. 43, 109; Ch. I,
lect. III, n. 50, 109; Ch. I, lect. III, n. 55,
110; Ch. I, lect. III, n. 58, 109; Ch. XII,
lect. 2, 35; Ch. XII, lect. 3, 35–37

Subject Index

abortion, 60–62, 185, 238, 339

action / act(s): Christian, 82–83, 269, 381; circumstances, 70, 201–4, 335, 349, 353; and end (finality), 96–97, 109–10, 175, 205–10; and free choice / freedom, 142, 171; divine, 95–96, 98, 169, 175, 175, 189, 373, 390; *fontes moralitatis*, 230–32; of the Holy Spirit, 39, 53, 68, 86, 95, 125, 139, 172, 174–75, 177–83, 206, 322, 331, 379, 385, 389–90; intention, 204–11; interior and exterior, 21–24, 179–81, 229–30, 291–93; intrinsically evil, 185–235, 238–39, 244, 247–52; object, 203–11; principles of, 171–72, 300; prudence and, 70–71, 352–55; Revisionists' understandings, 236–70; St. Thomas on, 167–84, 199–211; three levels of, 60–64; voluntary act, 210, 219, 310

agape, 34, 56, 58, 59, 88, 268. *See also* charity; love

Arab philosophy. *See* Islamic philosophy

Aristotelian, 12, 15, 85, 116, 133, 137, 174, 188, 255, 275, 288–89, 332, 343, 351

art(s), 98; compared with morality, 70, 191, 255, 266, 278, 295, 299, 307, 348

asceticism, 27, 48, 78–79, 121–22, 125, 136, 142, 183, 301, 316, 336, 340, 343, 371, 381

Augustinian, 140, 156, 174, 189, 193, 195, 199, 203, 207, 257–58, 310, 316, 363. *See also* *Name Index*, Augustine

authority, xiii, 3–11, 115–16, 239, 337, 339, 353–54, 366; civil, 32, 56, 160, 327–28; philosophical, 11–14; scripture, 7, 18, 22, 30, 52–54, 57, 68, 84–85, 87, 106, 108, 269,

373; theological, 17, 20–21, 27, 68, 70, 134–36, 200, 237, 293, 373

autonomy, xxi, 142, 167–84, 239, 267, 365, 375

Baptism. *See* sacrament, Baptism

beatitude, 15–16, 23, 49–50, 155–56, 158–59, 189–91, 207–8, 253–54, 258–59, 269–70, 273–77, 284–86, 333–34, 362–64; desire for, 49, 86, 94, 97–98, 102, 112, 122–23, 138, 174–75, 208, 393; Franciscan and Dominican views, 169, 211–12; St. Thomas's treatise, 65–66, 93–114, 115–29; three views on, 126–27; and virtue, 190–91. *See also* happiness, natural desire to see God

Beatitudes, 10, 22, 48–49, 57, 66, 82, 85, 93–94, 103–7, 110–15, 123–29, 138, 178, 286, 315, 333, 349, 381, 383; and the virtues and gifts of the Holy Spirit xii, 14–16, 26, 42, 94, 124, 128–29, 212; in the Catechism of the Catholic Church, 49, 66, 86. *See also* *Sermon on the Mount*

beauty, 106, 129, 160, 276

Bible. *See* Scripture, and *Scripture Index*

body, 19–20, 31, 58, 67, 71, 98, 101, 121, 131, 134–35, 139, 169, 205, 278–85, 311, 318, 322, 325–28; mystical body of Christ, 26–45, 56, 58, 155, 325, 334, 338; personal body of Christ, 31, 40; analogy of, 29, 32, 35, 43; in St. Paul, 30–38

Cartesian, 57, 263, 281–82

cases of conscience, 47, 57–59, 80, 111, 120, 183, 192–93, 216, 218, 244, 291–94, 297,

cases of conscience, *(continued)*
322–23, 327, 329, 335, 337–38, 343, 369. *See also* conscience

casuistry, 59, 71, 77, 80, 120, 183, 199, 216, 218, 223, 239, 243–44, 247, 251–53, 258, 264, 290, 293–94, 304, 307, 310, 319, 370

catechesis, 27, 30–31, 33–34, 52–54, 56–57, 59, 68, 79, 83, 321, 369; moral, 31, 34, 37, 47, 54, 56, 76, 259–60, 293, 302, 323, 340, 383

Catechism of the Catholic Church (CCC), vii–viii, 26, 30, 46–57, 66, 68, 86, 129, 290, 293, 304, 347, 349, 369–70, 380–84

categorical imperative, 117, 371

Chalcedon, Council of, 24, 153, 360

charism(s), 28, 32–37, 42, 83, 87

charity, 29–30, 32–38, 43–44, 51–53, 55–59, 67–70, 83–84, 87–88, 123–25, 127, 129, 279, 285–86, 315–19, 368; and conscience, 324–28, 330–34, 345–46, 348–49, 354; and the New Law, 177–82, 372, 378–79, 392, 394; and friendship with God, 12–13, 276; as friendship, 8, 12, 180, 193, 209, 255, 276, 285, 391; love, 32–33, 43–44, 50–52, 56–58, 96–103, 110–11, 119–23, 134–38, 154–58, 169–71, 177–84, 267–70, 276–77, 282–87, 295–97, 324–28, 332–33, 340–46, 366–68, 381–82, 393–94; love of Christ, 88, 328, 333; love of God, 50–52, 123, 134–35, 140, 158, 181, 345, 382; three stages of growth in, 113. *See also* agape; New Law

chastity, 58, 105, 106, 299, 385; and virginity, 67

choice and prudence, 343–45, 350, 352, 355–56; free choice (*liberum arbitrium*), 65, 99, 138, 182, 212, 278, 361, 363. *See also* free choice; freedom

Christ, 131–36, 138–46, 150–58, 162–64, 273–76, 278–79, 321–29, 331–41, 347–48, 360–61, 369–75, 378–84, 390–92; and beatitude, 94–96, 98–100, 102–18, 120, 122–29; and moral theology, 6–8, 10, 12–17, 22–23, 25, 47–50, 52–59, 61–69, 71–72; Body of, 26–46; Passion of Christ, 40, 155

Christian ethics. *See* ethics, Christian

Church, 325–29, 334–35, 338–39, 341, 369–70, 380–82; as Body of Christ, 26–45, 56, 58, 155, 325, 334, 338; and Christian ethics, 26–30, 41–44, 347–49

commandments. *See* Ten Commandments; precepts

communion, 18, 85, 99, 162–63, 303; with Christ, 162, 383; with the Trinity, 162; with the Holy Spirit, 23; with the Church, 26, 32, 56, 63

connaturality, between man and true good, 62, 84, 299, 302, 392

conscience, 49, 70, 77–80, 321–41, 342–56, 368–70, 372, 380. *See also* cases of conscience; prudence

consequentialism, 47, 63, 209, 244–48, 290, 292, 310, 340

contemplation, 94, 111–13, 121–22, 135–36, 156; Mary and Martha, 36; as highest human activity, 78, 99, 190; of God, 97–98, 105, 111, 140; of truth, 98–99. *See also* spiritual experience

conversion, 51, 104, 126, 315, 355, 356, 390

Council of Trent. *See* Trent, Council of

counsels (of perfection), 27, 70, 182, 183, 371, 381

courage, 88, 105, 139, 189, 209, 261, 279, 297, 314, 318, 332; exemplified in martyrdom, 14, 44, 67

covenant, 9, 26, 50, 69, 368, 378

cross, xv, 72, 78, 86, 88, 108–12, 114, 136, 363, 371

death, x, 72, 109, 111, 155, 160–61, 186, 194, 199, 238, 243

Decalogue. *See* Ten Commandments

desire, 117–23; for beatitude, 49, 86, 94, 97, 98, 102, 112, 122, 123, 138, 168, 174, 175, 208, 362, 393. *See also* natural inclinations, natural desire to see God

dignity. *See* human person

discernment, xv, 44, 57, 58, 62, 71, 113, 139, 197, 237, 297, 299, 330, 332, 335, 343, 345, 349–50, 353, 354, 387

discipline, xii, xiii, xxiii, 36, 304, 371, 377

disposition. *See* habitus

docility, 59, 63, 68, 316

Dominican(s), xii, xiv, xv, 73–90, 99, 225, 282, 309, 366, 369, 374, 380, 405

double effect. *See* principle of double effect

duty. *See* obligation

education: moral, 9, 69, 278, 289, 296–97, 314, 344, 354; divine pedagogy, 69

egoism, 119, 286, 291, 295–96

emotions. *See* passions

end, final. *See* finality

Epicurean, 4, 107, 275

ethics, Christian: and beatitude, 93–114, 115–29; and the Beatitudes, 111–14, 124–29; ecclesial context of, 41–45; Eucharistic context of, 26–45; Dominican, 73–89; historical studies and, 79–82, 186–87; and the image of God, 130–42; and New Law, 176–83, 369–84; and emotions, 273–87; philosophy and, 64–72; Scriptural bases of, 46–63, 82–89; sources for, 4–24; theological orientation, 14–16; two concepts of morality, 170–72, 274–76; and virtue, 288–303, 304–20

eucharist. *See* sacrament, Eucharist

eudaemonism, 66, 103, 117, 284–86. *See also* beatitude

evangelical counsels, 182, 183, 381

Evangelical Law. *See* New Law

experience, 7–8, 12–14, 19–20, 42, 44–45, 68–72, 84–87, 122–24, 131–32, 259, 261, 274–76, 278–82, 297–302, 337–38, 353–54, 360–61, 367–68; Christian experience, 14, 68, 72, 103, 113, 118, 123, 129, 131, 316, 338, 348, 388, 390; that forms wisdom, 35, 59, 63, 104–6; spiritual, 19, 44, 75, 86–87, 284–87, 315–16, 390–94

exteriority, 181, 197, 229, 234, 235, 250, 264, 343, 375, 391

faculties (capacities), 135–42, 308, 318, 329

faith, 108–12, 171–79; and the Church, 26–45, 175; in Jesus Christ, 26.45, 175, 378; and reason, 11, 64–72, 173. *See also* reason

Fathers of the Church. *See* patristics; *Index of Names*

fear, 104, 128, 274, 277, 279, 283, 297, 328, 350

Fides et Ratio, xxi, 64–72

finality (final end), 8, 15, 206–10, 253–59, 363; *ea quae sunt ad finem*, 209, 255–56. *See also* beatitude

forgiveness, 43, 63, 378

fortitude. *See* courage

Franciscan(s), 7, 76, 128, 134, 169, 200, 211, 278, 284, 309, 313–14, 317, 379

free choice (*liberum arbitrium*), 65, 99, 138, 182, 212, 278, 361, 363

freedom, 7, 60, 62, 69, 73, 79, 161, 235, 248–49, 270; and conscience, 331, 335–39, 342–47, 348, 350, 353; for excellence, 81, 137–40, 168–72, 176–77, 179–80, 182–84, 211–13, 235, 344–45, 365–66; of indifference, 27, 81, 130, 141–42, 163–64, 168, 217, 229, 233, 235, 308, 312, 335, 343–44, 365–66, 393; and grace, 361–68, 370, 381, 386–87, 389, 393, 394; historical perspectives on, 200, 211–17, 219, 221, 223–25, 229, 233; and virtues, 274, 276, 278, 286–87, 290, 296, 301, 307–8, 312, 318

friendship, 8, 12, 13, 44, 74, 102–3, 120, 128, 139, 145–46, 180, 192, 193, 209, 255, 257, 276, 285, 296; with God, 12–13, 276; and charity, 8, 12, 180, 193, 209, 255, 276, 285, 391

gift(s): and beatitude, 93–94, 100, 104, 106, 110, 112, 124–29; and the Body of Christ, 32–33, 35–37, 39, 42; of the Holy Spirit, 15–16, 28–29, 57, 68, 80, 82, 86, 93, 104, 110, 124, 135, 139, 162–64, 173, 212, 306–7, 315–20, 324–25, 331–43, 348–49, 371, 381, 385, 388–94; of understanding, 22, 106, 392; of charity, 35; of God, 51, 362, 383; of grace, 159, 367; of wisdom, 22, 104, 299, 392

good: and beatitude, 94–98, 101–3, 105–7, 110, 112, 119, 121–23, 128; conscience and, 325–26, 328, 330–34, 336, 338–40, 345–48, 350–54; divine, 286, 389; history of conceptions (good and evil), 188, 190, 192, 194–203, 205–10, 212–15, 217–18, 220–34, 251, 255, 258–60, 262, 264, 266, 270; and Holy Spirit, 387, 389, 393–94; inclination to, 348, 366; and joy, 286–87; Revisionists notions of, 238–49

gospel, 107–14, 172–73, 176–82, 327, 333–35, 338, 370–74, 377–84; as authority, 7, 14–15, 18, 22–24, 48–54, 57–59, 62, 84–85, 108, 269, 373; commentated by Fathers, 10–12; and morality, 46–63, 265–70; and philosophy, 12–14. *See also* Beatitudes; scripture grace, 12, 22, 53, 59, 61, 63–68, 72, 80, 83, 86, 95, 112, 117, 124, 126, 131, 134–35, 137–42, 152, 155, 158–64, 170, 172–73, 181, 183, 256, 268–70; and conscience, 323–25, 327, 331, 335, 339, 346–47, 357–58; and the Holy Spirit, 386–88, 390–91, 394; and nature, 112, 268–69, 359–62, 364, 366–68; and the New Law, 177–79, 371–75, 378–81, 384; and virtue and gifts, 273, 282, 285–86, 303, 315–16; and Christ, 26, 28, 30–31, 34–39, 42–43

habitus, xxi, 22, 67, 124, 291–94, 297–98, 306–13, 315–19, 330, 343, 350–51. *See also* virtues

happiness, 66, 119, 284, 294, 348. *See also* beatitude, natural desire to see God

heteronomy, vi, xi, xxi, 142, 167–71, 173

holiness. *See* Holy Spirit, sanctification

Holy Spirit, 32–35, 42–45, 57–58, 124–29, 172–84, 328–32, 367–68, 378–81, 385–96; gifts of the, 15, 28, 57, 68, 80, 82, 86, 93, 104, 110, 124, 135, 139, 173, 212, 290, 306, 316, 331, 343, 348–49, 371, 381, 388, 390, 391–94; human body as temple, 58, 71, 322; instinct of the, 100, 386–94; sanctification (and holiness), 37, 51, 59, 63, 135, 139–40, 347, 368, 378, 381

hope, virtue of, 14, 29, 58–59, 67–68, 87–88, 123, 135, 139, 158, 179, 189, 191, 277, 286, 315, 326, 331, 348, 378, 391–92

Humanae Vitae, 185, 236–37, 240, 244, 290, 376

Humani Generis, xiv, 74, 75

human nature. *See* nature, human

human person: dignity of, 144–63; end of, xvi (*see also* beatitude); happiness, 93–114, 115–29, 175, 189–91, 207; in the image of God, 130–43

humanism, 175, 218, 239, 267

humility, 13–14, 43, 56, 67, 85, 88, 97, 104, 126, 197, 278, 327, 333, 340. *See also* meekness

image of God, 130–43, 156–59, 331, 362, 368, 380; definition, 132–33

imitation: of Christ, 132; of God, 52, 96, 132, 140–41, 156–57

inclination. *See* natural inclinations

infused moral virtue. *See* virtue, infused moral

innovators, xvii, 237, 319. *See also* revisionism

instinct: animal instinct (impulse), 387, 390; of the Holy Spirit, 100, 386–94; rational instinct (*instinctus rationis*), 100, 330, 393; St. Thomas on, 385–94

intellectual virtue. *See* virtue, intellectual

intention, 204–5, 208, 210–11; Abelard on the primacy of intention, 194–97; Lombard on balancing intention and action, 198–200. *See also* action

interiority, 22, 62, 86, 139, 179, 180–81, 183, 189, 196–97, 204, 206, 208, 211, 216, 229–30, 234–35, 250, 258, 263–65, 282, 287, 291–93, 361, 368, 391

Islamic philosophy, 8, 100, 363

Jansenists, 77, 338

Jesuits, 117, 218, 338

joy, 94–95, 107–9, 129, 161, 181, 212, 255, 257, 261, 273, 275–76, 284–87, 327, 333, 340, 394; distinction between pleasure and joy, 94–95, 287; as fruit of the Holy Spirit, 368

justice, 13, 33, 39, 52, 58, 61, 80, 82, 88, 105, 112–13, 127–28, 159, 162, 168, 269, 288–89, 291–92, 315, 318, 324, 328, 333–34, 347–48, 378, 394; two concepts of, 294–97; and friendship, 44, 139, 145, 192

justification, 9, 172, 237, 323, 375, 378, 380

Kantian, xxi, 47, 57, 66, 86, 117, 167, 180, 243, 252, 263, 266, 267, 284, 286, 288, 290, 367

law, 9–11, 48–53, 56–57, 60–61, 168–85, 273–78, 292–97, 299–301, 333–40, 342–48, 350–58; divine law, 9, 69, 200, 319, 375, 381; eternal law, 11, 69, 168, 375, 383; and freedom, 182, 301, 335, 336, 344; Old Law, 28, 52, 69, 171, 178, 179, 181, 182, 379, 381; Roman law, 4. *See also* moral law; New Law; natural law

Law of the gospel. *See* New Law

legal obligation, 296; morality of, 27, 49, 78, 216, 233, 294, 355; and external acts, 234, 249, 336–37, 352, 371

liturgy, 23, 37, 41, 45, 57, 62, 95, 325, 327, 368, 379

Lord's prayer. *See* prayer
love. *See* charity

Magisterium, 232, 237, 239, 338–39, 376
manual(s) of moral theology, 10, 27, 47, 50, 66, 76–82, 186, 218, 227, 230, 321, 337, 340, 346, 369, 370, 371, 372
manualist(s), xiii, xv, xxi, xxiii, 232, 369
marriage, 49, 95
martyrdom, 44, 67, 112
meekness, 105, 127, 197. *See also* humility
mercy, 112, 113, 127, 128, 257, 333, 346
moral catechesis. *See* catechesis, moral
moral education. *See* education, moral
moral law, 27, 50, 60, 69, 86, 117, 170, 179, 187, 203, 213, 216–17, 239, 244, 248, 251–52, 259, 336, 338, 340, 342, 344, 346–47, 350, 354, 368, 370, 376–77, 381
moral obligation, 50, 171, 179, 181, 248, 292, 336, 339, 346, 372
moral precepts. *See* precepts
moral virtue(s). *See* virtue(s), moral
moral theology. *See* ethics, Christian
mysticism, 45, 48, 68, 86, 95, 125, 136, 183, 230, 276, 316, 336, 371, 381, 388

natural desire to see God, xiv, xx, 66, 97–100, 103, 106, 112, 121, 169, 174, 362–65
natural inclinations: according to St. Thomas, 224; as basis of natural law, 69, 70, 169, 214; as source of freedom, 139, 169–71, 345, 362; correspond to moral law, 346; first source of action, 70; perfected by New Law, 214; quality of human person, 158, 163; rejected by freedom of indifference, 163, 168–69, 213, 235, 393; influence on Capreolus, 312; to beatitude / spiritual nature, 169, 212–13, 235, 345–46, 363–65; to truth and goodness, 81, 138, 141, 158–59, 163, 169–71, 212, 300, 312, 346, 348, 362, 366; as basis of virtue of charity, 366; to social life / society, 44, 139, 158, 328; as root of justice, 296; to virtue, 159, 300, 307, 312; directed by virtue, 348
natural law: as self-sufficient morality, 239; as universalist perspective, 27, 174, 185; basis for human law, 69; basis for intrinsic (vs. extrinsic) goodness of actions, 187,

200, 214, 217, 233, 368; relationship to New Law, xvi, 28, 50, 69, 82–83, 214, 269, 372–76, 383; critiqued by those who reject intrinsically evil acts, 239, 252; directed by moral law, 27, 50; exists within us, 11, 22, 68; expresses divine wisdom/will, 212, 294, 372–73; expresses inclination to true and good, 22, 96, 363, 393; in post-Tridentine Catholic morality(moral manuals), 27, 173, 239, 252, 294; identified with Decalogue, 27, 49, 68–69, 172, 239, 343, 368, 370, 372; made peripheral by nominalism / freedom of indifference, 213–15, 233, 375, 379; in Suarez, 220; only part of Gospel morality, 172; proceeds from natural inclinations, 69, 169, 345; rejected by Reformation Protestantism, 172–73
nature, 12, 23; and freedom, 139, 200, 233, 361, 365, 367–68, 393; and grace, 12, 112, 160, 170, 269, 347, 366–67; and supernatural, 66, 100, 107, 199, 266–68, 279, 359–68, 375; divine, 134, 151, 153, 158, 366; incomplete, 123; laws of, 283; old and new, 133; state of pure, 359, 365; rational, 147–59, 162, 220, 222, 224
nature, human, 8, 23, 139, 233, 279, 283; according to Aristotle, 112, 137, 145; as autonomous, 239, 267–68, 270; as principle of action, 157, 339, 346; dignity of, 151, 157, 161; intrinsic desires of, 100; of Christ, 37, 39. 109, 144, 152–55, 157, 266; perfected, 112, 121; spiritual nature, 131, 169, 256, 368; and sin, 363; and grace, 12; and pleasure, 276–77, 287; and virtues, 233, 315; in inclinations to truth and goodness, 66, 138–39, 212, 235, 346, 393; and freedom, 169, 213, 235, 345, 346, 361–63, 393; of angels, 134
New Law (evangelical law, law of the Gospel), 50–53, 76–83, 86, 369–84; and autonomous morality, 176–77; and moral precepts, 172; and sacraments, 368; and the Sermon on the Mount, 104, 126, 206, 269, 368, 382–84; and the theological virtues, 50, 56, 172, 175, 206, 285; and Vatican II, 372–76; as grace of the Spirit, 22, 43, 61, 68, 83, 117, 139, 206, 285, 368, 386, 390–92; as an interior law, 9, 22, 51, 53, 83, 126, 374, 377, 381, 391; as perfect law, 69, 172;

New Law, *(continued)*
defined, 83, 139, 177; governs internal acts, 69; in St. Paul, 10, 269; in moral manuals, 27, 80, 86, 371; in the *Catechism*, 290, 380–82; natural law completed in, 28, 83. *See also* law

nominalism, 168–70, 215–17, 252–53, 319; and freedom, 200, 278, 393; and human nature, 19, 141, 365; and morality of obligation, 180, 252, 278, 353, 379; and reason, 99, 174, 177; and relativism, 252; against intrinsic morality, 200, 223, 230, 233; influence of post-Tridentine moralists, 316; of Ockham, 211–17; of Kant, 286

norms. *See precepts*

object. *See action*

objectivism, 263

objectivity: and beatitude, 97, 189–93, 208, 234, 253, 258–60; and morality, 187, 192–93, 208, 217, 233–34, 244, 259, 270

obligation, legal. *See legal obligation*

obligation, morality of, 42, 78, 253; and arbitrary morality, 183–84, 300; and conscience, 335–40, 352–53; and distinction between moral and spiritual theology, 78, 182–83, 242, 251; origin in Ockham / nominalism, 141, 170–72, 180, 212–16, 252, 379, 393–94; incompatible with intrinsic morality, 52, 180, 252; influence on Kant, 252, 288; narrowness of, 82, 142–43, 242, 259, 261–62, 270; and Suarez, 219–23

Old Law. *See* law; Ten Commandments

omnipotence, 198, 213

Optatum totius, 372–73

original sin, 43, 154, 159

Our Father. See prayer

paraclesis, 30–34, 54–56

parenesis, 27, 30, 48, 54–55, 323, 336, 340, 371

passion(s), 273–87; and morality, 17, 180, 297, 380, 394; and virtues, 95, 98, 105, 315, 332; concupiscible and irascible, 127; in Aquinas, 276–87; in Descartes, 279–82; rationality of, 316

patience, 61, 67, 88, 261, 279, 298, 332, 368, 391–92

patristic authors: moral method of, 49–50, 67, 171, 173, 234; influence on Aquinas, 67, 96, 123, 144, 168, 177, 208, 378; relation to medieval authors, 131–32

peace, virtue / gift of, 104, 129, 326, 333, 368; of Christ / God, 33, 38, 111, 126, 324; makers, 32–33, 37–38, 94, 104–5, 111, 126–27, 129, 324, 326, 333, 368

Pelagianism, 387

Pentecost, 22, 62

perception, sense, 122, 277–78

perfection: moral, 61, 69, 104–5, 125, 138, 148–50, 157, 171–72, 190, 240–42, 269, 307–8, 317–18, 332, 336, 343, 349, 371, 381, 383, 391. *See also* counsels of perfection

person, human. *See* human person

persons, divine, 133, 146–48, 152, 158–59, 162–63

philosophy: relationship to moral theology, 11, 20, 64–72, 138, 188–89, 267, 290, 322–23, 333; and theology in Aquinas, 11, 20, 107–8, 112–13, 118, 133, 319, 366

Platonism, 4, 61, 136, 168, 188, 275, 279, 284

positivism, 268

poverty, 104, 112, 128, 269, 278, 333

practical reason, 70, 329–35, 343, 349–51; first principle of, 330, 343, 345, 350–51. *See also* prudence

prayer, 24, 33, 38, 45, 179, 292; liturgical prayer and morality, 62, 325–27; Our Father / Lord's prayer, 116, 334

precept(s) / Norms, 215; and virtues, 125, 171–72, 183, 189, 206, 250, 261; formal, 250–51, 261, 263; material, 250, 261; moral, xvii, 60, 171, 194, 197, 231, 245–53, 294; of the Ten Commandments, 51–52, 65, 194, 213, 233, 374; of the Sermon on the Mount, 197; of the natural law, 185, 215, 233; three kinds of, 197

pride, sin of, 14, 278, 324,

principle of double effect, 238–45, 340

principle of cooperation in another's sin, 241

principle(s): first, 19, 21, 39, 98, 138, 313; exterior / external, 65, 206, 292, 391; interior / internal, xxi, 65–66, 181–82, 206, 211, 216, 275, 290, 292, 307, 353, 389

proportionalism. *See* revisionism

prudence, xxii, 13–14, 22, 67, 70–71, 78, 80, 82, 98, 109, 140, 189, 197, 203, 206, 226,

299–300, 313, 317–19, 330–38, 342–55. *See also* practical reason, wisdom
purity, virtue of, 61; of heart, 105–6, 126, 333

rationalism, 19–20, 99, 175, 267, 270, 276, 296, 374, 394
reason: autonomy of, 63, 239, 312; and faith, 71, 173, 175, 228, 268, 322, 366; and law, 259, 310, 314; and prudence, 335; and revelation, and sin, 160; and will, 65, 70, 137, 149, 195, 203, 212, 221, 231, 276, 350, 361, 364; and freedom, 142, 275; historical, 98, 148; human, 11, 108–11, 113, 158, 167, 170, 174, 176, 215, 219, 269, 366, 388, 392; light of, 129, 160, 373; order of, 58, 149, 160; proportionate, xxi, 238, 241–46, 248, 251; right, 58, 172, 174–75, 220, 222, 310, 312; theological, 34. *See also* practical reason
relativism, 252, 254, 266, 270, 373
revelation, 7–8, 14, 36, 66, 84, 152, 190, 192, 233, 239, 253, 324, 327, 340; and Aquinas, 11, 69, 82, 89, 99, 269, 348, 389; and moral theology, 47, 68–69, 82, 176, 232, 252, 267–69, 354; and reason, 9, 11, 13, 68, 339
Revisionism / proportionalism, xi, xv, xvii, xxi, 47, 54, 60, 209, 236–70, 290, 340, 376, 399, 404
rigorism, 242, 275, 282, 338, 344
Roman Catechisms (post-Trent), 80, 86

sacraments, 29, 40, 53, 61, 83, 135, 178, 368, 370, 379; reconciliation/penance, 80, 161–62, 218, 335, 369–70, 379; Eucharist, v, xx, 26, 29, 31–32, 40–41, 44–45, 325; baptism, 315, 323, 325
sacrifice, 209, 255; animal, 31; Eucharistic, 31; 'living', 31–32, 56, 325
Salamanca, theologians of, 223–25, 227, 249
salvation, 40, 46, 49, 315, 327, 391; in Christ, 23, 28–29, 33, 34, 38–39, 55, 59, 156; history, 96, 134, 154, 156, 159, 162, 191
sanctification. *See* Holy Spirit
scholastic method /analysis: medieval, 5–7, 10–11, 34, 57, 95, 115, 135, 194, 198–206, 233, 268, 304–20; modern, 227–32, 234, 237, 259, 267
science: moral, 54, 70, 78, 103, 300, 351; human / social, 120, 162, 236, 259, 270, 339,

368; modern, 20, 59–60, 120, 260, 270, 359, 367–68
scripture: and the historic method, 74, 79, 81, 187; and moral theology, xiii, 9–11, 46–63, 187–89, 252–53, 267–70, 338, 348, 371–80; and tradition, xvi, 236, 388; senses of, 23; use by Aquinas, 4, 68, 83, 95, 115, 133, 177, 253, 278, 329
Sermon on the Mount, xii, 10, 16, 27, 30, 32, 42, 47, 52–57, 63, 69, 83, 85, 104, 117, 126, 178–79, 188, 197, 206–7, 269, 302, 326, 333, 338, 368, 371, 377, 379, 381–84; Augustine's commentary on, 104, 383; Aquinas's commentary on, 15, 49, 66, 85, 103–6, 112, 123. *See also* Beatitudes
sin, 59, 159–63, 192, 220, 224, 226, 310, 335–36, 349, 362–67, 387; according to Abelard, 194–96; Adam's / original, 14, 132, 154, 159; "against own body," 58, 71, 322; atonement of, 40; consciousness of, 324, 327; cooperation in, 241; effect of, 160–61; in manuals of moral theology, 50, 51, 76, 78, 80, 372; liberation / healing from, 29, 42–43, 178, 315, 324; mortal, 117; satisfaction for, 225; slavery to, 180
spiritual experience, 19, 44, 75, 78, 103, 315, 390; and Kant, 286–87; and morality, 86–87, 285, 315, 394; and reason, 19; and love of truth, 99, 122
spirituality, xv, 45, 75; and morality separated, 27–28, 30, 48, 54, 125, 136, 230, 242, 251, 265, 267, 336, 338, 340, 371, 394; and morality reintegrated, xii, xv–xvi, 78–79, 88, 125, 171, 234, 268, 323, 325
spontaneity, spiritual, 139, 172, 180, 282, 39; result of virtue / interiority, 171, 207, 282, 291, 394
states of life, 28, 41, 42
Stoics, 4, 88, 107, 188, 190, 275, 279, 318
subjectivism, 189, 192, 208, 234, 270, 300, 373
substance, 7, 16, 62, 96, 98, 100, 106, 145–50, 155–56, 158, 201–2, 203, 205, 259, 268, 278, 280, 354
suffering, 72, 103, 257, 269–70, 279, 338
synderesis, 11, 70, 330–31, 343, 345, 350–51, 352, 354. *See also* conscience

technique, 84, 209, 254, 265, 266

teleology. *See* revisionism

temperance, 13, 42, 44, 88, 105, 139, 189, 210, 250, 279, 297, 299, 312, 314, 318, 348

Ten Commandments, 27–28, 47–52, 54, 65, 68–70, 80, 172, 178, 206, 213, 216, 233, 239, 269, 289–90, 306, 338, 343, 346, 354, 368, 370, 372, 374, 379, 381, 382–83

theological virtue. *See* virtue, theological

theonomy. *See* heteronomy

tradition: Aristotelian, 85, 116, 174, 288–89, 332, 334, 343, 351; Augustinian, 199, 310, 316, 363; Catholic moral tradition, 170, 188, 238, 340; Franciscan, 211, 284, 317; Kantian, 167, 180, 252, 343; manualist, xv, xxi, xxiii, 237, 343, 369; patristic, 52, 145, 168, 171, 208; philosophical, 18, 116, 177, 188, 201

Trent, Council of, 47, 80, 86, 218, 239, 268, 321, 335, 369

Trinity, 28, 43, 140, 144, 146, 152, 158, 178, 360, 363, 364; and image of God, 134–37

truth: and goodness, 21, 70, 97, 102–3, 110, 122–23, 138, 141, 159, 163, 170, 172, 183–84, 208, 212, 270, 307, 345–46, 348, 350, 362–66, 395; contemplation of, 98–99; inclination to, 138, 141, 159, 163, 169, 170, 182, 212, 345, 346, 350, 366; longing / desire for, 98, 100, 102, 103, 123, 375; moral, 344, 353

utilitarianism, 66, 209, 245, 247–48, 254, 257, 286, 290

values: and revisionism, 242–43, 246–48, 251–52, 254, 257, 265–66; moral, 171, 344; philosophy of, 252

Vatican II, xi, xvi, xxiii, 46, 236–37, 339, 369; on new law, 372–76

Veritatis splendor, xviii, 26, 47–54, 57, 304, 308, 342, 344–46, 369, 376, 380, 382–84; and the New Law

vigilance, 14, 67, 88, 353

virginity. *See* chastity

virtue(s): acquired, 67–68, 70, 189, 212, 255, 289, 298, 306–8, 318, 348, 354; and gifts, 16, 42, 66, 86, 124–25, 127–29, 139–40, 178, 270, 304, 316–17, 319–20, 324, 403; cardinal, 61, 87, 171, 306–7, 348–49; infused, 68, 306, 315, 348; infused moral, xxii, 15, 67, 82, 175, 212, 315; intellectual, 98, 299, 352; moral, 8, 13–15, 37, 58, 67, 88, 98, 105–6, 163, 175, 251, 297, 299, 314–19, 343, 352; perfection of, 275; theological, 15, 50, 58, 82, 88, 117, 134–35, 163, 172–73, 183, 212, 250, 261, 265, 292, 315, 317, 331, 333, 338, 343, 348, 370, 379–80, 388. *See also* habitus, infused moral virtue

vision of God, 23, 65, 66, 94, 98, 100, 105–6, 111, 113, 155, 175, 257, 359, 362–63. *See also* natural desire for God

vocation, xviii, xx, 46, 49, 61, 66, 83, 112, 229, 329, 334, 355–56, 372, 389–91

voluntarism, 19, 82, 142, 177, 276, 282, 289, 313, 344–45, 372, 375, 394

wisdom, 62, 70, 106–11, 157, 168; evangelical / gospel, 108; gift of, 22, 83, 104, 299, 346, 392; human, 107–10, 323, 347; of God, 12, 23, 31, 51, 108, 110–11, 114, 134, 191, 212, 323–24, 347; of the word / Christ, 108–9, 138, 156, 188; of the world / of men; philosophical, 7, 106–7, 110, 118, 191, 324; practical wisdom, 301, 332; spiritual, 36, 59, 62, 72, 84, 323, 325, 332, 354; virtue of, 35, 63, 100, 140, 170, 190, 345, 351, 354; way of, 57